Tiger Tales

An Anecdotal History

Of

The Flying Tiger Line

Tiger Tales

by

LeVerne J. "Vern" Moldrem

Third Edition

Copyright ©1996. Revised edition second printing 1996.
Second edition third printing 2000.
Third edition fourth printing 2002
by LeVerne J. Moldrem
All rights reserved.

Published by Flying M Press
366 Milky Way
Prescott, AZ 86301

PH. 928-771-0382
FAX 928-708-0979

Library of Congress Control Number: 2002100603

Printed in the United States of America
by Sheridan Books, Inc.
100 N. Staebler Rd.
Ann Arbor, MI 48103

ISBN 0-9649498-8-1

DEDICATION

This book is dedicated to the employees of the former Flying Tiger Line and to the memory of all those who have departed.

To our spouses who have had to delay anniversary celebrations and endure many holiday meals with an empty chair at the table.

To our kids who had to observe innumerable birthdays, graduations, school activities and other important family events without the presence of their "Very Important Person."

TABLE OF CONTENTS

DEDICATION		V
DISCLAIMER		VIII
ACKNOWLEDGMENTS		X
PHOTO CREDITS		XI
PREFACE		XII
INTRODUCTION PART 1 AVG		1
INTRODUCTION PART 2 CNAC		13
CH 1 BEGINNING WITH THE BUDD	1945	27
CH 2 THE DOUGLAS DC-3	1946	37
CH 3 THE FLYING TIGER LINE	1947	47
CH 4 THE DOUGLAS DC-4	1948	57
CH 5 THE CURTISS C-46	1949	61
CH 6 REFUGEE CHARTERS	1950	69
CH 7 COBRAS IN COLOMBO	1950	81
CH 8 THE SLEEPWALKER	1951	91
CH 9 BURBANK TO BERLIN	1951	101
CH 10 THE SEVEN YEAR ITCH	1952	109
CH 11 DISSASTER IN ISSAQUA	1953	117
CH 12 THE DOUGLAS DC-6	1954	129
CH 13 "THREE ENGINES GONE..."	1955	139
CH 14 THE DEWLINE PART 1	1955-56	151
CH 15 THE DEWLINE PART 2	1955-56	163
CH 16 THE DEWLINE PART 3	1955-56	175
CH 17 THE ENGINE MECHANIC	1956	181
CH 18 THE LOCKHEED "CONNIE"	1957	189
CH 19 ENGINES—MORE OR LESS	1958	199
CH 20 FIRES TO FURLOUGHS	1959	209
CH 21 FINALLY THE FLIGHT LINE	1960	219
CH 22 THE CANADAIR CL-44	1961	225
CH 23 THE IDES OF MARCH	1962	235
CH 24 OUR WORST YEAR	1962	245
CH 25 FLYING LESSONS??	1963	253
CH 26 SAIGON VIETNAM	1964	261
CH 27 BACK TO BURBANK	1965	271
CH 28 THE KOSHER CAT	1966	283
CH 29 CL-44 COPILOT	1966	297
CH 30 3 DAY PASS, 6 DAY WAR	1967	305

TABLE OF CONTENTS Continued vii

CH 31 FINAL FLIGHT ON THE 44	1968	315
CH 32 DC-8 FIRST OFFICER	1968	323
CH 33 THE MOVIE "AIRPORT"	1969	329
CH 34 TIGER INTERNATIONAL	1970	337
CH 35 THE X ROADS ENDEAVOR	1971	343
CH 36 "WHERE'S THE PILOT?"	1972	347
CH 37 FLYING REINDEER	1973	351
CH 38 A WORRISOME THING	1974	357
CH 39 PHNOM PENH PNANCY	1975	361
CH 40 THE FALL OF SAIGON	1975	371
CH 41 BAX TO AFRICA	1975	387
CH 42 THIS SHEAR WAS NO BLISS	1975	395
CH 43 HIGH HOPES, LOW CEILINGS	1976	401
CH 44 COCKPIT TO BOX OFFICE?	1976	411
CH 45 EMERGENCY DESCENT	1977	423
CH 46 SOME BAD NEWS	1978	431
CH 47 AND SOME GOOD NEWS	1978	437
CH 48 A BOEING SNOWPLOW?	1979	443
CH 49 ARABIA TO AFRICA	1980	457
CH 50 HORSE FLIES?	1981	479
CH 51 BOEING 747 CAPTAIN	1982	485
CH 52 FATIGUE	1982	493
CH 53 WAY DOWN AND WAY UP	1983	501
CH 54 SNOW AND MORE SNOW	1984	509
CH 55 TIGERS IN THE JUNGLE	1984	515
CH 56 "THIS IS BAGHDAD CONTROL"	1985	523
CH 57 A WOLF AT THE DOOR	1986	531
CH 58 THIS LAMB IS A TIGER	1987	541
CH 59 THE DC-8-73	1988	547
CH 60 THE FINAL FLIGHT	1989	553
EPILOGUE		560
GLOSSARY		561
INDEX		562

DISCLAIMER

The author cannot personally verify all accounts in this book as being completely true. There is no reason, however, to doubt the veracity of the many contributors. Many of them are retired airline pilots or flight engineers, and therefore are known to possess the highest in personal character and integrity, even though some of them are reported to be suffering from C.R.S.[1] Others are retired flight attendants whose characters are known, of course, to be above reproach.

As for my own credentials, I am also a retired airline pilot, and in addition I hold that universally recognized certificate of truthfulness and responsibility, the aircraft and engine mechanic's license.

In some cases it is possible that the stories are correct but have been inadvertently attributed to the wrong person. If you feel this must be the case, "Because the someone you know would never do that!"...rest assured it probably is.

Now that any suspicions you might have had are laid to rest, there is something I would like to explain. You might come across several "Bar Stories," and I wouldn't want you to draw the wrong conclusions. Say for instance, you find 50 "Bar Stories." Take into consideration that the Flying Tiger Line was in operation about 45 years, or 16,425 days...and nights.

---

[1] **Can't remember shit.**

DISCLAIMER continued

Putting things in their proper perspective, it should be obvious that we spent most of our layovers in our hotel rooms studying the operations manual or revising our Jeppesen route manuals. Many of us also found time to visit the fine art galleries and museums around the world. For instance in Bangkok some of us toured the famous Reptile Gardens or Buddhist Temples instead of wasting time on mundane things like getting a haircut.[2] (After reading this, my lawyer commented, "Well, it might prevent you from getting sued, but it won't keep you from getting shot!")

The Author

---

[2]It has been reported that Bangkok had barbershops that were full service.

ACKNOWLEDGMENTS

I had the privilege of spending 31 years of my life with the Flying Tiger Line. Knowledge of the company absorbed through those years was extensive, but I didn't have "The Whole Story." The rest of the story was obtained through taped interviews with many pilots, flight attendants and mechanics.

If I were to name all the contributors, I would have another book right here. I will mention that I interviewed all five AVG men who were alive and well:

Duke Hedman, in Las Vegas.

Catfish Raine, at his ranch near Fallon, Nevada.

Dick Rossi, at several reunions and by phone.

Joe Rosbert, by a taped phone interview at his home in North Carolina, and by correspondence.

Link Laughlin, by phone and letters.

It's only fair that I mention J. P. "Goldy" Goldsmith, because I kept him talking into my tape recorder for nearly two days at his home in Panama City, Florida, in addition to numerous phone calls. Goldy has a fantastic memory.

A special thanks to Patty Bliss for the information from <u>41 Years Aloft</u>, the flight attendant book.

I thank Ann Marie Prescott for her generosity in sharing her personal views of important events in the company.

Also I thank Connie Sprague for the "Elsie the Cow" story by her mother, Edith Perrine.

The names of all contributors are included in the index in the rear of the book. I thank each of them.

PHOTO CREDITS

I thank the following for contributing photos for this book:

Jim Thomas and Fred Reeves, who spent half a day helping me to select 35 photos at the Flying Tiger Museum in Los Angeles. Many different people have donated these photos to the museum, so I can't credit them all individually.

R. C. "Andy" Anderson, maintenance supervisor in Hong Kong, who sent two Connie photos.

Captain Bob Baird, retired Tiger, two DC-8 and two 747 photos.

Captain Ron Burson, retired Tiger, a 747 sitting on its tail in Frankfurt, Germany.

Richard Danec of the Borden Company for permission to use the "Elsie" photos donated by Connie Sprague.
© 1944-1948, Borden Inc.

PREFACE

This is a story of the Flying Tiger Airline as told by its flight crews, mechanics and others. Included are personal accounts of bravery and boredom, promotions and furloughs, disasters and death. This is the story of a great group of men and women doing what they love to do, and having a hell of a good time doing it. Together their stories present a living history of the 45-year existence of the Flying Tiger Line.

The airplanes pictured in the graphics at the top of each chapter title page were the dominant ones in use at that time.

When I started this book I intended to include spouses and families, but this proved to be impossible due to the massive amount of information I have received. In addition the nature of flying, especially in the early days, made the survival of the most secure marriage improbable. As a result many pilots ended their careers with different spouses. I wouldn't want to cause hard feelings to anyone due to my inadvertent use of a wrong name.

Many readers may not be of the aeronautical persuasion, so I have tried to explain our normal pilot-ese with the use of plain English. For all pilots, if it doesn't sound right, <u>the editor made me do it!</u>

There is very little profanity (bad words) in this book. I wanted to save you the embarrassment of having to ask your children or grandchildren what those words mean.

INTRODUCTION PART 1

THE AMERICAN VOLUNTEER GROUP

A.V.G.

Curtiss P-40

Although this is <u>NOT</u> a story about the AVG, this is where the "Tiger" story must begin.

In 1941 Claire Chennault's American Volunteer Group was formed to help the Chinese defend themselves against Japan. Because the United States was not at war with Japan, all pilots were required to resign their U. S. military commissions before they could be accepted as volunteers. They were paid a monthly salary of $600 plus a $500 bonus for every enemy plane shot down.

There are many good books about the AVG, and I can highly recommend the three that I have read:

THE AVG   INTRODUCTION

The Pictorial History of The Flying Tigers
by Larry M. Pistole
Moss Publications, Orange, VA

Flying Tiger Joe's Adventure Story Cookbook
by C. Joe Rosbert
Giant Popular Press
452 Sylva Highway
Franklin, NC 28734

Destiny
by Erik Shilling
5641 Carol Avenue
Alta Loma, CA 91701

These are the ten AVG pilots who in 1945 formed the Flying Tiger Line (FTL):

Bob Prescott	Bill Bartling
Duke Hedman	Tommy Haywood
Link Laughlin	Joe Rosbert
Cliff Groh	Dick Rossi
Bus Loane	Catfish Raine

These men have combat records, which are nearly unbelievable even today. After looking into their backgrounds, however, it becomes clear that these superb pilots would have excelled at any career they might have chosen. They were college graduates, most near the top of their classes. They all graduated from flight schools, won their wings and were commissioned officers in their respective services. The following are a few personal recollections from some of the AVG pilots.

INTRODUCTION   TIGER TALES

ROBERT W. "BOB" PRESCOTT

by Duke Hedman

DUKE: Bob, from Fort Worth, Texas, resigned his commission in the Navy to join the AVG. He became an ace with six confirmed kills.

One morning Bob took off from Toungoo and climbed to about 20,000 feet and was circling slowly looking for any Japanese planes that might come by. Several of us were standing on the ramp watching, as a lone Japanese fighter appeared flying south. Bob dove down out of the clouds but was a long way behind him and was closing on him very slowly. We were all cheering and dancing around and betting on whether Bob could catch him. Just before both planes flew out of sight, Bob fired a short burst. The Zero exploded in flames and went down.

This is Duke's story as given to me in a taped interview in Las Vegas, Nevada.

DUKE HEDMAN: I graduated from the University of South Dakota in 1939. Four of my fraternity brothers wanted to join the Army Air Corps cadet-training program, so I drove them to Fort Snelling in Minneapolis, Minnesota. When we arrived, we found that the examination took four days. The military would give applicants all their meals and put them up in the dormitory for the three nights. (This was before the war, and the military was very fussy about whom they took—about one in every 20 applicants—and treated them very well.)

I couldn't sit in the car for four days, so I decided to take the tests too. Of the five of us, I was the only one accepted. I was inducted in 1939, and I received my wings in

March of 1940.

The Air Corps sent me to Selfridge Field in Michigan to fly the P-43, the forerunner of the P-47. Then we got the P-36, which was a P-40 with a radial engine. Later we got the P-40s, so I knew how to fly them before I volunteered for the AVG.

My biggest deal happened in Burma on Christmas Day, 1941. We got word that a large flight of Japanese bombers was headed for Rangoon. My airplane was out of service, so I just grabbed one that was ready. Its pilot was chasing me with his pistol as I raced for the cockpit, but he didn't shoot, so I got there first.

A huge wave of enemy bombers and fighters were coming in, and I went south of Rangoon to meet them over the bay. I came in behind a tight group of seven bombers, made a pass, giving each one a short burst before trying to shoot down the leader. By this time we were over the railroad yards, and several of those bombers started going down.

We didn't have gun cameras at that time, so we had to have confirmation from another source before we would get credit for a kill. I shot down four bombers, which fell in the rail yards, so I had instant confirmation. The rest of the bombers dropped their bombs and turned for home. I kept on shooting until I was almost out of ammunition. Several more bombers were smoking, but I couldn't get confirmation that they had gone down.

Suddenly bullets hit my canopy and shattered all the glass. With pieces of glass stuck in the back of my neck, I decided to get to hell out of there. I pulled up and rolled over to enter a dive. When I did, a Japanese fighter appeared right in front of me, so I fired, and he blew up. I had confirmation on that one, making that day's score five certain kills, and making me an ace in one day.

Diving down from 10,000 feet to about 2,000 feet I started for home. As I turned, I saw another fighter coming at me. Of course I turned toward him and just before we fired, we recognized each other. He was an R.A.F. pilot flying an American made, but obsolete, Brewster Buffalo fighter.

I landed at an emergency field northeast of Rangoon, jumped out and ran over under some trees. A group of Burmese guards who had seen me land came after me with rifles and bayonets. I was afraid they might shoot me, either thinking I was Japanese or just because they were nervous. Then their captain came running up and spoke to me in perfect American English. After establishing who I was, he invited me to his home.

When we got there he went to a creek, which ran behind his house, and pulled up a basket full of bottles of cold beer. I sure appreciated that! Come to find out, he had graduated from the University of Ohio a couple of years before. I stayed at his place for two days, enjoying the rest until a truck arrived to take me back to our base.

JOE ROSBERT

Joe graduated from high school in Philadelphia with a scholastic average that won him a four-year scholarship from Villanova. In 1938 he graduated with a degree in chemical engineering.

Of ten men in his class who applied, he was one of the only two who were accepted for Navy flight school. Both were sent to Pensacola for primary training.

Joe got his wings in the spring of 1940, and one year later became a plane commander flying PBY patrol planes out of San Diego, California.

After a while Joe started to get bored with the long slow over-water patrol flights, so when he was invited to fly P-40s for China, he jumped at the chance.

JOE ROSBERT: When I arrived in Toungoo, Burma, I was a PBY pilot and had never flown a fighter of any kind, let alone a P-40. Now I faced my first real problem. I busied myself studying the P-40 Flight Manual. Two days later I had my first flight, and it was fantastic. I climbed up to 12,000 feet and did a series of maneuvers to get the feel of the airplane. By the time I landed, I knew I had made the right choice. I was now a P-40 pilot.

On December 18 we evacuated Toungoo and moved our operation to Kunming. There my next-door neighbor was Bill Bartling.

I had my first combat a couple of days later when ten Japanese bombers approached Kunming. We only saw four bombers go down, but the Chinese Intelligence confirmed that only two bombers made it back across the border, and those two crashed before reaching their base. The Japanese never tried to bomb Kunming again.

I was transferred to Rangoon in February. On the 25th Rossi and I were playing Acey-Deucy in the alert shack when we got an alarm. We took off. After climbing to altitude, we saw two formations of 27 bombers each heading for our airdrome. As I closed on the nearest bomber, we were suddenly engulfed by a group of fighters. One appeared in my gun sight, and I gave him a quick burst. He caught fire and spun in. I fired at a second one. Though white smoke belched from behind his engine, I lost sight of him so could not get confirmation.

Dick Rossi got two, and our total for the day was 21 confirmed and 30 probables, with no AVG aircraft losses.
The next morning I shot down another fighter at Moul-

mein. That morning our total was nine in the air and two on the ground. We landed back at our base and just had time for a cold lunch when the alarm sounded again. We managed to get 12 fighters in the air in time to meet 54 Japanese bombers and 54 fighters. I got two for sure and two probables, and only lost half my rudder.

Rangoon fell in March so we pulled out for Kunming, where I was promoted to flight leader. On the eighth of March I was sent with the First Squadron to Chungking, where Rossi and I quartered together.

The expected raids on Chungking never came, but the city of Kweilin, which had no protection at all, was bombed every day. Chennault decided to put a stop to it. Twelve of us were sent there, timed to arrive just at dark to minimize the chances of our being seen.

Two hours before dawn we were ready for takeoff. Chennault had set up communications in a cave in a mountain near the runway. Our ground staff monitored enemy flights from this protected cave. The ground crew notified us when enemy bombers and fighters took off from Canton and headed in our direction.

As the enemy planes approached Kweilin, Chennault gave the word to take off. We climbed to 20,000 feet and circled, waiting for them. Our formation dove on the rear of nine bombers. I fired at one. His engine began smoking, but he didn't go down.

Pulling up for another pass, I saw three more twin-engine planes behind the others. I dove on the highest one, who also went into a dive. Then to my amazement he pulled up into a loop and came out of it with an Immelmann.[1] Strange tactics for a bomber, I thought. Then I

---

[1] A climbing half loop with a half roll at the top, which leaves an airplane going the opposite direction. This maneuver was made famous by Max Immelmann in WW I.

understood. This was no bomber. This was their new twin-engine fighter! Having sufficient speed, I was able to catch him and gave him a short burst. Part of his wing flew off, and he spun into the mountains below. A bomber appeared directly in front of me, apparently unaware of my presence. My guns must have found a gas tank, because there was a gigantic explosion, followed by pieces of the plane flying past my canopy.

To my left a twin-engine fighter was chasing one of our P-40s. I dove in to help. The fighter made a head-on pass at me, so close we almost collided. After this near miss he swung around and tried it again. By now the P-40 he'd been chasing was on his tail and blew him out of the sky. For that day we got nine confirmed and five probables.

CLIFF GROH
by
Catfish Raine, a close friend.

CATFISH: I met Cliff Groh in Pensacola where he had the bunk underneath me. For years after we called each other "Bunkie."

Cliff fell in love about every week. He had a car, and he always painted his current girl's name on the side. Every week Cliff's car wore a new name. One time, he must have had it real bad, the engagement lasted three weeks.

I started out a class ahead of Cliff, but I came down with a case of measles, and so I graduated with his class. Cliff was out on the town the night before graduation and slept right through the time of his scheduled check ride. At the graduation ceremony the commanding officer said as he pinned the wings on Groh, "This pains me."

That night at the graduation dance, Cliff's girl was wearing an open-backed dress with straps. During some wild dance steps one of her straps broke. Being a gentleman, Cliff did the only thing he could think of: He took off his wings and pinned the lady's strap back on. The commanding officer was furious.

The following is from a taped interview with Catfish at his home in Fallon, Nevada, June 30, 1993.

CATFISH: The reason I went with the AVG was that I liked living. I was in the Navy, in a torpedo squadron, and I figured the longevity wasn't too good there. I was one of those who got over there pretty late, so I didn't get the training that most of the pilots got.

Twenty-seven of us were sent over on a ship and Joe Rosbert was our leader—the one who kept track of the money, the names and addresses, and who tried to maintain some discipline. We had a few orangutans among us, and they were always in trouble of some kind. Trouble was the booze on that boat was so cheap you couldn't afford to stay sober. I don't know how Joe managed to find out, but the captain of the ship could never find Joe when there was trouble.

One time a kid went into port and bought a cobra. When he went to bring it on board, the ship's crew wouldn't let him, and he was determined he was damn well going to do it. Nobody could locate Joe to deal with the kid. At the next port someone bought a water buffalo and tried to get that on board. Joe disappeared then too.

I got to Rangoon in October, and I went right to Toungoo where we had our training base. Because of a shortage of spare parts, we got practically no training. We couldn't take the airplanes up for practice because of the lack of parts, especially tires.

When the war broke out, a couple of squadrons went to Rangoon. Cliff Groh and I stayed in Toungoo and picked up a couple airplanes when they were finished and ready to go, and we flew them to Kunming. Then we got into combat, down over Burma mostly. Then during the next spring we were down over central China in Kualing and Punyang. I was credited with three and one-half enemy planes shot down and seven probables, most of them over central China.

One combat mission that sticks in my mind took place in Burma. We were strafing Japanese trucks coming up through Burma. That was more dangerous than aerial combat, because you were so close to the ground, and everyone you were shooting at was shooting back. I got separated from the rest of the group, and on my way home I saw this Japanese plane coming. I was below him and off to his left. I stayed below him and cranked up a lot of power, intending to swing in behind him when he went by.

I don't know why, but just before I turned, I looked up. There was another enemy plane about three miles behind this one. If I had pulled in behind the first one, the second one would have shot me to pieces. I stayed where I was until the second one went by, then swung in and shot him down. I never could find the first one...I don't know where the hell he went!

One time, toward the end of the AVG, I was on a bomber run escorting B-25s. The bombers dropped their load on this airport, but it was obvious there were no fighters there, so I stayed up above them. I lost sight of them while they were climbing back up through the cloud layers, and when I saw them again, they were way the hell and gone ahead. I was trying to catch up to them when out of the clouds came some I-97s, those little Jap fighters. I pulled up behind one and let him have it, and he just rolled over and went straight in. I didn't follow him down because I was afraid if I lost the bombers I wouldn't know

INTRODUCTION   TIGER TALES

how the hell to get home.

In 1942 Chennault was recommissioned as a brigadier general. The bad part of that was he had to take orders from Major General Stilwell. In March Stilwell, who knew little of air warfare, decided he wanted a bombing raid on a certain Japanese facility. It was so far away that the P-40s couldn't even get there and back, much less protect the bombers. It was a sure suicide mission.

The R.A.F. had five old Blenheim Bombers that were to be used on the raid. The night before, we flew the P-40s to Lashio, which put us forty miles closer to the target. We had the airplanes all ready to escort the bombers when they came over. They never arrived. We found out later that the R.A.F. pilots had found a sensible way to avoid certain disaster—after takeoff they immediately became hopelessly lost, finding their way home only just before exhausting their fuel.

This, as the story goes, is how the AVG became known as the Flying Tigers. Erik Shilling, an AVG pilot, painted the mouth of a tiger shark on his P-40, and then stood with bated breath as Chennault stared at it with his usual stony expression. His jaw softened slightly, which could be interpreted as a grin, and he said, "Paint them all that way."

When the AVG disbanded July 4, 1942, the ten previously mentioned pilots were hired by the China National Aviation Corporation, commonly called CNAC.

Chennault's Curtiss P-40s

INTRODUCTION PART 2

CHINA NATIONAL AVIATION CORPORATION

(CNAC)

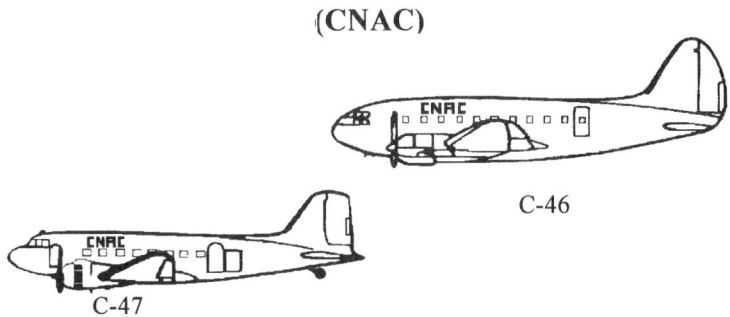

Flying the "Hump" meant the route from India across the Himalayas, bringing wartime supplies to China. This was the same war zone in which these AVG pilots had been flying P-40 fighters against Japanese Zeros. Now they were flying slow unarmed transports while the Japanese were still flying Zeros—not a comfortable situation.

At first they flew C-47s and C-53s. The C-53 is what the military called the passenger version of the C-47. Later they flew the Curtiss C-46 Commando, which hauled a much bigger load. The ten AVG pilots previously mentioned all accepted the challenge.

The Curtiss-Wright Corporation started CNAC in the 1920's. The Chinese government, tired of being taken advantage of by foreigners, demanded 51 percent ownership of the company. As the story goes, Curtiss-Wright wanted to dispose of their inventory of Curtiss Condor biplanes, which were becoming obsolete. They also flew Loening Amphibians on the Yangtse River between Shanghai and Chungking and Stinsons up and down the East Coast to Peking, Shanghai, Canton and Hong Kong.

DUKE HEDMAN: We all came direct from the AVG to CNAC except Bob Prescott. He went back to the States

and flew for TWA for a while. Because of his experience in Asia, he was picked for a secret mission to Moscow. A short time later he quit TWA and joined us at CNAC. We worked for a couple of months then were sent to the States for a working vacation and to pick up some new C-47s, which we ferried to India. We were based in Calcutta, and we lived pretty good down there. We had homes and apartments that were leased by the company.

Sometimes I was in charge of the entertainment. For instance on occasion I would go to Karaira Road and rent an entire house of pleasure, which included the bar and all the girls, for a weekend. We just went in and locked the doors behind us. The company knew how to keep its pilots happy but more importantly, they knew where to find us.

On the China side of the Hump we laid over in places like Dinjan, Kunming and Chungking. We flew about 150 hours a month and were paid $20 an hour, which was big money in those days. Then when we got back to Calcutta, we usually had a week or ten days off. The Royal Hotel had a golf course, and there was also a racetrack. The horse races were fixed, but we were on the inside and could sometimes make a little money.

The weather over the Himalayas was terrible, but it was better than flying in the vicinity of the Japanese fighters who were always looking for us. We were more concerned with the fighters than with the weather. We often flew the northern route where the weather was the worst. We flew mostly at night, and in the daytime we flew in clouds when we could.

Maybe Dick got hold of a bad ice cube the night before.

DICK ROSSI: During the war I flew the Hump in C-47s and C-46s. After the war I stayed with CNAC and flew out of Shanghai to most everywhere in China. Our copilots were Chinese who had practically no pilot training but were there because they spoke English, such as it was.

One morning I arrived at the airport about 3 a.m. and took off toward the west. We were headed toward the mountains, so I climbed up to 14,000 feet. I had awakened that morning with a bad case of the runs, and now I had to go again.

I said to the copilot, "Keep an eye on things while I go back to use the can."

Pretty soon I had the horrible feeling that we were spinning so, holding up my pants with one hand, I raced back to the cockpit. Sure enough, the copilot had the damn thing in a spiral dive! I got it out of the dive and climbed back up to altitude and back on course. Now I realized that I couldn't leave the copilot alone. I had to go back and get the crapper, which was just a tin can with a seat on it, and put it between the pilot seats. You had to have to go pretty bad to suffer those indignities.

You also had to be damn careful with that can. It was fitted with a clam-shell-type lid, so that when you got up, the lid slammed shut automatically. However, in turbulence you had damn well better hold on to the can, because if you bounced up off of it, the clam shell would slam shut, and you'd be singing soprano all the way home.

Talk about giving your all for the cause...but I guess a rough ride is better than a long walk any day.

JOE ROSBERT: CNAC kept their promise, and our vacations to the States coordinated with the delivery of new planes. My turn came in November. After visiting with my family and a terrific New Years Eve in the Stork Club in New York with my good friends Jeanne and Bus Loane, I found myself in Miami preparing to take a new Douglas C-53 back to India.

An item in demand but not available in China was cola syrup. It was sold in wooden casks, so I bought one for some friends in Kunming. This becomes important later.

Now it became apparent why this was called a working vacation. The trip to Calcutta, India, was via Miami, Florida, to Puerto Rico, Trinidad, Georgetown, British Guiana, Belem and Natal, Brazil. There we filled the extra gas tanks for the first time for the Atlantic crossing. We left at night headed for Ascension Island, a ten-hour trip to a place six by nine miles in size in the middle of the South Atlantic. Fortunately it had a powerful radio beacon which brought us straight in.

From there we flew to Accra on the Gold Coast of Africa, then several hops across the continent to Aden on the Red Sea. The rest of the journey took us along the south coast of Arabia, over the Indian Ocean to Karachi and finally to our destination, Calcutta. It was a relief to get away from airplanes for a while as we enjoyed two weeks off.

In April I took off from Dinjan in a C-53 with a load of medical supplies for Kunming. When we arrived at our cruising altitude of 16,000 feet, we encountered severe icing conditions. We could not maintain altitude and had to turn back. The C-53 kept losing altitude, and at 14,000 feet I knew there were mountain peaks higher than that in the area. To make matters worse, the crosswind was about double that reported, so we were much farther north than we thought. Suddenly there was a swirl in the clouds, and directly in front of us was a mountain. I made a hard right turn, but it was too late. The belly of the airplane scraped on the rocks, and we crashed into a mountain of snow.

My copilot had a badly sprained ankle and my right ankle was broken in several places. But the worst news was that the radio operator, Wong, was dead. There was no way we could walk in the condition we were in, so we stayed in the airplane for the next seven days. One of the things that helped to keep us alive was that cask of cola syrup I'd purchased in Miami. We made snow cones flavored with the stuff.

On the seventh day we made plywood strips to use as splints, tied them on tight with parachute cord, and started down the mountain.

Forty-six days after the crash we arrived at Dinjan, still on foot, and were flown back to Calcutta.

For the entire story of their survival, see <u>Flying Tiger Joe's Adventure Story Cookbook</u> as noted in the introduction.

Now we finally have the absolute true story of how Robert J. Raine became known as Catfish...maybe.

CATFISH RAINE: When the AVG was over, I went with CNAC and stayed with them until I came home in March 1945.

The real story of how I got the name Catfish is probably not as good as some that have gone around, but I'll tell the real one anyway.

I was flying for CNAC across the Hump, which was about the only way you could get from China to India and vice versa, because of the terrain and the Japanese army. I had some friends I'd known when I was with the AVG, and I took them a few fish some of us pilots had caught. They weren't catfish, but they resembled them.

When I returned to Dinjan the customs hauled me in and said, "Okay Captain Raine, we know that you're smuggling gold bars in those fish you took over there, so you might as well 'fess up and tell us all about it."

From that time on people started saying, how's the catfish business? Pretty soon everybody called me Catfish and today most people don't know me by any other name.

In 1942 CNAC constructed a 2400-foot dirt diversion strip at Balijan to hide the planes from Japanese attack. Then they found that dust was getting into the planes' carburetors and causing their engines to lose power. CNAC lost their first plane for this reason but fortunately the two crewmembers, Captains Link Laughlin and Bill Bartling, survived.

The chief pilot ran to the crash site and found Link and Bill sitting under a tree, badly injured. Bill had compound fractures and head injuries, and Link's face was all smashed up.

Link said, "Sorry about the plane."

"The hell with the plane, my concern is about you guys."

"In that case," Link said, "I think my love muscle is broke."

Link Laughlin left CNAC in 1944 and went to the Marines until the end of the war.

Bill Bartling was crippled up some in that wreck, but it sure didn't cripple his mind. He was always asking people, "What's the population of the town you're from?"

Ninety-nine out of a hundred would have no idea, then Bartling would tell them. He had a fantastic memory for ball players and their statistics. He could also multiply any three numbers by any other three numbers in his head. His answers were always correct.

Art Prendergast and his Chinese maintenance crew salvaged a C-47 that had crashed in the Manas River and had been abandoned. They had to walk to the river, and then make a raft to float downstream to the airplane. One Chinese mechanic fell off the raft and was eaten by a crocodile before he could be pulled out. Art hired local help with an elephant to drag the airplane to a dry riverbed where he could make repairs. Art acted as copilot when the plane was flown out.

Once Bob Prescott was checking out a new Chinese copilot and by way of conversation he asked, "When did you learn to fly?"
The man answered with a huge grin, "Me learn now."

Duke Hedman and Bill Bartling were flying a C-47 with $2,000,000 worth of gold bars from Kunming to Dinjan. Their worry was the weather closing in, until they noticed a Japanese Zero was closing in faster. They dove for the ground just hoping the wings would stay on, and then flew along the rivers, practically under the treetops. The Zero didn't want them that badly.
Bill Bartling flew 367 round trips over the Hump.
Dick Rossi had 735.

These additional ten pilots flew for CNAC and later joined FTL: Ray Allen, Carey Bowles, Bob Conrath, Don Hassig, Ralph Mitchell, Oakley Smith, Wayne Snyder, Dick Stratford, Dick Stuelke and Gerry Costello.

CAREY BOWLES: I learned to fly in the Civil Pilot Training Program at Texas A & M just prior to WW II. Just as the war began, I was accepted for instrument and multiengine training at the C.A.A. Standardization Center at Houston, Texas.
I moved on to become a flight instructor teaching the W.A.S.P. (Women's Air Corps Service Pilots) at Sweetwater, Texas.

As the war began to wind down, the W.A.S.P. School was closed. Fortunately, airlines were hungry for experienced pilots. I had offers from TWA, Eastern and China National Airways Corporation, which was operated by Pan-Am.

In the 1930's Pan American bought out Curtiss Wright's share of CNAC. I went to China with CNAC for two years, first living in India and flying over the Hump into China. I was flying C-47s and C-46s. The Hump route we flew was mostly from Dinjan in Assam in the northeast corner of India across Burma to Kunming, Yunnan, in Western China. It was approximately 500 miles in length. We flew a round trip every day, which took 7.3 hours, or one and a half round trips a day for two weeks. After that we had the rest of the month off in Calcutta. It was a great life if you could stay alive. We lost many airplanes and crews.

I arrived there in early 1945, as the war was nearing its end. Most of the Flying Tiger Line (FTL) founders had returned to the States. While in China I got to know Dick Rossi, Dick Stuelke, Dick Stratford and Bus Loane, all of whom later came to FTL.

In 1947 CNAC began operating six DC-4s, and I deadheaded home from Shanghai on the first Chinese Registered Airplane to ever land in the United States.

BOB CONRATH

Bob was in the merchant marine in 1939, where he met his wife to be, Martha, while they both sailed on the Grace Line. They were married in 1940 on the west coast.

Bob spent most of his pay on flying, because he wanted to accumulate 300 hours, the minimum required to join the Army Air Corps Ferry Command.

After the bombing of Pearl Harbor, he got a job as a civilian flight instructor at Blythe, California. When his contract there was up, he had his 300 hours, but they wouldn't release him. Instead he was transferred to Lancaster, California to teach instrument flying. He was stuck there until the war in Europe ended.

When the need for pilot training was reduced, he was allowed to join the Army Air Corps as a flight officer. He requested the Air Transport Command and was sent to the CBI (China-Burma-India) theater. Bob flew 75 trips over the hump before the war ended. While he was there, he met many of the AVG and CNAC pilots including his best friend, Dick Rossi.

After the war, Bob returned to China and flew with CATC until the communists took over the country in 1949. CATC was a Chinese airline left from the remains of the old Lufthansa outfit that was there before the war.

DON HASSIG

It was the morning of January 30, 1949, and the Red Army was overrunning northern China. Captain Don Hassig was highjacked by the Communists while en route from Shanghai to Tsingtao. The flight was diverted to the Communist held city of Tsinan where the crew and passengers were held for 34 days.

One officer asked Captain Hassig, "What flying did you do during the war? Were you a bomber pilot?"

"Sorry, I'm not allowed to give out that information."

"Well then, what do you think about Communists?"

"I don't think about Communists, I just fly airplanes."

Hassig could have told him he had flown 35 combat missions. He could have mentioned the time over Germany when he ran into heavy flak, which blew the rudder and one elevator off his plane, the Liberty Belle. The blast cut most of the control cables, killed the radio operator, one of the gunners, and nearly blew an arm off another gunner. He might have described how he fought the crippled bomber for an hour before landing on a fighter strip in Belgium, saving the life of the wounded gunner. He also could have told them he received the Distinguished Flying Cross for that day's work.

He could have, but he didn't.

When they were released, they were put on a train for the first night, and then transferred to an ancient truck until it ran out of tires. From there on they rode sidesaddle on the backs of bicycles until they nearly froze. Then they got off and walked. A couple of hours of walking was deemed sufficient when they came upon several farmers with wheelbarrows loaded with pigs on their way to market.

After walking alongside for a while and watching the pigs ride, Hassig produced some Communist paper money and soon a deal was struck. Money changed hands, the pigs walked and the weary travelers rode. They rode two to a wheelbarrow, one on either side of a big menacing wheel.

Hassig muttered under his breath, "I wonder what they've been feeding those pigs? I can't believe this. I started this trip in the left front seat of an airliner, and here I am in a wheelbarrow. Well, at least I'm still on the left side."

Many miserable cold hours later they passed through the Nationalist line and were then taken by truck to Tsingtao. Hassig and his crew were dropped off at the Dutch Villa, where all the flight crews stay on layover in Tsingtao. They arrived about midnight, and some of his buddies still at the bar nearly fell over when they saw him.

Hassig gave them the gist of the story, while inhaling a few belts of good Scotch.

When he finished, one of his friends exclaimed, "I'll bet you're sure glad that ordeal is over."

Hassig replied with his usual dry humor, "Slightly more than somewhat."

RALPH MITCHELL: I flew C-46s during WW II, but after the war I tried everywhere I could think of to get a flying job. I had no luck, so I went back to college for a year and a half. My oldest brother flew for CNAC in China in the early thirties. Ernest Allison, who was one of the early airmail pilots, was the chief pilot for CNAC. He did the hiring, so on a long shot I sent him my application. I figured if it didn't work out, I'd give up and become a geologist, which was what I was studying in college.

I'd used my G.I. Bill to get my instrument rating and had just completed training when I received a large envelope from Shanghai, China. Mister Allison hired me on the strength of my brother's reputation, but I had to pay my own way to China. I bought a ticket on a cargo steamer for 270 dollars. I was the only passenger.

When the ship docked in Yokohama, the captain said, "We'll be here for three days, so have a good look around Japan but don't get lost."

I had some friends who were living in Tokyo, so I went to visit them for a couple of days. I returned to Yokohama well before our scheduled departure time, but the ship was disappearing over the horizon. At this time Japan was controlled by the occupation forces, so one had to have a military pass to enter the country. I didn't have one, so the captain had given me a crew pass—which was now illegal because I had no ship.

Pan American Airways owned half of CNAC at the time, so I went to their offices and told the manager of my plight. I asked him to wire Mr. Allison and ask him for a ticket from Tokyo to Shanghai, and also an advance on my salary. Mister Allison was kind enough to grant my request, so I thought my troubles were over.

Then the manager said, "Let me see your passport."

When I handed it to him he said, "Where is the Military occupation authority permit? You need one to leave here."

I explained why I didn't have one, so because of the fact that there was no official record of my having entered Japan, I was allowed to leave the same way and finally arrived in Shanghai. Chinese immigration wasn't happy to see me either because I had no luggage and only 53 cents in my pocket.

I had to fly as copilot for about a month, then flew as captain for the rest of my time in China. During the war with the Communists we flew in supplies for the Nationalists and brought refugees out on the return trips.

CNAC needed a few crews to fly out of Peking, so I was sent up there. I rented a very nice home with three servants. The only beds in the house were small single cots. King size beds had just become popular in the States, and I had one before I left. It was not possible to have one shipped over, so, Pong, my number one servant, had one made for me in Peking. It was brass and cost about three hundred dollars, which was an enormous amount of money at the time.

I was flying trips into Manchuria. As time went on the Communists kept gaining ground, so the trips kept getting shorter as we had fewer and fewer places to go to. After about two months the company said we would have to pull back from Peking. It was about the end of 1948, and I was given only one day's notice, so I couldn't rescue the brass bed. It was bad enough that the Nationalists were losing the war, but it really hurt to lose that bed.

We had to evacuate the Chinese mainland in 1949 when the Communists took over.

Here are a few words about the exploits of Dick Stratford as told by Catfish.

CATFISH: Dick Stratford left CNAC and went with CATC. Dick was always kind of pugnacious. The customs officials pulled him and his crew in at Lanchow. They started roughing up one of Dick's Chinese crewmembers, so Dick decked him. With that they threw the whole crew in the pokey. Things looked pretty tough for them, so that night Stratford bribed the guard. They got out, jumped in the airplane and flew it to Shanghai.

Moon Chin, the American born Chinese manager, gave him a pretty good settlement and flew him to the States. He knew Dick couldn't fly into Lanchow anymore. Anyway, that took a lot of guts to buck authority, because when you're out there in the interior, you're at their mercy.

Dick Stuelke was sitting on top of the world when...

DICK STUELKE: I lost an engine on a C-46 while I was with CNAC. At the time I was flying at 15,000 feet, and the mountains beneath me were 14,000 feet. That was a little exciting for a while. I landed at Kunming and Art Prendergast brought a new engine and hung it on there, but we didn't have any oil. They sent another airplane with a barrel of oil, but Air Traffic Control ran them into a mountain...killed everybody on board, of course. Besides the loss of three good men, we still didn't have any oil. It took two more days before we could round up enough oil to get out of there.

After I left CNAC, I went to the Philippines and ran an outfit called the Commercial Airline Corporation, until 1948.

This is probably the longest introduction that has ever been put in a book, but I wanted to show the caliber of the people who started the Flying Tiger Line (FTL). They were adventurous young men, but were not foolhardy. They had vast experience in flying heavily loaded airplanes in bad weather with poor or nonexistent navigation facilities.

Every person who joined the company later had to make a choice. They could bring their performance up to the standards of these men, or they could leave. After they made the appropriate choice, the new company benefited from the services of an exceptional group of people.

TIGER TALES

CHAPTER 1   BEGINNING WITH THE BUDD   1945

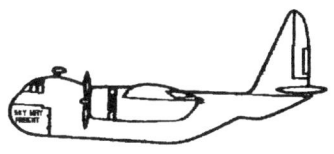

Budd Conestoga

When Bob Prescott returned to Fort Worth, Texas, in 1942, he was interviewed as a returning war hero. The reporter was a Texas girl named Helen Ruth Verheyden. An on-again-off-again courtship followed while Bob took a job flying for TWA.

It was during this time he made the secret mission to Moscow. The trip must have made him homesick for world travel, because he quit TWA and went back to China and joined his old AVG buddies flying for CNAC. Bob couldn't keep his mind off Helen Ruth, so he gave up trying. He got a leave of absence and went back for her.

"We can get married and live in Calcutta until the job is over."

This did not elicit the enthusiasm he had hoped for, but her protests were no match for his persuasion. They were married in 1944 and honeymooned in Mexico.

The founders of the company are getting on in years at this writing, and so they tend to remember details from their own perspectives, not exactly the same way. Here then, are several views of how the company started.

CATFISH RAINE: A group of investors including the Signal Oil Company were trying to start an airline in Mexico to be

called Aero-Azteca. Bob Prescott gave up his plan to return to China and hired on as their chief pilot. He was negotiating for three Budd Conestoga Airplanes from the War Assets Administration.

The Budd Railroad Car Company manufactured these planes, and some of the pilots have commented that they flew somewhat like a railroad car. Due to the aluminum shortage during the war, they were made of stainless steel. These twin-engine airplanes with tricycle gear and a rear-loading ramp were new, having been rejected by the Navy for MINOR mechanical flaws.

Prescott was back east to pick up a Budd for the Mexican airline when his brother, George, in Washington, D. C., said, "You guys are veterans. Why don't you buy those Budds yourselves?" (Veterans had preference in purchasing surplus items. The AVG was a civilian outfit, with no connection to the military, so technically none of the AVG pilots were military veterans. Due to their combat records, this detail was overlooked.)
I, too, was back in Washington at the time, and Bob and I ran into each other. When he left for California with the Budd, he took me along as copilot, giving me a free ride home. When we arrived in California, we began to form our own airline, National Skyways Freight. Bob was president, Duke Hedman vice-president, and I was chief pilot. The Aero-Azteca guys were mad as hell at us, and we didn't dare go down there for a while.

Prescott knew that after the war there would likely be many new airlines starting up and competition would be fierce. His best chance for success was to get organized while the war was still in progress. The big problem was that no airplanes were available anywhere in the world. It was this in-

CHAPTER 1   TIGER TALES

side knowledge that the entire production run of the Budd Conestoga had been canceled and the airplanes rejected by the Navy that made the airline possible. They felt that if anyone could make the Budds into reliable airplanes, they could. If not, the Budds could be replaced when DC-3s became available after the war.

The Budd Conestoga, rejected by the Navy—for minor technical flaws—but the only thing with wings that was available

JOE ROSBERT: Early in 1945 I was in Hollywood working on a picture at Paramount Studios about flying the Hump. That project lasted about three months, and just at the end of it I got a call from Prescott in Washington. He wanted to start a cargo airline and needed $10,000 from each of ten former AVG pilots. When I hung up the phone I checked my bank balance and found I only had $4,000

I called Catfish and said, "Did you get a call from Prescott?"

"Yes I did."

"Are you in?"

"Yes I'm in."

"Well I'd like to get in, but I've only got $4,000 in the bank."

"Don't worry about that. We'll go to the bank tomorrow and fix it up."

He loaned me the $6,000 and I gave him an IOU. Later I paid him back in full.

We all met in Pasadena at the home of Allen Chase and put the deal together. We each put up $10,000 but agreed that Bob Prescott should be given his shares for having promoted the project. Sam Mosher and his group matched the $90,000 and the National Skyways Freight Corporation was formed with $180,000.

The new company bought the entire fleet of twelve Budd Conestogas and immediately sold four of them for a price, which paid for them all. The remaining eight Budds departed Augusta, Georgia, for Long Beach, California. Seven arrived. The other one crashed in Fort Worth, Texas, and was sold on the spot for $500. It remained in service there for many years...as a hamburger stand.

DUKE HEDMAN: Concerning the ten of us that formed the airline, it is hard to think of things to say that haven't already been said. We all respected each other very deeply. I loved Bob Prescott. We all did. He was a brilliant guy who knew how to get things done.

Bill Bartling was a little different personality, but he was extremely intelligent. As an example—you could write down any number like 992 times 159, and he would multiply it in his head, and he was always right. I think he was the smartest man I have ever known.

CHAPTER 1   TIGER TALES

New Budd Conestogas at Long Beach

When we first started the company, I was vice-president for about two months, but then I told Bob I wanted to go back to flying, so I resigned that position.

Our first charter was a load of flowers for Detroit flown by a new guy—Gordon, I think. Then a load of grapes to Atlanta flown by Paul Kelly, a pilot who had flown for Chennault after the AVG disbanded. Next was a furniture charter that I flew from New York to California. It was hand to mouth for a while, and things didn't look so good.

Bartling never could pass his instrument checkride, so he couldn't check out as captain. He was given the job of running operations and worked his way up to vice-president. He would work 24 hours a day, whatever it took to keep things going. Without Bart we probably wouldn't have survived. He was that important. Bart ran the office at first and did all the scheduling. He remembered everything in his head. People would call all hours of the day and night, and he knew where all the airplanes were and who the crews were.

Janet Olson took over the scheduling functions as the company grew.

The new company did not intend to cash in on their "Flying Tigers" fame, but they couldn't escape it. The newspapers and radio reports gave a great deal of coverage to the new cargo airline. They seldom mentioned the name of the company, but referred to them as "Those Flying Tiger Pilots." As a result when they answered the phone saying "National Skyways Freight," there was often a pause, then the confused potential customer would say, "I was trying to reach the Flying Tigers."

LINK LAUGHLIN: Bob Prescott called me asking for an investment in a cargo line. I sent him $10,000 and drove my wife's Plymouth to Long Beach, California. She divorced me shortly after.

I was flying Budd Conestogas from Long Beach to New York for $400 a month. The flight crew had to help load and unload freight because we couldn't afford to hire enough loaders. One day an attorney called me saying, "Your ex wife wants $600 a month. Have you got it?"

I hung up. I never could tolerate obscene phone calls!

As one might imagine, things were not always done in a way that pleased everyone.

CATFISH: Red Holmes, an ex CNAC pilot, was one of the original investors until one time Prescott's wife was driving their car to California when it broke down in, of all places, Prescott, Arizona. Bob flew a Budd over there, and they

CHAPTER 1   TIGER TALES

pushed the car into it and hauled it back to Los Angeles.

Red said, "If that's the way we're going to operate, I want my money back."

Cliff Groh showed up looking for work, and we wanted to hire him because he was an old buddy.

Prescott said, "I don't want anyone flying these Budds upside down."

We assured him that Cliff would be a good boy, so finally Bob relented.

After a phone call from a bunch of homesick sailors in San Diego, the new airline was in the passenger business. The war was over and these sailors wanted to get to New York, and they wanted to leave NOW! This provided temporary employment for five Budd airplanes and their crews. Bob Prescott himself flew one of the planes, and Duke, Rosbert, Haywood and Groh flew the others.

CATFISH: The first few years were really tough. One time we couldn't pay the fuel bill so I put up $4,000 for which my partners gave me stock. At that time Duke and I were the largest stockholders.

We had a lot of trouble with the Budds. The worst thing was that the exhaust stacks kept falling off and causing engine fires. The first Budd we lost was bellied into a graveyard in Detroit. No one was hurt, but the copilot picked up his suitcase and walked off into the night. He was never heard from again.

Joe Rosbert's accident happened on New Year's Eve. We were having a party in Los Angeles at Prescott's house. About one o'clock in the morning the phone rang. Bob's wife answered it then called Mary Ann, Joe's wife, to the phone.

She said, "They crashed on a golf course back there in Virginia, and Joe wants to talk to you."

Mary Ann went to the phone real upset, and of course everyone was listening to hear what happened at the wreck.

About half way through the conversation Mary Ann's attitude changed, and she said, "You son-of-a-bitch! Where are you?"

Mary Ann could hear all the partying and goings on in the background, which of course gave rise to her suspicions.

We gave the airplane to the golf course and they made a bar out of it. We thought that might keep them from suing us.

Now the details from the first one to arrive at the accident, Captain Rosbert:

JOE ROSBERT: My copilot that night, John Pinny, had served with the R.A.F. during the war, even though he was an American. We took a load of flowers to New York, and on the way back we stopped at Washington, D.C., for fuel and to check the weather. While there we picked up six sailors who wanted to get to Los Angeles. We were always looking for a way to pay our gas to get home.

We left Washington heading west, and when we were over Knoxville, Tennessee, we began picking up ice. The radio reception was terrible, and after we tried a letdown at Knoxville and couldn't see anything, we headed back to Washington, D.C.

Our gas supply was getting low, and all I could see was the glow of lights down below as we passed small towns. I let down over a couple of towns hoping to see a rotating beacon or landing strip but had no luck.

On the third try I spiraled down over this little glow of lights and broke out of the clouds. It was like landing in a teacup with hills all around. It was snowing like hell, which made

CHAPTER 1   TIGER TALES   35

it hard to see with the landing lights on. I picked a spot that looked pretty flat, and when I turned on base leg we ran out of gas on one side. I managed to get the plane around on one engine and made a wheels up landing.

There seemed to be a murky shadow a short way ahead of the airplane, and out of this shadow came a dark figure. As he approached, we could see he was wearing a tuxedo and carrying a fifth of whiskey.

He handed it to me and said, "Here, you need this more than I do."

We had landed on a golf course in Bluefield, Virginia, right on the eighteenth green next to the club house where a New Year's party was in progress.

The first chance I got I called the C.A.A. I told them where we were and that everyone was okay. They congratulated us on a good job of getting it on the ground. Then I called Prescott's house...but you've heard that story.

There was one more serious accident with the ill-fated Budd Conestogas and the first to result in loss of life.

CATFISH: We had a contract hauling Newsweek Magazine out of Dayton, Ohio, to Los Angeles. This crew had flown all the way to the East Coast with a load of freight, then back to Dayton to pick up the load of magazines and head for Los Angeles. They apparently fell asleep. It appears that something woke them up, because they pulled the airplane out of a dive and bellied it in just below the airway beacon light at Acameda, New Mexico.

The crash threw the captain and copilot out through the windshield. Then the plane slid forward and crushed them. The flight engineer, Doc Lewis, was not wearing his seat belt, and he was thrown quite a bit further, but he survived.

The copilot on that flight was a glider expert. He had suggested to Prescott that we pull freight-hauling gliders with B-26s. You could buy a B-26 brand new from the factory in Long Beach for $900. His death ended that right there, however, because we had no more glider experts.

There were a lot of landing gear accidents with the Budd, but they were not all the Budd's fault.

CATFISH: Cliff Groh took off from El Paso in a Budd. He pulled the gear up a little too soon, then the airplane settled back on the runway. That meant some sheet metal work on the belly, but once that was done, Cliff flew it out.

The landing gear on the Budd had a serious weak point. Pilots of that time were accustomed to applying the brakes after takeoff to stop wheel rotation before retracting the gear. If they did that on a Budd, its sway brace would buckle and the wheels would become jammed in the wheel well.

CHAPTER 2   THE DOUGLAS DC-3   1946

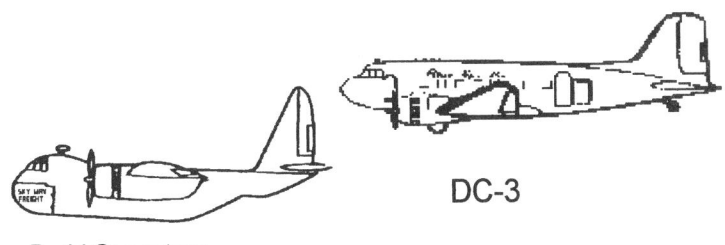

Budd Conestoga   DC-3

By this time the war had been over for a few months and surplus DC-3s were becoming available.

The Douglas DC-3

With the new airplanes added to our fleet, we had outgrown our facility in Long Beach and moved to Mines Field, which later became Los Angeles International. The company sold one Budd to the Tucker Motor Car Company. They used it to transport their car to various auto shows. Another was sold to a company in Cuba, and the last two eventually went to South America.

We improvised as we went along and made a lot of specialty flights that were profitable—such as, Borden's "Elsie the Cow" promotions.

Tiger DC-3 with Miss San Mateo Co., Edith Perrine, and Elsie

Edith Perrine and her sister, Anne, were involved in the "Elsie the cow promotions." A Borden's representative was impressed by the way they handled animals and also had the poise required for dealing with the public.

EDITH PERRINE: Flying Tigers had the contract to provide air transportation for the tour. Teterboro airport was fogged in and the tower would not clear our airplane for takeoff. The captain, Cliff Groh, said the weather was okay with him, so he took off anyway. I thought, well, this should be an interesting trip.

CHAPTER 2 TIGER TALES

Everything went fine until we crossed the Rocky Mountains. We noticed that Elsie was not feeling well. Her nose was dry, and she was not acting herself. Cliff radioed ahead, and a veterinarian was waiting when we landed at Salt Lake City. Elsie had pneumonia, but due to the quick medical treatment she came out okay.

Hedda Hopper, Elsie, Ginny Simms and Cliff Groh

We made stops at Albany, Detroit, Chicago, Omaha, Cheyenne, Salt Lake City, Elko and San Francisco. The westbound trip took 25 hours and the longest ground time was 2 ½ hours. There were only two pilots, captain Cliff Groh and copilot Don Clark, so I don't know if, how, or when they slept.

Yeah, but they were young then…and when they reached California, the trip was only half over. The tour lasted about a month, including stops at San Mateo, Los Angeles, Winslow, Amarillo, Dallas, Oklahoma City, Kansas City, St. Louis, Dayton, Albany and Teterboro.

I guess there were more cow rests than crew rests, after all, Elsie was paying for the gas.

When the company began hiring additional pilots, they attracted many exceptional young men, people who wanted more out of life and were willing to put more into it.

Among them was J. P. "Goldy" Goldsmith. Link Laughlin hired him in Oklahoma City in February 1946. This is how it came about.

GOLDY: I was flying C-54's on the occupation of Japan airlift in September '45 when I was called in to our operations office.

Hap Arnold sent a letter to his local commanders saying he wanted two pilots for a special instrument program. He wanted to set up standard procedures for flying the new Instrument Landing System, "ILS." The letter went to John Long who was my commanding officer. He recommended me and one other guy for this work.

We were flying DC-3s up and down the East Coast in zero-zero weather. Our job was to fly from La Guardia Airport, NY; to Newark; Presque Isle and Bangor, Maine; Manchester, New Hampshire; Boston, Mass; and back to La Guardia. We did our best flying when the airlines shut down because of weather. We really went looking for zero-zero conditions. We shot the approaches and touched our wheels down on each of those airports every day, no matter what the weather, for five and a half months. Most of the ILS procedures we still use today came out of that test program. That's what I was doing just before I got out of service.

A friend of mine, Al Pfeifer, who had just come back from China, stopped in at Long Beach to look up some Tiger guys there. I got a letter from him saying he had taken a job with

CHAPTER 2   TIGER TALES   41

the Tigers as a salesman at no pay, just commission, and was starving, but hopeful. He said he met Prescott and was convinced he would make a go of the airline, and he asked if I was interested. When he told me about the operation, I said that it sounded like a challenge I'd love.

I went to see my commanding officer, John Long, and told him I had a job offer if I could get out of the service. I was out the next day.

I went to Oklahoma City, where Tigers had just opened an office. Link Laughlin was the chief pilot, and when I showed him the letter, I was hired. I had logged a lot of time in a DC-3, so I was hired as a captain. Link gave me a check ride in a 3, and I was supposed to get checked in a Budd that Cliff Groh was bringing in from Los Angeles that afternoon. Cliff couldn't get the landing gear locked down, so he brought it in on its belly. That was our last operational Budd, so I never did get to fly one.

The wreckage of the Budd in New Mexico was right on the airway, and we used to look down at it as we flew over. Then we noticed that it seemed to be getting smaller as time went on. Come to find out, the Navajos were taking the stainless steel skin and were using it to make silver bracelets for the tourists.

Bill Thompson had taken his discharge from the service and had read an article about the Flying Tigers in the Readers Digest. He wrote a letter to Les Berryman, who was in charge of maintenance at Tigers, explaining how they would benefit from his services as a mechanic.

Les wrote back and said, "Okay, if we need you that badly, I guess you're hired."

BILL THOMPSON: I really enjoyed it; I was working maintenance with Jack Studer and Buck Buchanan. A few months later John Dewey and Jack Dupree came on. We used to work as teams and would challenge each other to see who could get our jobs done first.

We got an airplane in every evening and had to finish it that night. When the maintenance was done, we loaded the flowers or what ever else the cargo was. Bob Prescott came out and helped us load flowers on several occasions. We didn't care about shifts—we just stayed until the airplane was done. It was really enjoyable. We looked forward to coming to work, and from then on we just grew.

CATFISH: Ray Allen came with us in 1946 and was based in New York for a while. I was the chief pilot at the time, and I had set Ray up with Ralph Hedden to get checked out as captain on the DC-3. They got along like two cats with their tails tied together. They were on one of those Newsweek trips, and if I remember right, they flew from New York to Denver then Seattle.

I got a call from Ralph Hedden from Seattle, saying, "I don't want to fly with that so an' so anymore! He does this and that, and he makes me so mad I just don't want to fly with him!"

I said, "Well, I just want you to check him out. When he's checked out you won't have to fly with him."

"You mean I have to fly with him until he's checked out?"
"Yes."
"Okay, he's checked out!"

BUCK BUCHANAN: I hired on in Long Beach as a mechanic. Later, after we moved to Mines Field, my wife, Jerry, went to work in the tool crib. After we moved to Burbank, I went into the Engine Buildup Shop as a lead mechanic and foreman, and Jerry became the secretary.

CHAPTER 2   TIGER TALES

Buck Buchanan looks a little leery of that lousy lion

That year the company could have become part of a large international operation, but for a tragic accident of fate.

JOE ROSBERT: Chennault came by in the summer of '46 and talked to us about an airline he was starting in China, CAT. Prescott and the rest of us were interested; because he said we could do this together...form a big operation with what our airline was doing in the States and what he was doing in China.

We all agreed that it was worth looking into, so Prescott said, "I'll send my brother to Shanghai to check it out, and if it looks like you say, we'll go ahead with it."

Catfish and I had already talked to the old man (Chennault) about going back with him.

I told him, "I'm the superintendent of flight operations here, and I would like to get into that part of the operation in China."

He said, "Within a year we should be able to do that."

Prescott's brother, George, who was an accountant, packed his bags and headed for China. He laid over in the Manila Hotel in the Philippines on the way. While George was in the lobby, some Filipino gangsters came by looking for someone they were supposed to rub out. They sprayed the lobby with machine gun fire, and George Prescott, an innocent bystander, was killed. That completely squelched any incentive that Bob Prescott had for the project.

Catfish and I went in and told Bob that we wanted to go to China anyway and help the old man out, since we had already committed ourselves.

The airline could have gone under very quickly had it not been for the ingenuity and the will, if not outright devotion, these pilots had for Prescott and the company.

GOLDY: I was the chief pilot in Kansas City when we bought those 15 DC-3s in Walnut Ridge, Arkansas. I flew as much as 150 hours a month just checking out new pilots. These were on-the-line checkouts. When John Long got out of service, he bought a new Aeronca Chief and came taxiing up to our hanger. I hired him before he could get away. John was 36 years old and the company thought that was too old. The first chance I had, I got him a trip to Los Angeles where he met Bob, and fortunately, they got along great.

CHAPTER 2 TIGER TALES

When we started out we were on a cash basis, because we didn't have much credit. We had a cash box, and as we'd leave on a trip, we'd reach in and get some money, stuff it into our pockets and go. We kept the company's money in one pocket and our own in another. When we got back from the trip, if we could put back more money than we took, we knew we had made a profit. No one would even think of taking five or ten bucks for himself because we were all trying to keep the company afloat. Sometimes Cliff Groh would forget which pocket was his money and which was the Company's, but I think it worked out pretty much even.

In the early days the freight was often unloaded in Chicago, then we had to ferry the airplane to Newark. The planes had folding metal drop down seats along the sides of the cabin. We used to go to the terminal and round up people who wanted to go to Newark. We charged them $30 cash, which we would then use to fill the tanks with gas.

About that time the company acquired a four engine DC-4 and moved from Mines Field to larger facilities at Lockheed Air Terminal in Burbank. The employees were greeted by a sign that read, "Your Company has moved to Burbank. Park your cars and board the DC-4."

CATFISH: Tommy Haywood had been flying for Consairways out of San Diego. This outfit was flying under a lucrative government subcontract. Prescott had Haywood get all the information he could, so we could bid on the contract. Tommy went back and flew for them for another few months until he had the information, then he quit and came with us. They were sure mad when they found out about that. We won the contract, and that really pulled us out of the hole.

This was a typical move by Bob Prescott. He knew when the contract was up for renewal. He made the necessary preparations. Then he had the audacity to bid on the contract with no pilots and minimum facilities.

GOLDY: The Air Transport Command contract was for the military to provide 32 C-54s, and we would provide the flight crews, maintenance and operations support. We had two departures a day to Tokyo and two departures a day to Honolulu. All these flights were from Travis AFB, California.

When Bob announced that he had this contract, there were only two Tiger pilots who had flown the C-54. Neither one of us were current according to the military requirements. So Bob had no choice but to go out on the street and hire pilots. Because a lot of Air Corps pilots at Travis had inside information, several of them got immediate discharges from the service and hired on.

JOE RAFFERTY: I was a former 6th Ferry Group pilot at Long Beach and a C-54 instrument instructor at Homestead, Florida. I had my ATR and was qualified as captain.

I heard about the ATC contract from a friend at Slick Airways. I gave Tigers a call and was told to report to Lockheed Air Terminal for a 07:00 January 1, 1947, departure for a route check to Tokyo.

With the route check out of the way, I was on my way to Tokyo again. We had crew changes at Honolulu, Kwajalein, Guam and Tokyo. Sometimes we also had mail stops at Johnston Island and Iwo Jima. At Tokyo we stayed at the Meisner House, formerly the German consulate.

I was getting up one morning for an 06:00 departure when I heard water running and lots of giggling from a stall shower which was obscured by steam. They were Tiger pilots who said they were doing research, but I never did identify them.

Good thinkin' Joe. It wouldn't do to interrupt basic research into the baser business of the bath.

CHAPTER 3   THE FLYING TIGER LINE   1947

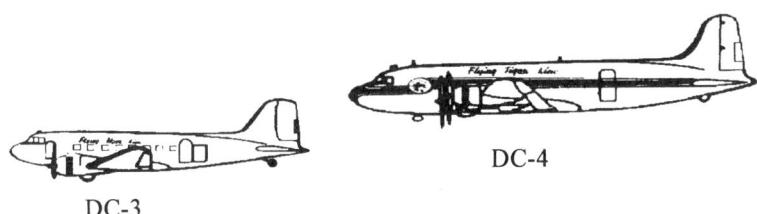

DC-3

DC-4

By this time everybody called the airline "The Tigers" anyway, so the company name was officially changed from National Skyways Freight to the Flying Tiger Line.

BOBBIE THARP: After being discharged from the Navy, I went to Los Angeles. On New Year's Day 1947 my wife and I were at the Rose Bowl game in Pasadena on our honeymoon. I had a letter of recommendation in my pocket to give to Western Airlines who I hoped would hire me, but I was much more interested in our honeymoon than the job and kept putting off the contact. Eventually financial reality dictated that I come down out of the clouds...or should I say, get up into them.

As I walked up the stairs to the Western Airlines office in the old Burbank terminal building, I met a guy coming down. It was Dick Story, one of my navigators from my days in the service.

He said, "Bob, what in the heck are you doing here?"

"I'm going to deliver this letter of recommendation and try to land a job. What are you doing?"

"I'm on my way to Tokyo with the Flying Tiger Line. They just got a big military contract, and they're hiring pilots."

I went on up the stairs to the office and found that Western had moved out the day before and Tigers had moved in during the night. I recognized some of the guys from China, and they recognized me.

One of them said, "Hey, you're a four engine driver."

"Yah."

"Well here, fill this out and bring it to my office. Don't bother standing in line."

When I went in he glanced at my application and said, "You'll get your check-ride tonight, then take your first trip out in the morning."

I went down stairs where my wife and Dick were talking. She said, "What happened? Did you get the job with Western?"

"No," I said, "I'm going to Tokyo in the morning with the Flying Tigers."

"You've got to be kidding!"

"No he's not," Dick said, laughing, "and I'm going to be his navigator."

So I was on the company's first C-54 flight across the Pacific. Those were exciting times.

Flying Tiger C-54 on Wake Island

CHAPTER 3   TIGER TALES   49

When I returned from my first trip on the Pacific, crew scheduling asked if I could go right out again. I said sure.

"Okay, we'll turn you around in Honolulu and get you right back."

They did, and when I got back they were setting me up for another trip.

I said, "Hey you guys, I'm on my honeymoon! Couldn't you let me go back to Seattle to at least get some clean clothes?"

"Sure," they said, "why don't you just take the whole month of February off?"

I about died right there. I thought I was being fired.

"No," they said, "you helped us, now we want to help you."

I was treated that way through all my years with Tigers.

While Bobbie was on his honeymoon, along came Joe.

JOE RAFFERTY: We were going into Johnston Island, which looked like a carrier deck from the air. Art Seymour was my copilot, and I had him land the airplane while I took an 8 mm movie of the beautiful approach to the short strip.

Some of the new-hire C-54 pilots tried to ride roughshod over the old Tiger pilots. They should have known better.

GOLDY: At that time we had no seniority list, so the guys who were hired for the ATC contract set up their own and had their own chief pilot. As far as they were concerned we were out of a job. I went to Bob and pleaded our case, telling him we had been with him since the beginning and certainly should have some priority on this. He assured me that as soon as the operation got going and we were checked out, we would be phased into the system.

I volunteered to come in with no pay to set up the training program, thereby insuring that we got checked out first. I got John Long and myself qualified, then I turned it all over to Herb Wall and John and I went flying. Because of the way the ATC guys tried to treat us, when the contract was over in the fall of '47 and we won the politics of it all, we said okay, now you're out. Now we set up the seniority list, which did not include anyone hired for the ATC contract.

Elgen Long was hired as a radio operator on C-54s. When the contract was over, the company had one leased DC-4, which is the civilian designation for the C-54, so they kept one navigator and one radio operator. Elgen turned out to be whichever one of these they needed.

Soon after the move to Burbank, Tigers built an engine buildup shop, a battery shop and a propeller shop inside the old concrete Lockheed P-38 revetments.

BILL THOMPSON: We hired a lot of people, but those that weren't much good were soon gone, and the good ones just seemed to stay on all the way through.

The DC-3, the only airplane available, was not a great cargo airplane. It couldn't haul a very heavy load, but in the beginning we were lucky to have anything to haul anyway. We had a lot of flower charters from California to the East Coast, and soon we were also hauling fresh fruit and vegetables.

We improvised as we went along and many specialty flights that were profitable. We transported Roy Roger's horse, Trigger, and several racehorses. A DC-3 was billed as the World's Greatest Horse Ship. That led to the realization that we could haul most any kind of livestock.

CHAPTER 3　　　TIGER TALES　　　51

AL MOBLEY: "Colley" Colquette hired me as a mechanic in February 1947. (Colley had been Prescott's crew chief on his P-40 in the AVG.) Bill Thompson, Joe Cuppet and O. C. Stubbs were there—in fact Stubby was my lead man at first. Jim Thomas and Rademacher were also there.

A Budd horse charter

Although wages and working conditions may have left something to be desired, there was no shortage of applicants.

GOLDY: In the early years sometimes the company would hire a copilot on a trip basis. They paid them three dollars an hour, and when the trip was over they were gone.

We flew those early DC-3s in the winter when the heaters would only work during descent. Many a night we froze our butts off. Tommy Haywood had found a hell of a deal on some military surplus Janitrol heaters. They were cheap, but we couldn't get them to work during climb or cruise. Maintenance went through them and found that they were made for the P-51 Mustang. They had a safety switch operated by ram air, and would not light until a relatively high airspeed was reached. When they reset the switch for the DC-3 airspeed, the heaters worked okay.

Wouldn't you know it, just when they got the heaters working they wanted the airplane converted to a walk-in freezer.

BOBBIE THARP: I often flew a Pacific trip in a DC-4, then a domestic trip to Kansas City in a DC-3. One day I got a phone call from Tigers saying, "You're set up to go to Kansas City tonight, and you had better bring warm clothes."
 I thought that was kind of strange. It was in the fall but wasn't that cold. Come to find out the company had been experimenting with hauling strawberries. They took a DC-3 and made a refrigerator out of it. It was so dammed cold in the cockpit that we had a light bulb on a cord and I stuck it down inside my shirt to keep warm.

What did the copilot shove down his shirt? Or did he take their advice and wear his long handles?

GOLDY: In 1947 we bought five DC-4s. We used two of them for charter work on the north Atlantic and the others on domestic routes. Now we could offer nonstop service to New York in only 13 hours. After the ATC contract was over in the fall, they cut back to five crews on the West Coast for domestic freight, and Bob sent me and Ralph Hedden back to Newark to set up the DC-4 charters.

CHAPTER 3   TIGER TALES   53

John Long was made superintendent of flight operations for the company, so I guess age and experience count for something after all.

ELGEN LONG: (no relation to John) In October when the ATC contract was over, Milt Lange, the chief navigator, and I went to the East Coast and were flying out of Teterboro, New Jersey. I was the only radio operator, so I guess that made me the chief. My first trip on the North Atlantic was to Oslo, Norway, with Goldy.

At Oslo they had a big celebration at the City Hall for us. Of course we were dead tired and about to fall asleep in the soup after the first few glasses of Aquavit, or whatever we were drinking. The big celebration was because we were taking the first Norwegian crew to Norfolk, Virginia. There they would pick up the first of many ships that would rebuild the Norwegian merchant marine. Before WW II Norway had the world's largest merchant fleet.

On the way back we changed flight crews in Shannon, Ireland, and Ralph Hedden was the captain on the return trip. Because I was the only radio operator the company had, I had to continue on to Norfolk. I believe that was the first Flying Tiger trip on the North Atlantic.

George survived the early days of aviation, survived the war and was ready for some peace and quiet. Then Janet Olson found him.

GEORGE BOCK: I started flying in 1932. I soloed and passed my flight check for my ten-hour private license in an OX-5 Challenger. I received Massachusetts State license number 16, issued by the Registry of Motor Vehicles.

My first real flying job was with Wiggens Airways at Norwood, Massachusetts, in 1939-40. I was an all-around hand, gassing airplanes, hopping passengers and ferrying airplanes.

When the war came along, I went to work for the Air Corps Ferry Command as a civilian pilot. I was based at Baltimore, Maryland, for a short spell, then transferred to Long Beach, California.

In June 1942 I received a commission as a second lieutenant. I ferried BT-13s, Hudsons, Venturas, B-25s, B-24s, B-17s, A-20s, P-38s and a few more.

I took A-20s across the South Atlantic to Abadan, Iran, and took a P-38 across the North Atlantic to Prestwick, Scotland.

After completing instrument school at Homestead A.F.B., Florida, I flew the Atlantic on the "Crescent" run to Africa and India.

In 1944 I transferred to Hamilton Field, California, and flew the Pacific in C-54s. I transferred to Travis AFB, California, in 1946 and became director of flight training. I separated from the service in 1947 as a Major.

I worked in the San Joaquin Valley as a crop duster, until Janet Olson, from Flying Tigers, called and offered me a job.

Now that the ATC contract was over, the company returned to nearly its former size, but many lessons had been learned along the way. Money could be made flying charters overseas if certain political problems could be solved. The pilots themselves, kept many small legal technicalities, from becoming large problems...if they couldn't be ignored altogether.

CHAPTER 3   TIGER TALES   55

GOLDY: It was pretty grim that year, and we didn't know if we were going to make it or go out of business. In the spring we began passenger charters on the North Atlantic. Then we started getting refugee charters and, before it was over, Tigers hauled more refugees than any other airline.

Passenger flights at that time used only one steward or stewardess. The first chief steward was John Weil, appointed in 1948.

Tigers also hauled a lot of combination passenger and cargo loads. Some were not very good combinations.

AL MOBLEY: We had a DC-4 with a load of carnations and strawberries plus a couple of racehorses in stalls. When the plane arrived in Chicago, the crew found that the horses had eaten all the strawberries. I hope those horses didn't have to race for a few days.

They unloaded what was left of the cargo and converted the airplane to passenger configuration. The combined smell of carnations, strawberries and horse manure is really hard to get rid of. I sure hope the passengers all had colds.

The Orchid Odyssey

JOHN "DOBBIE" DOBSON: One night in the late forties I was flying a DC-3 from Phoenix to El Paso with a full load of orchids. About 3 a.m., between Phoenix and Tucson, the left engine caught fire. I couldn't put the fire out, and finally the burning engine fell off the airplane.

During the fire the hydraulic lines burned through and, due to the loss of hydraulic pressure to hold them up, the landing gear extended. This extra drag made it impossible to maintain level flight on one engine. The airplane kept losing altitude until we crashed in a field near Eloy, Arizona.

After the airplane cartwheeled to a stop, I sat there for a moment thinking, ten minutes ago I was flying along without a care in the world, and now I'm sitting here in this field with the damned airplane on fire.

My copilot who had gone out the escape hatch yelled, "Dobbie, get the hell out of there 'fore it blows up!"

I climbed out of the burning airplane, and then remembered that my wife had just bought me a new suitcase. I figured I had better not come home without it, so I ran back and opened the cargo door. Several boxes of orchids were in front of the door, so I threw them out and grabbed my suitcase.

While the townsfolk stood in the field in their nightgowns watching the airplane burn up, I passed out orchids to all the ladies.

CHAPTER 4   THE DOUGLAS DC-4   1948

ELGEN LONG: In 1948 we started flying the DC-4 to Puerto Rico and hauling passengers from there to New York. To save money, weight, operational problems and time, I was made a combination radio operator and navigator. I didn't work for Tigers all the time. Sometimes there was no job. Quite often I would be called when they had an international trip.

A couple more old China hands were hired that year, Dick Stuelke and Bob Zalusky.

DICK STUELKE: In 1948 I returned to the States, hired on with Tigers and went out on a trip that same night. I was based in Denver for a while, then Burbank, Los Angeles and finally San Francisco.

I guess Dick wants us to think that was the extent of his career with Tigers, and that nothing exciting ever happened to him. I wouldn't want to leave the impression that trouble followed him around, but we'll come back to him several times.

BOB ZALUSKY: When I went into the Army Air Corps, the brass said my frame was too large to fit in a fighter, so they put me in twin-engine cargo planes. I went to China and flew C-46s out of Kunming, and that's where I first met the Flying Tiger guys.

After the war I tried to get a flying job but couldn't, so I went back to the University of Minnesota. After I graduated I took my wife and child and went to California, where I bought a bar in Thousand Oaks. I dropped in at the Flying Tigers in Burbank once in a while to visit some of the guys I knew from China, but there were no jobs.
Several months later Janet Olson, who ran crew control at Tigers, called.

"Bob could you take a trip from San Francisco to Kansas City for us tonight?"

I said, "Sure."

I rode up to San Francisco on United Airlines while trying to remember how to fly a DC-3. When I got to the Tiger ramp, there was Captain Tony Machado waiting beside a DC-4. I had never been in a DC-4 in my life, but that's the way we did things in those days.

When the military contract was over, the maintenance people had a lot of odd jobs to keep them busy. They converted several C-47s to passenger configuration, which were then flown to Egypt. They also overhauled and modified two Lockheed Lodestars for customers. Of course sometimes the pilots contributed to the mechanics' job security.

GOLDY: We had a DC-4 with a fairly new guy checked out in it. The short runway at Midway Airport in Chicago had a huge concrete abutment to keep airplanes from overruns onto the city streets. In this case it worked just fine. He hit it and destroyed the nose of the airplane.

This was an early model DC-4, and it was not built in sections like the later models. There was another DC-4 on the East Coast that was salvaged, so the company sent some mechanics back east to get it. They took the damaged

CHAPTER 4   TIGER TALES   59

nose off of our airplane one piece at a time and managed to replace all the damaged parts. That DC-4 was flying again in sixty days.

Talk about getting your nose tweaked

Tigers also began a lucrative transcontinental charter passenger operation using two DC-4s.

GOLDY: We got some additional overseas business and flew trips into Tel Aviv. John Dewey and Joe Cuppet and several mechanics went over there. We had five airplanes flying about 35,000 Yemenite Jews from the desert to Israel. Many of these people had never been near an airplane, but calmly took their seats.

As I understand it, their Scriptures promised, "Ye shall be taken up on silver wings and carried to the land of David."

Or words to that effect. It must be have taken a lot of faith.

AL MOBLEY, mechanic: I spent two months in Tel Aviv on the Yemenite operation. Curt Steiner, Phil Gold and I were over there. It was a very unhealthy place then, and at least one of us was sick most of the time.

I used to get called for a lot of field trips like that, because I lived too close to the airport. Some of the pilots were Johnny Holmes, Bill Korth, Skip Lane, Glen Myer, and Al Silver was there for a while.

Problems came up form time to time that required expertise not usually possessed by the average pilot.

DUKE HEDMAN: In addition to being a captain, Tommy Haywood also served as an engineering officer from the day he came with us. He figured out how to keep things cool in the cargo planes and all kinds of things like that.

I knew Tommy very well; in fact when I got married, we held the wedding and reception at his house.

Cliff Groh was invited. He was driving to the wedding in his convertible, but he must have started celebrating early. He was going so fast that he missed the driveway completely and drove his car clear up on top of the mountain and couldn't get it down. He had to hire a crane to lift it off the mountaintop.

CHAPTER 5   THE CURTISS C-46   1949

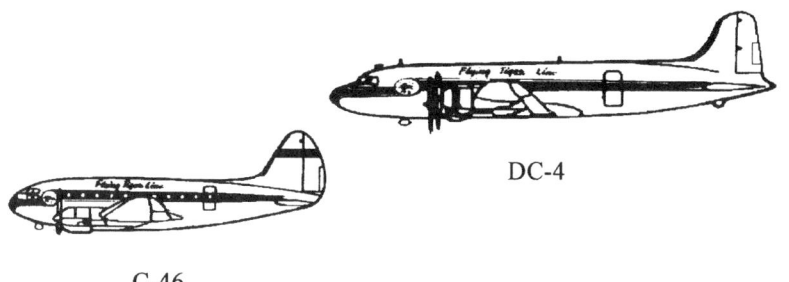

DC-4

C-46

Tigers located a couple of C-46s, which they leased. They knew from the China days that they were tough airplanes and could haul a good load, but until now they had not been available. By this time the military began declaring some of their C-46 cargo planes surplus and put them up for sale. Tigers won a bid on eighteen of them, which were parked in Pyote, Texas. Now came the hard part.

Rattlesnake city

Al Goldberg and a crew of his Tiger mechanics went to Texas to get them in shape to be flown to Burbank. Most of the C-46s had less than ten flying hours on them, but many had been stripped of parts and equipment. Some had their wings removed and had engines and propellers lying on the ground. The local inhabitants of the area did not welcome the mechanics: hundreds of rattlesnakes.

You realize this could take all week

The mechanics had a tough job, but they managed to get the additional airplanes flyable. They arrived in Burbank just in time. In April the C.A.B. (Civil Aeronautics Board) awarded Tigers Airfreight Route 100. It had been applied for in 1946, but that's the government. Route 100 provided all cargo service from California through the northern states to the East Coast.

CHAPTER 5   TIGER TALES   63

Soon to be a new C-46

Well, nearly new

GOLDY: John Long was head of operations, and Herb Wall was chief pilot in Burbank then. Part of that time I was chief pilot in Newark. Sometimes Burbank and I hired pilots on the same date. We always attempted to be fair about pilot placement on the seniority system, so when more than one was hired on the same day we would record the exact minute they were hired.

I was lucky to get some fine pilots in the early days...people like Ralph Hedden, Jack Russell, Doug Buskey and Ken Henderson. All you had to do with guys like that was give them an airplane, tell them to take it to Timbuktu, or anyplace else in the world, and they would just do it. Nobody had to tell them <u>how</u> to do it.

In the fall we had five airplanes in Europe, but only one credit card for fuel, and it had reached its limit. One day a mechanic, Tommy Reese, walked in looking for a job.

I asked him, "Do you have a credit card?"

He swallowed and with some trepidation admitted that he did. I hired him, and used his credit card to fill all five DC-4s with gas.

Later the director of maintenance said, "Why did you have to hire another mechanic?"

All I said was, "Believe me, it was necessary."

When our European operation was over, Tommy wanted to stay there, so he hired on with TWA in Rome.

If Bob Prescott could be presumed to have any faults, it would probably be that he couldn't say no.

DICK STRATFORD: Dianna Bixby came to Bob with a business proposal. She had a DC-3, which she was willing to lease to Tigers, on the condition that she came with it. She wanted to fly it as captain and have Tigers provide the other crewmembers. I was new with the company, so I was assigned to fly with her as her copilot. We flew from Newark to Hartford and Boston, then back to Newark. I'm sure she was the first woman to fly captain on any part 121 (airline) operation.

There is an interesting story behind all this. Dianna was a Converse, of the Converse Rubber Company, before she married. As I understand it her grandmother, who was a rugged individualist, became a steamboat captain on the Mississippi River. I guess Dianna wanted to take after her grandmother, so she became an airline captain.

I flew with her for about two months, and then I was checked out as a captain myself. About that time Dianna got bored with it all and went back out to the West Coast. I continued to fly that airplane along with Dobson and others of that seniority group. We were not particularly enthusiastic about making that trip, because it took all day and earned us only very few hours pay.

All I can say about the DC-3 operation is that it was a lot of work. We flew the trip to Boston five to six days a week. Although we were based in Newark, New Jersey, and would depart at six a.m., the company had set the schedule so that we were required to return to Newark at nine p.m. The reason for this was so that the cargo from that flight could be transloaded on a flight to the West Coast that same night.

At that time, you got no per diem pay unless you were away from home for more than 16 hours. To make matters worse, we got our legal rest in Boston. On these trips we would land in Newark about nine p.m. or later, drive 45 minutes to get home, then have to get up at three a.m. for a six a.m. departure. This gave us a maximum of five hours at home. I got most of my legal rest, especially in the summer time, down in the old Howard Burlesque House. It was dark, quiet and air-conditioned. As a copilot I was paid only $210 per month, so I couldn't afford a hotel room. After I checked out as captain I think I made about $400 a month.

GOLDY: I negotiated the first ALPA (Airline Pilots' Association) labor contract in 1950. When we were nearly done with it, the company got a contract in Bremen, Germany, hauling Displaced Persons to Australia. Bob asked me to go over there to set up and run the operation.

I said, "I don't like to do that because we're still working on our contract negotiations."

Bob thought it over for a minute and then said, "What do you really want?"

So we negotiated the terms of the contract over the telephone before I would accept the assignment. I took all this information to Ken Henderson, who was a new pilot at the time. He had indicated a desire to get involved in union work and had had some experience with it when he was with United. Ken took over the negotiations and the contract was signed soon after.

The following story by Pete Peralta happened just before he hired on with Tigers as a navigator. Though it is not a Tiger story, it might help to explain how Pete got to be like he is.

PETE PERALTA: I was doing some freelancing for an outfit called Skyways. We were ferrying a DC-3 to the Republic of Cameroon just north of the old Belgian Congo. I was with a guy named Bill Taylor. We took off across the North Atlantic to Shannon and spent the night there. Then we headed for Algiers, where we arrived late. We fueled the airplane as soon as we arrived, then spent the night in

CHAPTER 5   TIGER TALES   67

the American Embassy.

As we left the next morning I asked Bill, "Did you check the gas tanks?"

"Yes, I checked them last night."

We took off and headed across the Atlas Mountains. About half way across the Sahara Desert, I thought I'd better go back and check our reserve fuel. The reserve tanks were dry. The Algerians had fueled us the night before, and then stolen the fuel while we were asleep. This was when the Communists had taken over Algiers.

There was a little airport there in the middle of the Sahara called Insalah. It meant "God be willing." We circled around and tried to call the tower, but there was no answer.

We landed and taxied up to the pumps, but the pumps were dry. A four-engine plane was sitting there, but its engines were missing, the tires were flat and the windows were all shot out.

Bill looked at me and said, "Let's get out of here!"

It was 3 p.m. and the temperature was over 130 degrees. The needle was off the scale, so we didn't know how hot it was.

We tried to take off, but the plane wouldn't fly.

Bill said, "I'm going to bounce it three times. On the third bounce pull up the gear."

The third time it bounced into the air. I pulled the gear and we went out over the desert, about five feet above the sand with the props stirring up dust devils behind us. There was nowhere else to go, so when we gained a thousand feet of altitude we turned back to Algiers. This time I took care of the gas myself. We had been heading for Niamey, in the southern Sahara, so we sent a message to cancel our flight plan. The next day we flew down there and arrived 45 minutes before they got our message from the day before.

In all my years with the Tigers I don't remember any problems with any of the crews or anyone else.

THE FAMOUS BILL ICE STORY

DOBBIE: I was flying copilot for Bill Ice in a DC-3. We were grinding along when Bill began to get stomach cramps and had to use the can. That's literally what it was, a five-gallon can. Only in this case someone had forgotten to put it aboard. Bill just had to go, so he went back in the cabin and found an old newspaper. He did what nature demanded, but now that he had gotten it out of his system, what would he do with it? He came back to the cockpit, opened his side window and carefully thrust the heavily laden newspaper out the window. The 160 mph slipstream snatched the newspaper—leaving Bill standing there with his hands full.

CHAPTER 6   REFUGEE CHARTERS   1950

C-46

DC-4

Tigers had established a considerable passenger business and hired a number of pilots and stewardesses, even before the North Koreans embarked on their misadventure. Experienced pilots who had flown C-46s and DC-4s during the war were readily available.

When Tigers obtained a large government contract to fly displaced persons (DPs) out of Europe, they leased some DC-4s from Viking Airlines. Billie Welsh, a stewardess for Viking, came with the airplanes as part of the deal. This was fortunate for Tigers.

Billie's reputation of having a high moral standard, a hard work ethic, and a track record of "doing the paperwork right," earned her a position with Tigers. After about six months she was promoted to chief stewardess. She was strict on new hires, and made high demands regarding neatness, moral integrity, punctuality and loyalty to the company that signed their paychecks. She designed the stewardess uniforms and placed the contract for their manufacture.

This was one night Prescott probably wished he had gone straight home.

GOLDY: Dianna Bixby wanted to set a record by making an around-the-world solo flight, and she was looking for some backing. One night after Prescott had a few drinks in a bar, he bought a de Havilland Mosquito and gave it to her for her attempt.

He asked me to help set up the flight, so I hired Danny Danielson, an experienced and well-regarded navigator. He made up the flight plans for the entire trip. She couldn't get the performance she wanted from the airplane and eventually the plan was scrapped.

Sometime after that, Dianna and her husband had a contract hauling lobsters from Mexico to California. Her husband, Bill, I think, was flying a DC-3, and Diane a B-25. She flew into weather on a landing approach and was killed in the crash.

Here is more information from a pilot who would later become very well acquainted with the Mosquito.

This Mosquito can really bite!

CHAPTER 6 TIGER TALES

JACK TALKINGTON: Dianna Bixby did attempt a round the world speed record in April 1950. As I recall the effort failed in India, due to an overheated engine. On the aircraft's return to Burbank, it was purchased by Claire Waterbury of Aircraft Export Sales Ltd. The aircraft went to the Tiger hanger for a cockpit and nose modification.

The modification included an aluminum forward fuselage section, which permitted the aircraft to be pressurized for high-altitude flight.

Some guys start out at the top.

DON SANDERS: I hired on with Tigers in July 1950. When I filled out the application and gave it to John Long, John said, "Go see Herb Wall, our chief pilot."

This was mid-afternoon. At 5 p.m., Herb sent John Murray, who had just been hired the day before, and me up for a check ride in a DC-4. When we came down we were qualified, me as captain and John as copilot.

Herb said, "Don't go too far away. You're both set up at five in the morning to go to Chicago on a passenger load with Captain Graff."

We slept in double-deck bunks in Herb's office until three in the morning when we were awakened for the trip. I flew my first trip with Tigers as a relief captain, and I felt I had found a home.

Dick Rossi did a round-the-world Argosy flight, part of a program that awarded college kids credit for world travel. On this trip he got to lay over in a lot of interesting places. One of them was Tokyo, where they stayed for a week. He had just landed there when the Korean War broke out. His airplane was commandeered to go to the States for a load of ammunition and hand grenades. Rossi, his crew and passengers had to just sit it out in Tokyo until the airplane came back.

DICK ROSSI: When we were over India I flew to Agra so the passengers could see the Taj Mahal. While circling around it, one of the engines blew a jug (cylinder), so we landed at Delhi. Of course no one had a spare jug, so KLM sent one down from Amsterdam, and we had to wait for it. Then it turned out to be a dash 13 jug and we had a dash 11 engine. The basic jug was the same, but we had to take a hammer and chisel and cut some of the fins off so it would fit. We did, and got ourselves back up and on our way.

In addition to the European and charter business, Tigers operated seven DC-4s on the Korean Airlift.

BOBBIE THARP: I was furloughed in '48, so I flew for some nonskeds (nonscheduled airlines) for a while. When the Korean War broke out I called John Long.
    He said, "You're hired! Get down here as quick as you can. Do you know any radio operators and navigators?"
    I said, "Why, yes I do."
    "Hire them and bring them with you."

At the same time Tigers had an operation hauling migrant workers from Puerto Rico to New Jersey and New York to work in the fields.

GOLDY: We had one DC-4 on the East Coast that we put 100 seats in. We had the seats miniaturized and put them six across. That was amazing to have 100 seats in a DC-4.

CHAPTER 6 TIGER TALES 73

We got a lot of publicity out of that.

On a return flight one time Ray Korty radioed in that he had lost his hydraulic system and wouldn't have any brakes on landing. I was operations officer in Newark at the time, so he asked what I wanted him to do.

I said, "Take it to Idlewild, where there are longer and smoother runways."

I thought he would have a lot better chance of getting his plane stopped over there. He landed and held the nose as high as he could for what aerodynamic braking he could get, and that's the way it stopped, with its tail on the ground and the nose pointing at the sky.

DC-4s have a tailskid, which has a small hydraulic cylinder inside to cushion an inadvertent tail strike. In this case the airplane slid along the concrete until it ground the skid through and the hydraulic fluid caught fire. The passengers thought the airplane was on fire and began jumping out. As people began leaving the tail, the airplane settled back down on its nose wheel and no one was hurt.

Then along came Bobbie.

BOBBIE THARP: We had a DC-4 fitted with 100 seats for hauling Mexican farm workers. I was sent to Grand Forks, North Dakota, with a new copilot. We were doing our paperwork in the office when a CAA guy came in.

Everything was okay until my copilot said, "We've got a DC-4 out there with 100 seats in it."

Now the CAA guy had to see it, and I had a hell of a time convincing him it was legal.

Finally he said, "With all those people on here, I want to see some cabin attendants."

Where in the hell would I find cabin attendants in North Dakota? I called my wife's sister and her husband, who lived near Grand Forks, and explained my problem.

They came on as steward and stewardess for five days. We flew from Grand Forks to Saginaw back to Grand Forks to Travers City to Milwaukee, and we completed the contract. Of course Tigers approved it and paid them.

That's just an example of the way things had to be done. Every situation was different, and we were expected to do whatever was necessary to get the job done. No one told us how to do it, just do it.

If you work for an airline, you have to be prepared to do a lot of moving around. When someone quits or gets promoted, you may have an opportunity for advancement yourself.

DON SANDERS: Art Seymour was chief pilot in Salt Lake City while I was based there. He moved out to Burbank to take the chief pilot job there and asked me to take over in Salt Lake. Later, when we closed the Salt Lake City crew base, I went on the line in Chicago for about a month. Then Ed Pinke, who was the Chicago chief pilot, went back to Burbank to take over as director of flight operations. He asked me to take the chief pilot job in Chicago.

Six months later they moved the entire domicile to Detroit. I was there for about two and a half years.

Harry Taulbee, a highly qualified pilot, hired on in 1946 at the urging of his good friend, Tony Machado. He became number four on the pilot seniority list and was soon promoted to assistant superintendent of flight operations serving under Captain Joe Rosbert. Harry, always interested in trying something new, left Tigers in 1948 to fly for El Al, the new Israeli airline.

CHAPTER 6 TIGER TALES 75

In 1950 Harry returned to California and was offered a job with Consolidated Vultee Aircraft Company. They were experimenting with an air-to-air refueling program. He was riding as a passenger in a Lockheed Lodestar owned by Jacqueline Cochran and leased by Consolidated, when it struck a mountain on approach to the Burbank Airport. All aboard were killed.

Harry lived a full life and was well liked by all. He left behind his wife, Roseanne, and baby son, Jay.

All the China hands had to leave China when the Communists took over. Many of them found their way to Tigers when the Korean War broke out. Catfish rejoined Tigers but had lost five years of seniority. They strapped his long lanky frame into the cockpit of a DC-4 and sent him right back out to the Orient. He flew regular runs on the Korean Airlift.

Bob Conrath and Tom Cotton came with us that year. Some people get into flying the hard way, and then find that it can be even harder with Tigers. Tom Cotton, a slim, wiry, redheaded guy, joined the Naval Academy in 1939 with thoughts of becoming a Naval Aviator. Then he found that he would have to put in two years of sea duty as a deck officer before he could even apply for flight training. He resigned and joined the Army Air Corps as an aviation cadet. Some colonel flew over the field in a P-40 and did some pretty fancy aerobatics, and Tom was hooked. He wanted to be a fighter pilot.

He went through advanced training and was sent to China as a replacement pilot for the AVG. By the time he arrived, the AVG had already disbanded and their old P-

40s had been taken over by the 14th Air Force. Tom inherited Bill Bartling's P-40 which was in terrible shape but still flew. Tom served in China until the end of '44 and was flight leader for ground cooperation work. His group did strafing and rocketing work against the Japanese army coming down the Yangtze River.

Tom came back to the States and was the operations officer at Castle Field, California. A short time later he married his staff car driver, so I guess he really was operating.

After taking his discharge he started a small airline flying oil field equipment. That went well until all the drillers moved to Venezuela, and he was out of business.

TOM COTTON: One day I stopped in at Flying Tigers in Burbank to see if they were planning any hiring in the near future.

John Long asked me, "Can you go to Denver tonight?"

I had my wife and kids in the car, but I figured I could leave them at a motel for a day or so, so I said, "Yeah, I guess I could."

"All right, the pay is $270 a month."

Herb Wall checked me out in the airplane, a C-46, and I flew it to Denver that night. Ed Lowe went with me on my first trip. He was one number above me in seniority and had just come back from flying for Panagra (Pan American Grace) in South America. I thought a Burbank to Denver flight would be a quick turnaround, but I was gone for two and a half months. My wife got tired of Archers Motel, so she went to her family in Avenal, California, until I finally got back. I was on the Chicago Denver run on a C-46, so I never got a chance to get home.

One night I was scheduled for a Los Angeles run but because L.A. and Burbank were weathered in, we had to

CHAPTER 6   TIGER TALES   77

land in Palmdale.

I called Janet Olson and said, "I just have to get home and get my car. I've been riding a bicycle to work, and it's getting cold in Chicago."

Anyway, that's how I started with Tigers.

Later on I was on the operation hauling Hungarian refugees from Europe to Australia in DC-4s. One night after a fuel stop in Kuala Lumpur, Malaysia, I was coming into Waga Waga, Australia. When I landed, I saw another Tiger DC-4 on the ramp, so I thought, oh my God; he must have problems of some kind. He should have been out of here before now. Ken Henderson was the captain, and he put his people on my airplane and took off.

I put my people up in the hospital, the only place to stay because there were no facilities there. Then I had to three-engine ferry his airplane to Karachi, India, the nearest place where we could get the engine changed. When it was done, we flew back to Waga Waga and took our passengers to their final destination.

Loading at night

The Curtiss C-46 proved to be an excellent cargo airplane. It could haul almost as much as a four-engine DC-4. The Pratt and Whitney R2800-75 engines were very reliable.

The company used to give check rides out on the line. One night Art Seymour was giving Tom Cotton a check ride in a C-46. While they were over Nebraska, Art said, "You got a fire in the right engine."

Tom began reciting the memory items on the emergency checklist, "Firewall shutoff lever..."

Art said, "Pull it."

"What for?"

"Pull it. This is for real now. Pull it."

Tom pulled it, shut down the engine and feathered the propeller. When the exercise was complete, they couldn't get the propeller unfeathered, so they made an emergency landing at Omaha.

Tigers contracted with an overhaul shop in Oakland, California, to overhaul the C-46 engines. That turned out to be bad news. The engines began to fail almost as fast as our mechanics could hang them on the wings. The company had to find out what was wrong, so they sent Buck Buchanan up there.

BUCK BUCHANAN: I watched the operation, and saw that the work being performed was according to accepted standards, and that the men seemed to be well trained. Come to find out that though they were charging us for new parts, they were not installing them in our engines. Oakland Overhaul was tried and found guilty of using unserviceable parts. The company was heavily fined and some of its officers went to jail.

CHAPTER 6   TIGER TALES   79

Here's an example of one such engine problem.

BOB HAMBY: I was based on the East Coast for about six months, and then transferred to the West Coast to fly the Korean Airlift. After making one trip as copilot, I went in to see John Long.

"I see junior pilots to me flying captain on domestic routes. Frankly John, I need the money. I'd like to fly captain."

John said, "Well I haven't had any reports on you. I don't know if you can fly captain or not."

But he put me on domestic where I flew what I guess you'd call on-the-job training. About six weeks later he gave me a check ride and called me a captain.

My first trip out, while I was over Eagle, Colorado, where I had to climb to 15,000 feet, I lost an engine. So, I had to go back to Grand Junction. I got there and landed safely, so I guess I was a captain. The company thought maybe I had just let the engine ice up. Just in case there was nothing wrong with it, they sent Bob Hawes over from Denver to test fly it. He started it up, and it seemed to run fine, so he took off. Just after takeoff it quit, and he barely managed to get it around and back on the ground. So anyway my actions were justified.

Sequel to Bob Hamby's Engine Failure.

JOHN LAMPING: Bob Hawes and I were in Denver, so they sent us to Grand Junction to check Hamby's failed engine. Maintenance had a new engine there, but they weren't convinced that the engine needed to be changed. They ran it up and it ran good, with 25 to 30 inches of manifold pressure. I don't recall all the details, but they talked us into taking it up, using less power on that engine.

We took off to the north and got maybe 100 feet off the ground when it started coughing and backfiring.

Bob said, "Shut it down and feather it. It's more of a detriment than a help."

We must have wakened the whole city of Grand Junction as we made a sweeping turn and managed to climb on one engine high enough to get back around and land.

Come to find out, the internal blower bearing had failed. At a certain power setting the impeller moved forward enough to disturb the intake airflow, causing the engine to backfire and lose power.

I hope Penny's had a sale on underwear.

BOB HAMBY: During that time we were using those Oakland Overhaul engines on the C-46s. Because of all the engine problems I ended up taking six different airplanes to get from Denver to Chicago and back. Fortunately, they all crapped out on the ground. I never really lost another one in the air. Once I took a load of migrant workers from Chicago to Brownsville, Texas, with a fuel stop in Fort Worth. On takeoff from Fort Worth I lost an engine. I never got off the ground—just ran out across the prairie and bounced over a railroad track, which tore the tail wheel out of the airplane.

No one was hurt, but I never heard so many Mexican expletives in one place in my life!

CHAPTER 7   THE KOREAN WAR   1950 PART 2

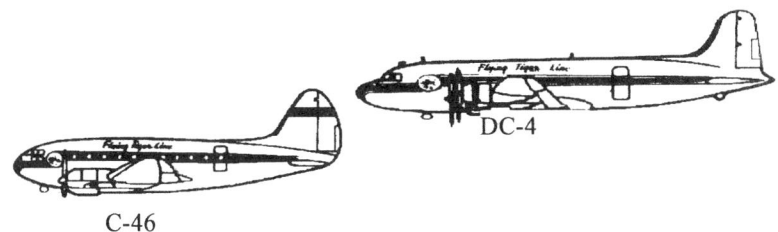

Among many pilots hired after the outbreak of the Korean War—er excuse me, police action—were Jim Bledsoe and Starr Thompson.

STARR THOMPSON: After WW II I worked for several outfits around the Caribbean, flying out of San Juan, Puerto Rico. I flew C-47s for a while then C-46s for about two years.

Finally I wound up in Greenwood, Mississippi, flying for Delta Airlines crop-dusting division. Jim Bledsoe was there, and we became pretty good pals.

After a couple of months Jim got a letter from the Flying Tigers out in California, who needed pilots for the Korean Airlift. Jim and I pooled our money and he called the chief pilot, John Long, on the phone.

"Hi, John, this is Jim Bledsoe. I'm answering your letter, and I would like the job."

Pause.

"Yes, I have my Air Transport Rating."

Another pause, then Jim said, "No, I can't make it by Wednesday. Will Thursday be okay?"

"Okay, John, I'll see you Thursday."

As Jim was about to hang up, I said, "Hey, what about me?"

Jim said, "Oh yeah...Hey, John, I've got a buddy here, Starr Thompson, who wants a job too."

"Yes, he has his ATR."

"Okay, thanks John," and he hung up.

I said with considerable excitement, "What did he say, Jim, what did he say?"

"He said he's putting our names on the seniority list, and he'll see us on Thursday."

Jim has always been one number senior to me. He says that's because he made the phone call.

While we were driving through Arkansas in my '37 Ford 60, I noticed a Highway Patrol cruiser behind us with his gumball machine all lit up. I pulled over and the officer walked up to the passenger side of the car.

He said to Jim, "Aren't you Jim Bledsoe?"

Jim was looking straight ahead as he said, "Yes, I am."

The officer said, "Uncle Jim, don't you recognize me?"

He was General Chennault's son, and Jim used to bounce him on his knee when he was a small boy. The general and his family were from that area.

Sometimes you take off from an airport, but don't arrive at your intended destination. Captain Doug Robbins and Monte Treft took off from Denver one night in a C-46. George Donahoe was deadheading with them. I don't know if they were overloaded, lost an engine or what, but they crash-landed in an alley in Denver. The pilots were not seriously hurt, but investigators found a body in the cockpit. He was wearing a full dress suit and was dead as a doornail, with an obvious broken neck. The mystery continued until they searched the cabin and found an empty coffin, which had broken open in the crash. The death certificate stated that the person had died of a broken neck.

Meanwhile Goldy had his hands full in Europe. The company had an operation out of Bremen, Germany, haul-

CHAPTER 7   TIGER TALES

ing displaced persons to Sydney, Australia. The operation started with one airplane, but ended up with five. Goldy sent a message back to the States telling them to make sure the airplanes had been cleared by the health department in Idlewild before departure. The people who got the message didn't know what he was talking about and the airplanes arrived with no certificate.

GOLDY: We filled out a blank form and got an official looking stamp of some kind from a military guy. We stamped the paper then turned the stamp slightly and stamped it again to make it blurred.

Lou Le Clere was one of our captains and Jimmy Powers was the copilot. I gave the form to Le Clere and said, "Here, this should get you through."

It did, as far as Calcutta.

When they got to Calcutta, they were nearly thrown in the clink. The officials there recognized that the stamp was not legal and held the airplane, passengers and crew. Lou was smart enough to know that he had to get rid of the evidence, so he swiped the phony health form and destroyed it. Then he went to a higher authority and convinced the man that the local officials had lost his health certificate and were afraid to admit it. His ruse worked, and they let him go.

Le Clere delivered his passengers in Sydney, and then flew back to Colombo, Ceylon, for a crew rest.

GOLDY: The bell captain in the hotel in Colombo gave Le Clere a box to deliver to me for transshipment when he returned to Bremen. No one told him what was in it, and he didn't ask. The box was the size of a cigar box, so it was

reasonable to assume that is what it was. Lou stuffed the box into an old canvas B-4 bag he was using as luggage, and promptly forgot about it.

Le Clere returned to Bremen, and a couple of days later he noticed a suspicious stain on his bag. He remembered the box, so he opened the bag and took it out.

GOLDY: Jimmy Powers was there as Le Clere unwrapped the box and found all this weird brown mess. He was going to stick his finger in it and taste it, but suddenly it dawned on him what it was.

He'd heard a rumor about a copilot—a real kooky guy who had flown one trip over there and was no longer with us. Seems this copilot got drunk in Colombo on a layover and mentioned that he thought his wife was fooling around on him. He asked one of the local boys to get him some Cobra poison. He was going to get her and whomever she was fooling around with.

There in the box was a broken vial, which still contained the Cobra fangs. The brown mess was the poison and was now all through Lou's bag. The idea was you could dip the fangs in the poison and pop somebody with them and in seconds that person would be dead. Lou called and told me about it, and I called a military doctor that I knew.

The doctor asked, "Is he still alive?"
"Yes. He just called me."
"How long ago was it that he touched the stuff?"
"More than thirty minutes."
"Well if he's still alive now, then he's all out of danger."

Once in a while a company will have somebody at headquarters they want to get rid of, so they'll send that person

CHAPTER 7   TIGER TALES   85

overseas. Goldy had one like that one time down in Colombo, Ceylon.

GOLDY: The guy was supposed to get us landing rights at Negombo, another airport there. He wouldn't tell me what was wrong, but every day he'd send a message saying they were still having problems, but that he was working feverishly.

George Edge was sitting in Bahrain with a load of passengers and had been told not to proceed. I told him to go anyway, and that I would try to take care of it from here.

Goldy was known to take a little gin now and then, for social or business purposes.

GOLDY: Fortunately, we had made a deal with Australian National Airways to handle us on that operation which terminated in Sydney. Their regional manager, Harry—I don't remember his last name—came to Bremen one time, and we shared a few bottles of gin getting to know one another. This came in handy. I called him to find out what the hell was going on down in Colombo.

He said, "Well, the airport is closed and all flights have to go into the new airport at Negombo, which is run by the military."

I said, "We don't have landing rights in Negombo, and I have two airplanes en route to Colombo."

Harry said, "Don't worry, I'll fix it."

Within the hour he called back and had the landing rights approved.

"How did you do that so quickly?"

"It wasn't so hard," Harry said. "I promised the adjutant's secretary that you would send her a package of silk stockings. They aren't available here."

I went to the PX and had a GI buy a Christmas gift package containing three pairs of silk stockings. I put them on the next airplane for Negombo.

Just for laughs when I sent in my expense report I listed $5.00 for three pairs of silk stockings for landing rights in Negombo. When I got back to the States after the operation was over, Fred Benninger, the company treasurer, called me in.

With a smirk on his face he said, "Okay, tell me the true story of the silk stockings."

I did, but I don't think he ever believed me.

Here, as the saying goes, is the rest of the story. Can you imagine just sitting in an airplane that long, much less flying it?

LOU LE CLERE: As far as those Bremen trips are concerned, we did some things that were almost beyond human endurance. We'd fly from Bremen to Rome, then to Athens and Karachi, then Ceylon, Jakarta and Sidney, Australia. The first trip we had a multicrew, and we flew the whole trip—about 50 hours of flying with no rest.

On the later trips we planned a layover in Colombo, Ceylon. That made it a little more bearable. Colombo is a lovely spot. We stayed in the Mt. Lavinia Hotel, which is right on the Indian Ocean and has one of the most beautiful beaches in the world.

I think we had two engine failures during that time. Both were on the return trips and on one of them we just shut the engine down and kept on going. We had a spare engine sitting in Amsterdam, so we flew there.

I was based in New York at that time, and the company came up with a Marseille, France, trip. It was a DC-4 freighter trip, so we flew that. Then they got three trips from Marseille to Tel Aviv, so we flew those. The airplane needed some maintenance, so we flew it to London and thought we were on our way home.

The company said, "Get the maintenance done, but don't go home. We have an Australian trip out of Germany, so take the airplane to Bremen."

I thought we would take the plane to Bremen and somebody else would take it from there. That somebody turned out to be us. All together we were gone about two and a half months. I had a wife and a relatively young son waiting in New Jersey, a strange place for her. But she was still speaking to me when I got home.

Looking back on it, we had great fun. You couldn't do that today if you had to.

At least Le Clere had radios with knobs on them. All Luccio had was one frequency.

LARRY LUCCIO: I was flying captain on the Newark, Bradley, Boston run. We had an old C-47 with a military five-channel radio. The only frequency it had that we could use was ground control. We flew this trip twice a day, so the control tower people all got used to us. We used the ground control frequency for everything—tower, approach and departure control.

There were a lot of other things going on in Burbank at that time. The C-46s from Pyote, Texas, were going on the line as fast as they came out of the hangar.

BOBBIE THARP: One day I saw Goldberg, the vice-president of maintenance, coming out of his office. He shook his head and said, "We got problems. I just had a meeting with Prescott. He wanted to know how many of

A normal C-46 load

the C-46's we could fly."

I said, "Oh, maybe ten or twelve."

He said, "How many C-46s did we buy?"

"Eighteen."

"We bought eighteen, and we're going to fly eighteen."

And you know, we did. We flew all eighteen of them. Our maintenance department is what helped make this company great. We also did a lot of outside maintenance through the years and the money that brought in helped keep the company solvent through lean times.

One of the reasons the maintenance department was so great was Charley Pryor.

CHARLEY PRYOR: I was hired in September 1950, and worked on the C-46 overhauls. At least they had left the rattlesnakes in Texas. When that job was done, I was on the modification (mod) crew overhauling DC-4s.

CHAPTER 7   TIGER TALES

Here are two more stories about pilots' circuitous routes before joining the Tigers.

MEL SMITH: We lived on Catalina Island when I was a little boy. My father took pilot training in WW I, and a friend of his, a WW I combat pilot by the name of Holliman, had a couple of airplanes. He used to give sightseeing rides around the island. Sometimes he would take me for a ride and let me handle the controls. His plane was an old Wright Pusher Seaplane with a Liberty engine. That whetted my interest in flying.

After graduating from high school I went to San Luis Obispo and started college. In 1940 I quit college and entered the civilian pilot training program there. I also got married at that time, so when I tried to enlist in the Air Corps, I couldn't get in. They didn't take married men at that time. Later they lifted that ban, but still didn't take married men with dependents, and by now we had a little one, so I still couldn't get in.

I got a job instructing primary students at the Army Air Corps School at Santa Maria, California.

After the war I got on as an instructor at a GI Bill flying school in Los Angeles. Paul Grace, who worked for the Flying Tigers, kept his plane there.

He said, "Come on out, maybe you can get a job."

I had gone to Long Beach and gotten my ATR and multiengine ratings, so I went to Tigers and was hired.

JOHN LAMPING: I started in December 1950. In those days you started on the extra list, not as a full-time employee. Art Seymour was the chief pilot in Denver, and he gave me three bounces in the C-46. I had never flown one, so I used the same procedures as for the DC-3 and it worked out great.

I made three pretty good landings, and he said, "You can go out Monday night if you want to."

So I did. A short time later I was put on the full-time list.

CURLY DICKINSON: I believe Dick Bently and I were the first mechanics to be hired as pilots off the floor in Burbank. As mechanics we were pretty familiar with the C-46 cockpit and its operation, at least on the ground and in taxiing out for run up at the far end of runway 15. You could get a lot of speed up in that short distance.

Captain John Long was doing the hiring at that time and the poor guy couldn't step outside his office without being bird-dogged by us for a flying job. I had just come to work on the swing shift when he walked over and asked if I <u>really</u> had all my tickets. I whipped them out. He took a quick look and told me to see Janet Olson in crew control. She told me to lock up my tools and go home and get some rest. I was being transferred to flight and would be going out in a few hours. I made my first trip at 0400 with Russ Kelly.

You gotta watch what you're standing on...

BOBBIE THARP: Art Seymour was deadheading with me in a C-46 when he had to use the relief tube. It's located on the left side of the cockpit and the hose is long enough for someone to use while standing behind the pilot's seat. So art is relieving himself when suddenly he starts yelling, "It's froze up! The hose must be froze up!"

I looked down at the mess on the floor and saw that the hose wasn't frozen...Art was standing on it.

CHAPTER 8   THE SLEEPWALKER   1951

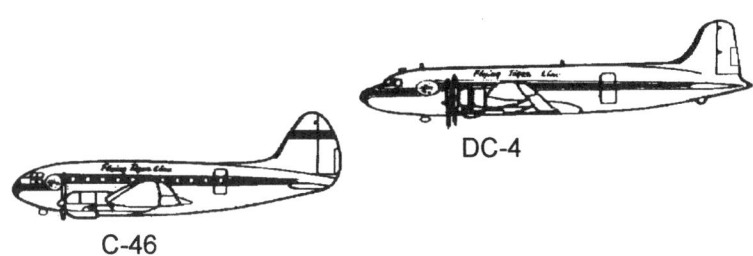

Among the new hires that year were Don Hassig, Pete Rinne and Carey Bowles.

DON HASSIG: I'd returned from China about a year before, and when I was ready for a job, I went to Burbank and looked up Fred Heckman, a navigator I'd known in China. He was working for John Long, the Tiger chief pilot, as a go-fer and general handyman. He introduced me to John and I asked for a job.

John had me take Herb Wall, a check captain, around the field three times, and once that was done I was a qualified copilot. I had about 200 hours in a C-46 in China, but I still got the same checkout as any new hire.

I was to be based in Denver, and when I arrived there I reported to Art Seymour, the Denver chief pilot. He briefed me on the way things were done around there, then told me I was on the schedule for a trip that night. I left for Chicago with Woody Woodward on my first trip with Tigers.

PETE RINNE: I'd been flying C-46s for Panagra in South America, but my wife wanted to return to the States, so we came back. I stopped in Denver and talked to Art Seymour at Flying Tigers, but he wasn't hiring.

After we talked for a while he said, "Hey do you know Ed Lowe? He flew for Panagra."

"Sure, I know Ed. Give me his address, and I'll go see him."

Art said, "Here fill out this application before you go. It won't hurt to have it on file."

I went out and spent the evening with Ed and his wife. A short time later Art hired me.

CAREY BOWLES: After the war I came home and returned to Texas A&M and finished my Aeronautical Engineering Degree in 1948. While in college I opened a small flight school and crop-dusting service nearby. I also worked part time after graduation with the Personal Aircraft Development Center of Texas A&M. This was interesting work, but I knew I'd be happier flying with an airline, particularly one that flew overseas.

The Flying Tiger Line was busily engaged in the Korean Airlift and had just bought 20 or more C-46s, so I decided they would be a good bet. I'd heard a lot about Flying Tigers since they began operations in 1945 when I was in China.

John Long hired me in February 1951. I made a couple of trips on the freight system before being sent to San Antonio to fly C.A.M.'s (Civilian Army Movements). There I met my wife to be, Cynthia Neathery, from New Zealand. She had been hired as a Tiger flight attendant the same day I was hired.

After a few months flying C.A.M's and six months on the Pacific, I bid captain at Newark, New Jersey. Through the years I was based in Newark, Denver, Salt Lake City and Chicago.

CHAPTER 8   TIGER TALES   93

Sometimes a house just seems to grow on you.

LARRY LUCCIO: I was with Ken Henderson in a C-46 going into Detroit one dark night. We were both tired and the visibility was poor. After we landed I looked over at Ken and said, "Geeze, Ken, look how close that house is to the runway. Even the laundry is hanging out there pretty close to our wing tip."

Instead on landing on the runway, we had sort of landed on the parallel taxiway.

Ken Henderson and I flew together quite often, and we lived pretty close together. I only had one car, but he had an airporter, so he picked me up and we drove down to Newark together. Once the weather was so bad, icing and whatever, that the flight was canceled. We had no defroster in that old coupe, and soon the windshield was coated with ice and we couldn't see to drive home.

We pulled in to this confectionery store, and I went in and bought some candles. We stuck them on the dash and lit them and soon we were on our way. The ice was melting off, and we congratulated ourselves on our ingenuity. Then BANG, the windshield shattered.

One day Bob Souers, the chief pilot, grabbed me and said, "If you are going to be a pilot in Newark, you need a type rating in the C-46, let's go."

We went up and did all the procedures, and I had my C-46 type rating, just like that.

As the company grew so did the need for office workers, and soon headquarters outgrew the available office space in the hangar. A new Flying Tiger Headquarters was built on Sherman Way, about two blocks from the Burbank Airport.

Tigers negotiated a number of lucrative DC-4 international charter flights. One of these was with an Indian shipping company, which was involved with a seamen's strike while one of their ships was berthed in San Diego. They chartered a Flying Tiger DC-4 to fly that crew back to Bombay, India, and to pick up a replacement crew. Dick Rossi and his crew picked up the Indian seamen then flew to New York, planning to fly east all the way around the world to take advantage of the prevailing winds.

Elgen Long was the navigator, and just after they took off from New York, they received a message requesting their E.T.A. in San Diego.

"For Christ sake," Dick grumbled, "we're just starting on a round-the-world trip and they already want to know when we'll get back."

DICK ROSSI: We sat down and figured and figured. You know there's a lot of things can go wrong and a lot of ways to be delayed on a round-the-world trip. Anyway, we came up with an ETA of 3 o'clock the next Friday afternoon.

When we arrived in Bombay, the new Indian crew was not ready, so this was our first delay. To make up time, we wanted to overfly Calcutta and go direct from Bombay to Bangkok, Thailand. The local officials wouldn't give me a clearance. No matter what I said, they just wouldn't clear me. They said, "All eastbound flights from Bombay always stop in Calcutta."

Dick gave up on them. In frustration he called the Minister of Aviation:

DICK ROSSI: As soon as I got the minister on the phone I said, "We want to fly from Bombay direct to Bangkok.

CHAPTER 8   TIGER TALES   95

There's no reason for us to stop in Calcutta when we have plenty of fuel. The officials here say they won't clear me because every flight eastbound out of India stops at Calcutta."
 The minister answered, "You're right, there is no reason to stop in Calcutta. You can go direct."
 "Sure, you can say that, but these guys won't clear me."
 "Don't worry, they won't give you any trouble."
 When I got back to the flight line those locals were saying, "Yes, Captain. Whatever you say, Captain."

So they got out of there and things went smoothly until they arrived in Guam, where they were reminded that incompetency and senseless red tape can be found in American government also.

DICK ROSSI: The airplane was refueled at Guam, but we couldn't get a clearance to depart.
 "Why not?" I asked.
 "Because you didn't have clearance to land," the young naval officer answered.
 "But I don't want to land, I want to take off," I pointed out.
 "Well, you can't take off when you didn't have a clearance to land."
 I could see logic would have no effect on this guy, so I said, "Well, can I talk to the admiral?"
 "You could try that, except that he's in a meeting and can't be disturbed."
 That was nine in the morning, and it took till about noon before I got through to the head guy. He found out that our clearance had been sent from Washington, and that we certainly could land and certainly could take off.

So we finally got out of there and got to Honolulu. Our destination, of course, was San Diego, but since we couldn't carry enough fuel to legally file for it, we filed for San Francisco instead, which is a little closer. After takeoff we took up a heading for San Diego. About halfway across we were doing pretty good on fuel, so we refiled for Los Angeles while still heading for San Diego. A while later we were still doing well on fuel, and the San Diego weather was good enough so that we could file for it.

Our passengers, these Indian sailors, had never been to the States and were really looking forward to a night on the town. They had their own Chinese cook with them who ran around the plane in his skivvies and tee shirt. But you should have seen this guy. About an hour out of San Diego he was all dressed up in a coat and tie and ready to do the town, and all the other guys were sprucing up.

When the DC-4 landed and pulled up to the ramp, it was exactly three o'clock on Friday. The funny thing was, the officers from their ship were parked on the ramp with a bus, ready to take the crew right out to the ship. They were scheduled to sail in thirty minutes. Those poor guys never even got to town.

The Korean war was in full swing, and Tiger flights were loaded in both directions—fresh young kids full of confidence westbound, and tired, sick and wounded men returning home.

CYNTHIA NEATHERY BOWLES, stewardess: There were sixty or so men on this unpressurized DC-4. They were unusually quiet for soldiers returning to the U.S....returning home. A lot of them had come down with amoebic dysentery; some had bandaged legs, arms, feet,

CHAPTER 8   TIGER TALES

hands and heads. Some looked worn and vague. Their corpsman had looked tired, so I had given him coffee first. I was surprised that it wasn't an AIREVAC flight with so many injuries. At least there were no stretchers, and I was grateful for that, since I was the only stewardess.

I'd had to switch flights in Tokyo, and that's why I had such a short layover. They wanted a stewardess with some medical background on this flight in case the corpsman needed help, and I was it.

Two hours after we leveled off, the copilot told us that he'd heard our passengers talking in the men's room at the airport. Apparently these soldiers and some others had captured an enemy position and had been pretty well shot up.

After the box lunches were served, I dimmed the lights. It was one a.m. and I was exhausted. I'd had only twelve hours on the ground in Tokyo and about four hours sleep. For half an hour there was movement in the cabin—men wanting more coffee, a drink of water, or someone making a last trip to the blue room before settling down.

Finally all was quiet, and I was able to doze intermittently, conscious of each man who passed me on his way to the blue room. My main concern before we left Haneda Airport in Tokyo was fear that the honey-buckets might overflow before landing at Wake Island. I had questioned the corpsman about those soldiers who had amoebic dysentery, making sure there was medication aboard for any who might need it.

Suddenly I was aware of feet running down the aisle. "Poor devil," I muttered, trying to throw off my drowsiness. "He'd better make it or we're liable to have a stinking mess to clean up," I shuddered at the thought.

The running stopped short of me. I shot to wakefulness as I realized that the soldier had swerved and was bending down on one knee in front of the main passenger exit.

I leaped from my seat and was at his back as his hand forced the door handle from the closed position to open. I tugged at the bulky coat clad body.

"Get away from the door!" I gasped, still pulling at him. "What in God's name do you think you're doing?"

He stood up, all six feet of him. It was then that I saw his eyes; they were glazed with sleep.

"We're on the ground...we're home," he muttered in his sleepwalking state.

I grabbed his arm and shook him.

"Get back in your seat. We are 7,000 feet in the air."

He wandered back toward his seat while I hung onto the door. I tried to tie the ditching rope around my waist while holding onto the door with one hand, but I couldn't manage it. After an eternity, which I suppose was only about fifteen minutes, the copilot came back.

He looked at me and said, "What in hell are you doing down there"

"The door is open, and I can't close it! Tie this rope around me so I don't get pulled out!"

He very bravely tied the ditching rope around himself, then put his hand over mine and closed the door.

The next morning I walked past the sleepwalker who was now awake.

He grinned and said, "I should give you one of my medals."

I said, "No thank you, I would prefer instead that you tell the next stewardess that you walk in your sleep."

Sometimes on a long night flight it is almost impossible to keep one's eyes open. Unless of course, one has the proper inducement.

CHAPTER 8   TIGER TALES

DON HASSIG: By now I had been with Tigers for two or three months and was again flying with Woody Woodward. We were on our way from Chicago to Denver. We'd made the usual fuel stop at Grand Island, Nebraska, and I was flying the leg in the left seat. It was very dark and very sleepy out. An hour or so after we'd taken off, Woody had tilted his seat back, and I thought he was asleep.

I was having a hard time staying awake myself, but I knew I had to, because there was no autopilot. On the C-46 there is an Aldus lamp, which is stored beneath the window on the right side of the cockpit. The Aldus is a very bright light, about six inches across with a pistol grip and a trigger to turn it on.

What I didn't know was that Woody was sitting there pretending to be asleep, but watching me nod off every few minutes. He slowly worked the Aldus lamp into his lap, pointing it directly at my eyes. Just as I nodded off again, he flashed on the light and hollered, " BANG."

If it hadn't been for my seat belt I might have gone right through the roof! Woody was still laughing when we got to Denver, and I couldn't close my eyes for three days.

One thing about flying with Howard in a hurricane, it's real easy to stay awake.

ARNIE BREDON: One of my early trips as a Tiger copilot was with Howard Bayne, hauling migrant workers in a C-46. We flew from Brownsville, Texas, to San Luis Potosi, Mexico, where the runway was built over an old graveyard. A hurricane was approaching; so all the other airplanes were leaving for a safe destination. As we hurriedly parked on the apron, the concrete surface gave way and the left main landing gear dropped into a tomb.

There was no one at the airport to help get the airplane out, so Howard and I hitched a ride to town to try to borrow a tractor. On the way we saw a hardware store, where we stopped and bought some cable. That was dumb. We should have waited until we had something to haul it with, because now we had to stagger down the dusty streets with a big ol' coil of cable wrapped around our necks.

At a baseball game we finally located the owner of the only tractor in town. It seemed he was connected with LAMSA, a Mexican Airline, whose team was losing the baseball tournament. I guess we looked pretty good to him because he wanted us to stay the next day and play baseball for them. But there was no way we were going to do that.

When we finally convinced him that we were in a hurry, he tore himself from the game and unlocked his shop. Then we found that the tractor was completely disassembled. We stayed up all night and helped him put it back together.

By the time the airplane was finally out of the tomb, we had to fly through the hurricane to get back to Brownsville, Texas. When we landed at Brownsville, we were the only airplane there. The hurricane had changed course, and everyone else had evacuated and flown north.

Sounds like Arnie fits in pretty well with this outfit.

CHAPTER 9   BURBANK TO BERLIN   1951 PART 2

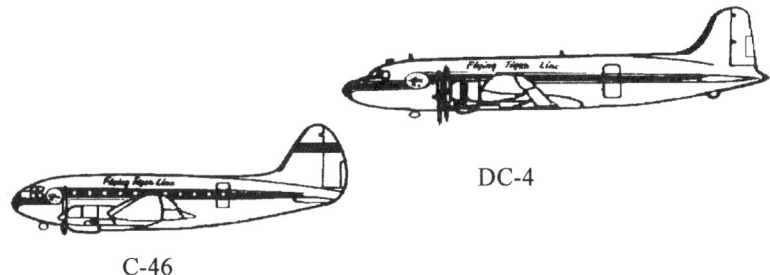

DC-4

C-46

ARNIE BREDON: I was flying a C-46 from Salt Lake City to Grand Island, Nebraska, with North Platte as the alternate airport. The weather was terrible all over the region. During climb out and upon reaching cruise altitude, we suspected some kind of fuel flow problem on the right engine. The mixture control had to be leaned way back to get proper exhaust flame and to keep the cylinder head temperatures in the green. Fuel consumption proved to be way too high, and after passing Cheyenne it was apparent that we would not have enough fuel to reach North Platte, much less Grand Island!

Every airport within reach was below weather minimums and Cheyenne was our only option. The tower was reporting 200 feet overcast, one half-mile visibility with winds out of the north at 40 knots and blowing snow. The ILS course was on the east-west runway, so we had to make the approach to the west, descend below the overcast and then make a left circle to land to the north. John White was along as check pilot. He had the final responsibility for the flight, so we swapped seats, and John flew the approach.

Suffice it to say, we made it—but I wouldn't care to do it again!! Under the circumstances, it was one of the best approaches I've ever experienced. But then it had to be. That kind of shared event tends to cement a lifelong friendship. John and I have toasted it several times through the years.

"They just had to have another cigarette."

GERRY TOWNE: We were flying across the Atlantic one night. Kirk Talley was the captain, Starr Thompson was the first officer and I was the copilot. Both of these guys were dying for a smoke. They had plenty of cigarettes, but no matches, so they spent half the night back in the electrical compartment, trying to short some wires so they could light a cigarette.

In late 1951 Tigers flew what was called the "Baby Berlin Airlift," to differentiate it from the "Berlin Airlift" of 1948. Instead of 1,000 DC-4s Tigers used two C-46s.

STARR THOMPSON: Oakley Smith took one of the C-46s over, and I think Brandenberg took the other one. They had three-man crews for the crossing because of the length of the trip. I think we had five crews over there. Jack Bliss, Jack Soloman, Brandenberg, Oakley and I were there as captains. We had guys like Andy Chambers, H.P. Watkins and Al Silver flying copilot. Dick Bentley and Curly Dickenson were mechanics for Tigers, but they both had their commercial pilot's licenses and got on that operation as copilots.

Pan Am had the contract, which they subcontracted to Tigers. Pan Am gave us about three months to move all the cargo. As soon as we got there, I went out and talked to the GI Radar Controllers.

I said, "You guys close everything up about nine at night don't you?"

"Yes, there's no one flying at night, so we shut it down."

So far so good, so then I asked, "If we want to fly at night, would there be any problem getting radar service?"

"None at all, we'll be here as long as you need us."

CHAPTER 9 TIGER TALES

We flew the military corridors from Berlin to Frankfurt, Hamburg and Bremen around the clock. Like, I would come out in the morning and take a trip to Hamburg and back, sign the logbook and walk over to the other airplane and take it down to Frankfurt and back. Then I was through for the day.

The next crew, Oakley's for instance, would take the first airplane (which was now reloaded) and fly it to Bremen and back. By that time the other plane would be reloaded and he'd fly that one to Frankfurt, or where ever it was going, and back. We kept doing that around the clock until we worked ourselves out of a job in six weeks.

CURLY DICKINSON: When we finally started for Berlin most of the continent had caved in weatherwise and we ended up crawling into Brussels. Barely! The second inadvertent layover had more going for it than the first one, Gander. Ooh la-la! Brussels is definitely not Grand Island.

Finally got to Frankfurt and settled into our new domicile. Wandered downtown to the Am Zoo. It was Christmas week and the lobby was loaded with holiday decorations. There was a huge Christmas tree with <u>real candles</u> ablaze. The candles were in little metal cage gizmos with a kind of heat shield on top. It was beautiful, nostalgic and romantic but I couldn't have slept a night in that place knowing the tree could light off at any time.

With Captain Jack Soloman we departed Frankfurt for Berlin, with Hamburg as our alternate airport. After we left Gunpost, the military tracking station halfway up the corridor, things like communications and navigation capability fell apart. Snow static blew any low frequency stuff like radio beacons clear out of the picture and our requests for a radar fix or DF steer went unanswered. We did a lot of wandering and scud running that morning. Then we found an airport that looked pretty good-sized with lights on it. We elected to land as we were getting "a little concerned" about our position. This was kind of like student pilot days where you could always land, inquire as to where in hell you were, and merrily proceed to destination.

We raised the tower using guard frequency but the controller had a pretty heavy accent, not like the US military controllers we had been working. Since I wasn't sure where we were, I was hoping it wasn't a Russian installation as I have a strong aversion to turnips or whatever their prison cuisine consists of. The wind was gusting and blowing so hard that it brought the visibility up to about a mile and we sailed right on in. In fact we sailed halfway down the runway before touching down. Braking was bad as the runway was wet, so as we got to the end, Jack cleverly applied the patented "Tiger Turnoff", a 180-degree ground loop finishing with a slide off into the goo.

We shut things down and waited. Soon the fire trucks arrived and one who spoke passable English advised us we were in Bremen! Not bad, we actually landed in the same country we intended to. Jack called Goldy who came steaming (literally) up from Frankfurt to conduct a hearing. Having done the necessary to satisfy the people who keep track of such things, Goldy told us to go back to base, get legal rest, and we would be due out immediately thereafter if not sooner. That's what I call a memorable Christmas.

STARR THOMPSON: Oakley brought one airplane back to the States via the Azores and across the mid-Atlantic. I took the shortest route to Keflavik and Greenland with the other one. I had Chambers and Silver with me. First we had to stop in Amsterdam to pick up our mechanics and have the cabin auxiliary fuel tanks installed. I had a navi-

CHAPTER 9   TIGER TALES   105

gator named Ted Smith; a radio operator, Frank Peters; and two mechanics, C.K. Doty and John Ciszlac. We got everything ready, took off for Keflavik and landed with a thirty-degree crab angle coming over the range station. The ILS was out of service.

Then we headed for Bluie West-1, on the southern tip of Greenland. Andy Chambers was flying that leg. It had been closed for weather for the past six weeks, but that day it was severe clear. We filled all the tanks with fuel, and I was making the takeoff. Andy was holding his hand up on the windshield to keep the sun out of his eyes, so he could monitor the engine instruments. The right engine only turned up about 2400 RPM, so I had to abort the takeoff. We got the thing stopped without sliding off into the fjord and taxied back to the ramp.

I said to Doty, "Have John take the face plate off the governor and clean the ice out of it, and it will probably be all right."

John looked rather skeptical, but he took the plate off and yelled down to Doty, "Hey, this thing IS full of ice."

I had that happen once before. We took off again and headed for Gander, Newfoundland. By this time it was dark, and we had icing like you wouldn't believe. To make matters worse, we got a message that Gander was closed due to weather and that we should divert to Presque Island via Goose Bay. I asked the navigator for a heading, time en route and so forth. He gave me a heading and an ETE[1] of 2:30 hours to Goose Bay—but hell, he had nothing to work with—couldn't get a fix in that weather, so he was really only guessing.

---

[1] Estimated time en route.

I flew the heading he gave me and tuned in the Goose Bay Radio. I got one good signal on it, but from then on there was so much static I couldn't hear anything. I left it on that frequency and watched the needle as it slowly moved to the left. When it showed 95 degrees to my left, I turned to the needle. We passed over Goose Bay one hour past our ETA. By then we were so low on fuel there was no way we could make Presque Island, so we landed at Goose Bay. We could have bought the big island in the sky on that one.

The international aviation language is English, and air traffic controllers are required to speak and understand it. Certain airport workers who do business with airlines also need a working knowledge of English. It is well known that many Frenchmen speak an English no one else can understand, mostly because they just don't want to learn it. They seem to believe that anyone in the world who has anything important to say should be speaking French.

One time Dobbie had a little problem in Paris. Our handling agent there at Orly was a Frenchman who had apparently learned his English out of a textbook. He had his verbs and nouns all mixed up, which caused a few communication problems. It was a rule among pilots to always climb up on the wing and check the fuel load to make sure the right amount of fuel was in the proper tanks.

GOLDY: Dobbie climbed up on the wing and saw that the fueler was doing it all wrong. This guy didn't speak English at all, so Dobbie headed for the office to get it straightened out. While he was up on the wing, someone had moved the ladder and Dobbie took an unexpected shortcut to the ramp. It would have hurt anyone else but Dobbie is

CHAPTER 9   TIGER TALES   107

so tough that it only tore the elbow out of his coat. He hit the ground running, got to the office, and proceeded to vastly increase the hapless agent's vocabulary. They say the agent's English comprehension improved considerably after that.

We all need a crutch now and then.

BOBBIE THARP: We bought two DC-4s from Resort Airlines that had Wright 9-cylinder 1820 engines. They were real dogs in performance. We refitted the cabins to our specifications and then put one of them on a military contract.

They picked up a load of troops in Seattle to take them to Great Falls, Montana. My copilot and I met the airplane in Great Falls to take it on to Chicago.

On board was Dick Stuelke, who had a leg in a cast, and was on crutches due to a motorcycle accident in Honolulu. He was supposed to advise us as to the many idiosyncrasies of this airplane.

So, we go to start the engines, and we can't get electrical power to any engine. Dick didn't know what the problem was either, so I called maintenance in Burbank.

The guy said, "Look in the forward toilet, where the main electrical buss is. Take the cover off and short across from the main power terminal to whichever engine you want to start. They're numbered, but be sure you use a heavy and well-insulated wire!"

Okay, but the fuel levers, magneto switches and whatnot are all in the cockpit, and I have to be back there in the toilet. So Dick gets on his crutches and stands between the pilot seats...and here is the whole airplane load of Air force mechanics watching and wondering what in hell is going on.

I holler, "Start 3!"

So we get it started, then the other 3 engines. I've always wondered what these guys thought—a guy in the front on crutches and the captain starting the engines from the toilet.

I guess this next crew figured out how to get the engines started.

JOHN NEWCOMER: We had this multi-crew trip just before Christmas. Jim Alexander was the captain, I believe Jack Bliss was the first officer, and I was the lowly copilot. We got into Stuttgart, Germany, and we were supposed to be there over Christmas, but the schedule was changed. I think Ralph Hedden had a little playmate over there and he didn't want to return this quick, so we took the trip.

This C-54 was one we got from Resort Airlines. It had Wright 1820 engines on it, and did not have extended range fuel tanks, so it was not normally used on flights to Europe. We made a lot of fuel stops because of headwinds on the westbound flight. We stopped at Bremen, Germany, then Prestwick, Scotland; Keflavik, Iceland; Bluie West-1, Greenland; Gander, Newfoundland; Idlewild and Newark. We made it home for Christmas, but just barely.

CHAPTER 10 THE SEVEN YEAR ITCH   1952

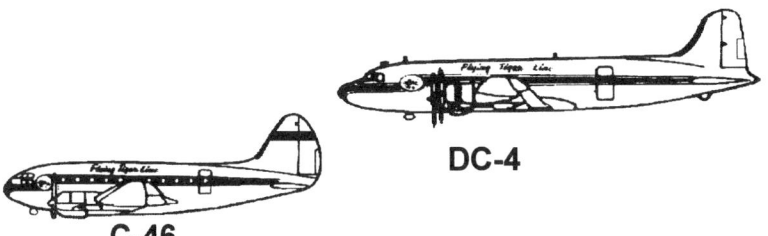

In January Captain Bob Barlow and Copilot Dick Taggart were fighting to keep the shiny side of their DC-4 up, while wending their way through an unforecast Pacific storm when...

FROM 41 YEARS ALOFT: Frances Drew once helped avert an air disaster by relieving tension in the cockpit while just trying to save a brand new cocktail dress. Frances was on a flight to Hawaii from Travis Air Force Base, when the plane encountered unforecast headwinds. For five hours it tossed about in a storm over the Pacific Ocean. They had passed their point of no return and were very low on fuel.

Sitting with her passengers in the cabin, Fran suddenly realized the horrible implications of a ditching at sea. In her suitcase were that brand new $70 dress, new shoes and a new hat. She visualized all these lovely things being lost forever and it was too much to bear.

She rushed forward to the cockpit where the pilot was sweating over the controls.

"Everything okay back there Frances?"

"Oh sure," Fran hesitated, "I just wanted to ask you something."

"What?"

"If we ditch the plane, can I take my suitcase with me?"

"WHAT?" The pilot exploded, "You have the nerve at a time like this to bother me about a stupid suitcase. Get out...go to the ladies room, put on your new dress and be the most glamorous survivor in the world, but just GET OUT!"

And now for the Captain's version of this story...

BOB BARLOW: We had an 11:58 flight plan, so I thought that was pretty ridiculous to start with. The navigator checked it out and he said it should be okay. By midpoint we were about a half hour behind, but we got a revised wind forecast, so it didn't look too bad.
 From then on nothing worked out. We found out later that someone had transposed the wind direction on the weather report. Our total actual flight time was 14:30.

And the handsome young copilot...

DICK TAGGART: We had passed equal-time-point when Honolulu radioed that we would have 120-knot winds on the nose for the rest of the flight. There was no way we could make Honolulu, so we turned to a direct heading for Hilo. We landed okay, but one engine quit while we were taxiing in to the ramp.

A lot of other things were happening in the company. We had outgrown the facilities at Teterboro, New Jersey, and moved our East Coast operation to Newark. The Korean Airlift was still going on, and more airplanes were needed for our domestic freight routes. It was fortunate for us that the remaining C-46s from Chennault's CAT airlines in China became available.

CHARLEY PRYOR: We got 18 of Chennault's C-46s. The wings had been removed, so they could be loaded on a ship.

CHAPTER 10 TIGER TALES

When they arrived in Long Beach, we hired a company to tow them to Burbank where we overhauled and reassembled them. We kept several of the best ones and sold the rest.

Sometimes you can fly across the ocean and never see any other air traffic; then again you might see one right in your windshield.

GOLDY: Ken Henderson was captain on a DC-4 flight to Ireland. He was in the right seat and the copilot was flying the airplane. The navigator was Jack Wanzer. During the descent into Shannon Jack was standing up, leaning on a cross bar behind the pilot seats, when a large bird came crashing through the right windshield. Ken had just leaned over to get an approach plate from his flight bag, so it missed him. The bird hit Jack Wanzer full in the chest and in one arm.

Jack stood there, dripping with blood and everything else that comes out of a bird, when a stewardess came up and asked what happened.

Jack said, "A bird came through the windshield."

She looked at all the blood and said, "Did it bite you?"

They say her youthful enthusiasm made up for her lack of comprehension. Sometimes a pilot would be better off with less enthusiasm and more skepticism.

BOBBIE THARP: On his first flight as captain, one of our guys took off out of Grand Island and decided he would give himself some single engine practice. He shut down an engine and feathered the propeller. So far so good, but when he tried to unfeather it, it would not unfeather. He landed in a cornfield a quarter mile from the runway.

Mel Smith and his copilot might have been white as the proverbial sheet if they had understood the problem.

MEL SMITH: We were taking off out of Salt Lake in a C-46 and, as usual, we circled for altitude until we could get over the mountains. It was dark and quite turbulent, and just as we cleared the crest, I saw a flash of light off to my right. Nothing happened, so I forgot all about it as we headed for Chicago.

After we landed, when the mechanic opened the cowling on the right engine, he said, "Come here. I want to show you something."

He was holding a cylinder head in the air by its spark plug leads. That head had blown clear off the cylinder. The cylinder barrel was still on, so the piston had still been able to move up and down, and the engine kept running.

Ray Foster landed in Salt Lake City also, and like to froze his berries:

RAY FOSTER: I had a C-46 with a load of strawberries bound for the East Coast. I landed at Salt Lake late at night in the middle of the winter. We were caught in a terrible storm—ice, wind and snow so bad that we couldn't go on. There were no other airplanes moving that night, so there was no one around.

I left the copilot with the airplane and started walking around the Salt Lake Airport to find some help. I damn near froze before I finally found some mechanics playing cards in a heated office. They helped me get the airplane into a hangar, so the strawberries wouldn't freeze. The next day we took them on to the East Coast. Taking care

CHAPTER 10   TIGER TALES

of the cargo was part of our job in those days. We couldn't just land the airplane and go to a hotel.

Bob Zalusky has figured out how to impress his passengers and save fuel at the same time.

BOB ZALUSKY: One night we took off out of Brownsville, Texas, with a load of about 40 Mexican farm workers. I was with a fellow named Art Peters, and we were bound for Cheyenne, Wyoming. About two o'clock in the morning, right over Fort Collins, Colorado, the left engine started acting up. The oil quantity and pressure were going down and the temperatures were going up. We went through the checklist and feathered the engine.

I called Cheyenne, and was told they had a ceiling of 500 feet and one-half mile visibility.

Oh boy! I thought. The Denver weather was below minimums, so we had no choice but to continue on. A few minutes later the whole airplane jumped sideways. The master rod on the right engine had let go with a KAPOW, and it suddenly got real quiet up there.

Art called Cheyenne and gave them a MAYDAY. He wouldn't have needed the radio; they could have heard him in Chicago. He told them we were at 12,000 feet and descending with both engines dead.

I said to Art, "You know that left engine was still running, maybe we can get it going again."

We had difficulty in getting the propeller unfeathered, but finally got it started. We were cleared for a straight-in approach, which would take us over the city. We didn't think we could make the airport, so we went around the city, hoping we could belly in on flat ground if we had to.

By the time we got there the weather had lifted to about a thousand feet, and we could see the airport. But as we came nearer the airport suddenly disappeared. The reason for this was that the airport is on a plateau, and we were below it. By this time the left engine was red hot and had caught fire from running with no oil. We knew it was seconds away from seizing. I called for half flaps, and the airplane ballooned up enough to put us above the runway. When it looked like we would make it, I called for gear down, and the green lights came on just as we touched the runway.

Having thought we wouldn't make it, we had decided that when we hit the ground Art would hit the crash bar. This would shut off all power and might help prevent a fire. The engine was already on fire, however, so when we dropped on the runway and Art hit the crash bar, which shut off our electrical power, so we couldn't discharge the engine fire extinguisher. I grabbed a hand fire bottle, jumped out of the airplane and managed to put out the engine fire before the fire trucks got there. The forty Mexican farm workers followed me out.

One who spoke a little English said, "You fly on only one engine, then only the other one. Do you always do that?"

"Oh yes," I said, "We save gas that way."

Sometimes you get to fly when the weather is good, and sometimes even in the daylight.

BOB ZALUSKY: I was en route from Seattle to Salt Lake City. On a bright beautiful day about two in the afternoon we flew over Pocatello, Idaho.

I looked down at a nice big runway and said to the copilot, "If a fellow had trouble, that would be a nice place to

CHAPTER 10   TIGER TALES

land."

The words were barely out of my mouth when—KAPOW—the left engine went. We circled around and landed, and then I had to ride a bicycle about five miles to town to find a telephone, so I could tell the company where I was. Bobbie Tharp has bitched about it ever since. He's the guy who had to ride a bus up there and fly the airplane out after the engine was changed.

Jack Russell was born in Ireland and brought to New York as a small boy. When a charter flight with a ten-day layover in Shannon came up, he jumped at it.

GOLDY: Jack got the okay to go to his motherland somewhere in South Ireland. We were staying at the Old Grand Hotel in Ennis. He gets on this train and is gone.

I was having breakfast in the hotel a week later when he joined me at the table. He was telling me how exciting it was to visit his uncle or whoever. They picked him up from the station in a horse drawn cart, which was quite a novelty for him. He talked about the train being so slow he got off and walked along beside it. While he's telling me this story he's cutting up like Jack can do, and all the while he's scratching himself.

I said, "What's the matter with you, you got an itch?" He rolled up his sleeves and I saw that his arms were all blistered, so I made him go to a doctor there in Ennis. The doctor looked at him and took a few steps backward.

He said, "You've got the seven-year itch."

I understand that's the term they use to describe scabies. The only thing he recommended was calamine lotion. We stopped at a pharmacy and Jack bought a quart of it, along with a two-inch paintbrush. We went back to the hotel, and he wanted me to go to his room with him and paint this stuff on. He weighed about 250 pounds, and that was a lot to be painting.

I said, "Hell no, I'm not going to paint you. I might catch it myself."

The only thing in the hotel worth drinking was gin and orange juice.

Jack said, "If you paint this stuff on me, I'll order us some drinks."

The bellboy brought the drinks, but they were gone before I got in the mood to grab the paintbrush, so he ordered more. That did the trick, so I dipped the brush in the calamine lotion as Jack ordered more booze. I held the brush as far from me as I could, but I had him completely covered when the bellboy came back with more gin.

I'll never forget the look on the bellboy's face when he opened the door and saw this huge man standing there painted completely white except for his eyeballs.

In the fall of 1952 all eight DC-4s were pulled off the Atlantic and put on the Korean Airlift. Prescott was still looking around for more airplanes.

BAR STORY by ZALUSKY
(After returning from a three week Pacific trip on a DC-4 with Pappy Huntington as the navigator.)

Boy, that Pappy Huntington sure could snore! We were staying in the dormitory on Wake Island, and one night we came back from the bar and Pappy was really sawing logs. We had to get some sleep, so we picked up his bed, Pappy and all, and carried him down to the beach and left him there. The next morning the tide was in when Pappy woke up to find himself floating in the ocean.

CHAPTER 11 DISASTER IN ISSAQUAH VALLEY 1953

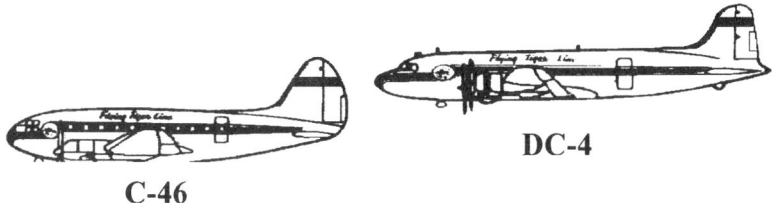

C-46   DC-4

GOLDY: The company leased an early model Connie from a pilot named Skinner. He had flown over in Tel Aviv, and owned it with another guy.

They came to Prescott with one of those, have-we-got-a-deal-for-you proposals.

They offered to lease him the airplane, as long as it was agreed that they came with it.

They were shooting touch and go's, and got tired of hearing the landing gear warning horn every time they closed a throttle for simulated engine failures. The instructor pilot told the flight engineer to pull the circuit breaker in order to silence the warning horn.

They busted their check ride.

They forgot to extend the landing gear, so they touched down with the propellers flailing at the concrete, until the engines stopped. Then the only sound was the underbelly screeching and scraping on the runway. Everyone on board got out safely, but the airplane caught fire and was destroyed.

I wish all stories could be humorous, or at least have happy endings, but in this business reality dictates otherwise. Tigers had their first fatal accident since the Budd crashed in New Mexico in 1947.

The following is from the C.A.B. accident report: "At approximately 9 pm local time on January 7, 1953, a Douglas DC-4 N86574, owned and operated by The Flying Tiger Line, crashed two miles south of Issaquah, Washington, during an instrument approach to Boeing Field, Seattle, Washington. All seven occupants were killed."

BOBBIE THARP: I went into Salt Lake to take a DC-4 eastbound with a load of troops the next morning. My co-pilot was a fellow by the name of McClendon. In the middle of the night I get a call from the chief pilot, Jack Martin.

"We got a problem," he said. "A DC-4 crashed in Seattle. I want you to go fly the C-46 up there in the morning to help with the investigation."

"How bad is it?"

"Bad. All seven people on board were killed. The crew was Chuck Greber, W. C. Lowe and B. M. Merrill. One of our stewardesses, Janet Woodmansee, was deadheading to Seattle. The other passengers were Mrs. McClendon, your copilot's wife, and two of their kids."

CHAPTER 11 TIGER TALES

When we arrived and flew over the accident site, my heart really went out to McClendon. You can imagine: his wife and two kids—gone. He wanted to visit the crash site right then.

So I got a car and we drove out there. The airplane had gone straight down into the ground. The tail was sitting on top of where the cockpit should have been. I took him back to town, and I'll tell you...that poor guy. Something like that is just totally devastating. There's just no way to describe it.

How the hell did it happen? Our investigation lasted about three months. We were able to reconstruct some of it.

This airplane had a history of the #3 fire-warning light coming on during acceleration. I had just flown that airplane out of North Platte a few days before, and on takeoff roll the #3 fire warning came on, so I aborted the takeoff. Maintenance checked it out and couldn't find anything wrong. We discussed it with maintenance and decided maybe during acceleration the exhaust collector ring moved aft enough to let some exhaust gas leak by and set off the fire-warning detector. They snugged up the bolts, and it was okay after that.

My theory is that the pilot was making a range approach into Seattle and had to make a go around. As they accelerated the #3 fire warning came on. Now they had to be busy pulling the firewall shutoff, closing the throttle and feathering the propeller—all that stuff while they were on instruments. Now he comes back around again. Renton lies to the east and south of Boeing Field. We don't know, but maybe he saw a break in the clouds. And seeing Renton, maybe he thought he saw Boeing Field so he started a premature descent into the hills? We can't be sure, but that's my theory.

During the investigation they tried to figure out how he wound up where he did. He must have been heading south, clipped the trees with the left wing tip and then rolled over to the left going over the mountain. He started out on the west side of the mountain and crashed straight down on the east side.

BOBBIE THARP: We started looking for engines and propellers. We found #2 propeller in a small waterfall. We couldn't get the propeller for #3, but I did find the firewall shutoff valve. It was in the pulled or closed position.

I still couldn't be sure they had shut down the engine unless I could find the firewall shutoff handles.

I said, "I want to get a back hoe up here and dig down where the cockpit is until we find the firewall shutoff panel."

Now came a very crucial question. There was little that had been found and sent home in the way of body parts. We knew who was sitting in what seats. If we started digging, we would surely find more body parts. What then? The coroner would have to be involved and what effect would all that have on their families? Would it be worth it all just to prove my theory? We decided it would not, and we ended the investigation there.

But life goes on. Now to more pleasant events. The reputation the maintenance department had established as C-46 specialists during the previous three years earned the company a very lucrative contract. The Air Force awarded the Tigers a contract to overhaul 107 C-46s.

BILL THOMPSON: This was an enormous undertaking and helped to keep the company afloat during a very lean

CHAPTER 11　　　TIGER TALES

period. It seems that it kept happening one step at a time. We kept getting better at what we were doing, and as a result we kept getting bigger.

In the early years the various employee groups could deal directly with Prescott, often just with a handshake. But as the company grew, things became more difficult and several unions were formed.

GOLDY: When I was director of flight operations in early '53, I negotiated the pilot, navigator and stewardess contracts all on the company side. Jack Martin, Vern Wastman and others were involved for the pilots.

BOBBIE THARP: Tom Cotton was scheduling chairman at the time. Tom and I were very close. We were trying to convince the company that we, the pilots, could have scheduled runs. Up to that time we never knew when or where we were going or when we would get home. The company agreed to let us set it up on a trial basis. It worked very well, and that's when our scheduled runs began. We showed the company that scheduling would actually save them money. I take my hat off to Tom. He was really the spokesman and the one who got it done.

The opening of a new station is always a big event, but if it is not profitable it can become a millstone for the company instead of a milestone.

BOBBIE THARP: I wanted so much to open a station in Seattle. I was from there, and I knew there was a lot of business to be had there from companies like the mortuaries and truck farming operations. George Cussins was vice-president of sales, and I talked to him several times about the potential.

One day Janet Olson called and said, "How would you like to swap trips?"

I said, "Okay, what do you have in mind?"

"We're opening stations in Seattle and Portland. How would you like to fly the inaugural flight?"

"How come you get to make the inaugural flight?" Art Seymour asked. "I'm the chief pilot, and I'm going along with you."

There were lots of signs proclaiming the inaugural flight plus planned speeches and what not. Portland had a woman mayor at the time, and someone had given me a lady's hat to present to her.

The airplane was late getting into Denver, which delayed our arrival in Portland. We were so late that the mayor had gone home when we got there, and all I had was the hat and no one to give it to.

We pressed on to Seattle, and by that time even the T.V. crews who were supposed to cover the inaugural landing had gone home. The only people who met us in Seattle were the mechanic that parked us, and my dad, mother and uncle. But I still cherish that. My folks would have waited all night for me.

Sometimes a pilot would arrive at Tigers, seemingly by accident after a long and circuitous route, then remain for an entire career.

Lamont "Shad" Shadowens had joined the Signal Corps during the war and was stationed in Hawaii on some top-secret project called radar. After WW II when everyone was coming back, he went into the real estate business out there. Then he decided he should learn to fly

CHAPTER 11   TIGER TALES   123

to facilitate the transaction of business between the Islands.

Shad went to the Hawaiian School of Aeronautics where he received his commercial pilot's license, and then Hawaiian Airlines hired him. He also had a Link trainer instructor's license, so he did that on the side while flying copilot for Hawaiian. This would also stand him in good stead later in his career when expertise at instrument approaches was mandatory.

By this time Shad had the flying bug. He would continue his interest in real estate, but he intended to make a career of airline flying. He sent applications to three airlines in the States and received two replies on the same day, one from Eastern and one from Flying Tigers.

SHAD: I chose Tigers and started in April 1953 flying C-46s. About three months after I was hired, I took part in what I thought was a very exciting event. I was copilot with Stan Hampton in a C-46 when we had a landing gear free-fall while in close proximity to a severe thunderstorm. We were a short distance from North Platte, Nebraska, our refueling stop. We couldn't get the gear to indicate double locked down.

We flew around for a couple hours burning off fuel while trying to get the gear double locked by the use of the mechanical crank. We tried shallow dives and sharp pull-ups, but we were never able to do better than single locked indication.

In the meantime the local radio station broadcast the news that, "An airliner is in trouble and will soon be landing at North Platte."

The local folks all drove to the airport to watch us crash. Some of them seemed disappointed when the land-

ing was normal and the airplane stopped on the runway. A tug came out and towed us in to the ramp.

We were wined and dined around town that night as surviving heroes. It was a big deal for me, being new in the business.

Shad and Hampton's problem was more serious than they might have thought. They had been in turbulence so severe that it had warped the wing spar, which had thrown the landing gear locks out of alignment.

Shad leaned back in his chair with a reflective tone in his voice as he continued.

SHAD: I think those were the days of the greatest esprit de corps of the Tigers, particularly among the domestic C-46 pilots. I had a lot of hero worship for the guys I flew with. I was absolutely certain I had chosen the right airline when I began to hear so many stories from other airlines about Flying Tigers making approaches to airports when other airlines failed to get in.

There was a policy in force at Midway Airport in Chicago that if three airplanes in a row missed an approach, they would close the airport. On more than one occasion, after two airplanes missed the approach, they called Tigers out of sequence to make the third approach so the airport wouldn't have to be closed.

I tended to take these stories with a grain of salt until one night I went into Binghamton, New York. I got to talking to one of the fellows working there. He was a tower operator and worked on the Tiger ramp part time.

He told me, "The reason I applied for the job at Tigers was that I wanted to meet some of those guys who make approaches in here when no one else can."

CHAPTER 11   TIGER TALES   125

Landing in bad weather can be a problem, but it helps to have good equipment and experienced controllers.

GOLDY: In my opinion the CAA controllers in Chicago in the early fifties were the best in the world. Many of them began their careers at La Guardia when the first ILS[1] systems were installed. Later, those who transferred to Chicago became supervisors and instructors for the new hires. One reason they were better was simply because they had more hands-on experience. They could tolerate, and many even enjoyed, the intense pressure of the job.

It's true that the Midway Airport was seldom closed to a Tiger pilot, but that's also true of some other pilots who flew in there on a regular basis and had proven themselves competent. At that time controllers relied more on common sense and their own discretion than on rigid rules.

Sometimes things look a lot different on the ground than they do in the cockpit when there's a red light on and a fire bell ringing in your ear.

HARVEY HELLER: I started out from Detroit for Boston one evening in a C-46. It was raining, and we were in the clouds. When I got to about 7,000 feet the fire warning came on for the right engine. I had always been told that if you didn't get a fire out quickly, you stood a strong chance of losing the wing. I shut the engine down, pulled the firewall shutoff, shot the fire bottle, and then went back to Detroit.

I landed all right. Then the mechanics found it was a false fire warning. They were real upset with me for shoot-

---

[1]Instrument landing system.

ing the bottle, because they didn't have a spare and now the flight would be delayed until they got one. I can tell you I was glad to be back on the ground no matter how they felt about it.

Some days it seems that you can't get anywhere without something being in the way.

DON HASSIG: One cold December morning I was scheduled to fly a C-46 from Salt Lake City to San Francisco. My copilot was a guy named Millard Berry. We took off to the south about eight a.m. Just as we got off the ground the left engine started backfiring, then the fire-warning bell came on. I looked out the side window and could see fire coming out from under the cowling every time it backfired, which was about every two seconds. I shut the engine down and feathered the prop. We were about 30 feet above the ground and never did get any higher.
    I was able to make a skidding right turn and get headed back north about two miles west of the airport. To our left was a high-tension power line on steel towers. Below the towers were wooden poles carrying more wires. Berry informed the control tower what was happening, and we were cleared to land on any runway.
    We were coming along pretty good, and I thought we might make it all the way around. Then I saw that the power line made a forty-five degree turn to the right. We couldn't get over it and there was no room to go under it, so I made another skidding right turn. As we straightened out again, I saw the towers of the low frequency range station directly ahead of us.
    It looked hopeless, so I told Berry to tell them we were landing on the lakeshore. I pulled the right throttle back, and we were immediately on the ground. It was a bit

CHAPTER 11   TIGER TALES   127

bumpy, but not too bad. We made sure everything was shut off, then jumped out and got about fifty yards away.

A few minutes later an old car drove up and an elderly man got out.

He asked, "Where are all the people?"

"There aren't any other people. Just the two of us."

"Are you sure?"

"Yes, I'm sure."

Then he said, "I work at a duck hunting club over at the lake and when I saw your plane go over I said, That thing is full of people and they're all goin' to be dead as hell in a little bit."

When he was convinced there were no dead people he snorted, got back in his car and drove away, leaving us standing there. A few minutes later a procession from the airport arrived. There was a fire truck, an ambulance and three or four cars. Art Seymour and a couple of mechanics, a couple of traffic agents and a CAA Inspector all showed up.

After seeing we were okay, Art asked who was in the car he saw leaving. I told him the guy was from the duck hunting club, and Art said, "What duck club?"

Art loved hunting and fishing, and I thought for a moment that he was going to drive off and leave us too.

The airplane was not badly damaged, so after they unloaded the cargo, the mechanics jacked it up, got the gear down and towed it back to the airport. They put two new engines and props on it and it was ferried to Burbank two days later.

When the cargo was weighed, the airplane was found to have been 1500 pounds overweight.

That particular airplane had gone through a major overhaul a short time before this happened and it was the only C-46 in the whole fleet that had two VOR (navigation) receivers. To this day, every time I see Dick Wilson, he reminds me that I wrecked the only airplane we had with two VORs.

BAR STORY

BY

BOB ZALUSKY: One night on layover in North Platte we went to a honky-tonk where the local cowboys hang out. We were having a few drinks, then a gal came by and asked me to dance. So I danced with her, and we were getting along pretty good. Too good, her husband thought. He took exception to that and came over and grabbed his wife, then he swung at me. I didn't really know what was going on, but it riled me a little, so I decked him. That's when the fight started.

Everyone was in on it. Fighting's what these cowboys do for fun. If there's no fight, someone will start one. Somebody swung at me, so I hit him.

About then a gal came up to me and said, "You son-of-a-bitch, you hit my husband when he was wearing glasses!"

Then she hit me with her purse and knocked my head right through the bass drum.

The bartender told me later, "I knew you were in a lot of trouble, 'cause Ida Mae always carries a flat iron in her purse."

Anyway I wasn't hurt bad until my copilot staggered across the floor to help me. As I was crawling out of the drum he stepped on my hand and broke my finger.

CHAPTER 12 THE DOUGLAS DC-6 1954

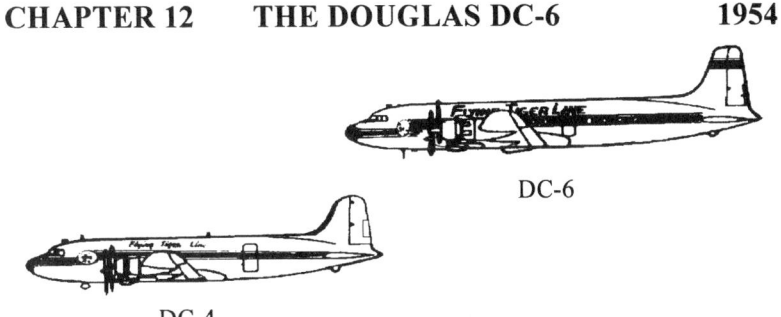

DC-6

DC-4

Often an event takes place, which in time has an unexpected and very welcome sequel.

GOLDY: Howard Brooks went into Rome with a load of passengers in a DC-6. He had a flat tire and also a magneto problem on one of the engines. TWA had a maintenance facility there, but they were mad at us at the time and refused to give us any assistance. Howard put the passengers in a hotel while we tried to figure out what to do.

In just a little while my phone rang. It was Tommy Reese, who had the badly needed credit card back in '49. He was still working for TWA there in Rome. He noticed the Tiger airplane sitting there with a flat tire and asked if we needed some help.

During the night the airplane acquired a new tire and a new magneto. Howard got his passengers loaded as quickly as possible and they were on their way.

I called Tommy. "You really saved the day for us on this one." I said. "What can I do for you in return?"

"In return for what? If I was caught helping you guys I would get fired, so I don't know a thing about it."

I sent him a bottle of Scotch.

There was a period during the year when it was doubtful the company could weather its financial problems.

LARRY LUCCIO: Bob Prescott came back to Newark and said, "Things are pretty lean. You guys may have to take a temporary pay cut."

He explained the problem, part of which was the cancellation of the proposed merger with Slick Airways.

When he was finished Ralph Hedden got up and said, "Okay boys, let's go flying."

So that was the end of that. We all took our pay cut, and sure enough, three or four months later we were reimbursed.

With Bob Zalusky and Jim Sanders it was not weather, but whether or not it would fly.

BOB ZALUSKY: Jim Sanders was my copilot out of Salt Lake City. Two C-46s bellied in at Salt Lake because of engine trouble. Bledso bellied one and Don Hassig another. The elevation there is high you know, about the single engine ceiling on the C-46.

Jim and I had a low manifold pressure reading on the left engine. It backfired a little bit then smoothed out. We kind of leaned it out, and then it seemed to run all right.

But I said, "Jim, you know we just might have some problems with this engine. Why don't we go through the feathering checklist right here, so that if anything goes haywire we can go right through it."

So we did.

Then I said, "Now Jim, if anything happens with this engine on takeoff, I'm just going to holler, FEATHER, and you go ahead and feather it and I'll fly it."

If we had taxied back to the ramp and said there was something wrong with that engine, they'd have said ground checks okay, because it was within limits. It just didn't act

CHAPTER 12   TIGER TALES

right though, and I had a bad feeling about it.

Well, we were just off the ground, just broke ground, and I hollered, "gear up" as the left engine went rower, rower, rower and quit.

I hollered "FEATHER IT," and he did. The gear was still coming up when we crossed the runway fence. There was a board across the top of the fence, and we hit it, but then we made it all the way around the pattern and landed.

Later the chief pilot called us in and asked, "How come you guys made it around, and the other guys bellied in?"

So I told him exactly what happened—that we had been all ready for it and had the engine feathered in about four seconds. We never got higher than about 60 feet; so we were almost in ground effect the whole way around.

A DC-4 at maximum gross weight is hardly a rocket in the best of circumstances. This was not the best circumstance...

DICK STRATFORD: I had a military cargo flight from Dover, Delaware, to Europe, with a fuel stop in Gander, Newfoundland. When we arrived in the area the Gander weather was down, so we landed at Stephenville. Bill Towner was my copilot, and it was his leg from there to Shannon, Ireland. The runway in use would take us toward a gap in the hills, and that gap was pretty damn close to the airport.

The weather was instrument conditions, and we could barely see the gap because of low clouds. We decided we didn't want to take off in that direction with the heavy DC-4. There was only a three-knot wind, so we requested the opposite runway, which would take us out over the water. The airport was very busy. Finally when there was a break in the traffic, we were cleared for takeoff.

Bill made the takeoff, but when we put the gear handle up the landing gear would not retract. Bill stayed low under the overcast, circled for a 180-degree turn and landed. If we'd taken off toward the hills, we'd never have cleared them with the drag of the extended landing gear. What was wrong with the gear? Nothing, the ramp service people had neglected to remove the ground locking pins.

There are always a lot of people being moved around in a growing company. Opportunity sometimes knocks at inopportune times.

DON SANDERS: One day Ed Pinke called me and asked, "Will you move to San Francisco as chief pilot? Dobbie just resigned."

I said, "Why didn't you tell me ten days ago? I just bought a house."

"I didn't know it ten days ago. Blame it on Dobbie."

I took the job and called my wife.

"Stop unpacking," I told her. "We're moving again."

While Don Sanders was working on his shipping problems, Bobby Tharp came up with one of his own.

BOBBIE THARP: I had a load of troops on a DC-4 headed for Morocco when we blew an engine. We were losing oil, so I shut it down and feathered the propeller. We went in and landed all right, but now we needed an engine. I swung a deal with the military to borrow one of their spare engines, which we would replace ASAP. By the time we got back to Newark, maintenance had an engine ready to ship.

"How will we get it to Casablanca?" they asked.

CHAPTER 12   TIGER TALES

"It's all arranged. We can ship it on an Air Force plane for one dollar."

The following account describes a normal international charter flight on a 200 mph unpressurized DC-4. Instead of holding the airplane while the crew laid over in a hotel, they used three pilots instead of two. The theory was that while two pilots were flying the third was sleeping, so the crew would always be well rested. Right!

DICK STRATFORD: We had some charters that had us leaving Newark at 3 a.m. and flying to Kingston, Jamaica. There we picked up a load of Jamaican immigrants and brought them through Bermuda, Gander and Shannon to their destination, London.

Then when the passengers were off-loaded in London, we flew the airplane to Melbourne, Australia, to pick up another charter. We only had one crew rest the entire trip, and that was in Karachi, India (now Pakistan). It was quite a privilege to see the sun come up three times before we got to see a bed.

Sometimes one has to strip down to the bare necessities.

CHUCK HAMMER: I had a trip with Cliff Groh from Honolulu to Tokyo on a DC-6. They had just put in that new rule that you couldn't land in Tokyo after midnight because of noise abatement. We were on a military charter going to Tachikawa. When we arrived the airport was fogged in and Yokota was fogged in, so we elected to land at Tokyo.

Cliff was sitting up there with his paperback book, while the copilot was taking care of everything.

All of a sudden he put his book away and said, "You know, we're going to have trouble getting out of customs down here. I don't want you guys to say anything. Whatever I do, you do, and we'll get out of this."

So we got in there and they said, "So sorry, no customs here now. They come in at six in the morning."

Cliff said, "Fine, that's no problem at all."

He walked over to one of those long wooden benches they had in the terminal and opened his suitcase. He took a pair of pajamas out, picked them up by the shoulders and carefully shook the wrinkles out and laid them aside. The Japanese guy took off like a shot, and by the time he returned, Cliff had stripped down to his shorts. We were a four-man crew, and the rest of us, as we had been told, had also undressed.

The guy said, "So sorry, you can not sleep here tonight!"

Cliff said, "Well we have to sleep someplace. We have to fly in the morning, and if you won't let us go to the hotel, we're going to sleep right here."

"You can go to hotel. Never mind customs. We put you in taxi and you go now."

Chuck remembered that little incident. Now he's on a trip with Glen Myer over in Honolulu.

CHUCK HAMMER: The Company had an entire floor blocked for us at the Waikiki Biltmore. We got in there during the height of the tourist season, and they had rented our rooms out to tourists.

Here we were, tired from flying in from San Francisco, and the gal at the desk said, "There will be a delay of about eight hours until your rooms are ready."

CHAPTER 12   TIGER TALES

Of course Glen was about to blow his cork.

I said, "Hold it, Glen, we'll never get a room that way. Don't say anything. Just do what I do. Trust me."

Glen was pretty skeptical, but he went along with it. The hotel had a huge open lobby with long comfortable sofas. I selected one and took my suitcase over and opened it. The rest of the crew did the same. I took out my pajamas, carefully shook out the wrinkles and laid them aside while I began unbuttoning my shirt. The rest of the crew did the same.

About that time here comes the manager, "What are you doing?" he asked.

"I'm going to bed. You rented our block of rooms to someone else, and we have to sleep somewhere."

By now we were unbuckling our belts.

He said, "Wait a minute," and hurried to the desk.

Soon he was back, "The only room we have is the penthouse suite. It has two bedrooms with two beds in each room. Would that be all right?"

We agreed that would meet our requirements, so he quickly hustled us up the elevator. We discovered a full bar in the suite that had been left open, so we proceeded to have a few drinks. Soon the phone rang.

"We forgot to lock the bar, so we would like to send a bellboy up to lock it."

I said, "Okay, but I just looked, and there is only one bottle of wine in there."

"Really! I don't see how that could be."

We had the booze hidden in a closet when the bellboy came. He confirmed that there was only one bottle of wine in the bar.

After he left we called all the other crews in the hotel and had ourselves a party. We felt the damned hotel made more money by renting out our rooms than what we drank cost, so they still came out ahead.

Maybe Cliff Groh was late for a party. He sure came down out of the sky.

BOB BARLOW: I was flying copilot for Cliff Groh on a DC-6 en route from Grand Island, Nebraska, to Burbank. When we reached our descent point, without saying anything, Cliff closed all four throttles, and then pulled the inboard propellers into reverse.

The airplane went through all kinds of gyrations. We had a deadhead on board who banged himself up a little, so he wasn't too happy. I'd had a clipboard on my lap, and I had to reach up under the instrument panel to retrieve it.

When we got on the ground, Cliff said, "Those inboards in reverse sure blocked out the elevator control. The next time I'll try the outboards."

I said, "Not with me on board you won't!"

Harry Hinshaw, the flight engineer, quit and went back to the maintenance department. I don't believe his comments were recorded.

No, in case you are wondering, reversing the propellers in flight is not a recommended procedure.

The following is a typical example of the actions of a Tiger employee.

MARILYN (SMITH) DREW, Stewardess: Captain Morris, Copilot Richards, and I took a load of passengers from Baltimore, Maryland, to Louisville, Kentucky, on DC-4 60V. The crew parked the airplane on the ramp, and took a commercial flight out, and I went to the hotel to await my next assignment.

CHAPTER 12   TIGER TALES   137

The next day dawned very stormy, and there were forecasts for severe weather including a warning that all aircraft should be hangared. I was the only one in town, so I called the FBO and asked, "Could you hangar our DC-4?"

He said, "Sure, but on who's authority?"

Mine wasn't good enough without pre-payment, so I told him I'd be right out with a check. In those days, stewardesses were issued company checkbooks, with each check having a maximum of $1,000. After seeing my DC-4 safely hangared, and enjoying the expression on the faces of the ground crew, I went back to the hotel and began to worry. Did I do the right thing? Would I have to pay the hangar charge or maybe they'd just abandon me in Louisville? Instead of worrying all day, I decided to call Pinke in Burbank and tell him what I had done.

He said, "So...we expected you to take care of your airplane. By the way, you're scheduled out tomorrow at 1620 for Vichy, Missouri, I forgot to call you."

A "BLUE GOAT" BAR STORY

ROBBIE ROBINSON: We had a DC-4 contract hauling G.I.'s from Guam to Casablanca, then to Tripoli, then we took replacement troops back to Guam. We were flying out of the North Shore Air Force Base in Casablanca, and were not allowed to go into town.

Anyway, we did get a few breaks between flights. I was rooming with a guy who was familiar with the area and knew how to sneak off the Base, so he showed us around.

He took us to a nightclub in Casablanca called the Blue Goat. The bar was quiet, and Captain George Edge sat unnoticed at a corner table nursing his drink. Suddenly two guys at the bar got into a fight, cussin' and swearin' and swingin' at each other. George Edge quietly walked up behind them, doubled up his fists and hit both of them behind the head, BAM! BAM! He knocked them both colder'n hell.

He pointed his finger admonishingly at the astonished barkeep and said, "I don't want any trouble in here."

CHAPTER 13   "THREE ENGINES GONE..."   1955

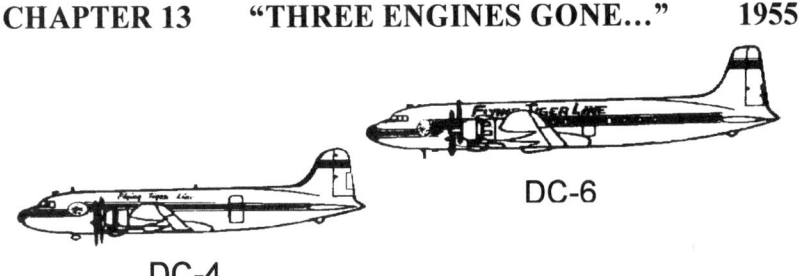

Some guys just have a broader view of the world.

JACK TALKINGTON: January '55 I left schedule line flying, to fly Tiger's Dehavilland "Mosquito". I took Paul Entz as photographer and to handle any maintenance problems that might occur on our operation. One occurred in February when Paul and I changed an engine in Palm Springs. Paul borrowed the mobile-A-Frame from maintenance in Burbank, and a couple days later we were back in business. We did photo work over Phoenix at 36,000 feet and Winslow at 37 to 38,000 feet.

By this time the company was operating six DC-4s, three DC-6s and 23 C-46s. The DC-6s were used on transcontinental cargo flights and on international passenger charters. One advantage in working for a growing company is the opportunity for rapid advancement.

AL MOBLEY: Joe Gaudino and I were both flight line mechanics and were walking out the gate one day when Art Seymour stopped us.
  "You guys want to be flight engineers?" he asked.
  "We sure do, and we have our written exams passed."
  "Okay, we'll give you the training and check ride on the DC-6."
  We started flying as flight engineers in February 1955.

With the advent of larger airplanes there was also a vast increase in the number of stewardesses. Here is a poem from the flight attendant book, 41 Years Aloft.

GIRL IN THE SKY

I wear silver wings
And a neat Flight Cap,
I've flown many times
Across the map.

The smile of a stewardess
I possess,
And my job in the sky
I know is the best.

I've traveled the world
Enjoying each sight,
And the world smiling back
Is my real delight.

When I take off
In a fine silver plane,
To be a good stewardess
Has been my aim.

For life is beautiful
Up here in the sky,
And I thank God
I am able to fly.

Pat Bliss, 1955

CHAPTER 13   TIGER TALES

Another girl in the sky...or maybe not.

GLORIA WISBAR: We had a group of French sailors on board and I got them all seated and belted and went up to tell the captain we were ready. On my way back I looked to the right and couldn't believe what I was seeing. One of the sailors had decided he wanted some fresh air, so he had removed the emergency exit window over the wing and was sitting there with his elbow resting on the window frame waiting for us to take off.

I ran up to the cockpit to tell the captain. I thought he'd be really mad, but he just laughed.

"These guys don't read or understand English, so do the best you can."

I didn't know whether to laugh or say, "I think I'll take the next flight."

You can take the boy out of Oklahoma, but you can't take Oklahoma...

CHUCK HAMMER: We had a passenger trip to Europe, so we had four crewmembers and three stewardesses. We had a layover in Paris, so that evening the seven of us were in the hotel bar having a couple of drinks and discussing where we wanted to have dinner.

Several suggestions were made and when it came around to me, I said, "I'm going to Maxim's."

"Maxim's? Hell, Chuck, you can't even afford a bottle of beer in that joint!"

I said, "Don't worry, they'll give me a free meal."

They laughed and said, "Yeah, yeah."

So we all took off, and I got a taxi and went over to Maxim's. I was properly dressed in a sport coat and tie, and I walked in and was seated. Soon the maitre d' came around to take my order.

I said, "I can't read the menu because it's all in French, but I'll tell you what I'd really like to have. I'd like to have some lamb's-quarters, a poke salad and I'd like to have some collard greens." (All these are greens, which are common in Oklahoma.)

He wrote it all down like he knew what he was doing and took off for the kitchen. They brought the hors d' oeuvres cart around with all the cheeses and crackers and what not.

When they brought the wine list I said, "I would like a bottle of white wine with body to it, but not too sweet and not too sour."

"Oui, Monsieur, we know what you want."

They poured a glass for me, but it was too sour. Eventually I had about ten glasses in front of me.

Then the chef came out looking perplexed. He and the maitre d' were apologetic as hell.

"Monsieur, I have looked through all my menu books and I cannot find lamb's-quarters. Also we cannot find how to make a poke salad. We are so sorry that we cannot serve you your order."

By then I had eaten my fill of the shrimp, crab claws and everything else they had put on the table.

I said, "Well I'm sorry, but that's what I came in here for. What do I owe you?"

"Oh, Monsieur, there will be no charge, and we would be privileged to provide transportation back to your hotel."

They brought around the limo, which had Maxim's emblazoned on the doors, and delivered me to the hotel. By then the rest of crew had returned from dinner and watched as I got out of the limo and thanked the driver.

"You really ate at Maxim's?"

"Yep."

CHAPTER 13   TIGER TALES

"What did it cost you?"
"Nothin'."

Chuck seemed to enjoy his free meal. Now if he could just find something to drink.

CHUCK HAMMER: Glen Myer was a very good friend of mine. Back in the beginning of WW II Glen was studying to become a priest. When the war broke out and they found out he had a pilot's license, they grabbed him and put him in a fighter group. That didn't sit too well with him, so finally he convinced them to transfer him to transports. He wound up at Fort Benning, Georgia, flying paratroop training flights in C-47s.

I was a jumpmaster back there on the tests. We were testing the new nylon chutes. We had been using silk chutes with the molded rubber rings, but then they came out with the nylon chute with the 21-inch hole in the apex.

The pilots were supposed to fly us directly over the runway, so we would land on the runway. Glen, being the nice guy that he was, let his copilot fly the jump course. This copilot flew across the airport at an angle, yet all the jumpers landed where they were supposed to, except me. I was the last one to jump, so I fell into the obstacle course along side the runway, and landed astraddle a log. That jump broke 58 of my bones, and I spent about a year in the hospital.

Years later Glen and I had a trip into Anchorage, Alaska. We were staying at the Captain Cook Hotel and were having a drink in the Crow's Nest. The two of us were sitting there telling war stories. Glen told me about letting his copilot fly during a parachute drop.

He said, "I am responsible for that jumpmaster being killed."

I said, "Did that happen to be the last test jump with the nylon chute?"

"Yes."

"Did you go over to the hospital to see the jumpmaster?"

"No, they told me he was dead."

I got off my stool and held out my hand and said, "Shake hands with him. I'm the guy."

From then on, I couldn't pay for a drink anywhere in the Pacific.

Some time later we were back at the Captain Cook, and I wanted to buy Glen a drink.

Glen said, "No, you really set my mind at ease knowing I didn't kill anybody, so I want to buy the drinks."

We were arguing pretty loud I guess, when Whispering Jim Martin walked in. He was a good friend to both of us, but he thought I was mad at Glen. That was in the days when Jim was real husky, and he grabbed me by the lapels and lifted me right off the floor.

I said, "Wait a minute, Jim. Before you hit me, listen to the story."

So we related the whole thing from the beginning.

Jim put me down and turned to Glen and asked, "Are you paying for my drinks, too?"

One can hear many humorous stories as old pilots recall their youthful experiences. I doubt that Perry was as bad as he says, but you never know.

PERRY DOVE: May 3, 1955, I believe it was, I had been getting my commercial and instrument ratings over at Northrup Field in Hawthorne. I had about 200 hours of tail-dragger time, and the biggest thing I had flown was a Stinson Voyager.

CHAPTER 13   TIGER TALES

One of my friends said, "Tigers are hiring pilots over at Burbank."

So I polished up my shoes and cleaned my fingernails and everything and went over there.

They felt of me, and I was warm, so they said, "You'll do."

There was about a dozen of us, and we were all in the same boat—no experience.

We marched into Art Seymour's office and he said, "You guys have to go to ground school on the C-46. Here's the address, be there at eight on Monday morning."

Tuesday at noon we finished the ground school and went back to Art Seymour's office. He was sitting there with his feet up on the desk.

"What do we do now?" I asked.

Art said, "You have to check out in a C-46. To do that you have to make three successful takeoffs and landings."

The next day they strapped my butt into the left seat of that big brute. (At that time the pilot doing the flying always sat in the left seat.) The check pilot was in the right seat, and he started the thing and taxied it out to the runway and locked the tail wheel.

He said, "Okay, you've got it."

I knew I was supposed to use a certain manifold pressure, 43 or 45 inches, something like that. But I couldn't find the manifold pressure gauges and watch the runway at the same time, so I just shoved the throttles open. He grabbed them and pulled them back to where they belonged.

About that time I was headed for the edge of the runway and was trying to get it straightened up, when he yelled, "I've got it."

He kicked the rudder a few times, got it straight and hollered, "You've got it!"

I pulled back on the yoke, and we were airborne. Good God Almighty, how will I ever get this thing back on the ground, I wondered. He coached me around the field and put the gear down, set the flaps and the power and pointed me toward the runway. I flew it in and hit the runway so dang hard I thought the instrument panel was going to fall right out of the airplane.

He pushed the power up and said, "Let's try another one."

The next one was a little bit better, and the third one was a little better than that, but not much.

Just as I was convinced I had lost my job, he said, "Okay, let's get the next guy up here."

I just can't remember who the check pilot was, but it might have been Don Sanders.

A few days after he was hired, they called him for his first trip. Jim Cullen was the captain.

PERRY DOVE: It was night of course, and I couldn't find anything in the cockpit. I knew I was supposed to help this guy, but he hasn't said a word to me. Pretty soon he was throwing switches and starting the engines.

I asked, "What do you want me to do?"

"Why don't you just sit and watch for this leg?"

I was never so relieved in my life.

We left Burbank for San Francisco on a crystal clear night, and I was lost from the time we left the ground. If he had dropped dead we would have crashed, because I would never have found an airport.

The next day was about the same, but the third day he said, "Look, if you're going to be a pilot for us, you're going to have to fly this airplane."

So he put me in the left seat, and I started flying my

CHAPTER 13 TIGER TALES 147

legs. Sometimes I was pretty good, but most of the time I wasn't.

I took off out of Grand Island, and had so much airplane in my hands that I forgot I was supposed to fly a heading!

The captain said, "It's not enough to just fly the airplane, you have to fly it <u>to</u> somewhere!"

Perry Dove has a sense of humor, and fortunately, so does Jim Cullen. But in the following story there is no humor to be found.

After flying the Pacific in DC-4s since 1947, Tigers lost their first airplane at sea in September. It was a MATS cargo flight, flying from Honolulu to Wake Island with Tokyo as the final destination. It carried a multicrew consisting of Captain Tony Machado, First Officer Warren Fong Gin, Copilot Robert Hightower, and two navigators, Dominic Ventresca and Richard Olsen.

After reaching their cruising altitude of 4,000 feet, Tony crawled into the bunk to take his turn at rest while Gin and Hightower were in the pilot's seats. Sometime later they apparently ran a fuel tank dry and an engine quit. While attempting to open the crossfeed valves, two more engines quit.

All this commotion awakened Captain Machado, but the airplane hit the water before he could get the engines restarted.

A distress message was being sent, but only the words "three engines gone..." were received by Honolulu Radio before impact.

One navigator, Dominic Ventresca, was trapped by the shifted cargo and was lost. The other crewmembers got out of the airplane, but they could not retrieve the raft or ditching supplies. Tony Machado was a strong swimmer, which was a good thing because he had not donned a life jacket. They floated all that day and the next night with Tony swimming from one to the other to hold on and rest.

That night a shark found them and bit Olsen's thumb off. While they were trying to stop Olsen's bleeding, Gin became delirious. He untied his life jacket and slipped beneath the waves. Tony retrieved the jacket and returned to help Olsen, but it was too late. Olsen was dead.

An air search was started when the distress call was received, and they were spotted on the second day. The search aircraft notified a ship in the area, and they found the survivors. They had been in the water more than thirty hours.

NOAH SMITH, navigator: This is one of those FICKLE FINGER OF FATE stories. I was scheduled for that trip with Tony Machado, but Nick Ventresca asked me to trade trips with him and I agreed. It's difficult for me to voice my feelings of "Man was I lucky to trade trips!" When I know the sorrow in Nick's family because of the trade.

I was with Tony when he made his first overseas trip after his splashdown.

We'd just reached altitude when a stew came up and said, "A passenger wants to know if this is the same Tony he'd fished out of the water."

It was, and they had quite a reunion there in the cockpit.

CHAPTER 13 TIGER TALES

Mess with Marilyn and you might get pounded.

MARILYN (SMITH) DREW: During the fall, most of my flights were from Newark, New Jersey, to Frankfurt, Germany. In Frankfurt our ground person was Bernt, a young man who desperately wanted to come to the United States. On our arrival he first proposed marriage, I'm sure to most of the stewardesses. When his offer was refused, he pleaded to be adopted. We might have found him more tolerable if not for the pound cake.

On every outbound trip he boarded several large boxes of pound cake, more than enough to be served for our three meals. It was fine for the first meal, dried out for the second, and hard as a rock for the third.

I had complained in flight reports to no avail. I had asked nicely and begged Bernt not to give us more than one box, which was all we could, and had room for. Finally, I threatened to throw out the excess if he ever boarded it again. He did and I did!

As soon as the steps were pulled away and the engines started, I opened the door and shoved out several boxes of pound cake. It was a beautiful sight—pound cake flying around in the prop wash with Bcrnt flailing around in the middle of it all.

I confessed my dirty deed in my flight report, and in a week or so got a summons from Mar Maguire, our Chief Stewardess. I was worried, and when I met her and saw the stern expression on her face, I was scared. I didn't want any more pound cake on our flights, but I did want my job!

After a few terse words, Mar broke out laughing. She did say that I shouldn't have done it but wished she had been there to see it. Bernt stopped boarding pound cake and also stopped asking me to marry or adopt him.

This logo known as the "Easter Egg" graced the forward side of the fuselage of the Curtiss C-46, Douglas DC-4 and DC-6 and the Lockheed Constellations

CHAPTER 14   THE DEWLINE   1955

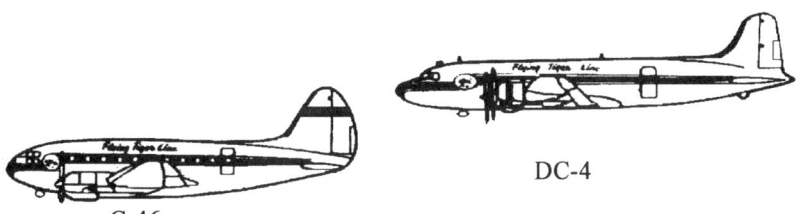

DC-4
C-46

The DEWLINE was the acronym for the Distant Early Warning Line of radar installations across northern Canada and Alaska. Flying Tigers was given a subcontract to haul supplies to the various radar sites during their construction.

The even-numbered sites were 100 miles apart, and the odd-numbered sites were 50 miles apart. The weather ran to extremes. In winter there were temperatures of 60 below zero, ice, wind, sleet, whiteouts and isolation. In the summer it was heat, rain and fog, along with lots of mosquitoes. But, I'll let the pilots and mechanics that were there tell about it

BOBBIE THARP: We were going to check out a few more pilots on the DC-6, and I was in class. During break I went up to Doug Robbins' office to shoot the breeze. He had a ruler out and was busy making up a form of some kind.

"What's up Doug? You took awfully busy."

"Yeah. We just got a big contract up in the Arctic, and I'm going to put a bid out on the Teletype."

Then he explained what the Dewline was, so I bid it right there. As a result I was pulled from the DC-6 class. We would be flying C-46s and DC-4s.

We took our NC numbers off the airplanes and painted Canadian letters on them. Then we painted our numbers over them with water-soluble paint. We flew them to Seattle and cleared outgoing customs, then flew them to Vancouver to clear Canadian customs. While we were inside with the paperwork, maintenance washed the water-soluble paint off, and now we had Canadian registered airplanes of Queen Charlotte Airlines.

It was colder'n hell and it was dark, and here we come into Hay River and land. One of the guys had a suitcase made of fiberglass. When the bags were dropped out of the baggage compartment onto the ground, the fiberglass bag was so cold it shattered like a pane of glass.

I took a DC-4 one time trying to find one of the sites. No one had been able to get in there, and they were running out of fuel and everything. We had to find them. There were whiteout conditions, and I remember I was flying that DC-4 standing up, so I could see down in front of the airplane. We found out later that we had flown right over them at about 50 feet, and we never saw them.

The buildings were built on permafrost. The heat from the buildings caused the ground to soften, and the buildings began to sag. It got so bad that there would be as much as a two-inch gap around the doors.

Gil Shelton walked into the hotel with ice on his shoes, slipped and broke his ankle. He insisted it was only sprained and sat around waiting for it to get better. It was turning black and green and hurt like hell. He couldn't fly, so all he did was sit around and get drunk.

One night while he was sitting at a table, someone took the bolts out and shortened his crutches. Gil was pretty well gassed when he got up. He grabbed the crutches, which were now way too short, and fell on his butt.

For some reason, he thought I was the culprit, and tried to beat me to death with a crutch. Some other bastard had all the fun, and I nearly got killed for it.

The airplanes weren't used to the severe cold either. Some winterizing would have to be done.

CHAPTER 14   TIGER TALES

GOLDY: When we first went up on the Dewline we had some real problems. The landing gear strut seals leaked in the severe cold, and the struts kept going flat. The seals all had to be changed to a cold weather type.

This was no easy task. The airplanes had to be jacked up and the landing gear struts removed to replace the seals. After reassembly the struts had to be serviced with hydraulic fluid and then charged with dry nitrogen. No big deal in a warm hangar, but outside in a howling wind it was another matter.

The new seals kept the struts from going flat, but they couldn't keep Zalusky's C-46 from going into a snow bank. The following is a good example of a pilot being commemorated for something he'd rather forget:

> **There was a young pilot named "Ski"**
> **Who's airplane was broken in three**
> **At a hundred per hour**
> **It became a snow plower**
> **He was painfully hurt in the knee.**
>   **Anon. (At least no will admit it.)**

There is more. This one was performed by the Tiger Dewline Choir to the tune of "On Top Of Old Smokey."

THE SAGA OF OLD NINE NINE TWO

> **Let me tell you a tale that has never been told,**
> **of a C-46 in the arctic so cold.**
>
> **A truly fine aircraft was old 992,**
> **She flew like an eagle way up in the blue.**

THE DEWLINE

On a cold April morning, a takeoff did start,
with Captain Zalusky and a guy named Art.

The crew didn't know just what was in store,
when they climbed aboard that pot bellied whore.

They ran through the check list and taxied on out,
at the end of the runway they turned her about.

The tailwheel was locked, they were ready to go,
to charge down the runway all covered with snow.

Zalusky was skillfully giving her juice,
to 52 inches, then all hell broke loose.

One engine crapped out, as quick as a flash,
old 992 in a snow bank did crash.

It gyrated forward, then up on her nose,
nearly flipped over, the tail end arose.

It came back to earth, with a terrible smash,
Zalusky was painfully hurt in the crash.

Don't laugh at my story of old 992,
Just bear this in mind, it could happen to you.

A word of advice to sum up the issue,
have plenty of paper, the kind made of tissue!

CHAPTER 14 TIGER TALES

This is what really happened:

BOB ZALUSKY: One night it had been snowing for several hours and, even though the runway was plowed, the left side had drifted over, so we had to take off on the right side. A cross wind was blowing so hard from the left that I had to start the takeoff roll, using full power on the left engine only, until I had enough speed to have rudder effect. Then I could bring up the power on the right engine. Just as I began to increase power on the right engine, the left engine failed. The airplane immediately turned left and went right into the snow bank.

Some guys just can't seem to stay away from buzzing things, especially mosquitoes.

JACK TALKINGTON: I went back on the Dewline and "in the now it can be told department," on July 22, '55, I took my wife and son on a Dewline flight with Copilot Jim Forsythe from Edmonton to Yellowknife, site #18 then to site #20, back to Yellowknife and Edmonton. The best part was my son being 12 yrs old, he was able to stand at the control wheel with my seat pushed back and fly the aircraft for almost two hrs. Every so often I'd have to add a little rudder to pick up a wing, but he was in his glory.

October '55 I went back on the "Mosquito" again with Paul Entz, working out of Denver. Most photo flights were at 40,000 ft. After we finished the photo work out of Denver, we moved to Cleveland for photo flights at 25,000 ft from Chicago-Cleveland-Cincinnati, and south to Louisville, KY.

The weather problems on the Dewline were bad enough without being compounded by poor communications.

One afternoon Dick Rossi flew a C-46 to one of the sites, but there was a blinding blizzard going on, and he never could find the strip. The next morning another crew took the C-46 loaded with fuel barrels, and Dick was scheduled to follow with a DC-4. The 5000-foot strip was supposed to have been plowed, but the ground crew had only cleared 3000 feet when the C-46 arrived. That was enough for the C-46, so he landed, was off-loaded and took off again.

Unfortunately, the loaders left all the fuel barrels stacked on the runway. When Dick landed the DC-4 on what he thought was a 5,000-foot strip, he soon found the end of the runway coming at him with all those barrels of fuel right in the way. He kicked right rudder and brake while pushing the left throttles forward. This spun the airplane around, and he went down the runway backwards with all four throttles wide open. The ground crew measured the distance from where he stopped to the barrels. It was 13 feet.

Navigation was very difficult at best, especially for pilots who had never flown up there before. Some said it got easier after a while, but others said you just get used to being lost. Bill wasn't lost; he just didn't know where the site was.

BILL PATTISON: On the Dewline they loaded us up with diesel fuel and sent us up to a site that no one had gone into before. Our charts were marked exploratory only, which didn't give us much confidence. We got up there okay, we thought, but then found we'd landed in the wrong place. We were on a ski strip covered with two feet of snow. Wayne Lowe was with me, and the only way we could get out of there

was to off-load the cargo. Wayne and I rolled all the fuel barrels off into the snow, then we taxied back and forth until we got the snow packed down enough to give us a runway so we could take off. That was quite a harrowing experience for us.

When we got back, we told our guys what happened. They said they knew about that ski strip, and that there was no way we could've gotten in and out of there. We said okay, but if you fly over it, you'll find eighteen thousand pounds of fuel oil drums on the ground.

BOB HAMBY: Dick Rossi gave me a briefing on the area and showed me how to read the maps. Jack Wibben was one of the best navigators up there, and he was assigned to be my copilot. On one of my first flights the airport was fogged in, so I flew over the airport and made an 80-degree reversal, all at 500 feet. After I found the airport and landed, the altimeter read 300 feet. I had been flying around at 200 feet above the ground. Luckily there were no hills in the way.

We were north of any area where rules and regulations were in force. You could do anything you wanted to. It was nothing unusual to cut a 200 and a half ADF approach (a 200-foot ceiling with half-mile visibility. A normal ADF approach would be about a 500-foot ceiling and one-mile visibility.)

At one of the western sites above Great Bear Lake, I came across the runway and they had a 100-foot ceiling. There was no cloud cover out over the sea, so I went out and ducked under the cloud layer and came on in and landed. When the cargo was off-loaded, I took off again. I talked to an inbound Canadian Pacific flight, but they were going by the rules so they couldn't land and had to go somewhere else.

We delivered a lot of freight up there, and one reason was that we were paid by the ton instead of by the hour. We couldn't afford to sit on the ground and wait for the weather to clear up. We made a lot of money for ourselves and also for the company. One day I made two round trips while a Canadian outfit was sitting there waiting for the weather to get better. That C-46 was one hell of an airplane. We left a few scattered around the Dewline, but nobody got hurt. Bobbie Tharp once cut one a little short and left the landing gear at the end of the runway.

Of course we started out landing on the ice. Sometimes the ground people would get a little too eager and would scrape the snow with their plows right down to the glare Ice. After that we got the guys to leave an inch or two of snow on the Ice. Later on they poured some gravel on the strips, but we never did have any decent runways.

I went up there in the spring of '55, but I didn't stay through the winter. I think John Lamping and Howard Bayne stayed all winter. I went back in the spring of '56.

I'll have to say that the Flying Tiger mechanics could fix just about anything anywhere so you could fly it out. They rebuilt two DC-4s up there, which were flown back to Burbank.

Landing on ice with heavily loaded airplanes could be exciting to say the least. Keep in mind that neither the C-46 nor the DC-4 had reversible propellers.

GOLDY: I think Wayne Peake was the captain and Morgan Hughes the copilot on one of the western sites, site 22 or thereabouts. They were landing a DC-4 on the ice and went off the end of the runway and tore the nose gear out. The company sent some maintenance guys up there to fix it.

They got some help from the Eskimos and cut slabs of ice and built an igloo around the nose of the airplane. I've seen pictures of it. They put Herman Nelson heaters in there but kept it cool enough to keep the Ice from melting. They repaired the airplane, and it was flown out. I think that was the

CHAPTER 14   TIGER TALES   159

most fantastic job of making do with what they had, which wasn't much, to get the job done.

Sometimes it actually goes from real bad to a little better.

JACK TALKINGTON: At first the crews stayed in a canvas Quonset hut at "Fox" on Prince Charles Island, located above the Arctic Circle. Then it got so cold the mechanics couldn't maintain the aircraft with nothing but a tarp to throw over the engines. We moved down to Coral Harbour on Southampton Island where we had much better facilities.

Much better facilities

For awhile the company couldn't get enough volunteer copilots to go up on the Dewline, so they drafted some from the bottom of the seniority list.

PERRY DOVE: Just as I thought I was getting the hang of the C-46, the chief pilot said, "We're sending you up on the Dewline for a while."

They put a bunch of us in a C-46 and sent us to Vancouver, to take the Canadian written test on air regulations, so we could fly in Canada. From there we went to Edmonton. The first trip I had was with Mark Devereaux. We called him Dusty then. Dusty wasn't feeling too good that day. He'd been partying a little the night before and was hungover pretty badly.

We got in this machine and headed for Fort Smith in the Northwest Territory for our first fuel stop. I had to crawl up a ladder with a five-gallon can of oil for the engines while wearing mosquito netting to keep from being eaten alive. We pumped the gas out of 55-gallon drums with a little engine-driven pump. Then I think we stopped at Hay River where we dropped off some freight and loaded some, and then we hopped over Great Slave Lake to Yellowknife where they off-loaded everything.

We were given a full load of freight at Yellowknife, and we headed north out of there. Now Yellowknife had a radio range station, which was good for about a hundred miles out. After that we had no radio navigation for about two hours as I recall. We had a drift meter in the airplane, so we were able to get some idea of our wind drift. We set our Directional Gyro, but then did not reset it because we were so close to magnetic north that our compasses were unreliable. Whenever we got on top of an overcast, we just flew the heading until it was time to let down, and then just hoped we could find the airport.

The sites that we were flying to had only 25-watt homers, so we couldn't receive them until we were real close. We took off out of Yellowknife heading north and were soon out of radio range. We had our contact chart out and were trying to

CHAPTER 14 TIGER TALES 161

keep track of lakes and rivers to help keep on course. Trouble was, with all the snow on the ground, we couldn't tell if there was one big lake with a lot of islands or a lot of small lakes. Then too, a lot of lakes look exactly alike.

Because of Dusty's partying the night before, he occasionally let off large amounts of internal gas. When that happened he'd light a match and hold it in the air. At first I didn't know if he was trying to portray the Statue Of Liberty or was burning off gas.

We were progressing pretty good when Dusty, looking at the map said, "You see that lake here?"

"Yes, I see that lake."

"You see that one up there?"

"Yes, I see that one."

"Okay, watch when we cross the first one and wake me when we cross the second one. I'm going to crawl in my sleeping bag in the back for a while. If you get lost, just kick the rudder. I'll come up and we'll try to figure out where we are."

So all of a sudden I was solo in this big airplane. The cockpit seemed about 20 feet wide, but I was going along fine. I was looking at the map and I knew where I was. This is really something, I thought. I'm pretty important around here now.

Everything went real fine until I ran a fuel tank dry. The engine started backfiring and chokin', and boy, I threw the map down on the floor and grabbed the throttle and got It back, got the tank switched and got throttle back up!

Of course Dusty knew what was going on, so he didn't bother to come up...unless of course he was asleep.

Then I hunted around on the floor and found the map stuck to the bottom of my shoe. I looked at it. Then I looked out the windshield at the terrain and looked at the map again, and said, "Oh crap."

I wondered if I ought to kick the rudder. Then I thought I'd feel real foolish if I had to do that. What in hell am I going to do now? I remembered being told when I got my instrument rating that if I ever got lost, I should just hold a constant heading.

So I said to myself, I'm going to hold this heading until it takes me to Siberia if he don't come up front.

When he finally came up, I was still holding that same heading.

He blinked his eyes in the sunlight a few times then said, "Well where are we?"

"I'm not really sure."

"Well let's try to find ourselves."

We fiddled around with the map for a few minutes, and he decided we were over a certain lake. He was right, and we arrived at our destination on time.

Anyway, that was my first trip in the arctic.

Cleared to land

CHAPTER 15   THE DEWLINE   PART 2 1955-56

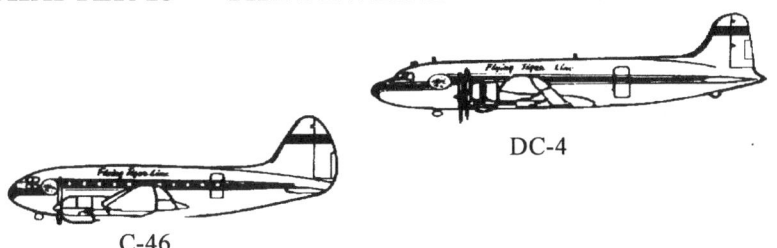

Well, considering the perspective we've just gotten from a junior copilot, let's see how it looked to an experienced senior captain.

BOBBIE THARP: Jack Wibben was with me when we came into an Arctic site in a C-46. We had a load of dynamite and jugs of acid that were used in the detonators. We had to get this stuff to the site. Other crews had tried to get in there, but the weather was too bad. We couldn't find it either and went to our alternate airport. Finally the weather cleared up enough, so we found the airstrip.

It was very short and was on a bluff. We had to land on the end of the runway, or we'd never have gotten stopped before running off the bluff. Just before touchdown we hit a down draft. It sucked us right into the ground. We hit one foot below the runway and tore the left main gear off. Then we slid down the strip until the wing tip dug into the snow bank, before we cart wheeled to a stop. Talk about a wild ride, that was it!

We scrambled out of the airplane through the copilot's window. The fuel lines had broken and the pumps were still on, and they were spraying gas on these hot engines. It sizzled like bacon frying.

We didn't walk away from it, we ran! The airplane didn't catch fire, not a single jug of acid was spilled, and obviously the dynamite did not explode.

Here comes another hairy emergency reverse thrust operation...the hard way.

DAVE VACHON: We were flying into Cambridge Bay, one of the better airports up there. Bobbie Tharp was the captain and Willy Parsons was in the engineer's seat. We were hauling this great big timber in the back, and it wasn't tied down. We landed on this runway, which was pure clear ice and when we put on the brakes, there was no braking action whatever. We were getting close to the end of the runway and there was a snow bank there, about four or five feet high. If we hit that snow bank at our present speed, that timber was going to go right out through the nose of the airplane, taking us with it.

Bobbie said, "Here, take the wheel."

I grabbed and held it steady while Bobbie grabbed the nose steering wheel. He turned it to the left while shoving the starboard engines to full power. As the DC-4 did a one-eighty, he went to full power on all engines. We slid backwards down the runway. All we broke was a taillight. I give Bobbie a hell of a lot of credit for quick thinking and having the guts to do that.

Now for a more relaxing account of a normal month's operation by another senior captain.

STARR THOMPSON: There were two crews in our area of the Dewline with Jimmy Powers and myself as captains. Karl Rader flew with me, and Curly Brumfield flew with Powers.

We had a good time up there and delivered a lot of lumber flying off those frozen lakes. We had no weather forecasting and seldom had communication with the sites.

CHAPTER 15   TIGER TALES

We would call on the radio and say, anybody been at site 28 lately? Somebody might answer and say, yeah, I left there about an hour ago, and we would get the field conditions and the altimeter setting that way.

We were up for three days one time. We had delivered our loads, then we wanted to pick up the loads that Jimmie Powers had to leave at Coral Harbour and Churchill when the weather was down at the sites. We got into one of the sites, and it was as bright and clear as noontime.

I was raisin' hell and saying, "Let's get this stuff unloaded before it gets dark, so we can go back and get another load."

The foreman said, "Good God, Starr, it's three o'clock in the morning!"

I had forgotten it didn't get dark, and we had been up two and a half days already. We had a three-man crew. I'd brought Brumfield with me, so we could keep going until we finished the job.

We had a lot of fun on the Dewline. I think I flew about 200 hours that month. Then I came home.

Art Prendergast, who had been one of the sharpest and most respected mechanics with CNAC, was on the Dewline. He was on the eastern section when he needed an engine for a C-46. In due time an engine crate arrived from Burbank, but when Art opened it, he found it contained a freshly overhauled DC-4 engine. Art sent a message, the crux of which was, "If you really want me to hang that engine on the C-46, I'll hang it on there!"

Burbank should have called Ed Abraham in Edmonton. He might have had two engines.

Gettin' a tune-up

ED ABRAHAM, mechanic: I was working out of Edmonton when Brandenberg crash-landed a C-46 at site 16. The airplane was written off by the insurance company, so Sam Agronin and I went up there to strip it of anything that was useful. We took radios, instruments and even the accessories off the engines—everything we could think of that we could lift.

We brought it all down to Yellowknife, where Doc Powell was running the operation. He asked if we could go back up there and remove the wing tips, because they were in short supply. We went back, but we were too late. The ice had thawed and the airplane was now on the bottom of the lake.

Sam, my helper, met a local girl in Edmonton, married her and stayed there. I went home a short time later.

Needs more than an engine on this one

They wouldn't let Perry go home, probably because he couldn't have found his way anyway.

PERRY DOVE: Some guys had some pretty wild experiences up there. I'd say mine were pretty routine, except one time. We were based at Coral Harbour then, on Southampton Island up in the Hudson Bay. We had Eskimos loading the airplanes for us there, and we were living in Quonset huts covered with snow.

After shuttling back and forth on the site line all day, we headed back to Coral Harbour. The weather was clear as a bell, and there was a Homer (a low frequency radio beacon) at Coral Harbour. The wind started picking up and blowing powdery snow and giving us this whiteout condition.

Crew hotel

The captain said, "We'll have to shoot an ADF approach. I can't see a damn thing."

So we shot the approach, and we missed. Then we shot another one and missed, and another one and missed. On the seventh approach we got a glimpse of the barrels along the runway and turned in and landed downwind. We were starting to sweat a little, because we didn't have enough fuel to go anywhere else. We had to land there! That was probably the hairiest experience I had up there.

There were a few minor events like getting lost. We heard that there was a herd of buffalo out there in the reservation that were used to feed the Eskimos in the winter. We were relaxing on the way home and decided to go hunt buffalo. We got lost doing that, of course, and it took

CHAPTER 15   TIGER TALES   169

about 30 minutes to figure out how to get back to Yellowknife.

One time I went up to Jenny Lind Island, which, as I recall, was about 300 miles from the magnetic pole. We had a lot of trouble with Jenny Lind Island. We seemed to be able to find it okay, but when we headed home, we would get lost. This happened to several crews.

One day, while one of the guys in the operations office was poring over the maps, he said, "I think I see the problem. Jenny Lind Island has been placed in the wrong place on the map by 40 miles."

I went up there with one guy (I think it was Bob Blanck) and on the way back we got lost...so lost that we didn't even know which way south was.

Finally, he held up his wristwatch and put the hour hand on the sun or something, I'm not sure how he did it, but anyway he pointed and said, "South is over that way." He was right.

But even if you learned to navigate up there, you still couldn't find your way out of the cold.

CATFISH: I was up on the Dewline one year. The biggest problem I remember was keeping the engines running when we were on the ground. The engine oil would congeal if it got too cold. But we had oil dilution systems on the airplanes and they allowed us to run some gasoline into the oil tank to thin the oil. Some of the guys got the oil too thin, and then the engines lacked adequate lubrication and would fail while they were at takeoff power.

John has a great sense of humor. You can tell because he thinks the following incidents were funny:

JOHN LAMPING: There were several funny things that happened. A DC-4, 010, had an APU (auxiliary electric power unit) in its nose, so there would be enough power to get the engines started up on the sites. Quite often the circuit breaker on the APU would pop when one of us was trying to start an engine, but we all knew that. If it popped, we just reset it. The trick was to not let the engines or the APU get too cold.

Yeah, it's cold out there

This next story sounds like what John was talking about, but you can't keep them warm if they won't start.

BILL SQUIRES: D. K. Hopkins and I took a flight into site 24. When we went to leave there we couldn't get number one engine started. We called the company on our H. F. radio and told them about our problem, so they sent a couple of mechanics up. They fixed the problem, which was a broken wire on the booster coil. Then they heated the cylinders. We went out and fired up, but we had very unstable oil pressure. We decided it was cold congealed oil in the lines between the pressure sensor and the gauge, so we didn't worry about it.

We took off, and just as we left the ground and pulled the gear up, all the oil pressures went to zero, then bounced back up again. We climbed to 1,500 feet, and suddenly number one engine stopped. It just quit turning. We shut it down, feathered it, and continued toward Yellowknife. Then we felt a jar.

Hoppy looked out and said, "Number one is turning again."

I hit the feather button again, but it was still turning.

Hoppy said, "Let's try unfeathering it."

Just as I reached for the button, the prop ran away. It really made a scream, and Hoppy nearly broke my wrist knocking my hand away. (The blades went to low pitch causing an over speed condition.)

Now we turned around and headed back toward the site. When we were all settled down in cruise, the oil pressure on number three went to zero.

I turned to Hoppy and said, "Will this thing fly on one?"

He said, "NO!"

The oil pressure kept bouncing between zero and just-a-little-bit until we landed at site 24, right where we started.

We parked the thing, and when we got out of that airplane, our knees wouldn't hold us up.

They must have been shivering from the cold.

JOHN LAMPING: Another thing happened to me. I took off from Sawmill Bay, and the oil pressure was oscillating on takeoff. In about two minutes the number three oil quantity gauge dropped to half a tank, so we thought we were going to lose the rest of it in a hurry. Then, when we leveled off, we didn't lose any more oil. We thought the smartest thing we could do was to get back on the ground while we still could. After landing we looked at the engine and the oil cooler was covered with oil. It wasn't unusual to have an oil cooler rupture due to the cold.

Our mechanics came up from Yellowknife to change the cooler, and then found there was a hole in the oil tank. We borrowed a Herman Nelson heater, and Paul Perry and I tried to keep the maintenance guys from freezing while they changed the oil tank. The temperature was -40 to -50F all the time.

You know, when you get too cold you tend to get careless. Instead of shutting the Herman Nelson down when it needed fuel, we set a big funnel on top of the heater and poured the gasoline in it. Unfortunately, the tank got full before the funnel emptied, so gasoline ran all over and caught fire. We had a hell of a fire right at the nose of the airplane. We had a rope fastened to the heater, so we tried to pull it away from the airplane, but the dammed heater had frozen to the ice.

While we were kickin' and stompin' at the heater, the maintenance guys (who were working under a tarpaulin) came plowin' out of there when they heard that big POOF. They helped us drag the heater away before it could burn up the whole damn airplane.

CHAPTER 15 TIGER TALES

One way to keep warm, light the heater

JACK TALKINGTON: I got lost on one flight when I thought I was tracking the Site radio station, then finding it was out of service. On let down through the clouds nothing looked right and we were unable to fix our location. The only real solid radio identification was the Thule AFB in Greenland. We worked the old ADF time/distance on it, located our position and returned to the site below the clouds and over the Arctic Ocean.

Another place one could get lost real easy was the Site at Bathurst Inlet. The compass would swing 360 degrees from one end of the runway to the other. Bathurst Inlet was right on the agonic line of zero variation. We set the Directional Gyro and flew the runway heading until the compass settled down.

Meanwhile back in the lower 48...

JOHN NEWCOMER: Captains Emmet Flood and Ken Henderson used to play tricks on each other. As is often the case, the pranks started small then became larger and more costly.

While Ken was out on a trip, Emmet went to a local music store and ordered a grand piano.

He said, "If I'm not home, there is a key over the front door, so just take it into the living room."

Then he gave them Ken Henderson's address.

Ken had to get even, so he ordered a truckload of coal.

He said, "If I'm not home, just dump it in the driveway in front of my garage door."

Then he gave them Emmet Flood's address.

CHAPTER 16 **THE DEWLINE** **1956 PART 3**

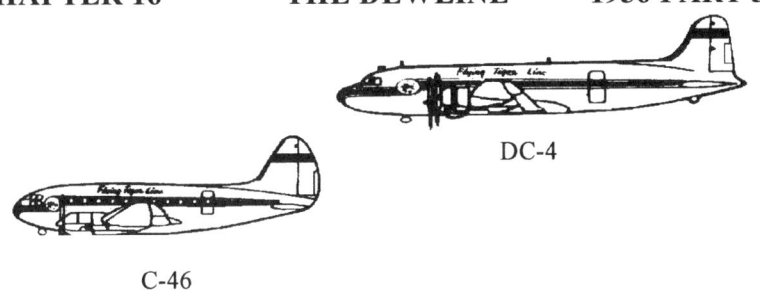

DC-4

C-46

The single most critical concern and the main cause of accidents on the Dewline was visibility—the lack of thereof.

GOLDY: I was in Coral Harbour with George Messinger when Ted Brondum crashed at site 26. We immediately went back to site 30 then had to wait for a break in the weather, so I could fly a C-46 over to site 26. Ted met us on the ramp, calm and collected like nothing had happened. There's no way to describe exactly what happened without seeing it, but here's the gist of it.

Ted had been coming around for a landing that night when a wingtip dug into the top of an uncharted hill and pulled the airplane right out of the sky. It slid down the hill between boulders as big as houses. You could hardly put an airplane between these boulders if you tried it on purpose. As it slid down the hill, one engine was torn off, the landing gear sheared, and one propeller blade came off and flew clear through the fuselage just behind the seat where a mechanic, "Oney" O'Neal, was sitting.

When the airplane reached the bottom, it turned slightly and went down into a ravine where it stopped. The only casualty was Oney, who bumped his nose as he ducked when the prop blade sliced through the cabin behind him. The entire nose of the airplane was ground off right up to the pilots' feet. The crew could exit right through the nose.

They had no idea which direction the airport was, but they knew they had to do something quickly or they'd freeze to death. They were hauling a load of diesel oil, so they rolled a barrel out and broke it open. It wouldn't light, so they cut the hose off a portable fire bottle and used the hose to siphon some gasoline from one of the aircraft's fuel tanks. When they poured the gasoline on top of the oil, it made a good signal fire.

Soon an old, thin priest with a long gray beard appeared out of the darkness.

Ted said, "I thought we'd had it, until I noticed he wasn't carrying a scythe."

The priest led the crew to the airport with his dog sled.

As might be expected, there is more to this story. Ted Brondum, the captain, fills in some details.

TED BRONDUM: We got to know the priest quite well. His name was Father Franz Van Der Velde. He was from Belgium but had spent much of his adult life in the Arctic. He could speak Flemish, French, English and Eskimo. He mentioned in one of his letters that he had salvaged the pilot seats from the plane for his own use. (Probably put them on his dog sled.) He retired and moved back to Belgium a few years ago.

In the last chapter John Lamping nearly burned 010 up during a heater fire. Now Mel Smith probably wished he had:

MEL SMITH: In April '56 I was flying 010, a DC-4, out of Churchill with Tommy Sullivan as my copilot. We had a load of 200 sacks of cement going to site 26. There was no airport at 26, just a strip where they scraped the snow off the ice so we could land. We off-loaded the cement then headed for site 30 to refuel, to go back to Churchill. When we were about halfway there, about over site 28, one of the

CHAPTER 16   TIGER TALES

fellows was on approach at site 30.

He said, "We're a C-46, and we're just barely going to get in. The weather really is getting bad."

So I thought, we better stop and get some more fuel. I called site 28 and asked, "You guys got extra fuel down there?"

"Sure," he said, so we landed. It was about 30 degrees below zero. We knew we had to leave the engines running, or we'd never get them started again.

The ground crew first had to dig the 55-gallon fuel drums out of the snow and put them on a flat bed trailer and tow it to the ramp. Now they were going to hand pump the fuel into the airplane.

I was burning more fuel keeping the engines warm than they were getting into the tanks. Then the hand pump broke. We still had enough fuel to get to site 30 and enough for our alternate but not a whole lot more, so we took off.

We had to overfly site 30 because the weather was below minimums. I called in the blind about the weather at our alternate. A Canadian Pacific flight answered.

He said, "Yes. Weather's clear up here. Come on in."

It was only about a 30-minute flight, so about halfway there he called again.

"Tiger, are you still there?"

"Yeah, we're still coming."

"Well you'd better hurry. The weather's moving in fast."

We had the ADF on the homer, which was located 3,000 feet west of the runway. There were no approach facilities, nothing to line up on. I looked down and couldn't see a thing. Everything was white. I looked again, and there was an airplane on the ground.

He said, "I see you going over, Tiger. I'll move out of the way so you can land. You better hurry...the wind's really blowing."

We circled the field and flew parallel to the runway, downwind. When we turned base leg we flew into the clouds. The front was just moving over the airport at that moment.

We couldn't see a thing and didn't know where the runway was but had to guess. We turned to the runway heading and let down to 400 feet where we broke out of the clouds but we were past the approach end of the runway, so we had to go around.

This time, on down wind leg, we ran into the clouds again.

The guy on the ground said, "I see you breaking in and out of the clouds. I'll shine my Aldus Lamp on you. Maybe that'll help."

We turned base, put the gear down, then turned final and let down to 400 feet again. I saw the flash of the light just off to my left, so I called for full flaps and started a slight turn to the left. When I did, the left wing hit the ground with a horrible noise, and it jerked the wheel out of my hands. Then the nose hit, then the right wing hit and straightened us out. I guess we ended up about 800 feet short of the runway.

Come to find out, when the front passed with the low-pressure area, our altimeter was reading two hundred feet high. If we had used the altimeter setting of the airplane on the ground, we would have been all right, but the guy on the radio was giving us readings from an old wall barometer.

Our airplane was written off as a total loss, then later Tigers bought it back from the insurance company and rebuilt it.

CHAPTER 16   TIGER TALES

Puttin' it back together

You forgot to shut the door, Mel.

Charley Pryor was on the Dewline in Edmonton, Churchill, and some of the sites. He worked on 010 and got it ready to fly to Burbank with the gear down. He was the lead mechanic on the whole re-build job after it came back to Burbank. At least he didn't have to re-build Bobbie's C-46.

BOBBIE THARP: Elgen Long was my copilot when we took off from Yellowknife in a C-46. About half way to Cambridge Bay we lost an engine and had to shut it down. The only place that had a C-46 engine was Hay River, but there were no mechanics there to change it. We flew in there on one engine, and they loaded the good engine on our airplane. We had to have two engines for takeoff, so we started the bad engine, got off the ground and shut it down again. We flew on down to Edmonton. Dick Rossi was in a DC-4, and he flew escort with us so in case we went down they'd know where the hell we were.

CHAPTER 17   THE ENGINE MECHANIC   1956

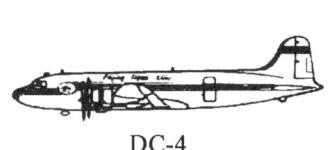
DC-4

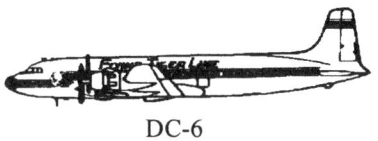
DC-6

Well, this is when I came into the picture. To fill you in on my aviation background, I joined the Air Force in 1948 and applied for the Aircraft and Engine Mechanic School.

I had a choice of Jet Engine School or Conventional. Of course we all knew that jet engines would never be practical for commercial use, so I chose conventional (meaning piston engines). I graduated and was assigned as an instructor in the school. After leaving the service, I worked as a propeller mechanic at Kelly Field, Texas, an instrument technician in Milwaukee and Los Angeles, and finally as an aircraft mechanic in Saint Paul, Minnesota.

There were a few more temporary occupations along the way, which are not relevant to this book, so I'll just skip them. After spending the bitter winter of '55-56 in Saint Paul, I quit my job at Northwest Aeronautical Company and returned to Los Angeles.

I looked in the want ads for a job and found two ads for aircraft mechanics. One was with the Flying Tiger Line and the other with Twentieth Century Airlines. I had never heard of Twentieth Century, so I stopped in at Tigers in Burbank.

I filled out the application and requested a job on the flight line. I was called in immediately to see Jack Studer, the general foreman of shops.

Jack said, "I see you've had experience as a propeller mechanic. We could use you in the prop shop."

"Thanks, but I really would like a job on the flight line."

Then Jack said, "I see here you've worked in instrument shops. We could use you there too."

I didn't say anything.

He said, "We need a man in the sheet metal shop also. I see you were doing airframe work on your last job."

I said, "Yeah I've always worked in shops. And now I'd really like to work on the flight line."

Jack pursed his lips. After a minute or so he said, "I don't see any engine experience on your resume."

"No, I've never worked on engines."

"Rhuel Trimble is the general foreman on the flight line, but he can't use you without some engine experience. Tell you what, I'll send you to the engine shop. After you've built up some experience there, you could transfer to the flight line."

I thought to myself, this outfit is willing to put me in a job I know little about, so I'd be more valuable in the future. I like that kind of thinking so I agreed. He sent me down to see Art Lawson, the engine shop foreman.

Art talked to me a few minutes then said, "You're hired. Starting pay is $1.92 an hour."

The Engine Buildup Shop

The shop itself is worth mentioning. It began as a set of concrete revetments built during WW II. Lockheed P-38 Lightning fighters were parked in them to protect the Lockheed Aircraft factory from any possible air raids.

Tigers, with their innate ability to make do with what is available, put roofs and doors on the revetments and

CHAPTER 17   TIGER TALES   183

turned them into shop areas. They served their purpose well for over 20 years.

At that time, in 1956, Tigers was operating about 15 Curtiss C-46s, twin-engine airplanes which use the Pratt and Whitney R-2800-75 engines. We also had eight Douglas DC-4s, which use four Pratt and Whitney R-2000 engines, and three DC-6s, which use four Pratt and Whitney R-2800-CB-16 engines. It sometimes became a logistical nightmare to keep spare engines available of all the different types.

Whenever we received a bare engine from the overhaul facility, we had to install all of its accessories, which included the magnetos, spark plugs, carburetor, generator, starter and tachometer generator. Other items such as exhaust collector rings, hydraulic pumps and, on the DC-6, a cabin supercharger drive might be installed depending on what position on the airplane the engine was to be hung.

Art Lawson left Tigers shortly after I came, and Buck Buchanan became foreman. Buck, a tall quiet man with a clear baritone voice, was one of the company's first employees. Gentleman is the descriptive term that comes to mind.

One of the mechanics I worked with was Art Prendergast, who was mentioned in the CNAC introduction and also in the Dewline chapters.

Art was a wiry little guy who might be the one who coined the phrase, "I'm not small, I'm just wound up real tight!"

One time Art was high up on a "Cherry Picker" working on the tail of a DC-6, when Bob Prescott noticed him.

Bob called up, "Hey Art, come on down. I want to talk to you."

Art looked down and said, "It's no farther for you to come up here than for me to go down there!"

Bob shook his head, laughed and climbed the ladder.

Another mechanic was Ed Hale, who later held a number of positions with the company and is mentioned many times in this book.

George Nau, a tall blond haired guy with a large family, worked in the oil cooler department while on furlough as a flight engineer. His name will appear later.

The lead mechanics were Jack Bobo, Wally Stevens and Walt Mroczec.

Next door to the engine buildup shop was the welding shop, Don Eatchel proprietor. If it was broken, he could fix it. If we needed a new type of engine stand or whatever, he could take our drawings and fabricate it. If we didn't have any plans, he'd figure out what was needed and make it anyway. Don was pretty close to being a magician. He spent some time up on the Dewline putting things back together.

The day I came to work the DC-4, 010, was in the hangar. It had just been ferried back from the Dewline and was being rebuilt. Two days later, Jack McClarty was hired.

JACK McCLARTY: Sheet Metal Shop: 010 was the first Tiger airplane I worked on. Shortly after that project was completed, I was drilling the rivets off the tail wheel support on a C-46. My tool chest was sitting directly under the tail just forward of the tail wheel. I don't know what I was thinking of, but I forgot that the airplane was sitting on its tail wheel. When I drilled the last rivets out, the airplane fell on my tool chest with a deafening crash. The only thing I hurt was my pride, but I never did live that down as long

CHAPTER 17   TIGER TALES   185

as I was with the company.

You need good sheet metal men when you have pilots like Perry Dove, who keep bending things.

PERRY DOVE: One day I came out of Dallas with Captain Brandenberg. We had a load of freight and a couple of deadheads in the back. We had one box on board that weighed 400 pounds. It contained the film of the first Atlas Rocket that was shot off of Cape Canaveral. We were at 8,000 feet and had no radar, of course, but the weather was supposed to be pretty good. We were hit by lightening once and then got into severe turbulence.
 Brandy was hanging on with both hands and said, "Get on these controls with me!"
 Once I looked back as our brainbags (pilot's flight bags containing charts etc.) flew up, hit the ceiling and came crashing back down. The can in the blue room (toilet) came flying out, and these poor guys in the back end were really getting beaten up. Some of the ropes holding the freight broke, including the ones holding the 400-pound box of film. It flew up and made a big dent in a heater duct. One of the deadheads got his arm broken.
 Brandy got on the radio and said, "We're getting the hell kicked out of us up here, and we need a lower altitude."
 They cleared us down to 6,000 feet, and we broke out of the bottom of a humongous thunderstorm right over Abilene, Texas. While all this was going on, we got a fire warning in a baggage compartment, so we peeled off and landed at Abilene. The airplane was a real mess. They took the guy with the broken arm to the hospital.
 The other guy said, "Hell, I'm not getting back on that thing! I'll take the <u>bus</u> to San Diego!"

The CAB renewed Tigers' operating certificate for another five years and also permitted the carriage of first-class mail.

That year Tigers became the largest passenger charter airline on the North Atlantic. After the Hungarian uprising we brought several loads of refugees to the States. It was time to hire a few more pilots.

George Kocisko was working seven days a week as a flight instructor at a small airport trying to build up enough flight time to be hired by Tigers. Every week he came in and pestered the chief pilot while claiming he was only updating his flight hours. Stuelke probably got tired of seeing him.

GEORGE KOCISKO: One day Dick Stuelke, the chief pilot, called and asked me to come in for an interview. Things went along fine until Ed Pinke, the director of flying, noticed that I had not yet attained the minimum age of 21 years. The dilemma was resolved by my getting a note from my mother.

I wouldn't want to suggest that George Kocisko's pestering drove Dick Stuelke to drink, but...

BAR STORY
by
DICK STUELKE: Goldy and I were in Johnny Valour's bar one night, and at closing time Johnny went home.

He said to the guy cleaning up, "Give these guys whatever they want, then lock up when you leave."

The swamper had a taste for "Vermoot," as he called it.

Every time he poured us a drink, we said, "Have one for yourself."

CHAPTER 17   TIGER TALES

By the time he locked up and went home, he forgot we were even there. Along about five in the morning Goldy looked around and said, "It sure is dead in here."

So we opened up. Guys started coming in, so we had people to talk to. The till was locked, so I told our customers they had to drink up what they put on the bar...because we couldn't make change. Sometimes they bought us drinks to help use up the money. Pretty soon we had several ones and fives, so we began charging customers as they left instead of by the drink. We'd decide what they owed by how drunk they looked.

About ten o'clock Johnny arrived to open up. Here we were, open for business and had a dozen customers at the bar.

He was mad as hell until he counted $245 under the counter.

Then he said, "All right, all right. But you guys could have gotten me in a lot of trouble."

I guess one could call this rocks on the Martinis?

BOBBIE THARP: Ed Pinke was the chief pilot and lived across the street from me in Denver. He had a nice house with a detached garage. His wife wanted a roof built to cover the breezeway between the house and garage.

He finally got around to building it and I was going to help him. We were going pretty well until a severe thunderstorm came up. It began to hail. The hailstones were so big that they broke the skin on our foreheads and we were bleeding. His wife knew that if we got down off the roof, she'd probably never get us back up there, so she started handing up martinis. I don't know how we finished the job without falling off the roof.

From Freezing to Frying.

BOB ZALUSKY: I was sitting in my hotel room in Kansas City, when suddenly a big ball of fire went down past my window. Come to find out Skip Lane, who had a room on an upper floor, had accidentally set fire to his mattress, which he then threw out the window. Well that was a hell of a lot better than keeping it in there with him.

CHAPTER 18   THE LOCKHEED "CONNIE"   1957

1049H Super Constellation

We nearly lost a DC-6 and its crew that summer. They took off from Idlewild, New York, and right after takeoff all four engines quit. The crew consisted of Captain Greg Thomas, Copilot Bill Seamans and Flight Engineer B. J. Palomar. The deadheads were Copilot Howard Amrhein, Flight Engineer Guy McAlister, Navigator Robert Dayton and Stewardesses Jeannine Cussen, Euginia Johnson and Berangere Reubens. Captain Thomas managed to put the airplane down on a sandbar. The three crewmembers were uninjured, but two of the six deadheads had minor injuries.

Here is the story from the copilot.

BILL SEAMANS: We were losing one engine right after the other until all four were gone. We were in the air probably four minutes at the most. The highest we got, if I remember right, was around 100 feet. The engineer and I checked everything. We checked the fuel system, everything, to try to find what the hell was wrong.

I knew we couldn't get back to the runway, so I yelled, "Head for the beach!"

Greg turned toward the beach and decided to land gear up, which was okay, and we never even got our feet wet.

But then Pinke (director of flight operations) was so pissed off at us that he was threatening to come right out from California to the East Coast and fire every one of us because he knew we screwed up. Frankly we thought we'd done something wrong too, but we didn't know what it could've been. When things happen like that it's terrible. And then the C.A.B inspector found that someone had inadvertently put deicer fluid in the ADI (Anti Detonation Injection) tanks, so we were off the hook.

(ADI is a system that uses a mixture of methanol and water to keep the engine cylinders cool during the use of takeoff power.)

The C.A.B. interviewed each of us individually, and from that interview I was offered a job. I turned it down because I'd have had to move to Alaska.

They didn't even get their feet wet.

The immediate problem was to get the airplane back to the airport. But before they could do anything, the tide came in.

CHAPTER 18   TIGER TALES

Then the tide came in

The recovery team dug a channel and brought in a barge, which they sunk beside the airplane. The airplane was jacked up and the landing gear lowered, then it was towed onto the barge by a large floating crane. The barge was refloated and towed to the airport. The airplane was hosed down with fresh water, washing out as much sand and salt as possible. The engines and propellers were replaced, then the airplane was flown back to Burbank where repairs were completed. Captain Thomas received the Daedalian Award for averting almost certain disaster.

General Billy Mitchell in 1921 urged the creation of an organization that would perpetuate the deeds and memories of American WW I pilots. The Order of Daedalians was formed in 1934 at Maxwell Field, Alabama.

The Daedalian Civil Air Safety Award is presented to honor ability, judgment, and/or heroism in difficult circumstances above and beyond normal operational requirements.

Here is another view of that event.

DICK WILSON: Gene Taylor was supposed to fly that trip, but the schedule was changed. Greg was new on the DC-6 and, though it was an empty ferry flight to Dover A.F.B., he made a wet takeoff. Gene, who'd had a lot of experience in the airplane, probably would have made a dry takeoff (would not have used the ADI system). Gene wouldn't have lost the engines there, but <u>would</u> have lost them on takeoff from Dover with a full load of cargo and without a handy beach nearby.

Elgen Long didn't win an award, but he could have received one for tenacity. He had served the company as radio operator; navigator and copilot and now he had reached that enviable position on the seniority list that let him check out as captain.

ELGEN LONG: I had about 2,000 hours as copilot when I checked out as captain on the C-46. My first trip was out of San Francisco in the middle of a winter storm. A whole bunch of real senior guys were deadheading with me, Cliff Groh among them, and they were all razzing me.
    "Don't you wish you were still a navigator in the sunny South Seas?"

In the fall Flying Tigers bought a fleet of brand new Lockheed Super H Constellations. I was there when the first one was towed over to our ramp direct from the Lockheed Factory. Seventeen Charlie arrived in a passen-

CHAPTER 18 TIGER TALES 193

ger configuration, and everyone present agreed that it was the most beautiful airplane we had ever seen.

They used the new model Wright R3350-EA3 turbo compound engines. With any new model of anything one can expect some problems, but this was ridiculous. We had 29 engine failures in one month. Captain Charlie Hicks and his crew were en route from Newark, New Jersey, to Burbank, California, one morning. They limped into Las Vegas, Nevada, with three failed engines.

Charlie's comment reportedly was, "Yeah, but the fourth one was running okay."

The new engines were equipped with a two-stage supercharger. The high position, known as high blower, was used during high altitude cruise. To help prevent engine failures, we changed our operating procedure and restricted the use of high blower.

We had more work in the engine shop than we could handle. For several months we worked 12 hours a day, six days a week.

Early one morning, before sunup, as I was driving home from work I asked myself, "Why am I doing this?"

Then I realized we were all doing it. The overtime pay was nice, but there was more to it than that. This was an emergency situation that could destroy the company. We would keep at it as long as it took. I don't recall anyone asking us if we would work overtime. They didn't have to.

When the problems were resolved and we were back to normal, John Dewey, the director of maintenance, came down and said, "Thanks, fellas." If he had made a big deal about it, we would probably have been insulted.

Goldy had been in management in various capacities in the States as well as in Europe.

GOLDY: About 1957 I went back on the line. From that time on, I negotiated every ALPA contract on the pilots' side until I retired.

I think the most exciting trip I ever had on the Pacific was a Connie operation when we were having all those engine failures. I left Travis for a six-leg trip ending in Tokyo, and ended up making six three-engine landings.

You don't have to go so far when you have two at a time.

DICK STUELKE: I was scheduled to take a Connie to Chicago, so I went to the airport a little early. Maintenance was working on two of the engines, and I heard one of the mechanics say, "I hope this thing hangs together."

I hoped so, too. We took off and crossed the mountains with all engines operating perfectly. Soon after crossing the Front Range abeam Denver, one of the engines maintenance had been working on belched a couple of times and quit. The hell with it, I decided, we're past the mountains. Instead of landing in Denver or someplace, we'll just three-engine it on to Chicago. As we passed abeam of Omaha another engine failed. We limped into Omaha on two.

When there's smoke there may be fire, but it is not always in an engine.

BOBBIE THARP: One night John Urnezis was with me when we took a Connie out of San Francisco en route to Seattle. We were in IMC (which means instrument meteorological conditions, which means lousy weather) and smoke started coming up into the cockpit—a hell of a _lot_ of smoke! We were up around Ukiah somewhere and on solid instruments. To get rid of the smoke we shut all the electrical systems down, pulled breakers and what have you. Now we had no communication or navigation radios. I headed west to be sure I was out over the ocean, and then headed south while letting down.

We finally broke out of the clouds, crossed the Golden Gate and flew down the bay and over the airport. I rocked the wings, and the tower gave us the green light to land. We taxied up to the hangar and shut down. I knew we couldn't fly until the cause of the smoke was discovered and fixed, so I went home. I got a call from the FAA.

"What happened?"

I told them what happened and how we'd gotten in.

He thought it was amazing that I could find my way back and land without radios.

I said, "What the hell do you think we did before we <u>had</u> radios?"

The old adage that if you want something done, give it to a busy man, applies here as well. Oakley Smith is a busy man. In fact he has been nicknamed Go-Go Smith, especially by those who have difficulty keeping up with him (most any normal person). When he was chief pilot in Newark, there was an organization for the blind there that Tigers helped out quite a bit.

OAKLEY SMITH: We were flying Connies at the time and had some cutaway models of power recovery turbines—models on which these blind kids could feel the inner workings. We took the kids into the cockpit and let them sit in the pilot and flight engineer seats and feel the switches and instruments, as we explained their functions. The organization put all this on tape and put it out nationwide, in fact worldwide. These were just some of the things we helped with after working hours.

Oakley spent most of his career with Tigers as a chief pilot, instructor pilot or senior director of flying.

OAKLEY: Regarding the new Connies and all the problems we had with the new Wright engines, Tigers did a good job of educating the pilots about those engines. They were sent to Caldwell, New Jersey, where the engines were manufactured. Those who were instructing or in chief pilot positions went through the whole manufacturing process. It was a good engine, but it had to be operated correctly. Eventually we overcame the problems, and those engines became more and more reliable.

As the reliability of the new fleet of airplanes improved, the company began selling the DC-4s and DC-6s. This freed up a lot of space in the engine shop. The company also sold all but two of the C-46s, which were used to shuttle up and down the West Coast. We bought a total of 15 Lockheed Super Constellations, each of which could carry 43,000 pounds of cargo.

The Connies also hauled passengers, and if they crossed the mid-Pacific they landed at Wake Island. Wake became the crew layover point of choice for most airlines. Airline managements, that is. The crews may have preferred Honolulu.

MEMOIRS OF A STEWARDESS from <u>41 years aloft.</u>

Before the advent of jets, every flight that crossed the Mid-Pacific used Wake as a refueling stop or layover point for

crews. Wake is comprised of three atolls, one runway and a big "most inviting" lagoon. It had a "low tide" country club (six holes at high tide) and an outdoor theater called the "Windy Palace" with free movies each night. This was situated next to the taxi strip, which drowned out all sound as airplanes passed by. The island had no fresh water, but champagne was relatively cheap!

With about 800 men living on an isolated island on which there were very few women and virtually NO single girls, it may well be imagined that the dozen or so stewardesses there on layover came in for a large share of masculine attention. Layover quarters on Wake, however, were referred to as the "Iron Girdle." A fence and powerful spotlights (provided by our airline to protect "their girls") shone upon the "Girdle" during the hours of darkness.

This led to a strange ritual. Any perfectly respectable man who wished to contact a girl inside the "Girdle" had no choice but to stand outside the fence yelling her name. Remember, there were no phones on the island.

Wake! Should always be written with an exclamation point, for to those who have experienced it, Wake is more than a place: it's an effect upon the senses. The mental image evoked by this name may be good or bad, but it is seldom indifferent.

Aircraft reliability had improved, but forecasting had not.

DICK STRATFORD: Johnny Newcomer, who was flying copilot for me, made the landing at Detroit. Our next stop was O'Hare but while we were on the ground in Detroit, Chicago's weather went down, so we delayed for a while. It was my leg, so when Chicago's weather opened up, I took off. This was all pretty uneventful. Things like that happened all the time on the East Coast and in the Midwest.

While we were en route, a fast freezing rain came through O'Hare. We were advised that the braking might not be so good, since they hadn't gotten the sanders out yet to sand the runway. We were landing to the northwest, and there was a slight crosswind. The landing went pretty well until I pulled it into reverse. Then the crosswind caused the plane to weathervane into the wind. I tried asymmetrical reverse and braking, but I couldn't keep the airplane from exiting the runway on the upwind side.

We were leaving the runway at about a 30-degree angle, and I didn't want to get stuck out there in case the ground was soft. I put the propellers in forward thrust and applied considerable power to the left engines. This put us into a 180-degree turn and we found ourselves back on the runway, headed in the opposite direction.

The Control Tower called us and said, "Tiger, one of the fellows here in the tower didn't see that. Would you mind doing that again?"

Johnny Newcomer picked up the microphone and said, "Listen, if he wants to come and sit down here, and I can sit up there in the tower, okay. Otherwise, no deal!"

Midway Airport in Chicago didn't need an ice storm to make it exciting.

GOLDY: One time at Midway a TWA passenger Connie was ready for takeoff when a Tiger Connie, loaded with freight, was taxiing out. The TWA pilot told the tower he wanted to let the Tiger takeoff first so he could watch it. That's how exciting those heavy takeoffs could be on that short runway. We often joked that we had to wait for the traffic light to be green when we crossed 53rd and Cicero at the end of the runway.

CHAPTER 19   ENGINES...MORE OR LESS   1958

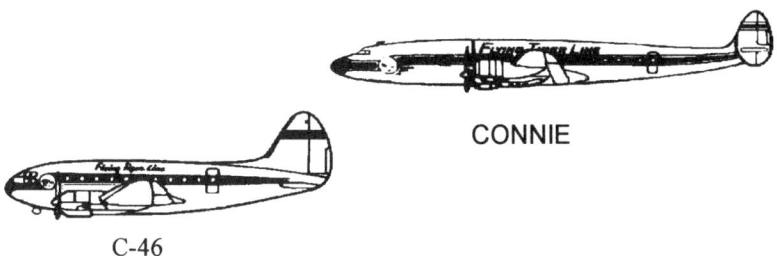

Tigers had a contract hauling jet engines from Pratt and Whitney on the East Coast to the Boeing factory in Seattle. This was when Boeing first came out with the 707.

BOBBIE THARP: John Lamping and I took this C-46 out of San Francisco, bound for Seattle. We had two jet engines in the fuselage in tandem. Because of their combined weight, we had to make two fuel stops. The first leg was a night flight up the coast to Arcata, California. The flight was uneventful, and we continued to Portland, Oregon, for our final fuel stop.

It was just getting daylight when we took off from Portland. We were rolling down the runway but did not yet have flying speed—when suddenly there was a loud noise in back, and the nose went up and the airplane leaped into the air! With both of us on the controls we could not hold the nose down.

I closed the throttles and the airplane nosed over and started down. All we could see in the windshield was concrete coming up at us.

We applied full power while using all the elevator control and trim that we had. Just before we would've hit the ground, the airplane leveled off. The tower, having seen all this, had already hit the panic button.

John Lamping said, "When I saw the fire house doors fly open, I knew we were in trouble."

The tower asked, "What's your problem, Tiger?"

"We seem to have lost elevator control," I said, "I don't know if we can get it around or not."

"You're cleared to land on any runway. The crash equipment is standing by."

The airplane kept oscillating up and down, with us making corrections as best we could with engine power. We considered putting it down straight-ahead but, with all the trees and buildings, that didn't seem like a good idea. We'd gained enough altitude to allow me to make a left turn, and I headed west over the Columbia River. We considered ditching in the water, but now we were down wind and didn't like the idea of ditching with a tail wind.

We turned onto final approach and got the gear and flaps down for landing. When we crossed the threshold I cut the power, and we hit the runway. The airplane bounced about twenty feet in the air and came down hard, but this time it only bounced ten feet. Finally it settled down and we managed to taxi back to the ramp.

There we found that the engine shipping bucks in the cabin had broken loose and had slid to the back of the airplane. The fuselage gets smaller the farther aft you go. The aft engine tried to make it bigger and couldn't, so it went right out through both sides of the airplane. What we had was not elevator problems at all, but an extreme tail-heavy condition.

We called the company and told them what'd happened, but then we had to wait for the FAA inspector. We were having coffee when he showed up about an hour later.

He said, "What are you guys drinking?"

"We're drinking coffee."

"That's what I thought. If I had been through what you guys have, I'd have probably drunk a quart of rye by now."

CHAPTER 19   TIGER TALES   201

Of course there's more ways than one to lose an engine. If it doesn't try to crawl out the back of the airplane, it just might quit running. For any reader not accustomed to airplane talk, the term "losing an engine" doesn't mean you can't find it, but generally means it is no longer producing power. The vast majority of flights begin and end with all engines operating normally, but we never discuss those. The following events are mentioned because they are unusual.

BOB ZALUSKY: I lost an engine on a Connie on takeoff out of Denver one day. I must have flown fifteen miles to the east before I could get high enough to dump fuel and go back to Denver. I was below the airport elevation and had to fly east where the terrain drops away.

Considering the following, it would seem that the good folks at TWA were no longer mad at us.

WALT SAHAYDAK: We were en route from Shannon heading for Gander on a Connie when the #2 engine failed. TWA also had an engine failure on one of their Connies, and we were right behind them. Bob Jenkins was our mechanic at Gander, so he and Marty Lewis and I took it upon ourselves to change the engine. We had no spare engine there, however, and neither did TWA.
 At that time TWA had a DC-4 rigged up as a flying workshop. That airplane flew up from Idlewild bringing TWA's spare engine and ours too. While we waited for it, TWA pulled their failed engine off. Then using their equipment, we removed our old engine. When the new engines arrived, they naturally hung their engine first because it was their equipment. Then we hung ours. With the

three of us working, we had our engine ready for run-up shortly after them.

In the meantime the rest of the crew and the passengers had slept in the hotel in Gander. Captain Buskey asked us what we wanted to do, because we hadn't had any sleep since we'd left Shannon. Marty and I said as long as we could take a shower and have breakfast, we'd be ready to go. We departed Gander about 45 minutes before TWA.

Some people would forget their glass if it wasn't attached to them.

DON SINGER: Doug Buskey was the captain, and Dan Hennessy was the copilot as we were climbing out of London with a load of passengers. Dan was asking me how the engine analyzer worked.

I said, "Well this is #3 engine and here is #1 cylinder"...right at this time the #1 cylinder failed.

I said to the captain, "We'd better shut this thing down!"

We feathered it, ran the checklist and began dumping fuel to get down to our maximum landing weight for our return to London.

There were no oil leaks or other evidence of any failure after we parked at the ramp. I thought oh, oh, I must have really screwed up.

The mechanics opened the cowling, and then we saw the problem. A master rod had let go, and the piston and rod had gone right up through the top of the cowling like a cannon shell. It was a good thing we shut it down when we did.

I had a bottle of Queen Ann Scotch. I was the only one who'd had time to get a bottle.

CHAPTER 19 TIGER TALES

When we got to the hotel, Buskey said, "Let's meet in my room."

I brought my bottle. Everyone else was sitting there with a glass, but I didn't have one. I went back to my room to get a glass, and when I got back my bottle was empty.

Sounds like these next guys never worked against each other before.

JOE CALTON: Starr Thompson was the captain, Rex Tripp the copilot and I was the flight engineer on this Connie. We were leaving Detroit about ten a.m., and it was already hot. We had a full load of cargo, and a #2 engine that had a history of running hot on takeoff. In those days we used to close the cowl flaps after we got going down the runway, but we were going to leave our #2 cowl flaps open until after takeoff.

During the takeoff roll, with everyone's mind on #2 engine, #3 propeller ran away.

I yelled to Starr, "#3 ran away!"

I was waiting for Starr to say, "Feather it."

He said, "S'matter with 3?"

I thought he said feather 3, so I did.

Then he thought I meant to feather #2 instead of #3, so he said, "Can you get it back in?"

I said, "Well of course."

I wondered why the hell he would ask me that. You would never want to unfeather that thing. But I cranked it back in, and it ran away again. Again I feathered it. Now he knew what was going on.

He said, "Dump fuel."

I hit the dump switch on the 260 panel with my foot. Then, when I stood up to grab the main dump valves, I looked out the windshield.

There was nothing but treetops ahead of us!

I said, "You mean <u>here</u>, Starr, can we clear the trees" (If you're going to crash you sure don't want to be dumping raw fuel on whatever you're crashing into.)

Star said, "Right here. We'll clear 'em!"

I slammed all four levers down, and we cleared the trees and came around and landed.

Rex said later, "You guys had that engine feathered, unfeathered and feathered again before we climbed 50 feet."

Of course a grossed out Connie on three engines isn't climbing all that fast.

On September 9 we had our first aircraft loss since I joined the company. Lockheed Super Connie, 20 Charlie, crashed during an approach to Tachikawa Air Base, Japan.

The flight was a Military Air Transport cargo flight from Travis Air Force Base, California, to Tachikawa Air Base, Japan. The Connie departed Wake Island after a scheduled fuel stop for the seven hour and forty-five minute flight to Tachikawa. The flight proceeded normally until they approached the Tokyo Area. The crew contacted Tokyo Control on schedule, and then was inadvertently given an incorrect radio frequency for the next sector. This caused the crew to be without radio contact with the ground for four minutes.

It is believed that during this time there was a navigation instrument failure. Due to the crew's distraction while trying to reestablish radio contact, the failure was not detected in time. The aircraft flew through its intended course and, while in clouds, struck Mount Tanzawa, 38 miles southwest of Tokyo.

CHAPTER 19   TIGER TALES

The crew members were George Donahoe, captain; R. J. Libra, copilot; B. J. Palomar, flight engineer and Robert Lowe, navigator. There were also two deadheading flight attendants on board, Geraldine Clemente and Yolanda Frey. There were no survivors.

(George Donahoe had been the deadhead on the C-46 that crashed in an alley in Denver in 1950. B. J. Palomar had been the flight engineer with Greg Thomas on the DC-6 that crashed at Idlewild, New York in '57.)

Serious mistakes do cause accidents. And then sometimes someone will make a dumb-ass mistake that puts the successful conclusion of a flight in serious doubt.

LOU LE CLERE: I was flying a Connie from Chicago to Burbank and was in high blower cruise at 18,000 feet when Center called.

"Your company wants you to call Airinc." (An aviation radio frequency for use between a company and its flight crews.)

I dialed in the frequency and called them.

The guy said, "Oh yeah, your company in Chicago wants to advise you that your airplane was inadvertently serviced with 100 octane fuel."

Of course we all knew it was supposed to use 115/145 octane. The engines were all running fine, but I decided to go to low blower and drift down to whatever altitude I could hold, then land at Grand Junction, Colorado, the nearest suitable airport. We shifted to low blower and found we could hold our altitude. The engines were running nice and cool, with no roughness or anything, so I decided to go on to Las Vegas. When we approached Vegas everything was still okay, so I went on to Burbank.

I landed at Burbank, where the FAA was waiting, Wright was waiting, Lockheed was waiting, and our people were waiting. Wright was going to tear one of the engines down to inspect for damage. I told them I wanted to go to the hotel and get some sleep, and then I wanted to be in on the tear down.

They took the engine apart and found no problems whatever with it. They replaced that engine with a new one and flew the other three on a waiver. I followed the records and all three of those engines ran their allowable time with no problems. I got a nice letter from the Wright Company. That kind of thing makes you feel good.

Sometimes just getting even makes one feel good.

CYNTHIA BOWLES: Fran Drew was on a trip with Frank Graff, who was always doing something to annoy the stewardesses. For some reason Frank kicked his leg backwards and actually kicked Fran in the shin. It hurt her, and of course her leg turned black and blue. But she got even. The next time they were on the ground, she took his flight kit into a blue room and peed in it.

Sometimes we would bring special food on board and cook it for the crew if we liked them. Fresh eggs for example were always welcome. This one time we cooked corned beef hash with a fried egg on top and served it to the copilot, who was a nice fellow.

Frank Graff, the captain, said, "That sure smells good. I'd like some of that."

Of course most of the girls hated Frank, and one of them had bought a can of dog food.

They heated it up, put an egg on it and gave it to Frank. He took one bite and knew it was not corned beef hash. He didn't ask for any more favors.

CHAPTER 19 TIGER TALES

Sometimes it doesn't pay to see the light.

BEN SHELTON, Radioman: A radio mechanic was installing wire bundles and coaxial cables in the baggage compartment of an airplane. It was dark in there, so he used a droplight and extension cord. The droplight cord was the same size and color as the coaxial cables. When he finished the job he had to return the droplight to the tool crib...that's when he noticed he had installed the droplight cable in the aircraft wire bundles.

To make sense of the joke hidden in the next story, you have to know that a "Castro Convertible" was the brand name of a very popular sofa bed in the New York area.

JOE FEMMENINO: Ray Korty was the captain, I was the flight engineer and the navigator was Harry Meyers. We had this gun running trip from Rome to Havana in October '58. There was an arms merchant in Rome who made the deal with the Cubans, so he was running the whole show, and he chartered the Tiger Connie to make the delivery. We were heavy as hell with the load of Garand Rifles, so we had to stop for fuel at nearly every airport we came to.

The State Department said that under no circumstances were we to land in the United States with the rifles on board. The guns were for Batista, but I guess they didn't help enough.

During the flight someone asked, "What would happen if Castro has taken over by the time we land?"

Harry said, "Well, I guess we would have to become Castro Convertibles."

Sometimes getting down on your knees can keep you from getting too high:

Jack Bobo Bourbon Story
by

ED HALE: One night after working the swing shift in Burbank, Jack Bobo said, "You wanna stop for a drink?"

"Sure, that sounds good," I said.

"Okay, follow me."

I thought we were going to stop somewhere for a beer, but instead Jack wheels into this liquor store. Then he comes out with two pint bottles of 100-proof bourbon. Good stuff too. He climbs into my truck, takes the cap off one bottle and throws the cap out the window and hands the bottle to me. Then he takes the cap off the other bottle and throws <u>that</u> cap out the window. Now we're going to have our drink.

We talked about one thing and another, then he drained his bottle and said, "See you tomorrow."

So now I'm out in the parking lot on my hands and knees, feeling around in the dark trying to find a bottle cap.

CHAPTER 20   FIRES TO FURLOUGHS   1959

1049H CONNIE

Though I had graduated from aircraft maintenance school in the Air Force ten years before, that didn't count for a civilian mechanic's license. So I went to school in Van Nuys, passed the tests and received my FAA Certificate. While this may not sound like a big deal in itself, it would prove to be a very important step in my career. Others also passed milestones in their lives. Some were disastrous.

DUKE HEDMAN: Tommy Haywood was on Wake Island on a layover when he met an old school buddy. The fellow was ferrying a light twin from the States to Australia, and Wake Island was one of his fuel stops. The twin had extra fuel tanks in the cabin, and all tanks were filled.

Tommy and the rest of his crew were watching the takeoff. Just after liftoff his buddy's airplane exploded and fell near the end of the runway. Tommy started running toward his friend to see if he could help, and suffered a severe heart attack. He never flew again, but served as manager of flight training for many years.

It was suspected that there were fuel vapors in the plane's cabin, which were ignited when the pilot keyed his microphone.

CATFISH RAINE: Tommy Haywood and I were very close friends, and we owned Mercury Aviation together in Los Angeles. Tom was a perfectionist in everything he did.

Like, he sent Duke and me up to Sacramento to survey a base so we could make a bid for a Mercury service spot. We wrote our report on the back of an envelope and sent it down to the brass. A couple of months later they were showing some people the difference between the report Duke and I sent on the back of the envelope and Haywood's. His was a neatly typed eight-page report.

Tommy did engineering work for us at Mercury service. He designed a baggage unloader and a lot of things like that.

This next event is from the flight attendant book, 41 Years Aloft, and speaks for itself.

KOREAN ORPHANS

On May 18, 1959, a flight was made which set the record for the largest number of persons ever flown overseas in a commercial aircraft. Flying Tiger Connie, 17 Charlie, flew from Seoul, Korea, to Portland, Oregon, with 144 people aboard.

This sounds preposterous since a super Connie in FTL's configuration is limited to 114 passengers and crew, but this flight was different. Of the passengers on board, 121 were children and 71 of them were each under one year of age. This in itself was probably another record for the largest number of children ever flown in an airplane.

The flight was another in the series that the airline has performed for Oregon's fabulous farmer, Henry Holt, in connection with his program for adoption of Korean War orphans. More than 1100 of them have now been brought to the United States.

The ship's manifest showed, in addition to the 71 children each under the age of one, 40 children ranging from 1 to 5 years of age; 10 from 5 to 10 years; 12 attendants representing the Holt Adoption Program; and a flight crew of 11, including 4 stewardesses.

The crew members were Captain Ray Allen; Relief Pilot Dick Rossi; Copilot Ralph Mitchell; Navigators Ernie Hickman and Bob Griffin; Flight Engineer Bob Zopfi, and Stewardesses Barbara Walmsley, Jeanine Frederick, Georgianna DuVander and Betty Starker.

The flight was made in an elapsed time of 23 hours with one stop at Shemya in the Aleutians. Flying time was 19 hours and 50 minutes.

Although 144 persons were aboard, with full tanks the airplane was 8,000 pounds below maximum gross weight, so it was well within safety limits.

The flight was routine except for some icing conditions near Shemya. The babies came through in splendid condition, with the crew winning plaudits from the doctors and nurses aboard.

The babies were carried in specially designed cradles supplied by the airline. Seats were folded down and the cradles laid across them.

Looking down the long cabin at all those children was a sight crew members will never forget.

Dick Rossi remarked afterward, "Boy, were those girls busy with the diapers. They must have changed a million!"

Flight is said to be mostly boredom with only occasional moments of excitement. Boredom is better.

ARNIE BREDON: We were leaving San Francisco one night in a Connie. Dobbie was the captain, I was the copilot, Willy Wilkins, the flight engineer, and Bill Towner was riding the jump seat. We took off on 28 and at 126 knots we got a fire bell on #3 engine.

As Dobbie made a right turn out over the United Airlines hangar, we got a fire bell on #1 engine. When we reduced power, the fire warning light on #1 went out, and we landed on runway 19.

After we landed, Bill Towner found that he had bitten his pipe stem in two. Dobbie had a new cigar in his mouth now. They never did find the one he took off with. After we parked the airplane, a mechanic from United Airlines raced up on a tug.

He said, "When you came over our hangar we heard a loud noise. We looked up in time to see the flames from your #3 engine going clear past the tail."

The main cargo door on a Connie was located aft of the wing, so when it was being loaded, a heavy concrete weight was hung on the nose of the airplane to prevent it from tipping on its tail. We were departing a Connie one night in Burbank, but when we went to remove the nose weight the airplane tried to tip over.

The foreman said to Captain Howard Brooks, "After you start the engines, we'll remove the nose weight. The airplane is a little tail heavy, but it'll fly real good that way."

Captain Brooks said, "That may be true, but I'd like it to stand still until I can get in it."

The lack of one of those pesky nose weights when you needed it was another problem.

DICK STRATFORD: I had a charter to Trapani, Sicily, with a propeller shaft for a ship. It was the largest single piece of cargo ever hauled on an airplane at that time. As I recall, Marty Lewis was supposed to be my flight engineer, but Tony Maiuro, who is Italian, insisted that he should have the trip and could be our interpreter. I stayed out of

CHAPTER 20 TIGER TALES

it, but somehow he was assigned to the flight.

Trapani was an old Italian fighter airstrip, and the main landing gear of the Connie would barely fit on the runway. After we parked, we found that there was no nose weight available. There was no way you could even consider trying to unload that immense shaft without the nose tied down. Tying the town fire truck to the nose of the airplane provided the solution. With that problem solved I went to the hotel.

Later I was awakened with the news that the airplane was damaged. The crane had broken when they had the shaft about half way out of the cargo door, and the shaft dropped down knocking holes in the floor and damaging the doorsill so badly that the airplane could not be flown.

The company sent a couple of mechanics over to patch it up enough so that it could be flown over to Rome where there were better facilities. Temporary repairs were made there before it was flown back to Burbank.

The same story as Tony recalls it. Turns out to be a real short story.

TONY MAIURO: We multi-crewed the Connie to Sicily. Stratford was the captain, Larry Luccio, the first officer and Howie Amhrein, I think, was the copilot. Femmenino and I were the flight engineers and the navigator was Hank Clark. The mechanic was Hank Haszko and the cargo rep was Joe Barberra.

Talk about C.R.S., these guys got it bad.

JOE FEMMEMINO: I was never on that trip. I was in Gander when I heard about it, and Tough Tony pulled seniority on me so he could go.

Let's leave well enough alone and go on to the next fiasco. It's the unexpected event, the one that you never dreamed would happen, that can pop up and grab you.

DICK STRATFORD: I had a ferry flight back to Los Angeles from a European charter flight. Tony Maiuro was my flight engineer again that trip. We made a fuel stop at Gander, as I recall, then as we approached Moncton, New Brunswick, at 18,000 feet, the yoke suddenly began to oscillate violently forward and aft. I disconnected the autopilot but that was no help. Tony jumped out of his seat, went to the aft end of the cabin and looked out the window at the tail. Here he found the problem.

The Connie has two life rafts installed in containers in the top of each wing. One of the doors had opened, and the raft had flown out and was draped over the left horizontal stabilizer. While Tony was back there, I was slowing the airplane to try to reduce the violence of the buffeting. Now we knew what the problem was, but we didn't know how the airplane would fly with the gear and flaps down.

We called Moncton Airport, declared an emergency and began our descent. With Carey Bowles, the copilot, and I both on the controls, we landed okay. When we got on the ground, we checked the airplane over and didn't find any structural damage. There were some holes in the control surfaces caused by the inflator bottle banging on it, so we patched them with dope and fabric and flew it to New York.

Now for the view from the right seat.

CAREY BOWLES: As I recall, we were over an airport called Seven Islands when the Connie began to shake violently. Looking out the window at the left wing, we could

CHAPTER 20   TIGER TALES   215

see that the life raft compartment door had come unlocked and the slipstream was lifting it partly open. This disturbed the airflow over the wing, which caused the near loss of control. I got on the controls and helped Dick to keep us right side up.

Suddenly we heard a THUMP, and the vibration changed. When Tony went to the back to look out a window, he saw that the raft had come out, flown back and wrapped around the horizontal stabilizer, which added to our control problem. The raft compartment door was still open and acting like a spoiler causing the wing to drop and the airplane to turn left. We had to counter with nearly full right rudder and aileron.

We landed okay, and while we taxied in, the raft fell off onto the ramp.

...and from the side saddle seat.

TONY MAIURO: I don't remember anything about that. I must not have been on that trip.

Guess I had better change the subject. Repairing damaged airplanes is what one would expect a mechanic to do, but if you want one, or in this case two, built, you had better call Charley.

CHARLEY PRYOR: Lockheed had made two turbo prop powered Connies for a Navy test program. After the Navy was through with them, we bought them for scrap. They were H models with the heavy floor and cargo door. The wings had been cut off with a torch just outboard of the landing gear.

We bought two G model Connies from some South American outfit and took the outer wings, center sections and tail and put them on the H model fuselages. Then, of course, we had to re-cable everything and hang new engines. It was a lot of work, but now we had two new Connies pretty cheap.

Charley's Connies may have been cheap, but I guess they could be called Cheep Connies when they were hauling baby chicks.

CHUCK HAMMER: They breed a lot of parakeets in California, and Tigers was asked if they could ship them by air. Tigers said sure, but you will have to package them. So they went and got a bunch of baby chick shipping boxes—those little paper boxes with holes in them. They filled all these boxes with baby parakeets and loaded them on the Connie. So we take off with them for a nonstop flight to New York. During the flight I opened the cockpit door and looked back. Our entire cargo was flying! Those little beaks are really sharp, and those little rascals had eaten their way out of the boxes and were all flying.
   I came back to the cockpit. Jack Morris was the captain.
   I said, "Jack, what do we weigh?"
   "Hell, I don't know. You got the weight and balance."
   I said, "No, no, I know how much we took off with. How much do we weigh now?"
   "What do you mean?" Jack asked looking puzzled.
   "Come on back here," I said.
   He crawled out of his seat and looked into the cabin.
   "There," I said, "our entire load is flying. Now how much does the airplane weigh?"
   "I haven't the foggiest notion." Jack answered with an impatient scowl.

CHAPTER 20   TIGER TALES   217

When we were on approach to Idlewild we called operations and told them, "Under no circumstances should anyone open the cargo door."

So we taxied in and parked, and the first thing we saw was the damned forklift coming up, and before we could do anything the guy opened the cargo door. Quick as a flash, about 100,000 parakeets went to Manhattan.

The end of the year historically brings a slowdown in business, which is often accompanied by layoffs and furloughs. (Junior mechanics are laid off, and junior pilots are furloughed.)

It's hard to explain the emotional letdown that can accompany a furlough notice, especially when received by a hard working and dedicated employee. Wayne Peake wrote the following on the back of his furlough letter.

> The moving finger writes, and, having wrote,
> Moves on: Nor all your piety nor wit
> Shall have it back to cancel half a line
> Nor all your tears wash out a word of it.
>   Omar Khayam

> MERRY CHRISTMAS 1959
> Comes the New Year, reviewing last year's debt,
> The simpleton relaxes...and forgets
> The furlough notice soon within the mail,
> "Dear Sir: The company regrets..."
>
> Behold, the Christmas rush is over:
> Behold, I greet you as before
> The thread of revenue grows thin,
> Your loyal service required no more!

FIRES TO FURLOUGHS

The grand career you set your heart upon
Flames, turns to ashes, and anon
Is not unlike Saint Elmo's fire,
Lighting a little hour or two and gone.

Why question ye the great accomplishment
Of revenues increased multi-percent?
The profits greater than before,
Must go to pay a new vice president.

A wheel that can with power absolute
The "ALPA" and C.A.B. confute.
And, knowing where the 'body' lies,
A dearth of talent into gold transmutes.

Nine years I took from your life, and well
I used your talents building F.T.L.
A puppet jumps to the strings I pull.
With hopes of paradise and threats of hell!

What matters that the winter winds blow chill
What matters that you have an empty till?
Your past performance helped to make us strong
Enough to furlough and recall at will.

Wait! For glory of contracts oversea,
Standby, and wait, in quiet poverty...
Standby, (while non-skeds [1] under bid),
To heed the rumble of an EA3.[2]   Wayne Peake

---

[1] Non scheduled airlines

[2] EA3 was the dash number of the Wright engines on our Lockheed Constellations R3350-EA3

CHAPTER 21   FINALLY THE FLIGHT LINE   1960

1049 H CONNIE

In the spring I transferred from the engine shop to the flight line. There were three crews on the swing shift of about six men each. The lead mechanics were Woody Lindsey, Ken Garber and Chris Ortega. I was on Ortega's crew most of the time, and Ed Hale, who had recently transferred to the flight line, was on Lindsey's crew.

There are all kinds of mechanics. Some will work methodically and do good work hour after hour, but wouldn't move any faster if the hangar was on fire. Many of this type will work their eight-hour shift and no more.

Others respond well to emergencies. If an airplane arrives with a serious problem, they will work as hard and as fast as they can and will stay as long as it takes to get the job done.

I'll have to admit that when I started with the company I was probably one of the former, but that didn't last long in this new atmosphere. The company was a very different kind of outfit than any other I had worked for. Here, it seemed like the more difficult the problem, or heavier the work load, the greater the enthusiasm and determination.

I soon became one of those that hardly ever refused to stay over if we had an emergency. I don't take credit for any positive change in my attitude. It was entirely due to the examples set by the old time Tiger mechanics. When you live and work with them every day, something has to rub off on you.

The fact that we all worked well together made it a pleasure to come to work every day. There were no inept mechanics on the flight line. They just could not bluff their way past Rhuel Trimble. And anyone who didn't want to work that hard had left long ago.

Like Bill Thompson said, "We were lucky that the good men stayed with us."

The Connie was our fleet airplane now, and we all knew it well. It had evolved into a very dependable workhorse.

Most of our overseas stations were manned by experienced people, and our crews could depend on good service...most of the time.

DAVE VACHON: Al Perreault and I were taking off from Wake Island at night in a Connie. Kenny Boyd was the engineer. We were screaming down the runway, and I was trimming it back and trimming it back, but nothing was happening. The airplane just didn't want to fly. Come to find out, the loaders had taken a spare engine out of the rear of the airplane and hadn't repositioned the cargo. It was so nose-heavy it couldn't fly. Fortunately we realized this while we still had enough runway to get stopped.

The trouble is that when things begin to settle down and become less of a challenge, one tends to get restless. After gaining some experience on the flight line, I felt that I should prepare myself for a better position in the future.

Historically, when the company needed flight engineers, they hired them from the mechanic's ranks. To be considered for those jobs, the mechanic had to have passed the F.A.A. Flight Engineer written examination. I bought the textbooks and a flight computer and began to

CHAPTER 21 TIGER TALES 221

prepare for the written test. Not that being a flight engineer is any piece of cake.

TONY MAIURO: I was pretty fortunate that during my flying career I'd never had any real problems...except for the one time when we iced up real bad. Frank Hawkins was the captain and we were en route from Gander to Shannon. We iced up so bad that we couldn't climb. If I hadn't put on about 500 gallons of Grandma gas[1] we'd never have made it. We had ice built up on the wings all the way back to the trailing edge of the flaps. We were in high blower just to keep the engines running, and of course we had gone under cowl[2] as soon as the icing started.

We began the crossing at 10,000 feet, but when we were supposed to go higher, we were in the ice and couldn't climb. We came down to 5,000 feet to try to get out of the icing and were burning a lot of fuel just to stay in the air. We called Air-Sea Rescue to escort us in.

It is a wonder that New York's finest didn't give Captain John Murray an escort.

CYNTHIA BOWLES, stewardess: One time John Murray bought a donkey in New Jersey to take home to his farm on Long Island. He tied its feet together and set the animal on the back seat of his convertible. He drove though the Lincoln Tunnel and all through Manhattan with that donkey

---

[1] "Grandma gas" is a term for the extra fuel added by the crew "just in case."

[2] "Under cowl" means the engines were getting heated air through the alternate air doors. This causes a considerable power loss, but at least the engines were kept running.

sitting back there braying. It was the funniest thing you could imagine. It was even in the newspapers.

I don't have long ears, but I was a real ass for believing this next story.

A notice was posted on the mechanic's bulletin board in the hanger saying that, in the future, flight engineers would not be hired from the mechanics' ranks. The company's reasoning was that such promotions would mean that the Maintenance Department would lose an experienced mechanic and would have to hire and train a new man. Like a fool I believed them put my books away.

HANK GERMAIN, mechanic: Tigers were doing a lot of modifications on Connies at that time, so when Thai Airlines went out of business with their Connies, Tigers bought them. Some of them were brand new, and some were really ratty. A bunch of us mechanics went to Bangkok and got them in flying condition. Then those Connies were flown back to Burbank where they were overhauled and sold to Air Mexico.

I remember hearing a lot more to that story. Of course, maybe Hank was not personally involved, so I'll tell it the way I heard it.

When the work was done, the mechanics went into Bangkok to clean up and relax. They hired a small three-wheeled taxi in which to tour the city. I assume they wanted to see the Temples, Museums and Art Galleries. This, of course, is thirsty work so they had the driver stop at a local watering hole. Maybe several. I don't know if the driver had been joining them or not, but at some point he drove his taxi into a clong (canal).

CHAPTER 21 TIGER TALES

Our intrepid mechanics pushed, pulled and carried the taxi out of the water and up the steep bank to the road. With their clothes sopping wet, shoes full of water and hearts full of cheer, they waved goodbye to the hapless driver and started walking. The driver then began shouting and demanded his fare. Our heroes looked at one another, paid the fare, then picked up the taxi and threw it back in the canal.

HANK HASZKO, Mechanic: We were scheduled to leave Newark for Argentina in a Connie loaded with cargo on Christmas Eve. We had a multi-crew with Bob Souers the captain, Art Flanagin, first officer and Frank Morrow, co-pilot. Tony Maiuro and Art Strassle were the flight engineers and Charley Bellows the navigator. Bob had not received the landing rights in Buenos Aires, so he wouldn't go.

On Christmas day Pinke called from Burbank and talked Bob into going, assuring him that the landing rights would be there when he arrived. They were not. After sitting in Buenos Aires for three days we were asked to leave the country with the cargo still on board.

We tried to land at Montevideo, but we had no landing rights there either. We were finally permitted to land in Rio, where we refueled and were supposedly cleared by Pan Am employees. All we needed was for someone to pull the crew entrance ladder away so we could start the engines, when customs came out to the airplane.

They looked around and asked Captain Souers, "Where are you going?"

"New York."

"Your bill of lading states cargo for Buenos Aires, Argentina. What are you smuggling?"

We remained in Rio for 22 days awaiting clearance or for someone to pay the right people under the table.

There have been a lot of stories going around about how much money I made on that trip. They were somewhat exaggerated. Actually I was paid eight hours a day, and my leadman pay rate at that time was $3.45 per hour. With all the heavy overtime around the holidays, some of the guys in Newark made as much as I did, and they spent Christmas at home.

There was a lot of talk going around about the possibility of Tigers getting jet airplanes. Lockheed had its new Electra, and they had proposed a cargo version. The Douglas DC-8, the Convair 880 or 990 and the Boeing707 were mentioned. None of those sounded feasible, and many of us chalked it all up to wishful thinking. Then we saw the modification on the C-46.

A C-46 in cruise with both engines stopped and the propellers feathered. Note the jet engine under the fuselage. Hmm, jet airplanes? Do you suppose...?

CHAPTER 22   THE CANADAIR CL-44   1961

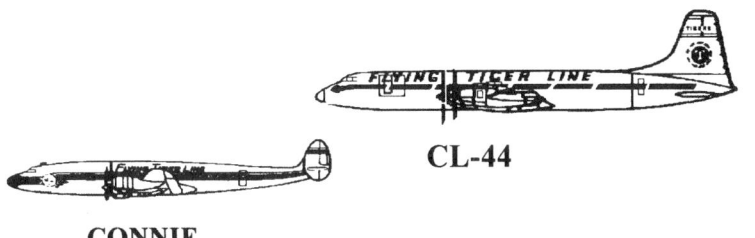

The Canadair CL-44-D4.

The good news of the year was that the jet airplane rumor turned out to be true. The bad news was that we had never heard of this airplane, the CL-44, and we were only vaguely aware of the existence of the manufacturer, Canadair of Montreal. The company bought a fleet of ten Canadair CL-44 swing tail Turboprop Airplanes. We took delivery of the first one in June, and it landed at Burbank amid half the news media in Los Angeles.

The crew parked the airplane and swung the tail open to the amazement of the crowd. Then came the first of many problems. The tail refused to close. There were so many safety devices to keep the tail from coming unlocked in flight that it could hardly be operated at all. The CL-44 was to be a long learning process. With a number of mechanics in school on the new airplanes, we were short-handed everywhere.

The CL-44 had a much greater range than anything we had flown before, so it could fly the great circle route from California to Japan with only one fuel stop. Tigers built and operated a refueling station and crew layover facilities at Cold Bay, Alaska, out on the Aleutian Chain.

To make our mechanic shortage even more acute, Flight Operations needed flight engineers and, wouldn't you know it, they hired them anywhere they could find them. This included from the flight line, but I wasn't eligible because I hadn't taken my written examination.

From time to time the company would select mechanics for the positions of maintenance representatives. These were management positions and were mostly on overseas stations. I was the union steward on the flight line at that time, and I had many complaints from mechanics.

"The same people are always picked for those positions. Why can't we all have a chance at them?"

I discussed this with the general foreman of out stations, Bill Thompson.

Bill said, "Some people don't realize that just because a man is a good mechanic doesn't mean he will be a good maintenance rep. There's a lot more to it. A maintenance rep has to do business with other companies, get tools and

CHAPTER 22 TIGER TALES

aircraft parts through customs, sign short-term contracts for emergency maintenance such as engine changes on off-route airports. He has to make decisions about which maintenance items can be safely carried over to a maintenance base, and what has to be fixed. However, there will soon be some openings in the Far East, and I'll try to spread the opportunities around."

At the end of July Bill called me into his office.

"We need a maintenance rep at Tachikawa Airbase in Japan. If someone wants to go, send him in to see me."

I went around to those who had been complaining.

One man said, "Gee, I can't go right now because my wife is pregnant."

Another said, "I'm trying to get rid of the crab grass in my lawn, but I'd love to go later."

I learned a lot about people that day.

My wife was pregnant too, but after I had made all the noise about the issue, I felt some responsibility.

I asked Bill, "Can I go for thirty days, until you can get someone permanently?"

With a bemused smile on his face he said, "That'll be just fine."

I was a little concerned about that smile, but I got a passport, visa and shot records, and left a week later. With my suitcase and toolbox I boarded a Connie. Goldy was the captain, Bill Hoey, the copilot, and Charley Hammer, the flight engineer. We flew to Tokyo via Honolulu, Wake Island, Guam and Okinawa, arriving in Japan on August 14, 1961.

Tachikawa was hot and humid, and there were few air conditioners. There were many open sewers at that time, and the smell took some getting used to. We were very short handed and sometimes worked 24 to 36 hours straight. It was challenging work, however, and I really enjoyed it. We had our own crews of skilled Japanese mechanics. Our job was to direct and oversee the maintenance and to take care of the paper work.

Harry Blackburn, the Rolls Royce representative, was a great help to us. He knew almost all there was to know about the Rolls Royce Tyne engine. Besides that, he was a good friend and pleasant companion.

When my temporary assignment was nearly up, I went to see Bill Curran, the senior maintenance rep.

"Bill, my thirty days are about up. Heard anything about my replacement?"

"What are you talking about? No one told me anything about a replacement. I've been over here a hell of a lot longer than you have, and if a replacement shows, up I'll go home myself."

<u>Now</u> I understood why Bill Thompson had been smiling when he said I could leave when they found someone on a permanent basis.

Ernie Boyer, from Detroit, came over to help out. True to his word, Bill Curran went home, and Earl Jolly took over as senior maintenance supervisor. Earl, Joe Lightner, Paul Shroeder, Ernie Boyer and I were the only maintenance reps in the entire Far East.

One of the flights we departed was a ferry flight to Burbank. If the flight crew had to have this problem, I'm glad it was on the other end of the trip.

DICK STUELKE: We were flying this CL-44 from Japan to Burbank. Don Hassig was my copilot, and he was flying

CHAPTER 22   TIGER TALES

this leg. Lloyd Moore was the flight engineer and Pappy Huntington was the navigator.

DON HASSIG: We were cleared to descend and cross Fillmore at 10,000 feet, so I reduced power and down we went. When I added power to level off, the #2 engine blew up and caught fire. It was dark and the whole damn sky lit up, illuminating pieces of the engine as they fell toward the ground.

They shut down the engine and shot the fire bottles to it, all to no avail. The fire was still burning.

STUELKE: Hassig and I discussed whether we should increase speed to try to blow the fire out, which might turn the fire into a cutting torch and cut the wing off, or just continue normal speed and maybe let the wing burn off. We didn't like either option, so we said the hell with it and just flew a normal approach. After we landed the fire seemed to be out, so we taxied to the ramp.

HASSIG: We had to clear Customs, but Customs had not arrived yet, so we couldn't get off the airplane. Maintenance didn't want to be held up, so they hooked a tug on us and towed the airplane into the hangar.

I said, "Hey, this thing was on fire a few minutes ago, and we want a stand pushed up to the door, so we can get out if it starts burning again."

About that time the mechanics noticed smoke coming out of the cowling. Some one hollered FIRE, and they all ran over to put it out, and we still couldn't get out of the airplane.

Stuelke looked at me and said, "The hell with Customs. I'm getting out of here."

Those were my sentiments exactly, so we went down the emergency escape rope.

When the mechanics opened the cowling, the damndest mess of hot smoking engine parts you ever saw fell onto the hangar floor.

Tigers sent some people to Fillmore to search for the missing pieces. One small garage owner opened up the next morning and saw a strange looking piece of metal lying in the road. He looked it over and threw it in his trash bin. Later in the day our people happened to stop and ask if he had found anything, so he gave them the piece. It was the main part they were looking for.

There was a hearing to learn the cause of the fire. The FAA, Canadair, Rolls Royce and Tigers all had people there. This was a very serious matter and everyone wanted to find the cause in order to prevent a reoccurrence.

Investigation showed that a bearing had seized which caused the shaft to break, disconnecting the turbine from the compressor. The turbine then wound up to such a speed in just seconds that it disintegrated. It broke into three sections, one of which had gone straight down out of the engine, cut through the constant speed drive unit and ignited its oil supply. As I recall, Rolls Royce modified the bearing and its lubrication system.

GOLDY: When we got the CL-44, I felt like I was a professional test pilot. There were very few flights where we didn't have an emergency of some kind. Some were very serious and could have gone the wrong way...locked elevators, locked rudders and whatnot.

CHAPTER 22   TIGER TALES   231

I spent a lot of grim days in Cold Bay, especially when they put us in old building #26, and the wind and snow blew in around the windows. We went off per diem while in Cold Bay because the hotel and all the meals were free. Not many ever complained about the food.

This next crew didn't get to Cold Bay, at least not on the airplane they started out with. They had landed in King Salmon for fuel because Cold Bay, Anchorage and Elmendorf were all weathered in. After they were fueled, they burned up #2 engine on start-up. The airplane was fully loaded with freight, and there was no way to unload it, so they could not three-engine ferry the airplane out.

ED HALE, maintenance: I got a phone call from Charley Pryor, who was at the hangar in Burbank.
"We need you to take a little field trip to change an engine on a CL-44."
"For Christ sake, I just got home last night from Germany!"
"Oh, I forgot about that, I'll get someone else."
A few minutes later he called back. "I can't find anyone who has changed a CL-44 engine. I really need you to go."
"Well where is it?"
"It's in King Salmon, Alaska, about half way between Anchorage and Cold Bay. Mike Drumwright will go with you from here, and Fred Reeves and Tom McClung from Cold Bay will meet you there."
We flew in there from Anchorage on a Reeve's Aleutian DC-6. As luck would have it, the CL-44 had a spare engine on board, which was being sent to Cold Bay as a station spare. All we had to do was figure out a way to get it out of the airplane. When we started working the temperature was -32 degrees, then a 40-knot wind came up. There was

no way you could work out in that weather. We borrowed a huge tarp from the Fish and Game Department. It must have been 100 feet long and 80 feet wide. After we took the propeller off, we made a windbreak with the tarp.

By the time we had the engine off it was three o'clock in the morning, but that didn't make any difference because it was dark all the time anyway. We hooked up the new engine, rigged the controls and ran the engine. It ran okay, but I couldn't hold the airplane on the ice long enough to check the propeller pitchlock, which requires nearly maximum power on the engine.

About ten that morning, Ed Pinke and his crew arrived on a local airline flight from Anchorage. He knew what we had been going through and was surprised that the engine was ready.

"What can we do to help?" he asked.

I said, "Well, I can't hold the airplane long enough to check the pitchlock."[1]

"How long does it take?"

"I think I can do it in 45 seconds."

"Okay, get in and we'll take it out on the runway."

I did the pitchlock check and the power run while we slid down the runway with the brakes locked and Pinke trying to keep it out of the snow banks.

That wasn't the end of the story. When the airplane landed in Tachikawa, all eight main landing gear tires blew out. The tread of the tires had been left in King Salmon...frozen to the ramp.

---

[1]The pitchlock is a mechanical safety device, which prevents the propeller blades from moving toward flat pitch in case of loss of hydraulic control to the propeller.

CHAPTER 22 TIGER TALES

DICK STRATFORD: There were so many problems with the CL-44 that I was afraid we couldn't overcome them all. It's the only airplane I've ever been in that, if you stood between the cockpit and the cabin, in the propeller arc, the vibration would tickle your feet so that you'd have to move. The propellers had a synchro-phasing system, but it didn't work. CL-44s came equipped with autopilots, but they didn't work either for the first year.

I was on a trip from JFK to Shannon with Bob Souers. when we first got the 44s. We started out each hand flying it for an hour, but by the time we arrived we were changing pilots every ten minutes. It's the only airplane I ever saw that you could trim up for level flight, then watch the trim wheel roll the airplane out of trim.

Some people sure spend a lot of time monkeying around.

MERLE KLEEN: John Ristaino hired me over the phone. I was in South Saint Paul, Minnesota, and he said get yourself to Chicago on Saturday morning, and I'll have a pass for you on the airplane. So I got to Midway Airport in Chicago and walked into the Flying Tiger Hangar. Somebody had dropped a crate full of monkeys off of a forklift, and there were monkeys in the rafters and all over hell.

I thought this is not a good sign. What kind of an outfit am I going to work for?

As the year came to a close I was invited to attend a Christmas party, the likes of which I'll probably never see again. Present were personnel from Flying Tigers, Slick Airways and Air America. I'm going to omit the names of the various culprits...er I mean participants.

The party was held in the home of one of the maintenance guys. Sometime in the wee hours of the morning we all went home and when the host went into his bedroom he found his buddy, an Air America pilot, in his bed with some girl.

The host was too drunk to do much about it then, so he crashed on the tatami floor where he slept it off.

The next night at the civilian club he confronted his pal about the indiscretion.

"What ever made you think it was okay to take some gal into my bed?"

His friend looked like his feeling were hurt as he said, "Hell, I thought you wouldn't mind us being in your bed, after all, she was your girl."

The new Tiger circle T came on the scene in 1961, adorning the tail of the new Canadair CL-44. It would remain the Tiger Logo for many years

CHAPTER 23   THE IDES OF MARCH   1962

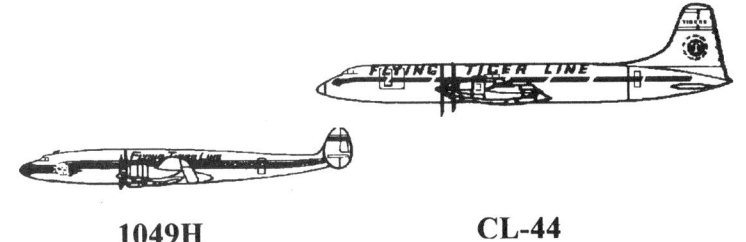

1049H   CL-44

This is what happened.

Our problems for the year began in January when one of our Connies, 11 Charlie, was taxiing in Grand Island, Nebraska, and fell through the taxiway. The right wing, horizontal stabilizer, landing gear and both right engines and propellers were badly damaged. They sent Doc Powell, Bob Opeggard, Willie Skaggs, Don Eatchel, Bill Smillie and Jack McClarty back there to fix it.

JACK McCLARTY, sheet metal shop: I was getting pretty good at it by then. When we were finished with the repair, I was ready to go home. Willy Skaggs had bought a '62

Mercury Comet there and wanted me to drive back to Burbank with him.

I said, "Hell, let's just load it in the Connie."

He said, "We got no way to load it, and it might not go in the door."

I looked around the field and saw this old forklift sitting in some weeds, so I asked the guy, "What would you charge to load that car on the airplane?"

The guy spit a wad of tobacco and said, "I won't charge you nothin'. It'd be worth it to see a car go in an airplane."

And this was the result.

Jack makes this all sound easy, but remember the accident happened in January and the airplane was flown out in late February. Not exactly the peak tourist season in Nebraska. The bitter cold was even more miserable to the mechanics, because they were all lived in southern California.

CHAPTER 23 TIGER TALES

Another view from the rear

At this time in the Pacific we only had maintenance people stationed in Japan, Guam, and Hawaii. If an airplane with a maintenance problem landed somewhere else, we would have to send someone to fix it. It seems that I was usually that someone. When we had a Connie down in Saigon, Viet Nam, with a blown engine cylinder, I gathered up the needed parts, rode one of our flights to Saigon and changed the cylinder.

Meanwhile on the other side of the world, Gene Taylor was a check pilot...

GENE TAYLOR: I had to give Tom Sullivan a check ride, and of course Tom is an ace of a pilot, and he breezed through all the maneuvers we had to do. There was a big rainstorm in the valley, and when we made our approach to Burbank, we took a lightning strike on the nose. It blew the nosecone right off the airplane, and the cone spiraled on down and landed on a golf course.

The funny part of this story is that this was when John Glenn was making his first orbit around the earth in the space capsule. He was right overhead when this happened and everyone had their radios tuned in. You don't realize how big that nose cone is until you see it on the ground. Some people ran up to it and, when they saw it was empty, started yelling, "Glenn, John Glenn, where are you?"

Back in the Far East I was still chasing broken airplanes. We had a CL-44 in Guam with an engine failure, and I went with a spare engine and parts and changed the engine. I hung the propeller then discovered a serious oversight. The parts kit didn't contain the O-ring seal for the propeller dome, and the dome cannot be installed with the old seal. It was my fault; I just forgot to check to be sure it was there. I wired Burbank and had one put on the next flight out.

You can imagine how I felt. Here we sat, the flight crew, cabin crew and a load of passengers for whom the Company had to pay hotel and meals, and an airplane that doesn't make any money sitting on the ramp.

While I was pacing back and forth berating myself, the captain said, "What's the matter, you don't want to be human like the rest of us?"

His comment sure helped to lift my spirits. I never heard a word about my oversight from anyone.

I had more problems. After spending a cold damp winter in Japan, I was not accustomed to being out in the sun. It was so hot in Guam that I received a severe sunburn. Fortunately for me, our flight attendants dragged me into the shade and doctored me up while we waited for the errant O-ring.

This job goes from hot to cold. Misawa was a Fighter Base in Northern Honshu, Japan. As a military contract airline, we used it as a fuel stop to and from Alaska. One of our CL-44s was on approach when the elevator controls

CHAPTER 23   TIGER TALES

locked up. The crew managed to get it on the ground, then called us at Tachikawa and demanded that it be fixed. Sam Royal was the captain and Stan Hampton the copilot.

There were no flights going to Misawa that day, so Earl Jolly and I went to Chofu Air Station, where Earl chartered a civilian Cessna 175 with two Japanese pilots. I took my tools and maintenance manuals and crawled into the back seat. The pilots spoke about as much English as I spoke Japanese…and that was none. As we flew north, the weather worsened, and about an hour and a half later we landed in Sendai for fuel.

The two pilots checked the weather, and there was much animated discussion in Japanese.

The first pilot pointed at the weather forecast, and sucking air through his teeth, made a loud, "Hisss!"

The second pilot looked at what the first pilot was pointing at and agreed with an even louder, "HISSS!"

After the obligatory hissing was completed, we again headed north. The ceiling was so low that we couldn't get more than about 500 feet of altitude. We were flying out over the ocean now, so at least we weren't likely to run into anything.

When we were a couple of miles south of Misawa, the ceiling lifted to about 2000 feet. As we entered the traffic pattern, I noticed a lot of airplanes. It seemed like there were F-101s everywhere I looked. After we landed and taxied off of the runway, we were met by more military police than I had ever seen in one place.

It seemed that we had flown right through the flight of F-101s, which were on approach and low on fuel. It turned out that my Japanese pilots had the proper paperwork and clearances, they just didn't understand the tower's instructions. They were finally released and flew back to Chofu.

I went to work on the airplane, and when I tried the elevator, it operated perfectly. Now I really had a problem. It can be very hard to fix something that's not broken. I could not duplicate the problem, no matter what I tried. I even froze the bearings with CO_2 bottles to try to simulate in flight conditions. No matter what I did, the elevators worked fine. I disconnected the artificial feel system, and it checked out okay. I was stuck. I couldn't release the airplane for service because it might lock up again.

I sent a message to Burbank saying, "Either send me the parts, so I can replace each component in the elevator and artificial feel system, or send a ferry crew."

The decision was made to ferry the airplane to Burbank, which was our main maintenance base. They sent Johnny Holmes, check pilot, and Hal Cerniway as check engineer. When the aircraft arrived in Burbank, maintenance there couldn't find anything wrong with it either, so they put the airplane back in service.

A few days later Goldy was on approach to Midway Airport in Chicago when the elevators locked up again. Goldy also managed to get the thing on the ground in one piece with help from the elevator trim tabs. I understand that the colorful language he used on the telephone convinced Burbank that they had better find what was wrong and fix it. I think it was Roy Cole who discovered there was an intermittent malfunction in the artificial feel system. After it was replaced there were no further problems.

THE IDES OF MARCH

Back in Tachikawa, I was scheduled to work the first flight that morning, 11 Charlie, just fresh out of overhaul after falling through the taxiway in Grand Island. When I arrived at the hangar I was informed that 11 Charlie had crashed while landing at Adak, in the Aleutians.

There was a multi-crew on board: Captain Morgan Hughes in command, Captain Tom Mitchell, Copilot Wayne Lowe, Flight Engineers Henry Guttman and James Johnstone and Navigators Michael Green and Kenneth Drusch.

The aircraft departed Travis AFB, California, with scheduled fuel stops at Cold Bay and Adak. After takeoff from Travis, the crew noticed a severe buffeting. They determined that it was probably caused by the hydraulic reservoir access door being inadvertently left open.

They returned to Travis where the door was closed and the fuel tanks topped off. Captain Mitchell, who flew that leg commented, "This airplane is extremely nose heavy."

The flight departed the second time with Captain Hughes flying. There was no further buffeting, and after landing at Cold Bay, he reported, "The landing was solid as I was unable to make a normal flare due to the nose-heavy condition."

R.C "ANDY" ANDERSON: That date, the ides of March, is etched in my mind. I remember from my high school Shakespeare, Julius Caesar, when the old Sibyl tells Caesar, "Beware of the ides, beware of the ides of March." In the ancient Roman calendar, the ides of March were the fifteenth day of March.

By coincidence in my personal life, many things I thought to be most unfortunate happened to friends and colleagues of mine on or near the ides of March. This year it would prove to be a very traumatic time for Tigers.

I was a member of the ground crew in Cold Bay that sent 11 Charlie to Adak, so I understand the emotions involved even to this day. The other mechanics at Cold Bay were Ray Millican, Jim Archer and Fred Reeves.

After refueling at Cold Bay, the copilot, Wayne Lowe, flew the leg to Adak. On final approach the airplane went below the glide slope.

Captain Hughes called out, "You're too low!"

Wayne added power as they both pulled back on the yoke, but the right main gear hit the rocks just short of the runway. A second later the nose gear hit the seawall four feet below the runway level. The force of impact drove the nose gear back and up into the cockpit floor. In so doing it struck the main aircraft control cables and pushed them up through the floor. The cables came up around the flight engineer, James Johnstone's leg, and then snapped back into their normal position. He was trapped.

The main landing gear and one wing separated from the fuselage and the wing exploded into flames. The fuselage slid off to the side of the runway and also caught fire. The fire truck arrived quickly and doused the fire in the fuselage. When they drove out in the field to douse the fire in the burning wing, the truck mired down in the mud.

A short time before this accident, there had been a hijacking in the States where the emergency crash axe was used as a weapon. The F.A.A. ordered the crash axes removed from all airliners to prevent this from happening again. As a result our crew had no way to cut the cables to free the flight engineer.

While the rest of the crew tried to free the engineer, the cabin fire re-ignited. With the fire truck now stuck in the mud, it could not get back to the airplane. As the fire came closer to the cockpit, the heat became unbearable. They put an oxygen mask on the engineer's face, but were finally forced to leave him as the airplane burned.

CHAPTER 23 TIGER TALES 243

As 11 Charlie was not coming, this meant that I would be working the next scheduled flight, 21 Charlie, a Connie passenger flight from Travis AFB. This flight also had a multicrew: Captain Greg Thomas,[1] First Officer Robert Wish, Copilot Bob Gazzoway, Flight Engineers George Nau[2] and Clayton McClellan, Navigators William Kennedy and Grady Burt Jr.

The stewardesses were Patricia Wassum, Hildegarde Muller, Barbara Wamsley and Christel Reiter.

They had made stops at Hickam Field in Hawaii and Agana Naval Air Station in Guam. The flight had departed Guam on schedule and made a normal position report about midnight, but was overdue at Clark Field in the Philippines. By morning the aircraft was officially reported lost. The following is an excerpt from the Civil Aeronautics Board Aircraft Accident Report:

That morning a message was received from the S/S T. L. Lenzen, a super tanker. The message stated that at 1:30 a.m. local time, she had sighted a midair explosion.

It was established, upon interrogation of five of the crewmembers, that shipboard lookouts had observed a midair explosion at the approximate position and time where N 6921C was expected to be. It was recalled that a vapor trail, or some phenomenon resembling a vapor trail, was first observed overhead and slightly to the north of the tanker and moving in an east to west direction. The Lenzen was cruising on a heading of 077 degrees at the time.

---

[1] Greg Thomas was the captain who landed the DC-6 in Jamaica Bay in 1957 after all four engines quit.

[2] George Nau was a mechanic I worked with in the engine buildup shop in 1956.

As this vapor trail passed behind a cloud, there occurred an explosion, which was described by the witnesses as intensely luminous, with a white nucleus surrounded by a reddish orange periphery with radial lines of colored light.

The explosion occurred in two pulses lasting between two and three seconds and from it two flaming objects of unequal brightness and size apparently fell, at disparate speeds, into the sea. During the last ten seconds of the fall of the slower of the two objects, a small bright target was observed on the ship's radar bearing 270 degrees, range 17 miles.

The ship reversed course and proceeded to the area of the radar target. They searched the area for five and a half hours, but found nothing.

In spite of the most extensive air and sea search in history, no trace of wreckage was ever found. Ninety-three of the ninety-six passengers on board were American soldiers and the other three were South Vietnamese officers.

NOAH SMITH, navigator: Darrel Jewett and I were set up with Greg Thomas on this trip. We were taken off schedule only hours before departure because we were high time for the month and were replaced with low time navigators.

This was a terrible time for all of us at Tigers. For days we went about our jobs without talking or looking at one another. Eventually we had to face the harsh reality that these things do happen. Life is always precious and sometimes is too short.

CHAPTER 24　　OUR WORST YEAR EVER　　1962-2

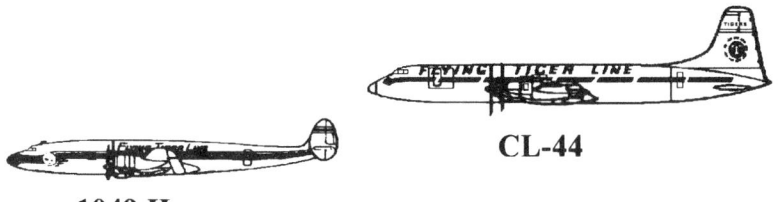

CL-44

1049 H

At least something went right for Bob Prescott that year when he married Ann Marie, from Stockholm, Sweden. She moved to this country in 1952 after finishing her medical training at the University of Lund, in Sweden.

Ann Marie operated the Golden Door, an exclusive health retreat in Escondido, California.

ANN MARIE PRESCOTT: Bob was a regular. He was like a Pied Piper—you know—he upset everything, which was fun, but that's how we met. People came to the Golden Door to get themselves turned around, both physically and emotionally.

Bob and Helen Ruth had been separated for a few years at the time, but you know how Bob was.

He said, "I didn't want to wake up one morning to find I had married somebody I didn't want to marry."

So he didn't take out his final divorce papers until the day before we were married. He just picked me up at the Golden Door and there was no if, and or buts. I was not in the marrying mood. I didn't ever think I was going to be married, so it was a reluctant capture. We married July 16, 1962. But Bob was wonderful; I mean he was such a wonderful entity.

You know Helen Ruth never considered herself divorced from Bob. She was always at every occasion... Thanksgiving and Christmas and Easter and whatever, she was always at the house. That was fine with me, because she had a need for that connection. Every time she showed up they just went into the same arguments they'd had when they were married.

From a Vibrant Romance to a Vibrating CL-44.

Charley Hammer: One day I sat there and watched the screws vibrate out of my new camera, and it fell apart right in front of my eyes. Why, I've laid my uniform cap on the coat closet shelf, and when I picked it up after we landed, the nut that holds the wings on had come unscrewed and the wings were lying on the floor. I've had screws fall out of the ceiling and drop on me in flight. It makes you wonder if any important things are coming apart.

Of course none of us who knew Charley would ever doubt his veracity.

Back out in the Pacific we were getting some help. In August Ed Hale came to Okinawa and took over maintenance at Kadena and Naha. Later he also became the station manager.

Everything went along pretty well until fall, when we found that the Company's bad luck hadn't ended yet. On September 23 another of our Connies, 23 Charlie, a passenger flight, went down in the North Atlantic. The flight crewmembers were: Captain John Murray, Copilot Robert Parker, Flight Engineer James E. Garrett and Navigator Sam Nicholson. The flight attendants were Carol Ann Gould, Ruth Mudd and Jacqueline Brotman.

The first problem they encountered was when a PRT[1] on the #3 engine blew its oil seal and poured oil into the engine exhaust, which caught fire. The flight engineer shut down the #3 engine and extinguished the fire. Then they left their cruising altitude of 21,000 feet and began a

---

[1] Power recovery turbine.

CHAPTER 24 TIGER TALES 247

drift down to 9,000 feet, the maximum altitude they could maintain on three engines.

The flight engineer was new with the company and our emergency procedures were slightly different from those to which he was accustomed. He apparently closed the firewall shutoff valve for the #1 engine by mistake. A minute later the #1 propeller ran away, meaning it went into an over-speed condition due to the lack of oil to the propeller dome. They shut down #1 engine and feathered the propeller.

This left them with #2 engine and #4 engine. They had to use METO^2 power as they drifted down to 5,000 feet, the maximum altitude they could maintain on two engines. They made many attempts to restart the #1 engine, but to no avail.

They now called Shannon Radio and requested the Keflavik, Iceland, weather. The weather there was not suitable, so they asked for a report on sea conditions in case they had to ditch. They also requested an escort. There was an eastbound Riddle Airlines flight nearing their position and also a westbound MATS flight, which changed course to intercept the Tiger flight.

There was no moon as they slowly made their way over the stormy ocean at METO power for another hour. Suddenly the red fire warning light illuminated and the fire-warning bell sounded for the #2 engine. When the captain retarded the throttle, the fire warning stopped, so he reapplied power but to a lesser manifold pressure.

At this time he changed course and headed for Ocean Station Vessel Juliett, which was 480 nautical miles away. He had the passengers don their life jackets and prepared

---

[2]**Maximum except takeoff.**

the airplane for a possible ditching. Again the fire warning activated and again power was reduced. They advised Shannon Radio that they could not maintain 5,000 feet with the reduced power. They drifted down to 3,000 feet, with METO power on #4, and reduced power on #2 engine.

Soon after both the Riddle and the MATS flight reported visual contact, the #2 engine failed. Now they were down to one outboard engine, and they couldn't go anywhere but down.

It was the middle of the night when they hit the water. One wing was torn off on impact. Sam Nicholson, the navigator, was an expert swimmer, and he dove into the ocean and retrieved a floating raft, the only one they could find in the dark. Fifty-one people boarded that single 25-man life raft. During the night three persons drowned in the bottom of the overloaded raft. Captain Murray, Navigator Nicholson, and Stewardess Gould survived. There were 76 military people and their dependents on board that flight, of which 45 survived.

Aircraft were overhead continuously from the time of ditching until rescue, six hours later, by the merchant ship Celerina.

SAM NICHOLSON, navigator: Three weeks after the hearings were over, I was the navigator on another Connie over the North Atlantic. My clothes had been lost in the previous ditching, and I still didn't have a uniform. We were in the middle of the ocean when suddenly we had an engine failure. The crew shut it down and feathered the propeller.

I sensed that it was unusually quiet in the cockpit. When I looked up, every crewmember was staring at me like I was hexed or something.

CHAPTER 24 TIGER TALES

Maybe Sam didn't have a hex on him, but he sure had his share of bad luck.

BILL SEAMANS: Sam bought a motorcycle and was tearing down the highway when he went over a steep bank and nearly killed himself in the wreck. Someone called the ambulance, and in the meantime Sam, who was all bloody and beat up, began crawling up the bank toward the road. On the way he slid his body across a hornet's nest and was stung by so many hornets that they had to wait in line to get at him.

He reached the highway at the same time the meat wagon did, so they rescued him from the hornets. With lights flashing and siren wailing they raced toward the hospital...and had an accident on the way. At least this way the doctors could fix everything at the same time.

An engine fire on an airplane can even cause the captain to light up.

BOB ZALUSKY: I took off out of Idlewild one night in a Connie headed for Frankfurt, Germany, when a power recovery turbine oil seal blew, and the flames lit up the whole sky. I had a load of passengers, and, of course, I had to dump fuel and return to Idlewild.

I'd quit smoking about a month before, and while the emergency was going on, I was busy just doing the job I was trained to do. But later, in the hotel, my hands are shakin'. I'm trying to drink a bourbon, and sloppin' it all over myself. The copilot fired up a cigarette. I bummed one off him, then went out and bought a pack. It took me two more years to quit smoking again.

An engine shutdown in the middle of the ocean seldom results in an accident, but it sure does raise the tension in the cockpit. In this case Starr couldn't blame it on Sam.

STARR THOMPSON: We came out of Chateauroux, France, in a Connie and went into Shannon for a fuel stop. While there we stocked up on Christmas booze in the duty free store, then went steamin' across the Atlantic. Andy Frampton was my copilot, Russ Vendini my engineer and Zimmerman was the navigator. Russ noticed that the #4 propeller was hunting a little bit, about a hundred RPM back and forth, so he brought it to my attention. I thought it might be the feeder spring in the governor 'cause I had that happen before.

We climbed to ten thousand feet and leveled off between layers. It was a nice moonlight night and everything was going pretty good. Just as we reached equal time point between Shannon and Gander, the #4 engine exploded and caught fire, lighting up the whole sky. It took about seven seconds to close throttle, mixture, firewall shut off, and shoot the fire bottle.

The fire went out. Then the panic was over, and we went to retard on the spark and auto rich and so on. We couldn't hold ten thousand feet on three engines, so we had to make a drift down. Now we were burning more fuel on three than we had been on four. We went down to six thousand feet before we could hold altitude. But now our problem was compounded because we were in the clouds and picking up a load of ice. It was one of those nights when you wished you were sitting in front of the fireplace in Alabama or someplace.

We rode that out until we got light enough (from burning off fuel) to go back to advanced spark and auto lean. Then we started making fuel (burning less per mile traveled). We were drivin' along, and old Andy Frampton was getting' a little antsy.

CHAPTER 24   TIGER TALES   251

I said, "Look, just think of it as going from Newark to Chicago. How long does that take in a Connie? Two and a half hours?"

"Yes, I guess so."

We ground along for another hour, and ol' Andy, who had a dry sense of humor, looked at me and said, "Ain't we ever going to get to Chicago?"

That broke the ice, and we all relaxed a little. We landed in Gander at dawn after five hours and eighteen minutes on three engines. Some of our Christmas booze didn't make it home. We went right to the hotel and drank a fifth of Scotch.

On December 14 in Japan we received the news that yet another of our Connies, 13 Charlie, had crashed on approach to the Burbank Airport in California. They were in heavy fog and crashed a mile and a quarter short of the runway. The captain was Karl Rader, the copilot, David L. Crapo, and the flight engineer was Jack Grey.

Also aboard was John Olson, the husband of Janet Olson, the long time head of crew scheduling.

The tragic end of 13C

The autopsy showed that the captain had severe coronary disease, and may have suffered a heart attack. Accident investigators believe he may have fallen forward on the controls making a successful recovery by the copilot unlikely. There were no survivors.

That was our worst year ever, and it would be fair to say that we all held our breath until the year came to a close.

CHAPTER 25   FLYING LESSONS?   1963

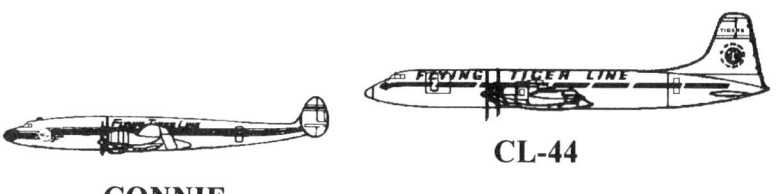

CONNIE   CL-44

We had a lot of military passenger flights out of Tachikawa, but the runway was so short that we couldn't put enough fuel on the CL-44 to make Elmendorf, Alaska. So we loaded the passengers at Tachikawa, then they flew over to Haneda Airport in Tokyo to fuel up.

One morning when the marshaller parked them on the ramp in Haneda, the left wing tip clipped a light pole.

I was on duty at Tachikawa, so our mechanic in Haneda called me. I told him to remove the wing tip, and that a CL-44 freighter had just arrived in Tachikawa and I'd send him the one off of it. It was quickly removed and I sent it and a mechanic to Haneda Airport in a taxi.

They installed the good wing tip and the passenger flight departed. Now the mechanic brought the damaged wing tip back with him. I inspected it and found no damage beyond the first rib. I had them cut off the damaged metal, form and rivet a patch over the end and install the navigation light.

While they were doing that, I wired Burbank and asked them to contact Canadair (who built the airplane) and get approval for my temporary repair. The approval came just as the mechanic finished installing the wing tip. His workmanship was so professional that I hated to tell to tell him he had put the navigation light on backwards.

We had enough help at Tachikawa now and could enjoy life a little more, but the forms of recreation available to us were limited. We did travel about the country sightseeing, but most of our free time was at the Civilian Club or some of the watering holes in town.

No one had access to a telephone, unless they lived at a hotel. Most people did not, on a permanent basis, because of the cost. So we devised a plan.

After each airplane departed from our base, at least one person with transportation would stop at the Dew Drop Inn, in Tachikawa. The agent on duty could then call there if he received a message that the airplane was returning. This didn't happen very often, but if a plane had any kind of serious problem and did come back, maintenance personnel had to be there.

Before long we were all stopping there. Equal time point was approximately four hours after departure so, except for the guy on duty, happy hour became several hours. It is the best excuse we ever had to hang out in a bar. Mama-San had a small T.V., and we soon got hooked on Sumo wrestling. Taiho, as I recall, was the hero of that time.

I felt like I was wasting too much of my free time and needed something a little more constructive to do. We had a radio man, Paul Hegstadt, who had been taking flying lessons at Chofu Air Station about ten miles from Tachikawa. It was an army post that had some small observation planes and also had a Flying Club. This was just what I was looking for.

I went to Chofu, joined the Flying Club, and had my first lesson in a Cessna 150. The flight instructor took me out to the Cessna, and after he explained how everything worked, we climbed into the airplane.

CHAPTER 25   TIGER TALES

He said, "What do you do for a living?"

"I'm an aircraft maintenance supervisor for Flying Tigers."

"Well, you already know all this stuff then. Just go ahead and take off."

I may have known "all this stuff," but I sure didn't know how to fly. I released the brakes and opened the throttle. When we reached about fifty miles an hour, I eased back on the controls and the airplane lifted off gently. Just as I was beginning to congratulate myself, the pilot's side window flew open with a loud bang, and the rush of air was deafening. As I let go of the controls to close the window, the airplane nose began to rise at about the same rate the airspeed was going down. I knew that wouldn't do, so I let go of the window and pushed the control forward to get the nose down where it belonged.

I shouted to the instructor, "Fly this thing till I get the window closed!"

I thought he'd be upset with me, but instead he seemed pleased.

He said, "That was your first in-flight emergency."

I didn't like the way he'd said, "first emergency," but it was also the last time I took off without checking that the doors and windows were closed.

It turns out I was not the only Tiger who was learning to fly.

ANN MARIE PRESCOTT: I flew quite often with Paul Kelly[1] in the Aero-Commander twin, so I thought I should

---

[1] Paul Kelly was the company executive pilot. He was an older man who had flown for Chennault in China after the AVG disbanded.

learn to fly, to be sure I could at least set the plane on the ground in case Paul should have a heart attack or something.

I took lessons from an instructor at Coffin Flying Service at Whiteman Air Park in Pacoima.

I asked him, "How do you spell that name?"

He said, "Just like it sounds."

I was afraid of that. As we taxied out in a Cessna 172 he said, "Let's pass that Piper Cub ahead of us on the taxiway. Give it the go."

He didn't say to open the throttle or anything, just "give it the go."

Well this is going to be interesting, I thought.

He was also a bit of a dirty old man. We were barely in the air before he was feeling me up, so I said, "Could we practice some takeoffs and landings?"

I wanted to be near the ground in case he got too close.

After the third lesson I told Bob, "I don't trust this guy too much. Get me another instructor."

Back to my own flying. I was having so much fun I almost hated to go on vacation, but it is just as well that I did. I would probably have had to go to Saigon.

ED HALE, maintenance: Bill Curran and I went from Burbank to Saigon to change a CL-44 engine, and we also had to change the anti-icing ring on the nose cowl. It had somehow shorted out and burned up, throwing pieces into the engine, which caused it to fail.

The only equipment we could find to lift the propeller and engine was an old A-frame type thing that Air Viet Nam had. It was about 16 feet high and had a huge chain hoist on it. It was towed over to the airplane, and we lifted off the propeller and lowered it to the ground. Then we

CHAPTER 25   TIGER TALES   257

hooked the A-frame to the engine sling, but now the tug was in use somewhere else, and we couldn't move the A-frame and engine away from the airplane.

Bill borrowed a big tug from Air France and pushed the airplane back, away from the A-frame. So far so good. We lowered the old engine and hoisted the new one up in the A-frame, but now an Air France flight had come in and they had left with the tug. Now we had no way to move either the airplane or the A frame.

Bill left again and soon returned with the most God-awful thing I ever saw. It was some kind of a high-wheeled tractor that must have been used in the rice paddies. Its rear wheels were about seven feet high, and it had a two-cylinder diesel engine, which shook the whole thing when it idled. It was all we had, so we had to make it work. We managed to get the engine and propeller installed without any damage, except to our nerves.

While Ed and Bill were vacationing in the Pearl of the Orient, Saigon, I took a month off and returned to the States for a vacation. While there, I went down to the Flying Tiger hangar to visit, then went upstairs to talk to Bill Thompson. I was going to ask him when my 30 days would be up, but I didn't get the chance.

He said, "There's going to be a big buildup in the South Pacific due to the Viet Nam war heating up, and we'll have to put people on more stations than in the past. Tokyo is too far away, and it takes too long to get maintenance people where they're needed. Would you like to move to the Philippines and try to cover the South Pacific stations from there?"

"Yes I would. I've been thinking along those lines. Jimmy Bracket and I could take turns riding on the flights to Saigon and Bangkok. We can cover the flights that way for now. If you put on more flights, we'll need more help." (Jimmy lived in the Philippines and worked for us.)

As soon as we returned to Tachikawa, I was transferred to Clark Air Base in the Philippines.

Gene Huntington was the Tiger station manager and Ernie Miranda was his assistant.

After renting a house and getting moved in, I went looking for transportation. New cars had to be ordered, and delivery could take several months. Ernie took me to downtown Angeles where I bought a 1949 Studebaker Commander. It was getting old, but was still reliable. I drove it for about a year.

I noticed an aero club just off the main road to Clark Field, but I never saw any planes flying. One day I stopped in and found that they had two good Filipino mechanics, but no one with an F.A.A. mechanic's license to sign off the maintenance paperwork. I became the maintenance officer for the club, and soon had two airplanes flying, then I decided to take flying lessons myself.

This wasn't easy because I had to spend so much time away from home to cover flights in Saigon and Bangkok.

During one such stay in Saigon, I was invited to an embassy party. Any Americans or Europeans who happen to be in town are always in demand for these functions. The excuse for a party this time was a going away dinner for a Philippine gangster who was being deported for smuggling. I was picked up at the Caravel Hotel in an embassy car and driven to a Chinese restaurant on the outskirts of town. It was a fancy place built over the water.

CHAPTER 25   TIGER TALES   259

The meal was a seven-course Chinese affair and it was excellent. I don't remember everything, but there was peanut soup, lobster, Peking duck, chicken with almonds, sweet and sour pork and more Scotch whiskey than I really needed to wash it all down.

The gangster's girlfriend sat on my left and he sat across the table from her. She was apparently very upset because he was not taking her with him. While we talked and drank, she reached down and held my hand under the table. I didn't mind that a whole lot, but suddenly, with no warning, she jerked both our hands high in the air, so he could see we were holding hands under the table.

I don't know what reaction she expected, but he just gave her a look that said he was done with her and didn't give a damn what she did. I was sure relieved to see that. I could have been found in the Saigon River by morning. I didn't want anything to do with her either, but I couldn't leave until the embassy cars did.

Back in the Philippines I flew every chance I got, and soon had my private pilot's license. No use stopping now, I began preparing for my commercial license.

They say it ain't over till the fat lady sings. Chuck was there when she sang.

CHUCK HAMMER, flight engineer: I was on a CL-44 passenger flight over the middle of the Pacific on our way home, when a stewardess came up to the cockpit and said, "We have a problem with one of the toilets."

That happened quite often, because the passengers threw a lot of junk in them. I would go back with the long screwdriver I used to check the fuel tank drip sticks, and I'd rummage that around and get the toilet working.

This time when I went back to see what the problem was the navigator, who was a helpful type of guy, followed me back to see if he could be of assistance. Here was this huge woman sitting on the can and she couldn't get off. What had happened was, the cap had come off the holding tank, so now the cabin pressure, being greater than that in the tank, was forcing her onto that stool. She couldn't get off, and she was moanin', groanin', screamin' and raisin' all kind o' hell.

The only thing I could think of was to depressurize the airplane, until we could get her off the can, then repressurize. So, I went back to the cockpit to tell the captain what I found and what I wanted to do. The captain notified the passengers that we were going to depressurize the cabin, and that the oxygen masks would drop down but there was no reason for them to get excited. "Just put the masks on and breathe until we tell you to put them back."

In the meantime the navigator took my long screwdriver and tried to pry the lady off the stool. She was beating on him because she didn't like any of his choices of prying points. With all the noise she was making, the navigator didn't hear the captain's announcement.

I reached up and flipped the switch, and <u>boom</u>!—the pressure was gone. This woman had both hands on the doorsill trying to get off the can, and the navigator was right in front of her trying to pry her off when the pressure released. She came flying off the can and knocked him right on his butt, then they both rolled down the aisle. We had to put him in the hospital for rug burns, sprains and what have you. We never saw that lady again.

CHAPTER 26   SAIGON VIET NAM   1964

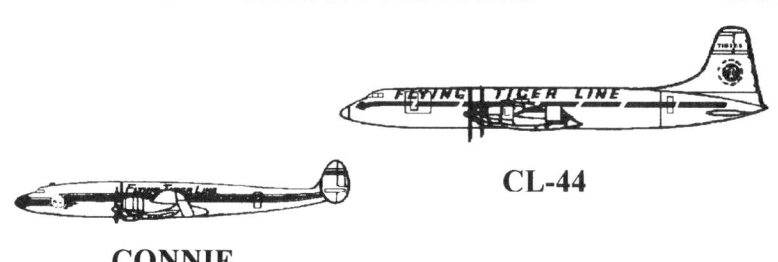

CL-44

CONNIE

Tigers had developed a sizable commercial business in Manila, in addition to the military passenger and cargo operations at Clark Field. It could take two hours to drive from Clark to Manila to cover a flight. In June the Aero Club bought a Cessna 180, a fast four-place airplane. Quite often I used it to haul parts to Manila for the CL-44. Once I had to remove the back seat so I could carry a main-gear wheel assembly.

Frank Graff landed at Clark and overheated all four brakes on the left side. After he parked the airplane, the thermal fuse plugs melted, and all four tires went flat. If that had happened in Manila, it would have taken four trips in the Cessna 180.

GOLDY: Frank Graff was bringing a CL-44 passenger flight in from Anchorage to Travis. It is said that Frank never landed the CL-44. He arrived. It was a hard airplane to land and Frank gave up trying. He just let it crash. I was deadheading on the airplane and Curly Olson was the copilot. Of course Curly was riding Frank unmercifully.

When Curly made the arrival announcement for Travis, he told the passengers to prepare for the their worst landing ever. Of course this time Frank was trying his best, but it didn't help. It was indeed the worst landing one could make without breaking the airplane.

Roy "Curly" Olson wrote the following poem for the flight attendants on his crew after a long international trip which included a layover in Honolulu.

COCKPIT TO GALLEY

We didn't get lei-ed, and 'tis sad that we are,
But we also wish to announce,
We can't always be as we wish,
And we accept the ball's bitter ol' bounce.

Perhaps not deserving is the way we should feel,
But honestly gals, we have tried,
To be gentle and loving and tender and good
Now evident-lax effort applied.

Some time in the future, not too far away,
We will meet again as crew,
And then, Mary and Betty and little Diane,
We will show you just what we can do.

There will be parties, gaiety and laughter and fun,
And dinners and dances galore,
And the tab for this fancy array of good times,
Will be paid by the front office four.

Some girls, suspicious, might happen to think,
Here is a danger in disguise,
But we can assure you it just isn't so,
We're harmless, just sweet little guys.

by Captain Roy Olson

CHAPTER 26   TIGER TALES

Back at Clark field, Gene Huntington, the station manager, left about this time and Frank Marble took over. He and Ernie Miranda, his able assistant, had their hands full too, especially when we had flights in Clark and Manila at the same time.

My next trip to Saigon was a little unusual. When we arrived, the weather was below minimums, so after circling in a holding pattern for an hour, we went to Na Trang, South Vietnam, for fuel. Before landing, we asked if they had an air starter on the field and were assured that they did. If they had not, we would have gone somewhere else, since an air starter is required to start a turbine engine. After landing and getting refueled, we found out that they were mistaken; there was no air starter on the field.

Dobbie was the captain and, fortunately for us, he had served in World War II with a pilot who was now the Na Trang Air Base commander. When he became aware of our plight, the commander had a starter unit flown from Saigon to Na Trang in a C-130. By the time it arrived, the weather in Saigon had cleared so we continued our trip.

The buildup in Viet Nam was increasing, and Jimmy Brackett and I had so many flights that we couldn't keep up any longer. R. C. "Andy" Anderson came out to take over the Bangkok station. I spent so much time in Saigon that I shared rental on a house with an Air America Rep., Rick Delman. One day he showed up with a big grin on his face and a Thompson submachine gun under his arm.

I said, "Where the hell did you get that and what are you going to do with it?"

"I bought it from a Tiger agent, John Schoumaker. We won't have to worry about the V. C. (Viet Cong) now!"

I was more worried about him.

Wouldn't you know it, while I was ducking machine guns and dodging hand grenades in the Far East, these guys were having a ball in West Palm Beach.

DOUG SHAW: These were the times of the great air shows by the "Tigers" during the Connie days in West Palm Beach, Florida. Joe Bower and Sy Goro were the maintenance reps and I was the Operations rep based in West Palm Beach in 1964. Tigers was operating passenger charters from New York to the Bahamas on Fridays and then ferrying to Palm Beach for layover. On Sunday, the aircraft would ferry back to Westend and Freeport to pick up the passengers and return to New York.

The ferrying of the flights presented several opportunities for some "out of the norm" flying, such as buzzing the crew hotel at departure. I sometimes received calls from the local police saying the citizenry was complaining of the noise. No one could ever say the Wright R-3350 engine was whisper quiet, especially at low altitude.

On this particular layover, we had Captains Jim Alexander, Frank "the hawk" Hawkins and Dick Rossi. I understand that a little wager had been placed as to who was the better pilot and could best buzz the hotel. Joe, Sy and myself heard about the competition that was to take place that Sunday. If we stood on top of a fuel truck, we could just see the Monte Cristo Hotel area.

Jim was the first to depart and we could see him make his pass. The next was Frank and he was slightly lower than Jim in his pass. The last was Rossi, and we lost sight of him below the tree line!!

CHAPTER 26　　　TIGER TALES

The next weekend, we heard that Jim made his pass at 500 feet. Frank was 250 feet above the ocean surface, and was sure he had won until he saw Rossi pass under him! I can't attest to the accuracy of the report as I didn't see it, but that is what we were told by (I think) Jim...

In thinking about the Palm Beach assignment, I'm sure I'll always remember Sy Goro and his poodle "Baron". Baron went everywhere with Sy and I think probably knew as much about the Connie as Sy did, perhaps more. I can recall Sy asking Baron if he thought the problem was a bad PRT or if the coil and plugs should be changed.

I don't recall Baron ever answering, but he and Sy seem to have their own communication link.

The flight attendants weren't wasting their time either. While splashing around the pond, they could have been up to their bikinis in alligators.

DOUG SHAW: I had been advised that the flight attendants in town were to have a wet ditching exercise during their weekend layover and that a raft was being sent.

I spoke to the airport manager and he had no problem with our conducting the exercise as there were several small ponds on the airport and one of them was suitable.

Joe and I drove to the selected pond and Joe suddenly exclaimed, "There's an alligator in the pond!"

I was doubtful, but I stopped the car and sure enough, there was an alligator sunning himself (herself?) beside the pond.

I had my doubts that I would ever get the flight attendants in a pond with an alligator in it and went to talk to the airport manager.

His response was, "Oh, don't worry, that's only old Fred and we will have the prisoner work gang (they still had work gangs in Florida at the time) come down on the exercise day and drive him away from the pond.

On the appropriate day, the work gang showed up and herded good old Fred away from the pond. I alerted the flight attendants and coordinated their pick up at the hotel Monte Cristo. Joe inflated the raft and the exercise was successfully completed.

I never told the girls about the alligator.

THE SWING TAIL THAT WOULDN'T

ED HALE, station manager: While I was stationed in Kadena, Okinawa, I had a CL-44 passenger flight arrive so, of course, we were parked on the passenger ramp for unloading. Then we converted the airplane to a freighter. We opened the swing tail, took all the rails and cargo tie-downs out of the bellies, then stored all the seats and galleys in the bellies. When we were done, the tail would not close.

We tried every trick in the book and a few that weren't. The tail refused to move. That evening the military had a passenger flight coming in and wanted our airplane moved. We were not supposed to move the airplane with the tail unlocked, but the military was getting very upset.

I told our mechanics, "Hook up the tug. We'll move this contrary son-of-a-bitch anyway."

When the airplane was positioned on the cargo ramp, the tail closed with no problem.

Now if we could just get the landing gear down...

ART GORHAM, flight engineer: Doug Buskey was the captain and Buck Waldo, the copilot, on this trip to Detroit. It was in the middle of the night, like it always seems to be when you go to Detroit. The flight was uneventful un-

CHAPTER 26   TIGER TALES   267

til we put the gear handle down and the left main gear wouldn't lock down. We had quite a lot of fuel on board so we flew over to Ypsilanti, Michigan, which had a searchlight in the tower. They advised, "The gear is hanging down and looks like it's on tiptoes." We knew that meant the bogie had not rotated and the gear was not locked down. We also could not retract the gear, so would have to land with the nose and right mains down.

While we flew around for a while, burning off some fuel, Buskey pulled out some of those smelly crooked black cigars he used to smoke. I think Buck even had one. When we went in and landed, it went pretty good.

Doug put the airplane down on the right gear and held the left wing up as long as he could. As we rolled out Buck said, "Hell this ain't nothin'."

Doug said, "Shut up, we're not stopped yet!"

About then the left wing settled down on the runway, destroying the left props and flaps. We slid down the runway pretty good, but at the last minute the left wing caught some runway lights and swung the airplane around.

When the airplane was raised with a crane, we found that the problem had been caused by the failure of the gear downlock housing. After the left props and flaps were replaced the plane was flown, gear down, to Burbank for permanent repairs.

As I recall, that was the only gear failure we ever had on the Canadair. It was difficult to consistently make good landings in the CL-44. In fact a few pilots never made any. As a result one might expect some landing gear problems, but not so. I have always suspected that the guy who engineered the landing gear sat next to the guy who designed the flight control system. Each time he looked over at the design, he added more strength to the gear.

Bill didn't have a gear problem, in fact he didn't know he had a problem.

BILL SQUIRES: I'd just come in from a long trip, so I had breakfast and flopped down on the couch and went to sleep.

When I woke up my wife was standing over me with her hands on her hips.

She said, "Are you keeping something from me?"
I said, "Well no."
"You're not telling me something?"
"No."
You know how a fellow would react to a question like that. Then as I woke up I thought, wait a minute, I really am innocent. How could I be in bad trouble?

Finally she laughed and said, "While you were sleeping, Dick Riemer called to say you had gotten a captain's bid."

Much to my surprise, I got it, got trained and checked out. Of course that meant I was off to Newark, New Jersey, where all junior captains have to go.

Back at Clark Field once again, on December 24 I was issued my commercial pilot's license. My celebration was cut short by the news that also on December 24 one of our Connies, 15 Charlie, had crashed. It had been on departure from San Francisco International Airport when it struck a hilltop near San Bruno. The crew was Captain J. Richards, Copilot Dan Hennessy and Flight Engineer Paul Entz. There were no survivors.

The flight was scheduled out at 9 p.m., but apparently the flight engineer had gone on sick leave. There were no engineers available in San Francisco, so they called Paul Entz in Los Angeles. Paul was not scheduled to fly, but though it meant giving up Christmas with his family, he agreed to take the flight.

The weather was rain and fog with high winds from the southwest, causing moderate to severe turbulence near the foothills.

The flight departed runway 28L at 12:28 a.m. Instead of going straight out through the Gap (the 287 radial), for some reason they turned sixty degrees to the left.

The crew suspected something was wrong with the instruments because they called departure control and asked, "How do you have us tracking toward the Gap?"

The controller, who had not been monitoring the departure, switched his scope from the 30 to the 10-mile range and asked their altitude. They replied nine hundred.

The controller then said, "Nine hundred, roger, it shows you going directly out on the...well, you're left of course, of the San Francisco 287 Radial."

There was no further communication from the aircraft. They struck the hill at 12:31:30, three and one half minutes after takeoff. The aircraft disintegrated on impact.

A faulty switching mechanism in the navigation system was the suspected cause of the heading error. As I recall, it was determined after the investigation, that proper monitoring by the controller could have prevented the crash.

When you get five pilots together, especially these five, the results are bound to be unpredictable to say the least.

RON WAY: Five of us, Bob Zalusky, Dave Wilson, Mel Ports, Tony Clasens and myself got together and rented a top floor apartment in Newark, New Jersey. It was in a nice new building with a view overlooking the projects.

The rooms were modern with lots of glass, so the first question was, who would wash the windows?

We were all afraid of heights, and it being twenty floors down to the parking lot, no one wanted to get that close to the windows. We played odd man out and, fortunately for us, rank and seniority only count in the cockpit, because Ski (Captain Zalusky) lost, so he washed the windows.

Later Mel Ports won a West Coast bid, so he asked us if we would see that his car got put on the airplane. He had a little hopped up Fiat sports car. We said sure, so Tony and I went out to put it on a pallet and tie it down.

Instead of pushing it onto the pallet, we decided to start it up and drive it on. The engine backfired and caught fire. Tony and I were running around like chickens with their heads cut off looking for a fire extinguisher. We found a huge one on steel wheels about three feet high. We were rolling it toward the car while Oakley Smith leaned against the hangar wall, laughing his guts out. We got the fire out and the car shipped to California. Mel had to figure out how to get it running.

Humor from the "Friendly Fighter Pilot" Wayne Peake:

DON HASSIG: Wayne Peake was chief pilot in LAX, and Jack Martin was the system chief pilot. I was in Wayne's office one day a few weeks after we got the first Boeing 707, and he said, "I'm going to be checked out on the 707 next winter."

"How do you know that?"

"I asked Jack Martin when I'd be checked out, and he said, that'll be a cold day…so that must mean next winter."

CHAPTER 27   BACK TO BURBANK   1965

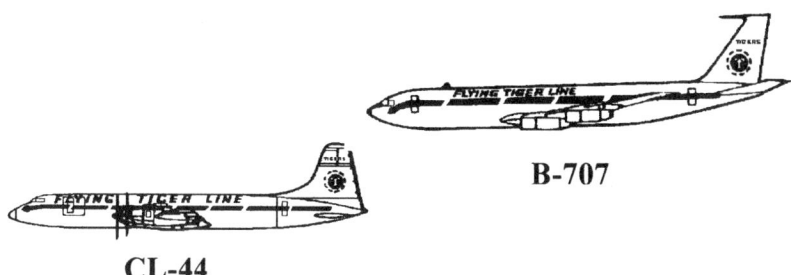

A number of people made career moves during the year. In April Ed Hale and his family returned to the States from Okinawa. Ed went back on the flight line in Burbank for a while, and then moved into the inspection department.

One night in Clark Field I wished I were in Burbank, too. A CL-44 had arrived from Bangkok with a serious fuel problem. When the crew tried to transfer fuel, the fuel in the transfer line went into the #4 main fuel tank. When we began to refuel the airplane, the same thing happened. We couldn't shut off the fuel to the #4 tank.

Now began one of the most trying times I ever had as a mechanic. I had to go into the tank, find and fix the problem. This wasn't easy. First we had to drain the tank of jet fuel. While the fuel was draining, I disconnected the aileron torque-tubes aft of the #4 tank to reach the wing access plate. After removing about fifty screws to remove the plate, I crawled inside the wing just outboard of the fuel tank.

When I looked in the maintenance manual for specific instructions, I found a warning that stated, "Do not use tools made of ferrous metal, because of the danger of sparks causing an explosion!"

I'm quite sure there was not a single nonferrous tool in all of Southeast Asia so I could forget that. Next I had to come up with some means of breathing while in the tank. I found an old air compressor. It seemed to pump about as much oil as it did air, but I taped the hose of a crew smoke mask to the end of the compressor's air hose with duct tape. The combination of the heat and humidity in the Philippines caused the mask to immediately fog up so I could hardly see at all.

After posting a Filipino mechanic on the ladder so he could pull me out if I lost consciousness, I tied a rope around my waist and I crawled inside the wing. Now I was ready to go to work. I removed about 100 screws then took off the fuel tank access door and set it aside. When I looked in the tank with a flashlight, I could see a three-inch aluminum fuel line elbow that had come off.

I had to crawl about 12 feet through the fuel tank to reach the elbow, and then try to reform the bead and replace the clamps. When this was done I backed slowly toward the door, making sure I didn't leave anything behind. In so doing, I backed right into the door, which fell over with a resounding crash.

After several seconds I realized the fuel tank had not exploded and I was still alive, so I crawled out of the tank into the dry part of the wing. I carefully installed the door and all 100 screws. I sure didn't intend to go back in there again. When I was done, I crawled over to the ladder to find there was no one there.

I was sick to my stomach and very weak-kneed as I walked away from the airplane. I took off my fuel-soaked clothes and sat down on the ground in the dark. I was completely exhausted.

When a mechanic came over I asked, "Where in the hell is the safety man I had posted?"

CHAPTER 27　　　TIGER TALES

"Oh, he became very sick from the fumes and had to go home."

It's just as well that he wasn't there. I was too tired to wring his neck anyway. I don't mind admitting that I was scared all the while I was inside that tank. Doing a dangerous job like that without proper equipment doesn't make one a hero, it's just something that has to be done. You don't ask someone else to do it for you. If you don't want any risks, then maybe selling shoes would be a better career choice.

The worst part of all this was that the next time that aircraft went to Bangkok, the elbow blew off again and Andy Anderson had to go in the tank and do the job over. He took the elbow out and went to a machine shop and had a new bead formed on it.

Come to find out the re-fueling pipes in Bangkok ran a very long distance underground and used more pressure than most airport systems. I understand there were no further problems after they reduced the pressure.

Back in Clark Field my pilot training had hit a snag. I had no books available when I took the written test for my private pilot's license, but I passed it anyway with a good score. I tried that again when I got my commercial license and just passed by the skin of my teeth. When I took the written test for the instrument rating I flunked badly. I had to have a book.

I mentioned it to Captain Bill Franklin and on his next trip he brought me an instrument course including charts and everything I needed. This time I knew what I was doing, and I passed the test. By March I was ready for my instrument check ride, but now the only F.A.A. examiner in the South Pacific was on vacation in the States. In July he returned to Manila, and I passed the check ride and got my instrument rating.

Bob Baird already had his.

BOB BAIRD: I had just completed three years as an ATC Controller with the FAA and I was eager to go anywhere to fly airplanes. In March of 1965 I had taken a job with an outfit called LAVCO to fly DC-3s based in North Africa. That should show how badly I wanted to fly.

I needed to store my car and gear with my mother in San Diego so I loaded up and headed south from San Francisco. I stopped at a coffee shop in Burlingame for lunch, picked up a paper to read, and automatically turned to the help-wanted section scanning under "A" for Aviation.

There was a nice ad stating the Flying Tiger Line was looking for pilots. Well I knew a little about this airline as I had seen their aircraft in and out of Honolulu when living there as a kid, and also working the boards on them at Oakland Center.

I decided to give them a call and was told by the Chief Pilot's secretary that it would take a week or so after submitting the paperwork to get an interview. I explained that in a week I would be enroute to Amsterdam to check out on a DC-3, and asked if they could make an exception?

She told me to hang on a minute, came back on the line and said they were doing a group of interviews right now and if I could come straight over I might get in. I was there within 15 minutes.

Dorothy Burke was the ladies name and she was a legend with the pilots of the FTL. She showed me down the hall on the second deck of the Tiger hangar and told me to take a seat with three other fellows that were sitting there outside the Chief Pilot's office. These guy's were all USAF pilots from Travis AFB near Fairfield, California, and all

CHAPTER 27   TIGER TALES   275

were four-engine qualified with several thousand hours of heavy time. Bummer, I thought, as I had 460 hours, all single engine, and a month-old instrument rating, not much chance here but what the heck!

After about an hour all the others were gone and the Chief Pilot called me in. As I entered the office a slim, trim, dapper looking gentleman rose from behind the desk and offered me his hand.

"I'm Don Sanders," he said, "Chief Pilot here in San Francisco."

I introduced myself and we got down to business with me showing him my logbook, pilots ratings, work history and a little about myself personally. He was quiet throughout most of this, asking a few questions related to my flying, and studied my logbook page by page.

"You don't have a whole lot of time here do you," he said indicating the log.

"No sir, I don't, it's darn hard to come by," I replied.

"Well, you do have one thing in your favor," he said, "Your ATC background is good, and you know for the first year you will be doing a lot of just talking on the radio and copying clearances anyhow!"

"Fine with me,"

Then he said, "What I like about your time in this log is it all looks good, I get a lot of young guys coming through here with a ton of P-51 time as in Parker Pen time, none or little of it real."

Don then told me he couldn't hire me on the spot as he would send his recommendations down to Headquarters in Burbank and they would make the cut there in about two weeks.

I now explained my other job and where I would be in a week. He asked if I could stall on going to Amsterdam, but there was no way I could do that.

I said, "I might then lose that job and if Tigers didn't take me I'd be out in the cold."

"Well Bob", he said, "I'm going to recommend we hire you and we will see what happens from there!"

I left the hangar feeling real good about the interview and headed on down to San Diego. Two days later the phone rang and it was a gal from Tigers in Burbank. She wanted to know if I could start a class in Burbank in three weeks time for a copilots position on the 1049H Connie.

I of course said YES and after getting the details, hung up, then called LAVCO and quit that job on the spot. Their reply is another story but no need to go into that. Three weeks later I was in Burbank, in school, and on my way to 25-years with the greatest airline to fly for in the world, bar none, the Flying Tiger Line.

By the way, none of the USAF pilots made the cut!

We had innumerable flights carrying troops into and out of Viet Nam. The flight attendants will never forget those special passengers.

"WE REMEMBER"
by

Linda Foster, flight attendant: Cam Ranh Bay, Danang, Saigon, five and a half hours down. You open the forward door; it was like walking into a blast furnace. The PAX all craning for their first look at "The Nam."

The Passengers: boys really—tough talk, comic books and loud laughter. You'd have thought they were going away to camp, except the truth was always there in their eyes and in the shaking of their hands. We cried some; we wrote to some, we kissed them all goodbye. Remember?

Then we loaded back up. The good part: bringing them out. Doing our Demo while the cabin temperature

CHAPTER 27 TIGER TALES 277

inched up to 120 plus. Our mascara ran, our hair frizzed, our in-flights were soaked with sweat.

But the guys didn't seem to mind. They were just so glad to be there, so grateful to be going home. The cheer they let out on takeoff was ear splitting, a roar of triumph and relief. You could actually feel their joy and it was impossible not to laugh. Remember?

Then a five and a half hour flight back. Plenty of time to clean. Clean the trays, clean the floors, clean the ovens, clean the coffee makers, clean the aft coat closet, and clean the lavs.

Hit Yokota running. Debrief in the never-empty lobby, and then collapse? Not us. We're just in time for Go-Go night! Remember?

A special time, those Viet Nam days. A nonstop party occasionally interrupted by heart-wrenching, backbreaking work. And in sharing that time we became more than fellow workers, more than friends. We became a family, remember?

By the fall of '65 we had more maintenance stations and more help in Viet Nam. I believe Frank Riggins was in Saigon, Bob O'Brian in Danang and Dave McElroy in Cam Ranh Bay.

My original 30-day agreement had now stretched to four years, and I thought that was about enough, so I informed the company that I wanted to return to California. I arrived in Burbank four years to the month from the time I left and returned to the flight line as a lead mechanic.

In November one of our more memorable jobs was to prepare a Boeing 707 fitted with extra fuel tanks for a record-setting flight around the world from pole to pole. The plane was called the "Pole Cat", of course. The flight took

62 hours and 28 minutes. At the time we were not aware of the events in Palm Springs.

ANN MARIE PRESCOTT: Tigers filled a Boeing 707 with extra fuel tanks and were going to make a nonstop flight around the world, leaving that day. Bob and I had attended an Air Show in Palm Springs, and after we saw Bob off, I took Peter, Bob's son, to our house in Palm Springs where I fixed him something to eat, then drove him back to the airport, so he could ride the Lear Jet back to Los Angeles.

Besides Peter, there were several prominent people aboard the Lear Jet. George Alexander, who was in the real estate business and actually started a big part of the Palm Springs development, his wife and son and daughter-in-law-were all on board. Bob knew George because they both had been regulars at the Golden Door. Bob called him the king of the Golden Horde. He was a very sweet man.

Dick Koret, a manufacturer of fine luggage, was there and then there was the pilot, Paul Kelly, and a copilot, a total of eight people.

I was very close to George Alexander because he was a constant guest at the Golden Door, you know. I drove home. It was a rain-slicked night, and just as I came to the house in Palm Springs and opened the garage door, I heard a voice. It was so distinctively George Alexander and I thought how in the world did he get out of the airplane and come up here? Then I went around all over the house, and he wasn't there. So I said, "Something has happened."

I called the Burbank Tower, which was about 30 minutes away from there, to monitor when they come in. That was about seven o'clock. I was totally aware at that moment that something had gone wrong. Then I heard on the radio that someone had seen a light, an explosion of some kind over the mountain. I tied it together, and I felt so desperate.

I stayed in touch with Sheldon Appel who was the closest relative to the Alexanders. Then, as that night unfolded and they never arrived, we assumed that they had crashed.

Bob was informed of the accident when his plane landed in Honolulu, so he returned on the next flight to California. Of course the plane and the rest of the crew went on and completed the Polar flight.

But I'll tell you what it did to Bob, I mean; it was the most traumatic experience of his life. Peter was his only son and all his hopes, you know, on whatever he hoped Peter would be. So it was devastating for him. It was unbelievable, because it was his only son.

You know, Kelly was about 65 years old and it was too fast an airplane for him. And you know the Lear is a very very fast plane. So I think the conclusion was pilot error. I don't think there was anything wrong with the plane.

The company was still hiring new copilots, and since I now had the qualifications, I applied for the job. They politely informed me that I was too old. The age limit was 29 and I was 35. Oh well, that's life, I thought. I should have started flying sooner. Anyway, I had a good job with ten years of seniority.

Most new copilots had to go to Newark, our east coast domicile.

BOB BAIRD: I went to Newark, New Jersey, for Connie copilot training. We had finished our ground school at Burbank and most of my class was assigned to the East Coast. I was pretty impressed by the size of the 1049H

Connie. The biggest airplanes I had flown in the past were single engine with fixed landing gear.

Oakley Smith was the chief pilot there and had the dubious pleasure of checking out the new guys. The first couple of flights were okay as most of the work was done by the flight engineer. Then we got down to some serious instrument work under the hood. The VOR and ILS stuff went well then we started on ADF approaches.

I chased the needle around for a while and when my missed approach time came, Oakley said, "Look outside."

I didn't see an airport anywhere. Oakley sort of pointed off to the right and behind and said he thought it was over there somewhere.

He asked me, "How many ADF approaches have you done?" "About three, six months ago."

Lucky for me, there were a couple of other guys not up to speed on ADF approaches either, so Oakley arranged for us to go over to Eastern Airlines to use their flight simulator.

It wasn't much more than a glorified big Link trainer, and it was set up as a Martin 404 cockpit. It did the job though. We each did nothing but ADF approaches in that thing for two days then went back to the Connie for a check ride, which we all passed.

A lesser man than Oakley Smith probably would have sent us packing. Thanks Oakley.

On the night of December 15, another Connie, 14 Charlie, crashed into a mountain near Alamosa, Colorado. The crew was Captain Pete Reed, Copilot Thomas Hunt and Flight Engineer Brian Ferris.

They were flight planned on Victor 210, an air route that is a straight line from Farmington, New Mexico, east to Alamosa, Colorado, and on to Lamar. The airplane was too heavy to climb to the minimum altitude required for the segment between Farmington and Alamosa, so they took Victor 210 South, which is lower. Now they crossed Alamosa heading northeast and should have made a right turn to follow V 210 to Lamar, but instead they flew straight ahead into a mountain.

Johnny Holmes, the chief pilot in Los Angeles, went to the accident site on the top of the mountain.

He said, "It was the worst terrain you could imagine. The snow and rocks were littered with bright colored wrapping paper from Christmas packages. There were not enough human remains to recover. We put a monument at the base of the mountain so no one would ever have to make that climb again."

BAR STORY
by

DICK MAXEY: Dobbie, Vern Mays and I had a trip into Anchorage and went to the Captain Cook Hotel. We agreed that we would change clothes and meet in the Crow's Nest for a drink. I rushed to my room, changed as fast as I could and hurried to the bar.

When I walked in, Vern Mays was sitting there with a martini in front of him and a glassy look in his eyes.

I sat down on a stool beside him and said, "You sure got up here in a hurry."

Vern said, "Who the hell needs you?"

I moved over to the other end of the bar and ordered a beer. Soon Dobbie came in and saw us sitting on opposite ends of the room.

He walked over to me and said, "What the hell's going on?"

I told him what happened and he said, "Look, I don't want any dissension in my crew, we're going to be together for the rest of this trip, so we'll have to get along."

I said, "Okay, you go sit by him."

Dobbie walked over and sat down by Vern saying, "What's with you and Maxey?"

Vern said, "Who the hell needs you?"

Dobbie came back and took the stool next to mine and motioned to the bartender.

"I don't know what you put in your martinis today," he said, "but I think I'll have a beer."

There was this handsome young copilot, but Diane wasn't impressed:

A Milk Bar Story

MIKE SWEELEY: I was new with the company and quite young when I had my first passenger trip in a Connie from San Francisco to Salt Lake. Mel Smith was the captain, Ed Herbert the flight engineer and Diane Hernandez was the stewardess. Diane came up to the cockpit, looked at Mel and Ed and said, "Two coffees," then looked at me and said, "Milk."

CHAPTER 28   THE KOSHER CAT   1966

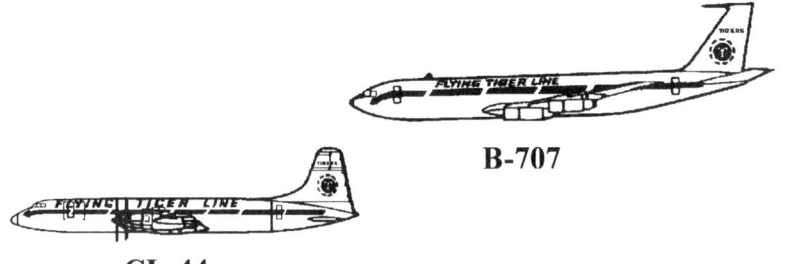

The weather outside was frightful...

JACK McCLARTY, sheet metal shop: We had another deal with a Connie, 16 Charlie, in Grand Island, Nebraska. It was caught on the ground when a hailstorm hit. The hangars there were covered with asbestos siding, and the hailstorm was so severe that it stripped the siding right off the hangar walls. The aluminum skin on the airplane was hammered like you wouldn't believe. It was a mass of dents from one end to the other.

I landed there the day after New Years from Los Angeles. Mike Healy met me.

I shivered and said, "How cold is it?"

"Seventeen below."

"Good God, what am I doing here?"

It turned out that there was no structural damage to the airplane, so we flew it with dents and all. Surprisingly, after that it was the fastest Connie in the fleet.

It was nothing personal Bill, just age before beauty.

BILL CHANEY: I was hired in January, and our class was told that we would fly that wonderful turboprop airplane, the CL-44. We were all elated and couldn't wait to get to school.

Upon arrival at Burbank we were split into two groups. The older group would be flying the CL-44, and I, being in the younger group, would be flying the Lockheed Constellation "Connie." I was very disappointed, but as it worked out the Connie was the best place to be. Our working conditions were better, and the airplane was a dream to fly. I am eternally grateful for having the opportunity to fly that airplane.

We flew trips to Newark, Binghamton, Detroit, and Cleveland one night, followed by trips to Newark, Chicago, Newark the next night. The first night was an extremely long duty period, and as it is sometimes, I wasn't able to get the proper rest for my next departure. My next trip was with Captain Ron Hall, who was getting a line check from Captain Oakley Smith, our chief pilot.

I was a little nervous having the chief pilot on board, but the trip seemed uneventful. I had the habit of looking out my side window at the right wing and number 3 and 4 engines. On that uneventful night I was looking out the window, and then my forehead touched that nice warm glass. With those gentle vibrations the Connie was famous for, I kind of went to sleep. You know how you catch yourself nodding? Well, I caught myself and snapped back straight in my seat. The first thing that greeted me was a question from Captain Hall asking if everything was all right?

I responded, "Of course, why?"

"Because you were looking out that window for an hour and thirty-eight minutes!"

I was terrified at what the results might be. Sleeping on the job and in front of the chief pilot, of all things. They had a good laugh at my expense and, of course, when we got to the hotel bar, I had to buy.

By March Flying Tigers had completed the move from the Lockheed Air Terminal in Burbank to the Los Angeles International Airport in Inglewood. I was a lead mechanic

CHAPTER 28 TIGER TALES 285

working swing shift on the flight line, and we were getting settled into our new facilities.

One day I got a call at home from Chuck Snoke in Personnel. "I understand you have your commercial pilot's license and instrument rating."

"Yes I have, but I applied for a pilot's job last fall and was told I was too old."

"That was last year. This year you're not too old. Do you still want the job?"

"Why, hell yes, next year I might be too young!"

"Could you come a little early today? Art Seymour wants to talk to you."

I thought I was there for an interview, but Art had already made up his mind.

He said, "I've decided to put you on as a copilot. I talked to John Dewey about you and he said, 'He's one of my best men, but I won't stand in his way.' "

I have always appreciated those kind words from John. I went through ground school and had my first CL-44 training flight on my 36th birthday.

I knew about all there was to know about every system on the CL-44. But then I should: I'd had to fix almost everything on a 44 at one time or another through the last five years. I would never know as much in detail about any other airplane. I had changed many engines and propellers; repaired fuel and hydraulic systems, flaps, elevators and wing spoilers; fought cantankerous swing tails and changed untold numbers of wheel assemblies.

Many a time, after working all night to get an airplane ready for scheduled departure, I would taxi it up to the passenger terminal and shut down the engines. The flight crew would take it from there.

Words can hardly describe my feelings when I made my first takeoff in training. It was almost like I was getting even with the airplane for all the grief I had put up with through the years.

Wayne Peake, "The Friendly Fighter Pilot," was my instructor. Wayne had flown P-51 Mustangs for the Israeli Air Force during the Arab Israeli war in 1948. I have heard two stories as to how he came by the "Friendly Fighter Pilot" nickname. One says a friend of his was flying a Messerschmitt for the Egyptians and during a dogfight Wayne shot him down, then followed his parachute down to be sure he was okay.

The other story was that during a dogfight he saw that his enemy pilot's guns had jammed. Peake waved a salute to the hapless pilot and broke off his attack. I think it is likely that both stories are true.

There was no flight simulator for the CL-44, so all flight training was done in the airplane. On a training flight there are usually two or three pilot trainees on board and two or three flight engineer trainees, plus the instructor pilot and check engineer. The trainees each fly for about an hour, then change seats. I made the takeoff from LAX, got the gear and flaps up and accelerated to the climb speed of 170 knots. To my surprise the airspeed stayed right where it was supposed to be. Wayne was even more surprised. He turned around to the others with a look of mock astonishment on his face, as only he could do. I think it was mock.

I had a few minutes of peace before we reached the practice area at Palmdale, so I indulged in some quiet contemplation.

CHAPTER 28　　　TIGER TALES

When Wayne gets through with me, I'll fly this damn thing as well as anyone. Come to think of it, I had better. If I ever bend anything, they'll probably make me fix it.

We arrived over Palmdale, and my reverie was over. Wayne tightened his seat belt a notch. My flight training had begun.

At least I didn't have to view the world upside down.

"I Didn't Think That Landing Was So Bad"

BOBBIE THARP: We were flying a Navy contract from Alameda to Indianapolis to Norfolk and back with CL-44s.

We landed in Indianapolis, and then crew control asked if we would deadhead with Carl Prentiss and his crew to Norfolk. From there we could fly the airplane nonstop back to Alameda. We said sure, we'll do that.

So we get on board. Carl is the captain, a young fellow named Jim Prescott (no relation to Bob) is the copilot and Ernie Belanger is the flight engineer. The copilot is flying the airplane. I'm sitting in the navigator's seat next to the engineer. It's a beautiful day, and we're coming in to Norfolk Naval Air Station. There was a small twin Beech ahead of us practicing approaches, which we were trying to keep in sight. I remember unhooking my seat belt, so I could stand up and see out the windshield.

We saw the airplane and everything was fine, so I sat down. I don't remember if I had my belt buckled, or was in the process of buckling it or what. Then we landed, and I didn't notice anything all that bad about the landing. I've ridden though a lot worse where it tripped all the circuit breakers off the line. Then CRASH BANG BOOM, and the airplane went all kittywampas!

What happened was the left wing came off, and then we rolled upside down and were going down the runway sliding on the top of the airplane. When it rolled over I went up over the circuit breaker panel and fell onto the windshield.

The crewmembers were all hanging upside down in their shoulder harnesses, with Ernie Belanger right above me. My face was right in the windshield, and all I could see was the blur of concrete grinding at the fuselage. I said to myself, the only thing between me and the runway is the top of this fuselage and when it wears through, I'm next. I tried to get up, but couldn't.

Ernie, hanging upside down, sees me and reaches down and picks me up by the shoulders.

He said, "Bobbie, are you all right?"

"Yes, I think so."

So he drops me, and I was right back where I'd been. For Christ sake, I'd had it made, and now I'm right back in the soup. The airplane was still sliding, and the concrete was still getting closer. Finally, we came to a grinding halt. The airplane was burning, and we could hear the fuel tanks exploding. As luck would have it, it was shift change for the Fire Department. The fire trucks were out and ready to cross the runway after we landed. As it was, we slid right up to the trucks and stopped.

The manuals had been thrown all around and there was dirt and dust everywhere. Man it was a mess to see anything in that cockpit. I started grabbing things in the way and throwing them back between my legs. Carl grabbed them and threw them out of our way. I got to the window and started to open it as the fire trucks began hitting us with foam. We started to exit the cockpit side windows, and then stopped.

We remembered the Slick Airways Connie that crashed at San Francisco International. The crew survived the crash, but the foam suffocated them.

I turned around and put my butt in the window. It was really getting smoky in there by then, but they saw us coming out, and directed the foam away from the window. When I got out, I counted the guys as they came out and we had everybody except Ron Penton.

I crawled back in the window and started calling, then I could hear Ron calling back. He was in the deadhead compartment where it was dark as hell, and now it was really filling with smoke. Ron followed the sound of my voice until we made it back out the window. When I could finally see him, he looked like he had been hit in the face with a tomato. He had cut his forehead and the blood was gushing all over. Believe it or not, when he got out of the airplane the soles of his shoes were smoking. That's how hot it had become in that damn airplane.

As we were walking away from the wreck, Carl Prentiss asked his flight engineer, "What time did you block us in?" (Flight crews are paid from the time the airplane first moves until it is blocked in, or parked, at its destination.)

We were taken to the base hospital, and we were all okay, so they transferred us to the civilian hospital. Now the concern was to keep us away from the press. We were sequestered in the auditorium.

We decided what we needed was some cold beer.

I said, "By damn, I'll get us some beer."

I was in civilian clothes so they didn't know who the hell I was. I walked out of the hospital to a convenience store about two blocks away, got two six-packs of beer and walked back right through a group of reporters.

While discussing the events of the day, Carl said, "You don't realize how wide the runway centerline is until you get a <u>real close</u> look at it."

While we drank our beer we watched our accident on the T.V. news.

Carl said, "Would you look at that. I'm sure glad someone took this video, or we would have missed the whole damn thing!"

I didn't think that landing was so bad!

Talk about Terrible Timing for Tom...

TOM CONSTABLE: This flight takes place on my CL-44 I.O.E. (Initial operating experience) We flew from LAX to Norfolk, N.A.S., Virginia. The crew consisted of Arnie Bredon, Scott Brown, Joe Rovegno, the check engineer, and myself.

When we arrived we saw a startling sight! As we rolled down the runway after touchdown, there off to the right we saw the remains of the FTL CL-44 that had crashed and burned the day before. It was upside down with the landing gear sticking straight up and very badly burned. This was a sobering sight indeed, especially to me being so new to airline flying.

After our layover at Virginia Beach, near the Norfolk Naval Air Station, we headed west to the Alameda N.A.S., near Oakland, California. These charters were called "Quick Trans" and were for the Navy.

This was my last leg of the line check and I was to be signed off as a bonafide flight engineer on the CL-44. As we made our approach to Alameda, N.A.S. the copilot was flying the plane. At approximately 50ft. he did something that should not be done in the '44, he pulled the throttles back to idle.

I was looking at my panel and Joe was standing behind me, all of a sudden I felt her sinking rapidly and looked forward. Arnie realized what had happened and tried to save the landing by shoving the throttles to the firewall. It was too late; there was nothing he could do. We were along for the ride. We hit very hard, so hard that Joe was knocked to the floor and all the bells, horns and lights were going off. Arnie stayed with it after it bounced into the air and we were hanging on the big 16-foot props.

I looked forward at the airspeed, which indicated 110 knots, we were swaying and wallowing down the length of the runway of which there was not much left. Captain Bredon did a masterful job of preventing our demise. He finally managed to gain enough airspeed to get her flying again. We went around and made a normal landing.

When we climbed down to inspect her, we were amazed at what we saw! All the engines were bent down, especially the inboards and the nacelles had wrinkles and the metal was torn. Amazingly none of the tires had blown as the struts had bottomed out and shaved the metal off the bogie.

We were fortunate to be with a fine pilot, otherwise I would probably not be writing this remembrance.

We had no simulator for the Boeing 707 either, and much of the training was done at Mojave, Ontario or Palmdale.

CHUCK HAMMER, flight engineer: I was with Dick Stuelke one-day flying transition over at Ontario on a 707. We were on our fourth or fifth takeoff when we blew a tire on the right main gear. We circled back and landed and blew the other three on that side. Dick had to use the brakes on the left side kind of hard to get stopped.

We stood around there a few minutes waiting for maintenance when I said, "I'm going to put the safety pins in the landing gear." [1]

So I walked over and put the pins in the right gear, then walked over to the left gear. I reached up and was just ready to insert the pin, when the thermal relief plugs blew. I didn't know I could jump straight up six feet in the air. I was way up in the wheel well. I got the pin in on the way down and when I came crawling out of there, Stuelke was lying on his back laughing.

So we advertised for a 707 expert ...

JOHN ADCOCK, Ground Instructor: I was working graveyard for Western Airlines as an electrician, when lo and behold, I saw a want ad for a ground instructor's job at Tigers. I had previously taught maintenance personnel in the Royal Canadian Air Force for four years, and I wanted to get back into instructing.

So, on my next day off, to Tigers I did go. Jack Martin was the chief pilot and Tommy Haywood was the manager of ground training. I had an appointment to see him for an interview, but he was out of the office when I arrived. Now I'm sitting in the outer office by Jack Martin's secretary, Pam, a real nice gal.

---

[1] Steel pins to prevent the landing gear from retracting accidentally on the ground.

CHAPTER 28   TIGER TALES

In walks Jack, sees me sitting there, and goes into his office.

I hear him say, "Pam, who's that guy sitting out there?"

"Oh, he's the applicant for the ground instructor's job."

"Where is Tommy Haywood?"

"He just stepped out for a few minutes."

Jack said, "Send him in."

I walk into Jack's office, we introduce ourselves, he sits me down and asks, "What do you know about the 707?"

"Nothing."

"You work at Western and they have 720s."

"Yes, but I just chase wires. Give me a book, I can read."

Then he said, "What do you know about the CL-44?"

"Nothing, but I can...

"Yeah, I know, you can read." With that he reached behind him and came up with the CL-44 maintenance manual, dropped it on the table and it fell open at the air-conditioning schematic. He swung the book around to me and said, "Show me how to get hot air to the cabin."

I didn't have a clue, but I figured it out and showed him.

At that moment in walks Tommy who says, "I hear we have a 707 instructor applicant."

Jack replies, "He doesn't know a damn thing about 'em."

"Oh well, it's no good then, we need a 707 man."

Jack snorted and said, "Tommy, hire the son of a bitch, he can read."

Others were in training also. Tigers signed a contract to provide two Boeing 707 passenger airplanes and several flight crews and cabin crews to EL AL, at that time the only commercial carrier in Israel. A home base for the flight attendants was to be established in Tel Aviv for the duration of the summer months.

BARBARA GRAHAM WAY, flight attendant: The airplanes were painted in the normal Flying Tiger Line letters followed by EL AL in both English and Hebrew. It looked something like a circus billboard, but we just called it the KOSHER CAT.

While the rest of the flight attendants were getting situated in permanent quarters, we landed in Tel Aviv and checked into the hotel. Rooms were assigned according to seniority, and Nancy Brennan and I were the junior flight attendants. The hotel ran out of rooms, so they said we could sleep in the sauna, but we had to be out by seven in the morning. The cost would be the same as a suite. This was impossible. We were totally exhausted and had to have a bed.

Ralph Hedden was the captain and Don Sanders was the check captain. They were sharing a suite, so they gave us the bedroom, and they bunked out on the sofas in the living room. We ended up with better accommodations than anyone on the crew.

A Boeing 707 had been dubbed the "Pole Cat" for its record flight over the poles the previous year, so it was natural for this one to become the "Kosher Cat."

INA COLLINS FINE, flight attendant: 41 Years Aloft. Great excitement prevailed during the bidding process. How intriguing it would be to live in the State of Israel—a

country few of us knew much about, save for occasional reports of border skirmishes with Arab neighbors. Successful bidders attended several days of classes organized and run by EL AL so as to acquaint our flight attendants with EL AL's paperwork requirements, kashrut (the country's very strict kosher dietary code) etc.

The initial settling in process resulted in a few mishaps with a less than honorable real estate agent, but after a couple of weeks, we all found suitable housing. Top on the priority list, of course, was to establish a favorite off duty "watering hole." Pat Conway, Lee Kyle, Treso Koken, et al put the "Red Rooster" on the map. To this day it probably has never enjoyed greater success than in the summer of '66.

Our passenger loads were undisciplined, difficult to control and demanding. A rather humorous situation, albeit unpleasant at the time, developed when Carol Collins was asked to store a salami in the icebox. At a refueling stop, however, the precious salami had been inadvertently removed by the ground catering personnel. After much verbal abuse from the irate passenger, Carol finally convinced the passenger she had not stolen the salami for her own consumption. Only one who has spent time in Israel could fully appreciate the importance of a New York salami to the average Israeli.

Travel within Israel was by bus—ala country style with animals and humans as passengers, by <u>sheruits</u>[2] or by hitchhiking. Buses and <u>sheruits</u> traveled along the major roads and tended to be crowded, stuffy and above all, SLOW.

---

[2]Shared jitney cabs which could always be made to accommodate one more passenger- ugh!

Save for eggs, cheese, fruit and bread, the food was generally unbearable. Filet mignon ended up looking like a Steak'um, and what wasn't dipped into hommus (chick pea derivative) was bathed in tehina sauce (indescribable).

Treso Koken came to the rescue by devising an ingenious way to smuggle in marvelous steaks from Stateside. By storing them in the nose gear compartment they stayed cool and the chef at the Hilton Hotel was bribed to keep them hidden in a corner of the frozen food locker, away from the prying eyes of the inspecting Kosher Rabbi.

As the contract neared completion we realized this had been a unique summer but it was not without problems. Yet sadness tugged at us as we prepared to depart from this land of stolen salamis; where in the summer of '66 the generators were powerful enough to light only one side of the street each evening; where the hot water supply became abruptly depleted half way through each shower; where bagels and lox were figments of New York imaginations; where private telephones were truly a luxury; where guns were commonplace; where negotiation, about anything and everything, regardless of how trivial the issue, was so refined that it is considered an art form; where international borders were indicated merely by painted stones; where numbers emblazoned on human arms denoting detention in a concentration camp became an all too familiar and tormenting sight; where lasting friendships were formed—not only with Israelis but amongst the closely knit group of participants in the FTL/EL AL operation.

The majority of us came away with greater insight into, and an appreciation for, the tiny country's daily struggle for survival. Though we are now scattered hither and yon, these flight attendants shall forever carry with them fond memories of a very special summer experience.

CHAPTER 29   THE CL-44 COPILOT   1966 PART 2

In initial airline training they teach all the emergency procedures and how to fly the airplane, but they don't teach you how to be a copilot. You will learn that on your own. You damn sure will. My flight training was completed, and I began flying the line in July. I flew my first airline trip as copilot with Captain John Urnezis. This was not a good start.

We left San Francisco for Chicago O'Hare with the captain flying and me handling radio communications. I called for our clearance, and then ground control for taxi and tower for takeoff. After takeoff I was talking to departure control and when we were over Oakland, they switched me to Oakland Center. That all made sense, so I began to relax. I had my chart out and found the first checkpoint, RNO, for Reno, so when we were overhead I called Reno Center.

The captain choked and yelled. "There ain't no Reno Center! It's still Oakland Center, and it will be Oakland Center until we get to Salt Lake Center!!"

John was just starting to calm down when he noticed I had maps all over the cockpit and was frantically searching for something.

"What are you looking for?"

"I can't find the next check point. I have LLC for Lovelock and BAM for Battle Mountain, but I can't find TOC."

The veins in his neck began to bulge again as he said, "TOC is not a check point; T-O-C means Top Of Climb!!"

On the return trip from O'Hare to Los Angeles, Rex Tripp was the captain. When I got the radios set up, I had another shock. The radio congestion at O'Hare was such that there was no way I could get a clearance, so I just sat there. Rex picked up his microphone, waited for a break, and calmly got our clearance. By the time we parked the airplane at LAX I had my confidence back.

My first international trip as copilot was with Captain Ralph Mitchell, and it began in utter confusion. Ralph had known me for many years—known me as a mechanic that is.

He arrived a little late and said, "Hi Vern, have you seen my copilot? I want to get a look at the flight plan."

I was standing there with the paperwork in my hand and a big grin on my face.

"I'm your copilot," I said, as I handed him the flight plan.

"Yeah sure," he laughed, "But I'm in a hurry right now, I'll let you know in a minute how much fuel I want."

"I'm not going to fuel it Ralph, I really am the copilot. I just don't have my uniform yet."

He finally was convinced when I showed him my name on the flight release.

We flew from Los Angeles to Cold Bay, Alaska, and laid over there for three days. Cold Bay is out on the Aleutian Chain and is cold and damp with usually poor visibility and high winds. Aside from that, it was a nice place. There was nothing to speak of within 500 miles, except bears and salmon. Flying Tigers managed the en-

CHAPTER 29   TIGER TALES   299

tire operation. We had a hotel and a restaurant with a bar, also pool tables and a small store. For breakfast they served the largest steak you ever saw, and eggs with potatoes and toast. The coffee came in huge mugs. It was hot and black, and it was free.

Ralph Mitchell loved to fish for salmon. He'd stand there in the icy water for hours. Bears also love salmon and quite often they and Ralph were fishing in the same place at the same time. Most other fishermen left when the bears showed up. Some left at full speed leaving their gear behind. Not Ralph. He continued to fish quietly.

He said, "If a bear gets too close and starts to get nasty, I just throw him a fish."

I don't remember him saying what he would do if he hadn't caught any fish.

Morgan Hughes is a fisherman too, but he spent a good part of this trip trying to stay out of the water.

Morgan Hughes' Three-Engine Connie
As Told By His Flight Engineer

BUCK JENNINGS: Captain Morgan Hughes, Copilot Frank Christian, myself as flight engineer and Navigator Pappy Huntington were ferrying an airplane from Norton A.F.B., California, to Clark A.F.B. in the Philippines for the Tiger Air Service (a subsidiary of Flying Tigers). They sent these old worn-out Connies to Kansas City to be overhauled at TWA, and then they were flown to the Far East.

These were supposed to be ferry flights but were filled with spare parts to the point of being nearly grossed out. This trip, in fact, was scheduled from Norton to Honolulu, but we were so heavy that we had to stop in San Francisco to get enough fuel on board. San Francisco was just that much closer to Honolulu.

This time the load of spare parts was to be dropped off at Danang, Viet Nam, and after off-loading, we took off from Danang for Clark Field in the Philippines. Just as we reached top of climb, we got an engine fire warning but no indication of which engine. While I scanned through the engine analyzer, the #2 engine indications went all to hell. We shut it down and feathered it, and Morgan looked out his window and confirmed that it was stopped and the propeller was feathered.

We finished going through the checklist, then suddenly the whole airplane began vibrating like it would shake itself to pieces. The first thought was that maybe the propeller had gone into reverse. In that case the checklist says to hit the feather button. I did that, and soon after the vibration stopped and everything smoothed out.

I said, "Well, I guess we saved the day. Is it stopped, Morgan?"

"It must be, but I can't see a blade. Frank, go back to the cabin and take a look."

The inboard propeller could stop in a position where a blade could not be seen from the cockpit, so Frank went back in the cabin to look out the window.

He was gone a couple of minutes, and when he came back he was white as a sheet as he looked at me.

I asked, "Well, Frank, is it stopped?"

"Stopped hell," he said using language usually reserved for mule skinners or maybe flight engineers, "THAT #!@^*%#son-of-a-#@*&% IS GONE!"

"What do you mean, gone, did it throw the prop?"

"Throw the prop hell, the whole #$%^&* #@%^ING ENGINE IS GONE!"

CHAPTER 29 TIGER TALES 301

In about three seconds Pappy handed the flying time to Clark and to Danang up to Captain Hughes. Danang was closer, so we turned back and sent a MAY DAY. The Air Force sent a C-124 out to rendezvous with us and flew underneath the crippled Connie to assess the damage. The landing gear and flaps appeared to be okay.

The drag of the flat frontal area of the nacelle with the engine missing was tremendous. Morgan put 20 degrees of flaps down, which helped to smooth out the flight. Upon arrival in Danang, the crash trucks and ambulances were all lined up just in case.

When we got on the ground and looked at the nacelle, the whole thing was a real mess. We figure it had all happened in about a minute and a half. The fire was so hot that it had burned the top engine mounts off, which let the engine drop down. This caused the severe vibration. The engine tore off and fell into the ocean about the same time I hit the feather button. When it left the airplane, the engine took the stainless steel firewall and the landing gear doors with it.

The base commander sent a staff car and took us to the Officers' Club where cold beer was set up.

We had to wait for the next Tiger Air Service flight to Clark, which left at midnight, so we just stayed at the bar. At midnight I was the last in line as we were going up the stairs to board the flight to Clark. An orderly came running to the airplane and handed me a TWX from Los Angeles. The message said to stay in Danang and wait for the airplane to be repaired.

He said, "Shouldn't we show this to the captain?"

"Hell no, put it in your pocket until we taxi out, then chase us down the runway with it."

A major amount of work would be required before the airplane could be flown. Most any other company would have sent a structural modification crew. Tigers called on Jack McClarty.

JACK McCLARTY, sheet metal shop: There was significant damage to the nacelle area that could not be repaired in Danang. Since the engine was gone, they needed a fairing made to cover the front of the nacelle to cut down on the aerodynamic drag. I got the call, so I designed and made one up in the sheet metal shop, then took it to the engine shop and fitted it to a Connie engine mount. Then I took the fairing to Danang and installed it on the Connie, so it could be three-engine ferried out of there.

On the way back I laid over at the Minami Hotel in Tachikawa, Japan. Another American came in and didn't have enough money to pay for his room, so they took his shoes (which are left outside the room) for collateral. I loaned him the money so he could get his shoes back.

Now back to my new career as a copilot. On layover in Chicago with Captain Rex Tripp I came down to the lobby in the evening. Rex was sitting in an overstuffed chair, apparently contemplating the design of the carpet.

I sat down and consulted my watch while saying, "A drink would sure go good before dinner, do we still have twelve hours?"

Rex said, "It's close, but the airplane will probably be late anyway. We can have one drink with dinner, and I know a good place."

We walked down the street about a half a mile, then went into this place and sat down.

CHAPTER 29 TIGER TALES 303

When the waitress came over, Rex said, "We'll have two specials."

The special turned out to be the largest Old Fashioned I had ever seen. We had one drink with dinner, after which I went back to the hotel and slept like a baby.

Bob Bax wasn't sleeping...

PETE OKICICH: I was flying copilot for Bob Bax on a flight out of O'Hare to Newark on the CL-44. As was his habit when the copilot was flying, he would handle the paperwork and copy the clearance.

He had requested our clearance and, as usual, there was a ton of radio traffic. We were waiting...and suddenly it began.

"ATC clears Tiger 454..." Well, typical ORD clearance delivery machine-gunned a lengthy clearance, naming every Victor airway there was. When they finished...Bob paused a few seconds before the readback and said.

"Say all after ATC Clears...MY PENCIL CAUGHT ON FIRE!!"

Danang, Viet Nam, was back on our minds again during the holiday season. One of our CL-44s crashed on approach on Christmas Eve. The crew was Captain Frank Hawkins, Copilot Mike Jackson, Flight Engineer Lloyd Moore and Navigator C. Tune.

The aircraft was on a precision GCA, (ground controlled approach) which was terminated due to a ground radarscope failure, at which time a missed approach was accomplished. The second approach was a surveillance GCA, which does not have precision capability. The aircraft began clipping the tops of trees about a mile and three quarters from the runway, then the left wing struck the top of a concrete temple.

They crashed in the center of a small village and demolished 42 buildings, causing 121 deaths. Three of the four engines had flamed out, but it is not known if the cause was damage by the treetops, or by the extremely heavy rain. About six inches of rain fell during the hour of the accident.

Bob Prescott was deeply concerned about the many accidents we had suffered. He wanted to be sure he had done everything possible to prevent further loss of life. Plans were being drawn up for a new flight-training center with modern classrooms complete with mockups and procedure trainers. We would also have the latest flight simulators when they became available. Tommy Haywood was put in charge of it all.

Bob also hired a highly respected TWA safety expert, Captain Robert Buck. He rode with several crews around the system to try to find areas where improvements in procedures could be made.

As I recall, the only real problem he found that caused concern was flight crew fatigue. Our aircraft did not yet have automated pallet loading, so the loaders had to handle each box or package one at a time, as cargo was transferred from one airplane to another. A crew could bring an airplane into Detroit, for instance, and wait several hours for it to be reloaded, and then fly it to Los Angeles. This resulted in very long duty times.

CHAPTER 30   THREE DAY PASS SIX DAY WAR   1967

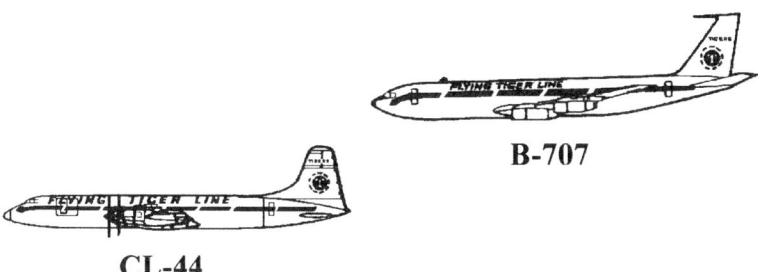

B-707

CL-44

I was learning this copilot business fast, but I had a lot of help from several senior captains. For instance, a Pacific trip with Starr Thompson, when he gave me seven legs in a row. That is a big help to a new pilot. One of those legs was into Seoul, Korea, in the middle of the night in an electrical storm. It was an ADF approach and every time the lightning cracked, the needle spun toward it. I was sweatin' and workin' like hell to keep us right side up when Starr looked over at me calmly and said, "Well, did you think the sun would be shining all the time?"

The next day when we got back out to the airplane there was a severe thunderstorm over the airport.

Starr said, "Well Vern, you got us this far, think you can find Haneda airport in Tokyo?"

So I started setting up the cockpit, then I noticed him staring at me with his eyes wide.

He said, "Are you planning to take off in this?" Pointing out the windshield.

"Considering what I was in last night, it didn't occur to me that I had a choice."

He said, "For Christ's sake Vern, when you're up there you have to come down, but when you're on the ground, you can stay here until you're damn well ready to fly!"

The next night it was my leg again from Haneda to Cold Bay, Alaska. After I leveled off at FL210, Starr yawned and said, "You got this thing wired, I'm going to go back and crawl in the bunk for a couple of hours."

Now here I am all alone up front. The flight engineer is busy at his station behind me. At regular intervals the navigator hands up our position report, which I transmit to Tokyo, or Anchorage Radio on H.F. As we burn off fuel, I decide when I want to climb to a higher altitude, call and receive the clearance, then report level. You can't imagine how much of a confidence builder something like that can be for a new copilot. Never mind that Starr was probably watching through the open cockpit door.

It's stories like this next one that make me glad I'm no longer in the maintenance department.

ED HALE, maintenance: We had a Boeing 707 in Yokota Air Base, Japan, which required a main landing gear strut change. I was a supervisor in maintenance training at the time, and George McGowen was the landing gear expert. I was supposed to watch him change the strut and write down all the procedures for the Maintenance Manual.

We arrived at Yokota from Los Angeles about midnight and had no visas, so we were given a 72-hour shore pass. It was supposed to take less than a day to change a strut. The next morning the fog was so thick, we couldn't even see the runway. The airplane, which was bringing the new strut, was sitting in Misawa, Japan, waiting for the fog to lift in Yokota and didn't arrive for a day and a half. Our 72-hour shore pass was already half over.

We had put the airplane up on jacks and removed the old strut and were awaiting arrival of the new one, when George came down with the flu, or something. He became so deathly ill that he threw up all that night, and he had a

CHAPTER 30   TIGER TALES

fever and couldn't even get out of bed in the morning.

When the airplane came in, I went out to the field to meet the Boeing representative. I took one look at him and thought, this guy has never changed a strut.

He said, "I'm a Boeing engineer. I'm here to find out why the strut broke, but I don't know how to change one."

Thankfully, I was present when we took the old strut out, and we had our own mechanics there, so we put the new strut in and hooked it all up. By the time we were ready for departure, we were well over our permitted length of stay.

Nancy, the owner of the hotel, said, "The police were here looking for you!"

We called the Tiger agent, Tommy Tomuro, who said, "Stay there and don't move until I get there."

He picked us up and said, "I'm putting you on the first flight out."

He took our passes to the Customs officer and explained what happened. They were mad as hell, but finally let us go.

The first flight out was this same 707 which was bound for Danang, Viet Nam, to pick up the remains of the CL-44 which had crashed there on Christmas Eve. Art Flanagin was the captain and when we arrived, Danang was under a mortar attack. The gun ships were circling the field and shooting the hell out of things. When we were cleared to land, I've never come down so fast in a big airplane in my life.

Charley O'Donnell met us and handed out flak jackets. They loaded all four of the engines from the 44 and whatever else they had been able to scrape up. We were out of there in about an hour.

If they would let Ed write all this up in the Maintenance Manual, it would be a lot more helpful...and interesting.

I flew a Pacific trip with one of my favorite people, Bill Hoey. We flew from San Francisco to Cold Bay, Alaska, where weather was marginal with a very severe cross wind, not too unusual for Cold Bay. When we arrived, we were informed that one of our navigators was seriously ill and had to go to the hospital in Anchorage. Bill had the airplane refueled, while the navigator was being brought on board, then we flew him to Anchorage. When we were refueled and the flight plan refiled, we flew back to Cold Bay again. That was a total of over 11 hours of flying.

There are many wild tales about Cold Bay Tigers, although perhaps some of them cannot be verified.

I am told that one of our senior captains may have spent a little more time in the bar than he had intended. It was after midnight when he made his way toward the back door to return to the hotel. In the meantime a black bear was enjoying a midnight snack from a garbage can he had overturned just outside the bar. Our hero opened the door and promptly fell over the garbage can and was now in the garbage with the bear.

The bartender said, "We heard a lot of loud grunts and then some cussin' and the sound of garbage cans bein' smashed agin' the building, then it got real quiet. Right after that, ol' Cap'n Anonymous walked back in and came up to the bar for another drink. He didn't smell too good, but I swear he was sober as a judge."

There were a lot of bears around Cold Bay, and sometimes they had to be chased off the runway before a plane could land.

CHAPTER 30 TIGER TALES

After two days there, we flew to Yokota Air Base in Japan. Next we went to Saigon, Viet Nam. After the airplane was off-loaded, we departed for Hong Kong. We didn't get far. On departure we had to shut down an engine due to a low oil pressure indication, so we had to go back to Saigon.

It was getting dark by then, and we could see flashes of artillery fire a few miles to the south. We departed about four hours later, after a defective oil pressure switch was replaced, and finally did get to Hong Kong.

While we were there, Bill bought a huge plank of exotic wood with which to make a new top for his bar. Every time we landed and went to a hotel, he and I carried the plank with us for safekeeping. It seemed like we carried the damn thing half way around the world.

Meanwhile back at the Head Shed, Prescott hired Wayne Hoffman as chairman of the board of the Flying Tiger Line while remaining as president. The way the company was growing there was some talk about diversification.

ANN MARIE PRESCOTT: Bob had sort of a mission. He was a visionary. I remember one time when Hoffman came on board, right? He was a railroad man and he had no understanding of airlines. A few months later he gave a talk at a party.

He said, "I have a lot to learn about the airlines. I went to Bob's office the other day,"

Bob said, "You know things are not going so good. We are losing money on the commercial routes, MAC[1] has cut

---

[1] Military Airlift Command.

us back 40% and the charter business is flat"
"What are we going to do about it?"
Bob said, "I just ordered ten new Douglas DC-8s."
"I have more to learn about this business than I thought."

My next flight was a long one with Captain Sam Royall. After stopping at about every place in the Pacific, we landed at Manila. There I got a chance to see many of my old friends who used to work for me. When the airplane was off-loaded, we departed for Hong Kong and a well-deserved crew rest.

When we were approaching Kai Tak Airport, we were advised that a Cathay Pacific Convair 880 had crashed on the runway and that the airport was closed, so we diverted to Taipei for fuel. By the time we were refueled the airport was open, so we flew to Hong Kong again. That was a very long day. Unexpected delays can turn what should be a pleasant flight into one of pure misery. This was one of those times. I was so tired when we arrived at the hotel that, as the saying goes, I felt like a package of raw hamburger.

It can be hard to get to sleep when you're overtired, but some guys I know could sleep on a stone wall.

RON WAY: I was the flight engineer on a CL-44 with Frank Jackson, the captain; Mike Sweeley, the copilot, and Glenn Lenarsic was the navigator. We started out at Kadena, Okinawa. At that time the package store on the base would not sell booze to civilians, but Glenn was retired military so he got us a bottle of hooch. So we went whistling over to Danang, Viet Nam, the next day, and we lost

CHAPTER 30   TIGER TALES

the hydraulic system and had to blow the landing gear down with the emergency bottle.

We were lying out there on top of the wing trying to get some rest. With all the screaming fighters coming and going and the C-130s blowing sand all around, it was a hell of a mess. Maintenance found the leak between number one and two engines, so now they had to have a new line made up. Since this was going to take time, they got us a tent in which we could get some sleep.

Glenn brought a quart of apple juice with him from the airplane and also the bottle of bourbon.

He said, "All right, have any of you ever heard of a Stonewall Jackson?"

None of us ever had.

"Well you have now. It's bourbon and apple juice. By the way, you guys owe me twenty cents each for the booze, because it cost me eighty cents."

So we all chipped in our twenty cents, had a couple of Stonewall Jacksons apiece and then went off to sleep. When we woke up the leak was fixed, and we took off for Cold Bay.

The next morning in Cold Bay we were playing pool and whatnot, waiting for the next airplane to come through, when someone came by and said, "The airplane has over flown and gone to Anchorage."

This meant we would have at least another day to wait for the next eastbound airplane. Frank Jackson had kept the other half of the bottle, so we all turned to him and said, "Let's have the bottle."

Without saying a word, Frank handed us each a dime. He had already emptied the bottle.

This next crew could have used that bottle; they already had access to the water.

GEORGE GEWHER: It was 4 p.m. on a hot summer day in 1967. I was departing from Chicago O'Hare on the 1049 Connie; my crew was Larry Drake, copilot, and Jim Hengehold, flight engineer.

We were fairly heavy on this takeoff, in the 135,000 lbs range. We were cleared to runway 9 left. On the departure end of that runway, there is a water tower, maybe a mile and a half from the end of the runway. It is one that looks like a golf tee and is right in line with the runway.

We were flight planned direct to Newark, so we had a good load of fuel on board. We were cleared for takeoff and started down the runway when just after V2, as I was rotating for takeoff, we had a fire warning bell and light in number four engine. I told Jim to feather number four and told Larry to tell the tower that we had shut down an engine and needed to come back and land. This was done, and the tower told us that we were cleared to land on any runway. I was still flying straight ahead, so I told Larry to start the flaps up as slow as possible. As we continued east, this water tower began to appear in front of us. I didn't want to make a steep turn, as we were still not climbing very fast. I continued straight ahead and passed over the water tower maybe less then fifty feet. After the flaps were fully up the airplane began to climb better, and I made a left turn down wind for runway 14 left. We leveled off at a sufficient altitude, came back around and landed.

When we taxied back to the Tiger area and parked the airplane, maintenance told us that it would take a while to fix the problem. Since we were pushing duty time, we decided to cancel and go to the hotel.

I said to my crew, "I'll meet you in the bar for a beer." We didn't take long to assemble at the bar and order our beers. Now mind you, not much had been said between us since we had parked the airplane.

CHAPTER 30   TIGER TALES   313

We all picked up our beers at the same time, as Larry Drake says at that moment, "That was the biggest #!%@*#% water tower I ever saw."

The Arab Israeli Six-Day War might have taken seven days if these guys hadn't been helping.

RALPH JARVIS: The captain was Jim Alexander, I was the copilot and Ernie Rice was the engineer on a military charter out of Loring A.F.B., Maine. The CL-44 arrived at Loring from a southern military base with a load of munitions. We were to deliver it in Rome, Italy, after a fuel stop in Mildenhall, England.

That evening, before our departure, Abba Eban, then Israeli Ambassador to the U.N., was very vocally denying on T.V. that the U.S. was aiding Israel.

Our flight to Mildenhall was routine. On arrival, however, we learned that all the U.S. military C-130s based there had flown to Wheelus A.F.B. in Libya. Either the Libyans were our friends at that time, or they didn't know about it. After refueling, filing a flight plan and checking the load, we departed for Rome. During our approach to Campino, the older airport, we saw a most interesting thing. We flew alongside an ancient viaduct. It was still supplying Rome with water after thousands of years.

After we parked, Ernie opened the swing tail, and Jim and I finished our paperwork. When the civilian cargo handlers saw the load of munitions, everything stopped. A rather lengthy meeting ensued—lots of paperwork, confusion and strained nerves. We agreed to take the aircraft to a NATO base about 200 miles north of Rome. We departed with an Israeli attaché who smoothed the ruffled feathers.

The military base had no traffic and little in the way of aircraft except an EL AL 707 that was waiting for us. We parked as close to the 707 as safety would permit. The night was very dark—no moon, lots of stars and a circle of about 15 interested parties with Jim Alexander in the middle. Everyone was expressing his own feelings: "Is it safe to move?" "Did you have any problems?" "How much does it weigh?" "How are we going to transfer the load?"

Finally Jim said, "You guys figure it out by yourselves. We've had a long day, and we're going to bed."

Everything went fine. The load was transferred safely, both aircraft were fueled, EL AL went to Israel, and we went to Ireland. The war ended the next day.

Instead of the winds of war, we had plain old winds...headwinds, that is. I had a Pacific trip with Bill Hoey. We left Cold Bay bound for Tokyo in the middle of the night and encountered much higher headwinds than had been forecast.

When it became obvious we would not have enough fuel to reach Tokyo, we returned to Cold Bay. We were in the air seven hours and forty-eight minutes and were right back where we started. While we were getting some sleep, they off-loaded 2000 pounds of freight and put on additional fuel. The next day we made it to Tokyo in eleven hours and twelve minutes. The following day we returned to Cold Bay in only seven hours, so you can imagine what the winds were out of the west.

A Bar Top Story

During the trip I asked, "Bill, how did the new bar top turn out?"

"It turned out just beautiful. My wife says it is the only thing I ever made that works."

CHAPTER 31   MY FINAL FLIGHT ON THE 44   1968

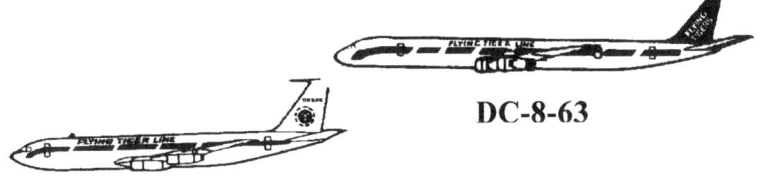

DC-8-63

B-707

I began the year flying CL-44s as copilot on our domestic routes. January is a nice time of year to enjoy the icy runways in places like New York, Boston, Chicago, Newark, Hartford and Philadelphia.

February was just as bad by adding Detroit, Binghamton and Cleveland, but fortunately I was back on international flying by the middle of the month.

The CL-44, also called the Canadian Edsel because of its lack of acceptance, was not a pleasant airplane to ride in due to the vibration from the propellers. The deadhead compartment was large enough and contained three bunks, but the vibration was even worse there because it was closer to the propeller arc.

After several hours one begins to ache all over. You try to keep your mind off it by doing something. Some people read or worked crossword puzzles. Clever people, such as Captain Wayne Pcakc, wrote poetry. The following poem was written for the crew he was with and is a good example of the silly things your mind can grab onto to relieve boredom. Of course none of these things really happened.

"PRESS ON"
They say there's an aircraft just leaving Saigon
Bound for Yokota Airdrome
Heavily laden with terrified men
Scared that they won't make it home.
When just at V.R. came a hell of a jar

MY FINAL FLIGHT ON THE 44

And the number four engine dropped dead
The captain was calm as he turned to Jack Swan
(his flight engineer)
And these are the words that he said.

We'll press on! We'll press on
To V ref, flaps up and beyond
We're off to Yokota, won't bend one iota
So cheer up my lads, we'll press on.

While still in the climb without reason or rhyme
The pressurization went out.
We stayed at ten thousand, kept right on a rousin'
Then we all heard the good captain shout.

Press on! (Chorus, "Sung Fracto Gusto")

As we passed Eagle Ray with a cry of dismay
Frank Christian (his copilot) jumped up with alarm
He said, "Number three is a sick S.O.B.
I think we are buying the farm."

Kadena came through like a bolt from the blue
Saying, "We're high thin scattered, and calm."
Then Wayne exclaimed, "Tell 'em flying's our game
We got two good ones left, lets press on!

Chorus (More gusto, less fracto)

Then Brigite (flight attendant) burst in with a sick looking grin
Yelling, "Wish us Godspeed and Good Luck"
Some bloody G.I. has passed out Spanish Fly
And the PAX are all running amok.

CHAPTER 31   TIGER TALES   317

But the captain's no fool, he was keeping his cool
He reached down and grabbed the P.A.
We're in for the weather, lets all pull together
Now here's what I'm planning to say.

Chorus (With feeling)

We're abeam of Yazu when we drop Number Two
Number One was just running on fumes
Now we're all out of gas, falling flat on our ass
So the girls had to mount their brooms.

They threw us a line and we fell in behind
With the passengers shouting "Ole!"
Their towing art mastered we planted the bastard
In the middle of Yokota's runway.

Chorus (With whatever's left.)

And pressed on, we pressed on
To the hotel, the bar and beyond
We went up to our room and sent up the balloon
And toasted the girls until dawn!

          Captain Wayne Peake

After flying a trip to Viet Nam and back to Japan, Captain Bill Hoey and I deadheaded nonstop to San Francisco. The flight would take about twelve hours, so after we were airborne, I made some remark about the long miserable ride we had ahead of us.

Bill said, "Oh I don't know about that, Lad. Why don't you grab us a couple of those paper cups?"

Then Bill opened a brown paper bag and pulled out a fifth of Old Grand Dad. He unscrewed the cap, looked at it intently, then with great deliberation he dropped the cap in the trash can. Who said it was a long way from Tokyo to San Francisco?

Bill Hoey was a homespun philosopher and writer who wrote western short stories in his spare time. Trips with Bill were always a lot of fun. He drank quite a bit, but he could hold his liquor well and was always sober when it was time to go to work.

Sometimes it does seem that history repeats itself, though this time the incident was over before the townsfolk could gather to watch them crash.

SHAD: Fifteen years after my experience in North Platte with Captain Stan Hampton, when we couldn't get the landing gear locked down on the C-46, I was captain of a CL-44 flying across the Midwest when I had an engine fire warning. We shut it down, and shot the fire extinguisher bottle to it but still had the fire warning. We shot the second bottle, but the obstinate red light remained on.

Now we had no choice but to make an emergency landing. Guess where we landed? North Platte, Nebraska. The field was actually a little short for the CL-44, but it worked out okay. When the engine was inspected they found, as is the case with most fire warnings, it had been a false warning.

There always has to be a wise guy…

PAUL REBSCHER: During initial flight training a sweet young thing from personnel came in and gave a short talk on filling out forms etc.
She said, "It looks hard but when you get used to it, it's easy."
Someone in the back row said, "Hell, I'm easy."

CHAPTER 31   TIGER TALES   319

As laughter erupted she regained control of the class by saying, "You may be easy, but I'm a cinch!"

In the spring of '68 Flying Tigers bought a fleet of Douglas DC-8-63Fs, which were more commonly known as stretched eights. They were stretched by adding one fuselage section forward and another aft of the wing. I won a bid for a first officer's position and was scheduled to attend class in June.

GOLDY: Bob Martin and I were in training on the DC-8 and flew from Los Angeles to Fresno for some practice landings. Dick Wilson was the instructor. I had no brakes when I landed at Fresno, so I had to use the emergency air brakes. After we taxied off the runway, the tower told us the left landing gear brakes were on fire. Dwight Metcalf was one of the second officers, and he went down the escape chute to put out the fire. He was wearing trousers made of silk or something, and as he slid down the chute they melted and burned him pretty badly.

We put the fire out (on the brakes, not on Dwight) then Dick rode back to the terminal with an emergency vehicle so he could call the company. While he was gone a reporter from the Fresno Bee crawled through a hole in the fence and wanted an interview. We told him about the brake problem.

Then he asked, "What's the captain's name?"

I said, "Jack Martin." (The director of flight operations.)

Then he looked at Bob and said, "What's your name?"

Bob held a straight face and said, "Ed Pinke." (Ed was the vice president of operations.)

So it came out in the Fresno Bee, that Jack Martin was the captain and Ed Pinke was the copilot. We told the reporter that Ed wanted a copy of the paper, so he sent one to Ed Pinke in Los Angeles.

Ed said, "It wouldn't have been so bad if I was listed as the captain, but here I was a copilot again."

Fred Benninger, the long time tightfisted keeper of the purse strings since the beginning, left the company. Tom Grogean, a young fellow brought in by Wayne Hoffman, replaced him.

In May I made my last flight in the CL-44. It was a multicrew trip from Los Angeles to Melbourne, Australia, to pick up a load of racehorses. The crew consisted of Captain Ralph Mitchell, Co-Captain Roy "Curly" Olson, me as copilot, Larry Partridge and Manny Morris, flight engineers and Len Jarvis and Bill Orlicky, navigators.

I flew the leg to Honolulu, Hawaii, Olson the leg to Nandi, Fiji Islands for another fuel stop, and then Ralph flew to Melbourne. We had an 18-hour rest at the Southern Cross Hotel, which was plenty of time to soak up the atmosphere of the hotel bar along with a fair amount of its contents.

It was my turn to fly the leg from Melbourne to Auckland, New Zealand. When we checked the weather, the forecast was for severe crosswinds at the Auckland Airport.

Ralph called me aside and said, "What say we play a dirty trick on Olson, and let him fight that crosswind in Auckland? Then you can have the next two legs."

When Olson got the word, he pretended he was being unfairly treated because it wasn't his turn to fly, but he grudgingly crawled into the left seat.

CHAPTER 31 — TIGER TALES

That's a nice thing about flying with senior captains who are also gentlemen. They were not about to let a copilot land the airplane in severe weather conditions with a load of high-strung thoroughbred racehorses on board, but they chose to be diplomatic about it.

We left Melbourne with a dozen racehorses on board and flew to New Zealand, where we stayed at the Intercontinental Hotel. The next day we picked up 14 more horses in Auckland, then departed for Tahiti.

Thoroughbred horses sometimes get very nervous and can hurt themselves or cause severe damage to an airplane. Because of this danger, the owners usually send handlers along to keep the horses quiet. Some of the horses have to be given tranquilizers, and occasionally one will go wild and have to be put to sleep.

When the 26 horses and three handlers were loaded, I flew the leg to Tahiti for a fuel stop. While we were there, we had an air-conditioning problem, so we went to the Taaone Hotel while it was being repaired.

The hotel grounds were covered with tropical shrubs and flowers, with the hibiscus and bougainvillea in full bloom. The rooms were individual cottages with thatched roofs and open windows with screens on all sides. It rained several times during the day, but that just made it easier to sleep. Ralph had been there before and knew the owners of a small French Restaurant, Le Relais "Chez Gaspard." We had dinner that night and were given the finest service.

We also walked to downtown Papeete and went to Quinn's, world famous bar, for a nightcap. There were no sidewalks, and because of the heavy rains we did a lot of leaping over mud puddles.

The next day I flew my last leg on the CL-44 to Los Angeles. It was just as well, because it was also the worst landing I ever made in the '44. At least I didn't bend the airplane. I don't know how the horses felt about it.

I'd Rather Be In A Bar, Story
Author is known (But he won't admit it.)

The new copilot was on an eastbound trans-continental night flight. He was a well-educated young man eager to do a good job, but was a little apprehensive about the grizzled and cantankerous old captain. After they crossed the Front Range near Denver, the captain went to sleep.

There were scattered thunderstorms over the Midwest and he watched for several minutes as they came nearer to a huge storm directly ahead. The lightening display was tremendous, and he knew he had to do something.

He gingerly woke the captain and said, "Sir, it looks like there is a severe thunderstorm ahead. Don't you think it would be advisable to circumnavigate the area?"

The captain rubbed his eyes with his knuckles, looked out at the storm and grabbed the controls as he said, "Hell no! We're going around that sum'bitch!"

CHAPTER 32   DC-8 FIRST OFFICER   1968

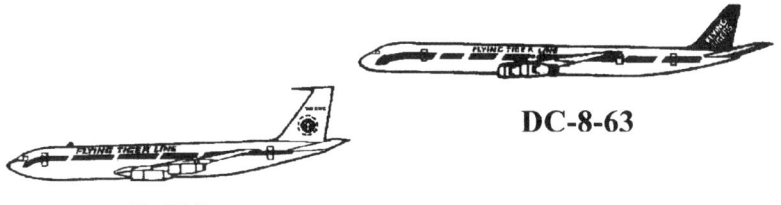

DC-8-63

B-707

TOM CONSTABLE: During the Vietnam War we were flying CL-44s to airbases in Vietnam. On this particular trip Bill McKenzie was the captain, and I was the engineer.

We flew to Saigon and landed at Tan Son Nhut Airbase. Since we had "real" milk (not powdered) on board, we thought it would be nice if we took it up to the guys in the control tower. They always appreciated it very much.

Bill and I gathered up what we could carry and walked over to the base of the tower, where there was a soldier on guard duty. He was in a sandbag bunker just outside the entrance and stairway leading up to the tower.

The stair well was lit with one light bulb, which had attracted about a thousand Geckos; they were all over the wall. Bill had a great aversion to lizards and such things, so he went up the stairs careful to not touch the walls.

We gave the much-appreciated supplies to the fellows working the tower and chatted for a while. They told us that the "High Altitude Artillery" was soon to arrive. By this they meant B-52s on a bombing mission from Guam. Their target was some miles northwest of Saigon. They thanked us and we said good-bye.

Bill preceded me walking gingerly down the long steep stairway. As Bill approached the last step, mischievous me gave him a little push and he stumbled forward flat up against the wall.

The Geckos were all over him like ants on a sweet roll, and he let out a yell that could have been heard in Hanoi.

About this time I was having second thoughts about what I had done. What if the guard was jumpy and thought we were the "VC"? We could have been shot.

The guard came running to see if we were O.K. We assured him that we were and walked back to the aircraft. We could hear the B-52s flying overhead towards the northwest. A few minutes later we could hear the thousand pounders exploding, and we could swear that we could feel the concussion moving our pant legs.

We fired up the old "Flintstone Rocket" and flew back to Japan. I don't think Bill will ever forgive me for that silly little prank.

There was a change in airline terminology with the coming of the jet airplane. Captains were still captains, but copilots were now first officers, and flight engineers, who used to be mechanics, were now called second officers. (Flight engineers were no longer required because with the new jet airplanes nothing could ever go wrong.) With the DC-8 we didn't have to stop in Cold Bay for fuel but could fly a load nonstop from Anchorage to Tokyo.

My first trip was a military passenger flight from Tacoma, Washington, to Anchorage, Alaska. Goldy was the captain, Larry Partridge, the second officer and Bill Roberts, the navigator. We left Tacoma about dark, and just after we reached V1, the speed beyond which we could no longer stop the airplane, we blew a right main landing gear tire.

I guess we all thought at first it was a bomb, but when we felt the severe vibration along with the right main landing gear indicator showing unsafe, we suspected a blown tire. We did not retract the landing gear, because we didn't know its condition and didn't want it to come up and possibly jam in the wheel well. We had to have more information before preparing for a landing.

It was dark by then so a flyby of the tower would not have been much help. We requested that a vehicle be sent out to inspect the runway for debris. For all we knew, we could be missing a wheel, or the entire landing gear for that matter. After they checked the runway, they reported finding a half of a tire casing but no metal parts.

The vibration during takeoff was so severe that we could hardly read the instruments. It caused the fuel transfer line to come apart and fuel from the center fuel tank poured overboard. We got a clearance to fly over the water and dump fuel down to our maximum landing weight of 275,000 pounds.

While we were dumping fuel, Goldy looked over at me and said with a grin, "Do you wish now you were still in the maintenance department?"

"Hell no. If I was, I'd have to work all night to put this thing back together."

Now that we knew the landing gear was probably intact, we returned for a landing. I say probably intact, because we didn't know why the landing gear safe light was not lit. We requested the emergency equipment to stand by and began the approach. Goldy set the DC-8 down on the runway carefully and kept the weight off the right landing gear as long as he could. As we taxied off the runway we could hear the entire planeload of G.I.'s applauding.

We found that one half of the tire had stayed on the wheel and the other half had flown off, breaking several wing flap hangers and shearing off some hydraulic lines and the landing gear down lock switch. We went to the hotel while the wheel assembly was being changed and all the damage was repaired.

This was the first airline trip for two of the flight attendants.

One of them said to me later, "I was sitting in the forward galley when I heard the explosion, and I thought it was a bomb. Then the airplane began shaking so badly, I was sure it would come apart. The coffee pot came out of its receptacle and was sliding toward me. I couldn't think of anything else to do, so I kept pushing it back in, and it kept sliding back out."

The next morning all the repairs had been completed, and we continued our trip with no further problems.

LARRY PARTRIDGE: I was told by McChord AFB people that during a runway clean-up procedure following our problem, a three or four foot piece of recently damaged angle iron was found just shy of our lift off point. It was assumed that was what caused our tire blowout.

The following is by a bored flight attendant stuck in some God-awful corner of the world. Anywhere can qualify if you've been there too long.

THE LAYOVER from <u>41 Years Aloft</u>

Well, we've been here a whole week now,
And boredom should have passed.
But everybody's wishing,
That we'd get home and fast!

The desk clerks are all nasty,
The hostesses are rude.
They'd rather see you starve to death,
Than give you any food.

CHAPTER 32   TIGER TALES

> Some rooms are hot as hell you know,
> And some are cold as tombs.
> Get pneumonia from the climate change,
> Just going room to room.
>
> There aren't any nightspots
> Where we could have some fun,
> The biggest thing in boredom town is
> Someone's fly undone.
>
> They do have booze aplenty, so
> We drink all night and day.
> The only thing that worries me now,
> Is finding the nearest A.A.
>
> Now what sadistic people,
> Would send us to this place.
> Doomed to spend the rest of the month,
> Cut off from the human race.
>
> What pisses me off the most, I guess,
> And leaves me all uncheered.
> Is recalling I wasn't assigned to this,
> But that I volunteered!!!

When the new DC-8s came on the line with a much higher payload, 110,000 pounds versus 63,000 pounds for the CL-44 and 43,000 pounds for the Connie, we didn't need as many airplanes. As the company began selling airplanes, we didn't need as many pilots. I was bumped off of international flying in October and had to fly domestic routes. Junior pilots began to be laid off. Soon it would be my turn.

A brand new Douglas DC-8-63

It was Paul's first trip with the Company, and was he impressive!

PAUL REBSCHER: When I was a new copilot I had a trip with Captain John Newcomer on a Cl-44.
John said, "Would you like a little stick time?"
Of course I said, "Sure," and I flew the next hour or so, keeping old 446 right on course and altitude. What I didn't know was that John never disengaged the autopilot.

CHAPTER 33 THE MOVIE "AIRPORT" 1969

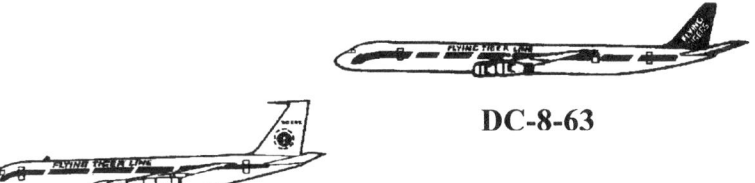

DC-8-63

B-707

George Bock would say this was the highlight of his long and successful career.

Universal Studios had chartered a Flying Tiger Boeing 707 and a flight crew to use in the filming of the movie, Airport. Captain George Bock, First Officer Dave Vachon and Second Officer Hal Cerniway flew the 707 to Minneapolis, Minnesota.

The movie was filmed in February at Wold Chamberlin Airport in Minneapolis. Preparations were being made to film the snowstorm accident scene. The snowplows had cleared the runway, and there were high snow banks on both sides. Sand was spread on the runway, and the flight crew made a trial run to test the braking action, which was good.

Now the movie people had to set up the klieg lights and the cameras, which took considerable time. All during this long interval it was still snowing. When they were finally ready, Captain Bock started down the runway and accelerated to the agreed upon speed of 70 knots. When he applied the brakes, he had no braking action whatsoever. He quickly applied maximum reverse thrust, which blew an enormous amount of snow ahead of the airplane. He had to stop using the thrust reverse for fear that the people up on ladders aiming the lights would be blown off.

As the Boeing 707 hurtled down the runway, all the movie people were busy doing their jobs. The cameramen were shooting pictures, and no one realized there was a problem.

Skidding sideways, the airplane slid to a stop at the end of the runway with the nose wheels cocked off to one side.

Henry Hathaway and his film crew were ecstatic about the pictures and congratulated the flight crew on a fantastic job. They were not aware just how exciting it nearly was.

Moon Bergman, the Tiger mechanic who was there to service the airplane said, "I thought for a moment I was going to be there until spring digging that thing out of the snow."

I didn't have to dig anything out of the snow, but there was sure a lot of it around. I was with Bill Hoey on layover in Anchorage in the middle of the winter. We had arrived early that morning, and I woke up about noon. Now I had to stay awake, so I could sleep at night to be rested for an early morning departure to Tokyo.

It was about three in the afternoon, and I had already had lunch, gone for a walk and solved the crossword puzzle. At the moment I was totally bored as I gazed out the window at the street below.

Just then around the corner came Bill carrying a large brown paper bag. I dashed from the room to the elevator and hit the down button. The door opened at the ground floor just as Bill was reaching for the up button.

Bill said, "Well hello, Vern, I'm glad you're up. If you're not doing anything in particular, come on up to my room, and we'll have a little drink."

I wasn't doing anything period.

CHAPTER 33   TIGER TALES   331

Bill opened the large paper bag and pulled out a quart of Old Overholt. He poured two water glasses about half full of whiskey. No ice, no mix, just whiskey. Then we began to talk. No particular subject, just pleasant conversation. Soon Bill refilled our glasses. He talked about the Korean War days and what Anchorage was like then.

About six o'clock he said, "Let's get a cab and go to dinner. I've been thinking about a restaurant where we used to hang out, the Saber Jet."

Bill made a phone call, then we drove somewhere on the outskirts of Anchorage. When we walked into the place, it was obvious we were expected. Bill was greeted with real affection. He put his arm around the beaming waitress and explained in detail what he had in mind. He introduced me and said we wanted a quiet table in the back room, and when she had a free moment she could join us and talk over old times. All in all, it was one of my most memorable evenings in Anchorage.

Probably one reason was because I knew I wouldn't be back there for a quite a while, but...Frank and Bob can handle it.

BOB BAIRD: Frank Graff was the captain and I was yanking gear for him in a -63. (DC-8-63) I can't recall the others but there was an oiler (second officer) and a navigator, of course.

We left Anchorage about midnight for a Cold Bay stop, then on to Tokyo. The weather was anything but good there and at our destination. About a hundred miles out of Cold Bay we were cleared for the approach and advised to contact Cold Bay Radio. We did so and were advised, "The current weather is 200-1/2 in blowing snow with a 20-knot crosswind.

Cleared for the VOR-DME ILS and report over the VOR outbound."

Frank is rummaging around in his brain bag, then asks if he can use my Jepessen as it appears he has left his in the hotel in Anchorage. I, of course, comply and hand him my approach plate, which he proceeds to lay on his brain bag where I can't see it.

Anyhow, we let down on the DME Arc, and I have no real knowledge of just where we are. I am fidgeting around and real uncomfortable and I ask Frank, "Where are we?"

He say's, "Not to worry—just call the Localizer alive for me to make the turn onto final."

I call the movement as soon as I see it, and we start a left turn to capture it but end up somewhat off as the crosswind component at altitude is way over 50 knots. We edge back and at Glide Slope Capture are about on it and showing about 15 degrees of drift. We get the gear and flaps down and I am looking for the lights, monitoring airspeed and altitude and giving the standard callouts.

At about 1000 feet the Engineer calls out, "Number three has flamed out!"

Frank is pretty much locked on by now and he says, "Just standby, we're going to land in a minute."

We break out at about 300 feet with the approach lights in sight, but offset quite a bit due to the drift. Frank calls the runway in sight as I call minimums, and he starts kicking the drift out. Well we arrive, no doubt about that, with a Frank Graff patented landing.

He yanks all four into reverse, and with the number three out and the max crosswind we just sort of turn sideways and slide down the runway, somehow still on center line!

We came to a stop some 7-8000 feet down the runway with the nose cocked about 40 degrees to the direction of travel.

CHAPTER 33 TIGER TALES 333

Franks says to me, "Tell 'em we are on the ground in case they can't see us and gi'me the after-landing checklist."

I do that and note as we taxi in that my right leg is having a nervous spasm, and I feel bad for being such a wimp. Heck, all I had to do was sit there while Frank did all the work, and it didn't bother him at all.

Of course we all have to take checkrides. They're always interesting and sometimes fun. A bunch of us showed up for ground school, and there were a lot of "there I was" stories from Jerry Petros telling how his B-24, C-124 or B-29 did this or that. Somewhere along the line we got into systems review of the DC-8, with a few raunchy slides thrown in just to see if we were awake. A couple of days of this was followed by an airplane check with Dick Keefer as check pilot.

Frank Halpin and I were paired off for the ride along with Dick, a check engineer and a pair of second officers.

We headed out to Bakersfield for the approaches and bounces (literally)!

Arriving in the airport area we are informed of the wind, runway in use and that the temperature is 107F. We began the approaches. I don't remember who went first, and it doesn't matter, as the yelling from Keefer was pretty loud for both of us. Seemed like all was pretty much okay until we got down around 200 feet, when he'd pull the hood, and we'd try to land the durn thing.

We'd be fighting the thermals from the excessive heat, which appeared to be trying to stream up to us thinking maybe the airplane was a place to cool off, not understanding how hot the cockpit was at times like this. Anyway, the airplane seemed to not want to go down at all, so we'd pitch it over a little more than usual, then fight it in the flare to arrive with a thump and bounce and much cussing, which along with Keefer's comments made for a rather noisy arrival.

A big furlough was pending and it looked like I'd soon be looking for a new job. The Connies and the CL-44s were being pulled off the line and sold. The first of the year I was bumped from first officer back to a second officer position.

Just before the furlough notices were sent out, I was offered the position of chief second officer. I should have taken it, but due to personal family problems at the time, I did not.

The chief pilot in San Francisco, Dick Stuelke, knew the chief pilot, John Lagerquist, at Capitol Airways in Wilmington, Delaware. He called him for me, and I had a job as a DC-8 copilot, before my furlough was effective.

I suppose someone might deduce that Chuck was a big pain in the neck, but I would never say that.

CHUCK HAMMER: I bumped my head on so many things in the airplane through the years, that I developed a problem in my neck. Three vertebrae fused together, so I lost my medical certificate, which eventually caused my retirement.

When I was in Cedars of Lebanon Hospital, they had me on so much painkiller that my doctor was concerned. Then he found out I liked to drink, so he prescribed Manischewitz Wine and beer. The prescription might have gotten mixed up somehow, but I got a quart of Manischewitz in the morning and a quart at night. Then I got a six-pack of beer at ten in the morning and another at three in the afternoon. I can't drink that much.

CHAPTER 33 TIGER TALES

Seymour, Goldy, and a lot of the guys used to come up and see me. I soon had a coat closet full of beer and wine, so I could entertain my friends when they came. I had a lot of friends.

Someone else left the company that year, but under more pleasant circumstances.

GOLDY: John Long was the first captain with the company to retire, so they wanted to do something special for him. The Douglas Company had given Prescott a big model of the DC-8, so Bob was going to give it to Johnny Long. He had Pinke set a party up in a private room. There were several couples there—Pinke and I, Wayne Hoffman, Bob, and of course John Long, all of us with our wives.

While we were standing there talking, I told Bob about the landing escapade up in Fresno last year when we gave Ed Pinke and Jack Martin's names to the newspaper as being the pilots. Bob thought that was about the funniest thing he ever heard.

Bob loved to needle Pinke anyhow. He liked Pinke and respected his intellect, but he still liked to needle him. Of course Bob liked to kid most anyone that he knew well.

The booze was really flowing that night. Prescott was at his best, and he got up to make a speech before presenting this big model airplane to Johnny Long. Trouble was he had been drinking so much that he forgot and got up twice to give the same speech.

There's nothing funny about this joke.

PAUL REBSCHER: I had an international trip with #1 Captain, Ralph Hedden, First Officer Spence Sidney and Navigator Joe Carr. I was the second officer, so I was in charge of the galley. In those days there was a special meal for the captain, usually a nice steak. The rest of us ate rubber chicken or meatloaf.

I heated the meals in the oven, but when I took the hot foil off of the captain's steak, I dropped the steak on the floor. It was such a mess that there was no way to cram it back in its container.

I said, "Ralph, I have bad news. I just dropped your meal on the floor."

Ralph thought about it for about two seconds then said, "No Paul, you didn't drop my meal, you dropped your meal."

CHAPTER 34   TIGER INTERNATIONAL   1970

DC-8-63

In May I was recalled by Tigers and began flying out of San Francisco as a DC-8 second officer. Now I had experienced my first furlough and recall, so I could consider myself a genuine airline pilot. Flying first officer for Capitol Airways on DC-8 passenger flights to Europe during the furlough was a lot of fun, but that's another story.

Because of the continuing growth of the company, it was felt there was a need to diversify. Tiger International was formed with Wayne Hoffman, an experienced railroad executive, as president. Tom Grogean was named one of the directors. The new corporation purchased North American Car, a railroad leasing company.

Half a world away in Taipei, Taiwan, a children's hospital was dedicated in honor of Peter Prescott, Bob's son, who was killed in the Lear Jet accident in Palm Springs in 1965.

ANN MARIE PRESCOTT: Al Cormier was heavily involved with the children's hospital in Taipei. It was in a sense a memorial to Peter, but it was also a thing that Al started by collecting toys and goods and things for the children. Then, after Peter died, we raised money to create the wing that was called the Peter Prescott wing of the Children's Hospital in Taipei.

    I remember we had a big service in Taipei, and Helen Ruth came also. Basically, the wing was maintained by Tiger employees and donations from different places for quite

a number of years. China and the Flying Tigers always had a strong connection.

And then, you know, Bob and I traveled quite often to Taipei on business and met the people there. Eventually from business it evolved into something more. It just seemed natural that Peter's memorial should be there. There was a need, and it fit right in at the time, I think.

Also in that part of the world on July 27, we suffered another aviation tragedy. I was in the Tiger crew room in San Francisco on the 24th, preparing for an eastbound flight when Captain Monte Treft, First Officer Bob Foley, Second Officer Bill George and Navigator Walter Roberts were leaving for Anchorage and the Far East. We exchanged pleasantries and departed on our respective flights. Three days later they crashed on approach to the Naha International Airport, Okinawa, in a heavy rain.

A witness reported, "The rain area appeared to be like a wall about 1/4 mile off the end of the runway. Visibility was so bad that I could not see the airplane until after the crash."

The DC-8 hit the water, broke in two and the forward fuselage rolled inverted in shallow water. The tide was coming in, and the rescue people couldn't get into the airplane in time.

Captain Treft died of head injuries. The other crewmembers drowned. Rescuers made a small hole in the floor of the cockpit and passed an air hose to Foley, who was the only one conscious, but he drowned before they could get him out. He was due to retire in three weeks.

CHAPTER 34 TIGER TALES

Sometimes the bad luck happens to the other guy.

BOB BAIRD: 10 August 1970. Sam Royall is the skipper and I am the first officer, along with Joe Rovegno as oiler (second officer) and Stan Jorgensen navigating us down South. It was my leg, and we were flying N794, a tried and true pax bird with a load of unhappy GI's headed for "Nam."

We launch from Yokota for a nice daylighter down to Camh Rahn Bay. It was an uneventful and routine leg with good service from the cabin crew, as usual trying their best to keep the coffee cups filled.

Approaching Quin Noun we start our descent and soon are talking to Camh Rahn Bay Approach and are advised to expect a straight in for the right runway. We are asked if we prefer a GCA but elect a VFR approach and at about 10 miles out we have a nice visual on the field. Approach hands us off to the tower as I call for gear and flaps, and we are set for landing.

Inside five miles the tower advises a C-123 will be on a short left base for the left runway and to report him in sight. Sam rogers that and at the same time calls the traffic. I note his position but am concentrating on airspeed and altitude, and as I am a little high on the VASI I'm bringing her down smartly.

Suddenly, Sam say's "That guy is going in!" I glance over to maybe 11:30 and see the C-123 inverted at about 400 to 500 feet over the beach. Within seconds he hits the deck and explodes into a giant fireball. We are maybe a mile out by now and the radio is silent.

Sam calls the tower and advises them of the crashed aircraft which is burning quite well off our left wing now. He then tells me to go around, and I shove the power up calling for gear up and flaps to the go-around position at the same time. The tower now also tells us to go around and to contact

Departure Radar. We do so and are directed to hold off shore VFR. We do that.

About this time the Senior Flight Attendant comes up and wants to know what's happening, and some of the passengers are curious about the fireball we just flew by. Stan gives her the dope, and Sam adds, "No need to tell them about the crash as they are pretty nervous anyhow!"

We hold for about 30 minutes and are then cleared in VFR and proceed back to the airport and land. Sam and I go to base Ops to brief those folks on what we had seen for their accident investigation. Some time much later I read the USAF Report on this accident, which was caused by a flap failure due to ground fire while these guy's were on a resupply mission. Amazingly the Crew Chief was thrown from the aircraft and, though injured, survived. The other five crewmembers did not. They, along with fifty thousand others, are commemorated on the Wall in Washington D.C.

I always remember how calm Sam was all throughout this experience. He wasn't even ruffled by my DC-8 landing! What a great guy.

Sunny days are appreciated, but are not always in the forecast. In this case it was fog that caught Ray Foster.

RAY FOSTER: I brought a DC-8 into Anchorage in zero-zero conditions. I had no choice. All the other airports within reach—Elmendorf, King Salmon and Fairbanks—were also down. I had made a couple of missed approaches, and now I had to land. I flew the ILS right on down until the wheels hit the runway, then I braked to a stop. We couldn't even see to taxi off of the runway. They had to send someone out with a tug to find us and tow us in to the ramp. I had two flight attendants deadheading with us, and one of them peed in her pants. I don't blame her a bit.

CHAPTER 34 TIGER TALES

In December I won a bid for a first officer position effective January 1st. That was a real nice Christmas present. I figured if things kept improving I'd soon be back to where I was in 1968.

Bob was already there.

BOB BAIRD: George Edge and I were operating one of the Canadian Passenger DC-8s, 624 I think. We were trying to make it non-stop from Yokota AFB Japan, to Seattle, so we're at max plus on the take off weight and sometimes even 10,000 feet of runway out front looks short!

Big George is flying, and I am calling speeds as we slowly but with much noise head down runway 36. "V1" comes and goes followed by "Rotate" which he does and not much happens.

Ol' George says to me, "Bob, have you ever had a tail strike in one of these?"

I sort of reply, "Well no, I don't think so".

I am really looking at the end of the runway coming up way too fast, and we still aren't flying!

George says, "Well this is what a tail strike feels like," and he pulls another few degrees on the yoke. The nose pitches up a bit and I swear I can feel the tailskid dragging...maybe not. Anyhow we fly and not a bit too soon as the end of the runway disappears under us and not very far under at that!

Yokota tower comes up and say's "Geeez Tiger you left a mile of sparks back there!"

I give them the "Sorry bout that" reply and we press on.

When George pulled that yoke back, he looked like a Big Teddy Bear playing with it. A super guy to fly with!

Later, much later, we found the weight and balance tables for these two aircraft (624 and 625) were way off on the loading charts. We were lucky not to have had an overrun accident with them when maxed out.

The war in Vietnam was still hot and heavy, and we had been advised that aircraft on approach to any of the South Vietnamese airports could be fired upon, so the captains should take all precautions.

Good news and bad news. The good news was that the aircraft logbook has heavy metal covers, which protect the book from damage. The bad news was that there was only one logbook on the airplane.

EILEEN "MRS. BILL" FRANKLIN: Willie Wilkins stopped by our house on his way home after an Asian trip with Bill.

Willie said, "We had some excitement this trip. The Viet Cong tried to shoot us down, but there wasn't much danger."

"Not much danger?" I said, "What did you do?"

"Bill just put the log book on his seat and sat on it."

"Well, that's pretty nice for Bill, but what did you do?"

"The only thing I could do. I sat on his lap."

Sounds like the well-worn term for a captain, "Old Iron Ass," really applies here.

CHAPTER 35   THE CROSSROADS ENDEAVOR   1971

DC-8-63

An event took place that year in which survival was anything but a safe bet. You wouldn't have to be a Tiger pilot to attempt something like this, but it would probably help...especially if one is also a navigator:

Elgen Long began his career with Tigers as a radio operator and a navigator, then became a copilot and later a captain. He would need all those skills to fulfill his dream, which was to fly solo over both the North and South Poles, crossing the Equator at the Prime Meridian and again at the 180th Meridian.

This would take money, so he had sold his boat and mortgaged his house. He leased his neighbor's Piper Navajo for the trip, and the only modification he needed was to add auxiliary fuel tanks to give him a 4,000-mile range.

With some help from Ed Pinke, vice president of operations for Tigers, he managed to have a Carousel Inertial Navigation System installed. This system was designed for the DC-8 and 747, but it worked just fine in the Piper.

There was an ulterior motive here. The company was interested in installing inertial navigation systems in our airplanes. Having one on a record-setting flight would be good advertising for the Carousel Company, and Tigers would gain firsthand knowledge on how well it worked.

Tigers also loaned a life raft and other emergency equipment. (Probably in case it didn't work.)

Elgen took off from San Francisco on November 5, 1971, on the first leg of the trip, which was to Fairbanks, Alaska. Over the Gulf of Alaska heavy icing clogged up the cabin heater intake rendering the heater inoperative. This caused Elgen considerable discomfort.

The next leg was from Fairbanks over the North Pole to Stockholm. During this leg the heater again would not work. This became extremely serious. Elgen thought there was a real possibility that his body temperature might drop so low that he would no longer be able to function. The weather at Stockholm was forecast to be below minimums, so he made a precautionary stop at Tromso, Norway, for fuel and a chance to get warm. (When you stop to get warm at an airport above the Arctic Circle, you have to be pretty cold.)

He continued to Stockholm, then on to London for a good rest. While there he bought another suit of long winter underwear and a heavy shirt.

His next stop was Accra, Ghana, and then he went on to his second objective, crossing the Prime Meridian at the Equator. He then crossed the South Atlantic landing at Recife, Brazil, and followed that with succeeding stops at Rio de Janeiro and Punta Arenas.

Next came the most dangerous and most demanding leg of his flight, across Antarctica to McMurdo Sound. He began the 3397-mile leg under clear skies, but with a storm covering the entire Antarctic. The weather was zero-zero when he crossed the South Pole but the crossing was verified by U.S. Navy ground radar. He was lucky to get into Williams Field at McMurdo just before a storm closed it down.

CHAPTER 35   TIGER TALES

The flight to Sydney, Australia, then to Nandi in the Fiji Islands was pleasant by comparison. On the next leg, which was to Wake Island, he passed the final crossroad, the Equator, at the 180th meridian.

At this point he had landed on six continents, so he headed west to Tokyo, Japan, to include all seven. Then it was back to Wake, then Honolulu and San Francisco.

Captain Long set eight records on this trip:
1. First around-the-world flight landing on all seven continents.
2. First solo flight around the world at the poles.
3. First flight crossing the Equator at the Prime and 180th Meridians.
4. First solo flight across Antarctica.
5. First solo flight Antarctica to Australia.
6. First Federation Aeronautique International (FAI) Class C flight around the world at the poles.
7. First FAI Class C flight North Pole to South Pole.
8. First FAI Class C flight Equator over South Pole to the Equator.

The flight covered 36,313 miles.

Tiger International was also keeping busy. They took over control of the Flying Tiger Line, Tiger Leasing and Tiger Air Service. Then they used our profits (probably) to purchase National Equipment Rental. Diversification had begun in earnest.

What'd he say?

This is the way I heard it. Wayne Elliot, a copilot, was flying his Cessna 150 when he inadvertently flew into a "dust devil," which is a large whirlwind, or a small tornado (depending on whether or not you are in one). He crashed and was banged up pretty badly, so he was on sick leave for quite awhile.

After he returned to work, he was in the crew room one day when Starr Thompson walked in. Starr had not seen Wayne since the accident.

"Hi, Wayne, good to see you back. How ya doin'?"

"Oh, I'm doin' pretty good, Starr, except that sometimes I can't remember things."

The more Starr thought about that, the more concerned he became. He decided he had better inform John White, the system chief pilot. John agreed that if this was true, Wayne sure as hell shouldn't be flying. John gave him enough time to get home then called him.

"I hear you told Starr you're having trouble remembering things."

After a hesitation Wayne answered, "Jeez John, I don't 'member tellin' him that."

CHAPTER 36 "WHERE'S THE PILOT" 1972

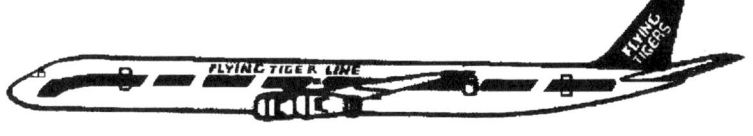

DC-8-63

A lot of people were moving around during the year. Ed Hale was promoted again, this time to supervisor of reliability analysis.

Sandra Ferguson, a Tiger flight attendant, moved about as far as one can go. She volunteered her services to the Tom Dooley Foundation and spent three months in Jawalakhel, Nepal, teaching English to the local children. Sandy was the fifth Tiger to join the Foundation over the years.

I flew a trip from Seattle to Chicago and New York with Captain Ron Hall and Second Officer Dave Freeman that turned out to be a real circus. A company traffic agent, who had never ridden in the cockpit before, was riding with us to New York. Chief Pilot Oakley Smith also rode with us as far as Chicago.

Before we left the crew room in Seattle, Ron said, "Oakley, if you'd like to fly it to Chicago, just crawl in the left seat." (A usual courtesy extended to chief pilots because having a desk job, they don't get a chance to fly as often as they would like.)

"Why thank you," Oakley said. "I'd be glad to."

Then Ron said to me, "Vern, if you don't mind, I'd like to take your seat. I have some things to talk over with Oakley."

"Sure," I said, "I don't mind getting paid for not working."

When we arrived in the cockpit, Oakley, a tall silver-haired man of obvious authority, sat in the captain's seat. Ron, a much younger man, sat in the first officer's seat, and Dave attended to his duties at the second officer's station. The agent sat in the observer seat behind the captain. Not having anything to do, I busied myself by making coffee, tidying up the galley and sweeping the floor.

After we landed at Chicago, Oakley went on his way, and Ron and I went to the crew room to take care of our paperwork.

When we came back to the airplane, Ron climbed into the left seat, and I took the right seat.

The agent's back stiffened as he said with considerable apprehension, "Where is the pilot?"

Without batting an eye, Ron turned and introduced himself.

He said, "Don't worry, I've been taking flying lessons, and besides, I used to be a baggage handler."

"And anyway," he said pointing to me, "Vern is going to fly it to New York, and he's a licensed airplane mechanic."

On the way to New York we ran into heavy weather, and I had to enter a holding pattern due to backed up traffic. One end of the holding pattern was in the clear, and while we were turning we could see several other airplanes. They were at different altitudes but I guess it didn't look that way to our passenger. I shot an ILS approach to runway 4 Right, and we broke out of the weather at about 300 feet.

Dave said later, "That guy was sure scared. I've never seen anyone with eyes that big. He was turning blue, and I was beginning to worry about him. Then when he saw

CHAPTER 36 TIGER TALES 349

the runway appear right in front of us, he finally took a breath."

We seldom have deadheads ride with us who are unfamiliar with airplanes and the normal weather we encounter. Ron really didn't intend to terrorize him... probably.

Ray Foster was back in the weather again. At least this time he didn't have any deadheads.

RAY FOSTER: I had a scheduled DC-8 flight from Hong Kong into Naha, Okinawa. The weather was forecast pretty good, but when I arrived the wind was blowing like hell, a 70 knot quartering headwind on final approach. I fought that thing all the way down and actually landed. Then the agent ran out and said, "What are you doing here?"

I said, "This is where I'm supposed to be."

"Didn't they get you on the radio? There's a typhoon coming in and it's going to get real bad here!"

I fired up again and took off for Tokyo before the typhoon could take us with it.

One of our crew schedulers became a second officer and began flying the line as a crewmember. Considering what he got himself into, he may have preferred a typhoon.

DOUG SHAW: The "ex-scheduler" had an active social life and was dating different flight attendants on each of his flights. Since he knew how the scheduling system worked, he would call crew control to see what flight attendants would be working on his flight legs, and if a favorite of the month wasn't scheduled, he would ask for a favor of the scheduler to see if their trips could be matched.

Jim Ossello was the manager of crew scheduling at the time and kept telling the "ex-scheduler" to stop calling and asking for favors. However, the calls continued and Jim figured he had a way to get the cooperation he asked for.

On the "ex-schedulers" next trip he found that all of the gals he had been dating were working the same trip. If you bid a passenger flight, you pretty well stayed with the same flight attendant crew for the entire trip, and they were long trips!

There were never any more calls to crew control for special scheduling favors.

What A Pilot Wants In His Union Contract

To make as much money as his relatives
think he makes.
To have as much time off as his neighbors think he has.
To have as much fun on layovers as his wife
thinks he has.
And he wants it all retroactively.

CHAPTER 37   FLYING REINDEER?   1973

B-747

DC-8-63

This is a horny story in more ways than one.

RALPH JARVIS: In early spring Captain Morgan Hughes, Second Officer Will Tjosaas and I flew a DC-8 from Portland, Oregon, to Nome, Alaska. We couldn't get fuel there, so we put on enough to fly to Nome and return to Portland.

The load was supposed to be 220 reindeer to be flown to Portland where they could adjust to the warmer climate, before being flown to their final destination, Taiwan.

Every spring the Chinese would go to Nome and pick up reindeer horns that had been shed during the winter. By importing the whole reindeer to Taiwan, they could assure the Chinese a dependable supply of horns—which when ground up were supposed to make an excellent aphrodisiac.

We parked close to an old WW II type hangar with a closed in ramp to help keep the reindeer from escaping. The reindeer were in the hangar—all 130 of them.

"Where is the rest of the herd?" I asked the handlers.

No one would admit to knowing anything about them.

A young lad came up in the cockpit, so we showed him around. We gave him a sandwich and an apple, and then asked, "Where are the rest of the deer?"

"Oh! The helicopter pilots rounding up the herd got thirsty, so they stopped for a beer and never finished the job."

Morgan and I were invited to take a tour of the city of Nome. There were nine churches and nine bars. (That seems like a fair arrangement.) Everything was very expensive because it all had to come from Anchorage by barge. The coastal waters around Nome are very shallow, so everything is off-loaded from the barges and put on flat bottom boats and rowed to shore—more expense.

Soon the mosquitos would be hatching. They are Texas size, or Alaska size, so maybe it is just as well the Alaskan winters are so long.

In the meantime the herders were having a tough time coaxing the deer up the ramp into the airplane, so Will jumped in to lend a hand and ended up with a badly sprained wrist. Eventually the DC-8 was loaded, Will's wrist was bandaged, and off we went to Portland. We were the largest airplane that had ever landed in Nome, and the whole town turned out to watch us take off.

During the last couple of years the company installed and ran testing programs on inertial navigation systems (INS) for the airplanes. When this new equipment, which had been developed for the space program, became operational, the pilots could do their own navigating on trans-oceanic flights. As a result all of our navigators were soon out of a job.

HAROLD MULVANEY, navigator: The company got the okay to use the Inertial System as of June 1, 1972. They kept us on salary until our contract expired November 1, 1973, and then gave us severance pay.

I went to Los Angeles to INS school, and then had my first overseas flight without a navigator. With Captain Jack Morris I flew from San Francisco to Anchorage, Tokyo and Naha, Okinawa. Then to Seoul, Korea, back to

CHAPTER 37 TIGER TALES 353

Tokyo, then we flew nonstop to San Francisco. We found our way home, so we must have learned something at the school.

I flew numerous international flights to Southeast Asia that fall and winter. Several flights were to Saigon, Viet Nam, with layovers in Bangkok, Thailand. I really did enjoy Bangkok. I like the Thai people, and they seemed to like us. I toured the Temples, saw the famous Reclining Buddha, the Reptile Gardens and viewed the river traffic on the clongs (canals). I had seen all these things when I was there in the early sixties, but I enjoyed them again. Of course my living accommodations were much better than Carol Bassie's.

From the flight attendant book, <u>41 Years Aloft</u>:

Phi Beta Kappa, Carol Bassie, didn't wear her Tiger hostess uniform during her four months in Laos. She slept on a bamboo pallet, washed in cold water and often went to bed "with the same dirty feet" for several days in a row and thought nothing of it.

Carol took a three-month's leave (that turned into four), from her flight attendant duties with FTL to work in a 50 bed Dooley Foundation hospital in North Laos.

She returned from Ban Houei Sai where she learned to teach English to the Lao, plan and supervise the preparation of meals for 54 persons, shop in the native markets across the Mekong River in Thailand and care for patients.

Carol taught the Lao to make American pancakes, and in turn learned that some palates prefer fish and chicken heads to a juicy slice of roast beef.

One morning very early mini-sized Carol was the only person awake when a patient died. It fell to her to wrap

the body and carry it from the hospital with the help of a Lao technician, to prevent evil spirits from invading the hospital, a disaster which the Lao believe would have required all other patients to leave.

"I did a lot of things I'd never done before," Carol said.

So did one of the flight attendants with Bobbie Tharp.

BOBBIE THARP: For a while in Anchorage, the company put us up in a small hotel near the airport, rather than downtown. The hotel people were very happy to have our business, so they put a van at our disposal in case anyone wanted to go fishing. Among a group of us who went, was Zalusky, who thought we might take some food with us, and of course, something to wash it down with.

The hotel folks said they would be glad to cook up any fish we caught at no charge.

So we go down to the river, some of us are fishing, others eating sandwiches and drinking martinis, beer and whatnot. I was doing pretty good, caught several salmon, so we go back and have a nice salmon dinner at the hotel.

The next day I left on a trip to the Orient somewhere, and get back to San Francisco a few days later. Marge Houge, the chief stewardess for the company said, "Bobbie, I want to see you in my office."

I thought, "Now what?"

She shut the door and said, "What were you doing to my Stewardesses up in Anchorage?"

"Nothing, I was only fishing...for salmon, and that's all I caught."

"Well," she said, "while out there along the river one of the girls had to go to the toilet, and of course, there was no place to go but behind some bushes, so she did. Then later, on the way to Saigon she came down with poison ivy or

CHAPTER 37   TIGER TALES

poison oak. Can you imagine how uncomfortable that would be in that heat and humidity while wearing a girdle?"

"No, I don't wear girdles, but I can imagine it would be miserable. I didn't know they had poison oak or ivy in Alaska, but if they do, I don't see how I should be responsible for where she drops her drawers."

A DC-8 at Anchorage

I managed to stay out of trouble all year, probably because I was too busy to go fishing. By December 11th, I had already flown the maximum hours allowed annually, so happily, I had the rest of the year off.

Bob Conrath was the third Tiger pilot forced into retirement by the FAA age 60 rule. Now he would have the rest of his life off, but he was not happy about it. Just when you get enough seniority to be able to hold desirable

<u>bid lines</u>, you're sent to the <u>sidelines</u>. Bob flew for Tigers for 23 years.

This next is not a bar story, but that's where I heard it.

One of our flights, which was equipped with the new INS system, left San Francisco for Chicago about midnight. A United Airlines cargo flight, also bound for Chicago, took off right behind the Tiger. United did not have INS.

During climb-out Center said, "Tiger, you're cleared direct to Farmm." (an intersection on the approach to O'Hare Airport in Chicago)

A few minutes later United said, "Center, could you give us a compass heading for Farmm?"

Center: "Tiger, what's your heading for Farmm?"

Tiger cheerfully replied, "270" (which, of course, is due west).

When the laughter died down, he gave the correct heading which would be about 060 degrees.

CHAPTER 38   A WORRISOME THING   1974

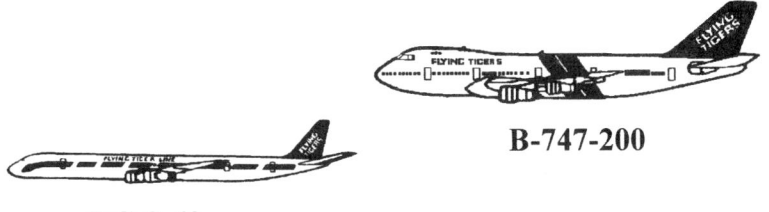

B-747-200

DC-8-63

Several other companies, most of them related to Transportation, were purchased by Tiger International. Along with all this came the addition of many new faces in upper management. This caused an undercurrent of concern among old time employees. Experienced airline people were being replaced by bean counters, whose only concern was the bottom line. They didn't appear to give a damn about the airline or its employees. But not to worry: Bob Prescott was still running things.

The mysterious east can be even more mysterious to a new copilot.

ERNIE THARP: My first international flight to Tokyo, Japan, was quite an experience, as no one told me what to expect upon arrival in Japan.

After we completed the shutdown checklist, I put all my things in my brainbag and closed it. I had noticed that a few well-dressed Japanese men had entered the cockpit. They seemed very formal and wore white gloves. I had turned to the front of the cockpit, and when I turned back, my brainbag was gone!

My initial reaction was, some dirty bugger stole my brainbag! The rest of the crew laughed and said not to worry about it. I thought, that's nice. It's my brainbag that's stolen, not theirs. I was upset about it all the way from the airport to the Tokyo Hilton.

We walked into the lobby, and lo and behold, there along with the rest of our luggage was my long lost brainbag. We went to the front desk to check in, where I was told to give my room number to the bellboy, and he would take the bags to my room.

I walked up to the bellboy, showed him my room number and asked if he would take my bags up to my room. He said, "Hi."

I said, "Hello, would you please take my bags to my room?"

He said, "Hi."

Of course the rest of the crewmembers were laughing their heads off.

I later found out that he wasn't saying hi, he was saying hai, which is Japanese for yes.

Every time you get to sleeping good, someone wants to wake you up.

BRENT SENSABAUGH: It was a long trip from Anchorage to Chicago to New York. I had dinner and a couple of beers and went to bed in the nude. During the night I got up to go to the bathroom. I opened the door. Whoops, wrong door. Here I was on the 40th floor of the Americana. I woke up as I heard my room door close behind me. Now I knew I was in a bad way here. I walked down the hall, but had no idea where the rest of the crew was. I saw a flowerpot at the end of the hall, so I did what I originally had to do.

I walked back to my door and lay down and curled up on the floor and went to sleep. An hour or so later a security guard came by and saw me lying there. I told him my story while he wrapped a towel around me. Then he checked my name and room number in the register and let

CHAPTER 38 TIGER TALES 359

me back in my room. The story is not over yet.

About two weeks later I had the same trip, went to the same hotel, and took the elevator going up to the 40th floor. This time I am in my uniform. I got to the 39th floor and the damn elevator quit. I'm really tired so, after a short while, I lay down and went to sleep. Some time later they got the elevator door open, and the guard shook my shoulder, "Are you all right, Sir? We were worried about you."

I turned around and looked at him. He was the same guard that had found me before.

I said, "I'm in a hell of a lot better shape than when you found me in my birthday suit."

"A couple of beers," Brent says. I'm sure he wouldn't try to kid us, but I worry about his arithmetic.

> Life gets tedious sometimes.
> From the flight attendant book, <u>41 Years Aloft</u>
>
> You've Been Flying Too Long If:
> You bake everything at 350 degrees for 40 minutes.
> You close your car door and try to put the girt[1] bar in.
> You can sleep sitting up, surrounded by people.
> You install a life vest under your favorite chair.
> You hand a guest a cup with water for an ashtray.
> You subscribe to Stars and Stripes.
> You buy only support hose in lingerie departments.
> You ask riders in your car to fasten their seatbelts and extinguish all smoking material before going downhill.

---

[1] A metal bar installed on all passenger exit doors that will deploy the escape chutes automatically when the door is opened.

Your biceps are bigger than your boyfriends'.
You think shoes come with milk spots.
You stomp garbage at home.
You hide your passport at customs so no one will see how old you are.
You write a letter, address it, and stick it on your wall.
The cockpit crew begins to look good.
You meet the man of your dreams on the airplane.

You're a new hire if:
You believe Korean clocks are really antiques.
You eat crew meals and like them.
Your hearing is good.
You believe you're the only one available for a trip.
You think "MAC" (Military Airlift Command) is a hamburger on a sesame seed bun.
You check each call bell and reading light.

Unknown

A DOBBIE STORY, Probably at least 80% True

One Sunday afternoon Dobbie took his kids to a ball game. After they were seated, he noticed a group of longhaired hippy-looking guys sitting in front of them. That was okay until they started smoking pot and using foul language. Dobbie decided this was not proper behavior at a game where there were several families with children.

Dobbie reached in his pocket, pulled out a dime and handed it to one of his kids.

"Go call your mother and tell her I'm in jail."

Whereupon he proceeded to correct the flawed behavior patterns that had been exhibited. Strangely enough, while the dust, pot and hair were flying, all the policemen present just happened to be looking the other way. The applause Dobbie received was that usually reserved for a home run.

CHAPTER 39   PHNOM PENH PNANCY   1975 PART 1

During the siege of Phnom Penh, Cambodia, by Pol Pot and his Khmer Rouge, the population of the city was facing starvation.

TOM SULLIVAN: One of the recent activities concerning the Tigers was the rice lift between Saigon, Viet Nam, and Phnom Penh, Cambodia. We had a group of outstanding guys who volunteered to go over there. They were making four and five round trips a day. Communist forces surrounded Phnom Penh, and we were trying to keep the city from starving.

We didn't lose any airplanes or people, but we had to pull out just two weeks before Saigon fell. It was quite an experience and a fitting part of Flying Tiger history.

The following is an excerpt from an article in Tiger Review, the company monthly magazine, dated April 1975.

On March 2, under a contract with the U.S. Government, Tigers began flying rice from Saigon to Phnom Penh to support the people of war weakened Cambodia, whose food supply had been cut off by advancing Communist forces.

For 43 days volunteer crews and ground support personnel put their own welfare second as they flew and maintained the planes that were the Cambodians' only link with food. Flying two to six mercy missions a day, Tigers landed 176 times at Phnom Penh's Pochentong Airport amidst ex-

ploding rockets and artillery, bringing a total of 16,687,265 pounds of rice into the besieged city.

Saigon: Loading rice for Phnom Penh

Flying Tiger DC-8s being loaded with 45 tons of rice for the starving people of Phnom Penh, Cambodia

The Tiger office served as the Air Force command center and coordinating center for the other airlines involved. In fact, Kangieser said, Tigers supplied, upon request by the U.S. State Department, technical data, facilities and personnel that made the rice lift possible.

They were powerless to make possible the success of the Cambodians against the Communist insurgents. On April 12 the U.S. evacuated Phnom Penh and brought the rice lift reluctantly to a close as the city fell to rebel forces.

CHAPTER 39 TIGER TALES

"It's sad," said one first officer on the airlift, "knowing there's nothing more we can do. If we could, Tigers would be among the first back there."

Here are some personal comments from some of the people involved.

TED BRONDUM: When I served with the Royal Canadian Air Force during WW II, I was with a supply squadron in India. We dropped personnel and supplies to the Guerrillas in Southeast Asia. The supplies included a great deal of rice. Now some thirty years later I was flying rice in Southeast Asia again.

Larry mentions in his diary that I went back to the States after the seventh day. This is true, but I returned on April 2 and stayed until the end of the operation.

The following is from the personal diary of then First Officer LARRY PARTRIDGE:

Day 1

Up at 5 a.m. leave Caravel Hotel—go straight to Tan Son Nhut (Airport) through dark streets of Saigon, already cluttered with many forms of transport peculiar to Saigon.

We're apprehensive—very good that captain rode with Airlift the day before and got a look at the operation.

Captain Ted Brondum is Norwegian. Very capable. His two favorite statements...it's not easy being a Viking, and...Columbus who?

I am Norske also (sometimes my mother denies that. If she is right please forgive me, Norway, for adopting you). Jim Winterberg is our second officer-very good at it and an excellent pilot, too. He's Scotch, German and American Indian—I picture him wearing a kilt, waving a tomahawk and singing "Little Big Horn Ober Alles." However he's done so well working with the Cambodian unloaders in Phnom Penh that we've softened his image somewhat by calling him "Lord Jim."

Take off around 7—take a grand tour over Saigon to get our minimum en route altitude—above enemy A/A rockets and we're on our way. In just a few minutes we have radio contact with Phnom Penh. For the first time we hear the words we later learn to sweat about—"All Bunnies Incoming!"

This is the code word that means the airport is under rocket or artillery attack. Cloud cover is bad and we look hard to find a hole. Find one and down we go—pattern approach and landing are different but uneventful—air traffic is thick—all kinds of aircraft all over the place. Shelling continues, but it's on the other side of the airport. Very quickly we're unloaded and on our way, again climbing through a hole in the cloud cover and then back to Saigon...missions #2 and #3 are about the same, but the weather is much better.

Day 2

About the same as day one, but we fly four missions—shelling still sporadic and inaccurate on the airport itself. But a short distance from where we park is a grove of palm trees with little shacks. We call it "Sunnybrook Farm." Rockets hit it all day—there goes the neighborhood.

I feel pity for the poor farmer...if there is one. The tight grouping of the hits makes us nervous. What if they adjust a bit in our direction? Discovered that French style toilet paper stretches. Try to snap off a piece with one hand and you end up with 47 feet of it on the floor. That bothers me almost as much as the rockets.

Day 3

Some hits are close enough to shake the airplane—even with two engines running (we do this to be ready to "get

CHAPTER 39 TIGER TALES

the hell out"—which is standard departure for Phnom Penh). We hear the "ka-rump"—some give off black smoke and some brown, have to ask someone about that. Climbing out we hear the word that the ramp itself is getting near-misses. After we get back to Saigon, the message comes through that World Airways has been hit and is trying to get out—they make it back to Saigon and we congratulate them on a good job getting back. Tail section looks like Swiss cheese. Airplane parked for repairs.

Day 4

Only two missions today—decision to continue flights made about noon. Over Phnom Penh we notice that the only air traffic now is us, meaning Tigers, Trans International and World Airways and Cambodian fighters. Makes going in and out much safer. Reason: all civil traffic halted. Enemy action is light. Very few incoming. Up to 12 missions now.

Every day after the rice lift got started, Ernie Miranda from Manila sent a box all sealed up and marked COMAT (company material)—S. M. oil. It contained two or three cases of San Miguel Beer all packed in ice and ready to drink after the last flight of the day.

Day 5

We fly four missions today. Getting very tired—asking for relief crew but none on way yet. Hot day—up in 90s and very humid. Airplane still running beautifully. Tires badly cut by shrapnel, but holding up. Rockets and/or artillery fire is light, but some hits are close. Someone should invent an air—conditioned flak jacket. Can feel sweat running down my chest and back, 16 missions.

Day 6

Incoming still light and inaccurate. Very hot and humid. "Lord Jim" has Cambodian unloaders working very well. They smile and wave every time we taxi in. Before, very sullen and morose. Jim gives them cold water from our galley when he feels they deserve it. I feel they'd do anything for him now. Three missions today. Total now 19. Get word volunteer crew is on the way. Hurry up you guys!

Day 7

Other crew is here. Hooray! We fly first mission while they observe. Incoming very light. We have the rest of the day off. Twenty missions now.

Day 8

Day off—mad because I woke up at 5 a.m. as usual and couldn't go back to sleep—went to the swimming pool at Saigon Airport—to bed at ten, but didn't sleep well.

Day 9

Captain Brondum left for States. We lost our Viking. New captain is Dutch. About the same except maybe more stubborn. Captain Bob Bax, another very capable pilot and a good man to be around. Still very tired. We stop at three missions due to that and the fact that "Lord Jim" had a 6,000-pound rice pallet run up on his foot while unloading. His toe is purple but he says it should be okay. Incoming is getting more accurate and increasing in frequency. If nothing else, isn't very good for our nerves. Seeing and feeling and hearing many "ka-rumps" now. Other crew took 4th mission and got very heavy shelling. We say, "Welcome to the war."

Day 10

Enemy fire getting very heavy at times—and accurate. Two Cambodian G.I.'s riding bicycles across taxi-way beside us have a rocket hit very close to them (and us). I'm afraid they've had it as both of them fall off bikes and lie there. Bikes continue on. They get up again, run to their bikes. And I'm sure set a new record of some kind. (Evel Knievel would have been proud of them.)

That afternoon we find that "Tail Pipe Charley" (code name for the advisers based at Phnom Penh and living in a revetment made of sand bags at the airport) haven't had anything to eat or drink yet that day except warm water. Their supply plane didn't come in due to the action. We

CHAPTER 39 TIGER TALES

gave them all our sandwiches and donuts plus the hot coffee in our galley. They are all now wearing Flying Tiger baseball caps when they can. They wear steel helmets mostly.

After the military quit flying food in for Tailpipe Charley, we took their food orders and radioed them back to Tigers in Saigon. On the next trip we'd bring them bags of hot cheeseburgers or whatever they had ordered. It was probably the most unique fast food service ever devised.

Day 11

Enemy fire very bad. Finally on last flight we take a hit less than 100 feet from our tail. Shrapnel coming down all around us. Jim picks up a piece with a string. It's too hot to handle with hands. Mechanic standing under tail when round hits. Nothing hit him, but he saw chunks skipping through the grass and dirt all around him. Airplane inspected for damage back in Saigon. None—a miracle! We stop at hotel. All very tired now. Got permission to name airplane for my wife—calling her "Phnom Penh Pnancy." Company buys dinner and drinks for both crews. Have day off tomorrow. On our flights alone—not counting other crews or airlines—we've hauled 2,737,600 pounds of rice.

Day 12

Day off. Try to sleep in, but am foiled by habit. Awake at 5 a.m. Doze on and off till 10 then give up. Go and eat. Jim and I just sit quietly. I feel as tired as he looks. Maybe now that a regular schedule is here we will catch up. Meet other crew at hotel and they're still stuttering. The ammo dump was hit during their trips and shelling was very heavy. Shrapnel nicked their crew chief. Didn't know it till flight engineer saw the blood.

Day 13

Up at 5 a.m. again. All in clean uniform. ABC News was supposed to go with us. I guess they talked themselves out of it. First and second flights a breeze. But third something else. Many accurate hits on ramp area before we arrive. Then just as we're about to land we see a round hit right on the runway in front of us. Radio says, "Go around and hold." We agree. C-130 stops half off the runway. We think he has been hit. It's quiet for a while so we go in. All okay we think. But "ka-rump" right behind us where we parked yesterday! All on ground crouch a bit. Two there and one on the runway again. Why can't someone knock out those bastards? We get out okay. Land at Saigon and rush to hotel for debriefing. Another day another dong (Vietnamese money). Total 37 missions.

Day 15

Up at five—four trips—all uneventful—enemy fire very light but accurate—several hits on runway, but not while anyone was there—not much to talk about except the heat. I'm going to freeze to death when I get back to Seattle—a little homesick—miss wife and kids very much—stay at airport and put name on airplane. She's now officially Phnom Penh Nancy. DC-8s are good airplanes, but Nancy has got to be the best—still no mechanical problems. Total now 37 missions.

Day 16

While waiting in the hotel lobby to go fly my two trips get word that Phnom Penh Pnancy has taken a hit! It's minor (hole in engine cowling etc.) But I feel something for her. She's been a super lady and doesn't deserve such treatment.

I take her twice more into Phnom Penh with no problems. Ground advisers on our initial call say, "Is that Phnom Penh Nancy?" We laugh and affirm it. It looks like that's her official name now. No more Tiger 783. Total: 39 missions.

Day 17

Two afternoon flights today. No sweat. Very quiet and that's fine with us. Captain is Oakley Smith, our Director of Flight Operations. Another good man to sit beside. Don't know total poundage of rice flown in now, but must be phenomenal! 41 missions now for Jim and me.

Day 18

Day off—wake up at 5 a.m. as usual—lay awake listening to artillery fire on outskirts of Saigon—seems heavier than usual—count about thirty rounds and fall asleep—imagine, they used to count sheep and here I am counting shots. What's this world coming to?

Met a Norwegian journalist at the hotel. He gave me a beautiful book on his hometown of Alesund—made me homesick for my fjords in northern Washington State. I've got to visit Norway some day soon.

Day 20

Up at 5 a.m. again—curfew ends at 6 at the airport. Complicates things a little—two uneventful trips—incoming accurate, but very light. TIA (Trans International Airlines) takes a minor hit on the nose—third trip we have to go back to Saigon due to heavy shelling of airport.

We wait for a while—things seem to quiet down so we take Nancy back in—on short final approach rockets hit on both sides just ahead—very close—more falling as we land and taxi in—very sad news—direct hit in parking area, and Lord Jim has lost seven of his Cambodian friends.

They were waiting to unload our aircraft when hit came. Four killed outright, two lost both legs and died on the way to aid station—several others wounded and one more gone at aid station—now they are not smiling—Cambode "Boss man" comes into cockpit visibly shaken—practically on verge of tears—we talk a bit—I give him a pack of cigarettes and all his remaining crew ice cold Cokes. Many thanks, but still no smiles.

We are saddened and angered by the situation—almost wish Nancy was a bomber. At Saigon we cancel the last flight due to even heavier shelling. 45 missions now.

Day 21

Day off—nobody flying because TIA got bad hit on first flight of the day—fire started under wing, but crew very brave—they returned to airplane and taxied it away from fire—engine blast put out ground fire. Fire truck followed airplane and put out fire on wing. Military C-130 also hit—both disabled and all flights canceled till further notice—we have dinner at floating restaurant and watch boatloads of refugees coming up the Saigon River.

Day 22

Another day off—situation still the same—TIA and C-130 still in Phnom Penh—shelling light but accurate. We think they're trying to put both aircraft completely out of commission. Military says they'll try to push back rocket sites—but I wonder how in hell they can do anything with the tired old equipment they have—get word Jim and I might be able to go home tomorrow—be great to see Nancy and kids, but I hate to leave here and do no more for these people. I'm ashamed of the free world's reaction to this situation. It will be a long long time before I can try to sleep and not see that Cambodian "Boss man's" tearful face asking, "When are the people going to help us?"

If this is the Communist way of "liberating" the little people, I shall hate them with a passion till the day I die.

CHAPTER 40   THE FALL OF SAIGON   APRIL 1975

B-747

DC-8-63

Now an account of just one trip to Phnom Penh by Captain Ted Brondum, First Officer Bob Baird, Second Officer Larry Barrow and Flight Mechanic Jim Bartosiewicz, as told by:

BOB BAIRD: Military briefing. "Good morning gentlemen. Today's situation around Phnom Penh remains basically unchanged. The insurgent activity west of the airport continues and the perimeter is now about four and a half to five miles out. The Khmer Rouge (KR's) are moving approximately two battalions up from the Neak Luonq area, but it's estimated it will be two or three days before they are a factor.

The young Air Force captain (our briefer) walks to a covered aerial overlay of Pochentong Airport and lifting the cover sheet, points to numerous red dots penciled on the chart.

"Yesterday we counted about five 105 and thirty-six 107 rounds. A light day you might say."

Smiles flicker among the groups of pilots attending the briefing.

"What about anti-aircraft or Strella threats, anything new in that department?"

"Negative. As far as we know the KRs don't have Strella, and we have no reports of any significant anti-aircraft at this time."

I wonder what got that Cambodian AC-47 last night just west of the field...oh well, press on as they say.

"Takeoff times and call signs are posted on the mission board. Base Altitude is one five thousand and call Tail Pipe Bravo (operation headquarters) on the same channel as yesterday."

"The latest weather is reported VFR with a few scattered clouds at around fifteen hundred, and that should burn off early. That's about it, unless there are any questions."

There aren't, so we shuffle out into the next room, check our call sign and takeoff time. We are Klong 945 today and we're number four to launch, so there's plenty of time to check the paperwork, drink a cup of bitter instant coffee, and kibitz with the crew members.

Thirty minutes prior to launch we walk out to the airplane. She sits on the ramp looking clean and eager.

The morning sun radiates off her pale aluminum skin. She doesn't look very war-like, but then she never was supposed to. The cargo door is open and loaders are busy filling her belly with 45 tons of rice for the people of Phnom Penh.

Now, on up the high crew ladder and into the office where no day is the same and each sunrise and sunset a delight only a few are privileged to observe. Time now for the mundane task of pre-start checks and ATC clearances. Time check and five minutes to go. Engine start and all in the green, taxi clearance to two five right. (The left one's closed due to a VNAF A-37 running off the edge.)

Two flights of bomb-loaded A-37s are ahead of us, and we wait patiently in the run up area as C-46s, C-47s and assorted other aeronautical paraphernalia clang down in front of us. The A-37s canopies slide down, and they trundle onto the active amidst a babble of Vietnamese on tower frequency. Ok, we'll be next and about time too as the first drops of sweat run down my forehead and into my

CHAPTER 40　　　TIGER TALES　　　　　　　　373

eyes. The 37s, nicely spaced, begin their roll with a demure roar of engines.

Klong 945 taxiing out at Saigon

"Klong 945 cleared to line up"

"Roger, 945 into position." Checklist below the line and ready to go.

"Klong 945 cleared for takeoff. Climb instruction—climb on the 160 radial 24 DME then on course. Contact departure after airborne."

The clearance is read back and power levers up to takeoff EPR settings. Takeoff weight is 282,000 pounds, not anything near max, but the roll is still long enough in this heat and with the ever constant five-or-six-knot tail wind component. (I wonder if the bloody wind indicator in the tower is stuck. They always report the same value and that old-fashioned windsock always disagrees!)

Lift off. She hangs there for a moment as if undecided then begins to climb. Through three hundred a gradual left turn out with all hands scanning for traffic. Further left and the CDI (course deviation indicator) comes alive, a little further to center the needle, and speed adjusted for max rate of climb...not supposed to be any threats out here, but I consider anywhere outside Saigon as suspect.

Cleared from departure to center and "check out of FL80 please." Roger that, and through it with a call as 20 DME comes up. 24 DME and out of ten with a hard right turn to on course and continue the climb to FL 220. Check level and airspeed building to Barber Pole. Number two VHF turned to the tactical frequency of Tail Pipe Bravo, the airlift command post at Phnom Penh, and a listening watch begins. Phnom Penh's DME comes in and seventy out we cancel IFR with Saigon and ease the power back to begin a speed reduction.

The engineer brings up a nice cold cup of water, and downing it, a DME check shows we are coming up on fifty out.

"Tail Pipe Bravo, Klong 945, base plus seven, request your status."

"Klong 945 Bravo, we are clear at this time, five's the active, traffic one Big Bunny ahead of you (another eight)."

"Roger Bravo, we'll give you a call closer in."

Time waits for no man gentlemen, so now to work. Power all the way off and start down, planning on FL150 at 25 miles. Pass the flak jackets please...minor contortions getting into the thing and slightly pulled muscle somewhere in my back in the uneven struggle. Finally get it on and zipped up, and the temp shoots up another 20 degrees.

Drift down to 150 is okay and level with 28 DME coming up, continue the speed reduction now to 230 and call for flaps and gear. As the gear locks down and three green showing, flaps to 23 and complete the before-landing checklist to the line. Push her on over now and take her

CHAPTER 40 TIGER TALES

down is the order of the day. Ahead, Phnom Penh is visible and Pochentong Airport a scar on the green brown earth southwest of the city. Watch flap speed and begin s-turns to clear the area (look for traffic) and also give me a little more time to get down.

"Traffic at two o'clock low." The engineer's on the ball, and I check his call and pick up a C-47. At the same time I spot a pair of T-28s headed for the field. We're out of eight and a little close, so I swing around to the left and start another S-turn. Good. Going to work out fine.

"Lots of traffic down there," someone says.

Rog, I can see five or six aircraft in various parts of the sky, a couple of UH's (Helicopters) low leveling down a tree line, a Porter, T-28s, a 130, Man! All sorts of goodies floating around!

Downtown coming up on the nose, continue turning right planning a left turn back in on the downwind. Bravo is still quiet. Phnom Penh tower is up, and he's talking to quite a few folks requesting downwind and final reports. Sounds like your local airport on a Sunday afternoon. Even now I find it hard to realize there is a war going on down there, but a glance off at my ten o'clock brings the reality of the moment back as a pair of T-28s pitch up and break into a steep bomb run on a KR position west of the airport.

Check speed and approaching three thousand close in, low enough for now. One of the eights took some automatic weapons hits out here somewhere.

Bravo comes alive "Warning, Warning, Warning" Incoming. A puffy ball of dust erupts into the air in the center of the field. Trouble comes in pairs they say. Sure enough another burst in the military area near some parked C-123s.

Pucker factor increases rapidly now and the scan rate goes up accordingly. Hot in here, sweating like crazy, can feel the water trickle down my legs. Quickly scan the panel and then back outside looking for traffic and checking my position.

Roll into a left turn now and ease onto downwind. Look for traffic. I pick up Klong 930, another stretch eight, on a close in base leg coming down steeply. Normally we would be spaced 15 minutes behind the aircraft in front of us, but in this case we have caught up with it due to his being delayed by an aircraft emergency landing in front of him. Established on downwind still descending, whoops. A C-130 head on and going in the opposite direction. Stop descent, and we clear by about a thousand feet, no problem.

I set up the descent again, check right but can't see the runway. I ask Ted, who looks rather uncomfortable in the right seat, to call the turn for base leg. I don't see 930 either so he must be no factor. Ted gets our downwind call in to the tower finally between numerous radio transmissions.

"Roger Klong 945, report a five mile final."

Five mile final? Wasn't planning that but it's his ballpark. DME clicking three to four, lonely out here at this altitude, we make a good target.

"How does it look Ted?"

"You're okay, come on around."

I crank her around to the base leg. Still can't see the runway.

"Tighten up the turn a bit and you've got it made," says Ted.

Rog, check speed and sink rate, add a little power, and around she goes calling for gear down and flaps to complete the landing checklist.

"Uh, 930s there."
"What's that?"
"930s on the runway."

Runway is coming into view, and now I see 930 also, taxiing back on the runway. Tower seems uninterested in all of this. Well there isn't enough room for two down there so, "Going around" called, gear up and flaps back to twenty-three as power advanced and climb back to fifteen hundred with a right break to rejoin downwind again.

Ted calls the tower and again gives me the turn in point. We roll in on final with gear and flaps, add a touch of power and pitch for a little too much sink. Runway coming up...check speed and sink...right on down five hundred...four...three.

"DC-8 on short final. Go Around!" "DC-8 on short final. Go Around!"

Tail Pipe Bravo is screaming on the radio. At midfield a rocket impacts, followed quickly by another. Both are near the runway.

"Max power, gear up, flaps twenty-three!"

We're getting real good at this!
I re-establish a downwind, sliding in behind a C-130. He's a little slow for us, so we kick the gear out early and add flaps to slow down for spacing. He rolls off to the right for a short approach to the field.

Really sweating now, interesting trip so far. Ted says bring her around and tower calls—we're number one. Roll out on final with about two miles to go. The 130 is turning off at mid-field. Slight corrections to line up and check speed and sink rate. Everything looks good. Threshold coming up, very slight flare, power off. Slight jar, spoilers extend, throttles back and reversing as the in-transit lights come on steady, all four in reverse. Speed 135 slowing. Runway flashing by, but no braking yet. Max reversing, lots of noise and shaking, speed 105, good, brakes now, not too hard you clod, no tire changes at Phnom Penh if you please. Runway end coming up. Cancel reverse and slow for the turn around.

Ease all the way over to the left, not much room here, nose wheel steering engaged and crank her around 180 degrees and taxi back to the mid-field turn off point.

While I taxi, Ted sets the aircraft up for takeoff, and the flight engineer confirms we're ready to go. Taxiway coming up, slowing, we ease onto the PSP planking laid to reinforce the concrete pathway to the ramp. A ground marshaller, splendid in blue shorts, T-shirt, green-covered helmet and sweat-stained flak jacket, directs us to park near Bravo's Bunker as 930 is standing on the primary unloading spot.

I ease onto the spot, and the ground man gives me "Chocks In." Shut down one and two and the cargo door coming open. The Cambodian ramp crew rides the loader up to the airplane and scramble on board. The engineer has unstrapped and moves back to supervise the unloading. As his Cambodian is rather sparse he'll supervise by pushing and shoving the heavy pallets in the order desired and will be in ill humor while he catches his breath when we leave. What price fame and glory?

We are nosed in close to Bravo's Bunker, and I have a clear view of most of the ramp area. A dozen or so men and women are scooping sand into burlap bags to beef up the bunker's overhead protection. They haven't taken a direct hit yet, but you never know.

Bravo's radio man/manual controller is below me and some thirty feet away. He's standing in a sandbagged enclosure and looks distinctly warm. He has one hand on the radio mike and the other on the well-publicized red warn-

CHAPTER 40 TIGER TALES

ing flag that he waves like crazy when he gets an incoming report.

A pair of Cambodian T-28s taxi by, returning from a strike. Both are rather moth worn, and one in particular seems to have an oil leak of some magnitude. I notice one of the birds has the .50-caliber gun pods mounted below the wings. The pilots appear to be fairly young and both sport gaudy scarves in the best tradition of the fighter jock. I'd like to swap seats with them for a while, what a blast!

A dull "whump." A 107 lands some three or four hundred yards away. No one pays any attention to it. I decide to put my somewhat war weary SPH-5 on anyway. Another explosion with a nasty crack to it. It's on the other side of the airplane somewhere, must have been fairly close though as the folks on the ramp have all hit the dirt. The little red flag is waving madly in front of me. Not much you can do about it at this point!

The folks on the ramp are back up and about. No one is hit. Nasty things these rockets, no warning whatsoever. Peace and calm, then a mighty bang. Everyone here is wearing flak jackets and quite a few sport tin hats also.
The paper in Saigon reported that all the best-dressed people in Phnom Penh wear flak jackets while shopping and some very colorful designs are showing up.

A line of rickety looking trucks queue up beside the loader to off-load the rice pallets. They really look ancient, reminding me of the old wood burners we used to see in Tokyo years ago.

A small boy riding on the top of the cab of one of the trucks flashes me the international "OK" sign as he rides by. I wave to him, wish I had some candy along to toss his way. I'll try and get some before the next trip in.

Larry Barrow, the engineer, comes up and reports two pallets to go and negative onload.

Time to restart one and two. I bring the power up on three and four, and we light the two still engines. All four running and off-loading is complete, and the door is closing. Chocks are pulled. Crank the nose steering hard left. We're close to the bunker so use caution coming out. Clear right and away we go. Ground time ten minutes. Off load: 90,000 pounds of rice and one case of beer for the troops at Bravo. Very nicely done too, I might add.

Taxiing out we weave around some freshly filled craters on the ramp and continue on the PSP to the runway. Tower calls and advises "Cleared to line up and takeoff." His accent distorts the words just a bit. The first few trips in we were sure he was saying "Cleared to land or takeoff," and it always got a laugh in the cockpit.

The airplane is empty now and mid-field takeoffs are the order of the day, as traffic and incoming rounds preclude taxiing to the end with a slow turnaround and then launching.

A quick final check as we align with the runway centerline, max power, the airplane leaps ahead. The tree line off the end of the runway grows rapidly but no sweat as we reach Vr and rotate.

The airplane comes off quickly, and I continue the backpressure on the yoke, adjusting the pitch attitude for max rate of climb. No other traffic in sight for a change, but we won't relax until we're level at our cruise altitude. Reduce to climb power now and fly the briefed egress headings out of Phnom Penh.

Approaching FL-80 I call for gear up. We've left them down until now to assist in cooling of brakes and tires.

"Tail Pipe Bravo, Klong 947 inbound."

Another ricebird is on his way in. The air is cooling down now, and we struggle out of the sweat-soaked flak jackets and down a cup of cold water. Back to Saigon for

CHAPTER 40 TIGER TALES 381

another two or three trips today and we'll be done. Until tomorrow.

Tigers continued the rice lift until Pol Pot's forces overran Phnom Penh. We heard later that all the ground support people at the Phnom Penh Airport were beheaded.

The following Tigers were involved with the rice lift:

CAPTAINS	FIRST OFFICERS	SECOND OFFICERS
Bob Bax	Bob Baird	Larry Barrow
Ted Brondum	Dave Buckner	Art Dodd
Jerry Casey	Tom Fredericksen	John Franzone
Paul Crowley	J.D Johnson	Marv Griffith
Mark Devereaux	Ken Johnson	Archi Hall
G.(Dick) Riemer	Dave McDevitt	Joe Pacini
Sam Royall	Larry Partridge	Fred Peterson
Oakley Smith	Bill Popp	Mel Ports
Tom Sullivan	Al Taylor	Angelo Regina
Bill Towner		Jim Winterberg
		John White Jr.
		Ted Freedell

GROUND SUPPORT
Gary Kangieser, Terminal Manager Saigon.
Jim Bartosiewicz, Maintenance Rep Chicago.
Joe Bazan, Maintenance Manager Far East.
Dick Dunn, Senior Operations Supervisor Travis AFB.
Richard Hernandez, Maintenance Rep Chicago.
Norm Martel, Maintenance Controller Los Angeles.
Frank Riggins, Mechanic Los Angeles.
Gregory Slack, Flight Line Mechanic Chicago.
Grant Swartz, Maintenance Rep Saigon.

VIETNAMESE TIGERS

Tran Anh Kiet	Truong Khai Hoan
Nguyen Van Bich	Ho Van Sanh
Ngo Van Hai	Ly Van Tai
Nguyen Gia Hoc	Nguyen Van Hue
Nguyen Van Thanh	Nguyen Hoang Son

By April the situation in Saigon was deteriorating rapidly. The following account by Ralph Mitchell says it all:

RALPH MITCHELL: 4-18-75 My crew—First Officer Ted Freedell, Second Officer Rick Middle—and I were to fly from Seoul, Korea, to Manila, Saigon, and Bangkok tomorrow. We felt that the company might want to evacuate our personnel soon. I figured we could get at least 400 people into the DC-8-63F. They would be sitting on the cargo floor, but they wouldn't be complaining about the lack of amenities. I had some experience in evacuating refugees in China in 1948.

The biggest concern is panicky people trying to get on the airplane. Then there are the regulations. All kinds of rules have to be broken or ignored. Then there is the matter of carrying passengers without proper immigration papers.

4-19-75 The Station Manager in Seoul informed me that our flight was scheduled to overfly Saigon tonight. After leaving Manila for Bangkok, we called the Tiger station when passing abeam of Saigon. They reported all was normal.

4-20-75 At 8:00 a.m. at the hotel, I received a call from director of flying, Oakley Smith, in Los Angeles. He said

CHAPTER 40   TIGER TALES

time had come to evacuate our people from Saigon. Intelligence reports indicated that Russian SA-2 anti-aircraft rockets would be in range of Tan Son Nhut Airport within 48 hours. They expected an airplane would be shot down, which would effectively close the airport.

We were to have the Manila freight off-loaded from the airplane, and then fly it to Saigon arriving at 3:00 p.m. I called the FTL station in Bangkok, but got no answer. Then I called R.C. "Andy" Anderson, our super-reliable maintenance expert at his home and informed him of the change. He took care of everything, and we departed on schedule.

We were concerned about being swamped by too many demanding passengers, as the World Airways 727 was recently, coming out of Danang. World Captain Ken Healy, whom I had known with CNAC in Shanghai, left Danang for Saigon, and some refugees were still hanging onto the airplane landing gear as it left the ground.

When we arrived in Saigon, our people parked us in an area near the end of runway 25L and said to shut down the engines. They didn't seem to be in any hurry to leave. Dick Dunn, the FTL operations man, said all was well, but they didn't want the airplane to leave until after dark. A lot of the people didn't have passports or exit visas, so they had to sneak onto the airport without going through immigration. We didn't want our long ground time to raise suspicions, so we opened an engine cowling to indicate a maintenance problem.

We were driven off the airport to Steve's Cafe, run by an American, where we spent the afternoon drinking iced tea. Steve, the owner, told Ted he didn't intend to leave town.

Finally at nightfall, we were taken to the Tiger Operations building at the airport. It was full of Vietnamese relatives of Tiger employees, all looking rather nervous. The destination of our flight had been changed to Guam, but we were still filed for Hong Kong on our flight plan.

At 8:40 p.m. the crew went out to the airplane with some of the FTL family personnel and Gary Kangieser, station manager, who had a very hectic day trying to arrange all the details of our departure. Grant Swartz, maintenance supervisor, had taken care of the airplane all this time and supervised loading of company material, spare parts, etc. Many of our passengers had already been loaded through the main cargo door in large containers, as though it was a cargo loading operation. We took off at 9:01 p.m. After climbing out over the ocean and away from Saigon Control, we changed our destination to Guam. All passengers were FTL employees and families, World and Trans International Airlines and American Express employees and families or others who had in some way contributed to the safe departure of our Saigon staff.

4-21-75 After a smooth five hour and ten minute flight we landed at Agana Naval Air Station, Guam, which is run by the Navy, but is open to civilian airliners. Having arrived at four in the morning with little notice, we created quite a bit of confusion. Agana Tower at first refused us permission to land since we didn't have a proper clearance. We told them we didn't have enough fuel to go anyplace else, so finally they let us land.

The passengers were taken in quarantine to a local hotel. The District Director of Immigration in Hawaii sent word that they were to permit the evacuees to travel through Guam without processing them there.

The passengers were to board a Pan American flight to the States, so our part of the evacuation was complete. My crew and I went to the Okura Hotel to rest, in preparation

CHAPTER 40 TIGER TALES

for our planned 8:00 p.m. departure for Hong Kong where a load of cargo was waiting.

While I was trying to sleep I got phone calls one after the other. The FAA, the press, a ladies group wanting to get orphans out of Saigon, the Immigration Department and the Governor's office. The FAA man wanted to know if the radio navigation aids in the captured areas were operational.

I said, "Look, I've got to get some sleep, I have a flight out of here tonight."

"Don't worry about that," he said. "The Governor has a police car parked in front of your nose wheel, and the airplane has been impounded."

Seems this flight had been cleared by the State Department, but not with the Governor of Guam. The Governor finally agreed that we could depart after all the evacuees had departed on Pan American. This caused Tigers another day of needless delay.

So that was the end of it. The rest is history. Our people all did their jobs well as long as they were there, and we are relieved that they all got out safely.

DC-8 at Sunup

CHAPTER 41   BAX TO AFRICA   1975 PART 3

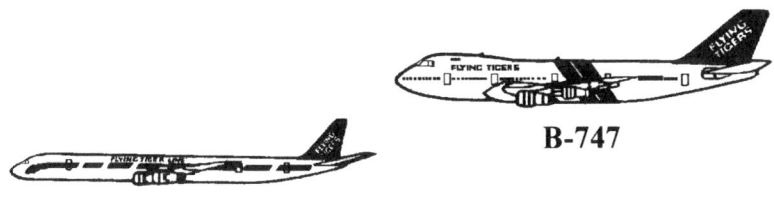

I had been flying domestic routes during the spring, so I missed out on the excitement in Southeast Asia. By June I was back on international, and I had three Pacific trips with three senior captains: George Edge, Bob Zalusky and Howard Bayne. I couldn't leave well enough alone.

In July I got a call from Crew Scheduling offering me several trips between Europe and Africa.

After a moment's consideration, I asked, "Who's the captain?"

"Bob Bax."

"All right," I said, "If Bax will do it, so will I."

"Fred Peterson will be the second officer," he added.

As it turned out, a Swiss charter airline, SATA, had a contract to move three DC-8 loads of cargo from Maastricht, Holland, to Lagos, Nigeria. They had leased a Flying Tiger DC-8 and intended to fly it with their own pilots. There were some paperwork problems with getting their crews certified, so they finally gave up and contracted for a Flying Tiger crew to fly it.

We boarded a United flight from San Francisco to New York, then a TWA first-class flight to Geneva, Switzerland.

I asked Bob, "What about the flight charts for the route we're going to fly?"

He said, "Don't worry about it."

The next night we arrived at the airport an hour before our scheduled departure and went to the SATA office where we presented ourselves to the operations supervisor.

He was very helpful and asked, "Do you have all of your flight charts for Europe and Africa?"

Bob looked at him with a blank stare and shrugged his shoulders. The supervisor then looked at me hopefully, but his only reward was another shrug.

The end result was that we were provided with a SATA agent, Rene, who accompanied us for the entire operation. He rode with us on every flight, provided all the required paperwork and charts and paid all the bills everywhere we landed. All landing fees, fuel bills and other charges in many of these countries must be paid in cash. He had the cash in sealed envelopes with the trip numbers, dates and airport names on them. He even arranged for hotels, taxis and provided the crew meals. All Bax and I had to do was fly the airplane. You can probably understand why I always enjoyed flying with Bob.

We left Geneva, Switzerland, about midnight and made a right turn out. This put us over Lake Geneva. The bright moon reflected on the lake and made the city look that much brighter. Though it was night, the snow-covered peaks of the Alps were clearly visible.

Six hours and twelve minutes later we landed in Lagos, Nigeria. The airport was the biggest mess I had ever seen. Cargo was stacked everywhere. Goods were coming into the airport faster than the local transportation facilities could move them out. The Nigerian government put out an order that cargo planes could not be off-loaded until the trucks were there to receive the load. We went to a hotel.

CHAPTER 41   TIGER TALES   389

Well, they called it a hotel anyway. It was terrible. There were only two rooms available, so Bax and I shared one, and Fred and Rene shared the other. The walls were greasy and dirty, and plaster was falling off the ceiling.

We left Lagos with an empty airplane and flew nonstop to Maastricht, Holland. It was a welcome relief. The hotel was spotless and the restaurants the same. Before we left the next day, Rene went to a supermarket and brought back two huge boxes. He had cold cuts, canned fruits and juices and about everything you could want to eat or drink. We left Maastricht with a loaded airplane and flew to Mallorca, an island off Spain, for a fuel stop. I was surprised to find the island covered with old-fashioned windmills like one would expect to see in Holland.

Me, in Mallorca

After leaving Mallorca, we crossed the Mediterranean Sea, Algeria, and then the Great Sahara Desert. The weather was clear, and I had been watching a road that ran straight south. It seemed like it must have gone at least a hundred miles with no turns and nothing in sight. Finally, in the distance I saw the road bend around something and then continue as before. When we were overhead, I saw what the highway bypassed. It was a village of about six houses, and that was all. I guess they wanted to avoid traffic jams during rush hour.

Loading the lorries in Lagos

CHAPTER 41 TIGER TALES 391

This time when we arrived in Lagos, we stayed on the airplane. This, it turned out, was not a good idea either. There were no bunks and no places to lie down, so we tried to sleep in our seats. Funny, we can sleep just fine in these same seats when we're in the air and are trying to stay awake.

During the night the trucks arrived, so they began unloading the airplane. With all the yelling and the noise of forklifts and trucks, we got very little sleep.

Night owls in Nigeria

We were on the ground 24 hours in addition to the time spent flying down there, and then, to make matters worse, we had to stop in Kano, Nigeria, on the way back.

Bob flew the leg from Lagos to Kano, and it was my leg from Kano to Maastricht. The Nigerian countryside was dotted with little clusters of mud huts, surrounded by low mud walls. I leveled off at about five hundred feet above the ground, and we got a good look at everything. As we accelerated through 300 knots, I began climbing to our assigned flight level. It wouldn't do to hit a buzzard, or anything else, at high speed.

When we arrived at Maastricht that evening, we were dead tired. We figured we deserved a couple of drinks before hitting the sack, so we dropped our bags, uniform coats and caps in the corner and went directly to the bar. Later, when we left the bar to pick up our bags, Fred noticed his expensive camera was missing. He reported it to the police while the rest of us went to our rooms.

A couple of hours later the police found the camera case down the road in a ditch. They said they knew who took it but didn't have any evidence. Fred never did get it back.

We left Maastricht again on the 22nd and stopped at Mallorca for fuel as before. We heard of another hotel near the airport at Lagos and decided to try it. When we got there it was full. We waited for a couple of hours, then finally gave up and went back to the original fleabag. This time we had individual rooms. They were also better rooms, better being a relative term.

Bob said, "When you guys get ready, come on down to my room."

CHAPTER 41   TIGER TALES

We did, and when we knocked on his door, he opened it wearing polka dot pajamas and a large grin.

He had a bottle of Jack Daniels on his nightstand and handed us each a glass. Sometimes it's the little things that make it all worthwhile.

This was our last trip to Lagos. We left at 1 a.m. and arrived in Geneva, Switzerland, about 7 a.m. Captain Bax added up all of our flying and decided it would take us two days to get legal (sufficient rest to proceed). As I walked into the hotel room, my eyes fell upon a welcome sight. The bathroom contained the largest bathtub I had ever seen. I filled it with hot water and took a long refreshing bath.

When I got out of the tub, I dried on a towel that was as big as a blanket. Then I put on a bathrobe provided by the hotel and went into the bedroom. There was a newspaper (in English) and a bar. I helped myself to a cold German beer (bier), while I read the paper. When I finished the paper and the beer, I went in and took another hot soaking bath. I finally felt clean and totally at peace with the world as I crawled into the big comfortable bed. About 30 seconds after my head hit the pillow, I was dead to the world.

I awoke about 5 p.m. and walked down the street to a small sidewalk cafe. The evening weather was perfect as I sat there and watched the street scene while enjoying a few beers.

I spotted a French restaurant down the street, which reminded me that a good meal was long overdue. I can't remember the exact name of the entree, but even if I did I wouldn't be able to spell it. Anyway, it was an excellent meal. I went back to the hotel and slept another eight hours. Bax was right. Now I was rested enough for the long trip home.

Bobbie had a trip that few pilots get to enjoy.

BOBBIE THARP: On a DC-8 Pacific trip, my son Ernie was set up as my second officer. Upon learning this, I got a pass for my wife, Harriet, and she went along with us from San Francisco to Anchorage, Taipei and Hong Kong. Later we heard that we were the first father-son team that had flown together as cockpit crewmembers with the airlines. This, I would say, was one of the highlights of my career.

BAR STORY
by
JIM MONTGOMERY: A group of pilots were at this bar talking about a difficult approach.

The bartender was listening and finally he said, "You know, I've been thinking about this."

He picked up a Budweiser bottle and placed it on the bar, then placed another Budweiser bottle a couple feet away.

"If you had something here," he said, indicating the first bottle, "and something over here," indicating the second bottle, "then some way to tell when you're on this line here, why, you could find the airport."

One of the pilots snorted and said, "It sounds like a Budweiser approach to me."

CHAPTER 42 THIS SHEAR WAS NO BLISS 1975 Part 4

B-747

DC-8-63

I've noticed that one of the best sources of humor is to ask a senior pilot how he started flying, or the circumstances of his hiring at Tigers.

BILL HEAPHY: It always interested me how some of our senior captains became Tigers and the varied backgrounds they had. One night (it was always, night) while tooling along with dear old Captain Harold P. Watkins, I asked how he arrived in this position of command aboard the Canadian Edsel, or the CL-44 to the uninitiated.

Not being one to sugarcoat things he replied, "Because I got fired from Pan American."

Now he had my attention and my admiration for his truthfulness, so I asked what brought this on?

So H.P. told me this story.

"I was hired as a third officer on the flying boats out of New York. The third officer was mainly what we now call a go-fer type position during most of the time in-flight, but upon arrival at the destination bay or in some cases a river, his skills were very important."

Laughing while telling me this tale he continued:

"I had to stand up in an open hatch just aft of the nose, which got pretty wet depending on the weather, waves, and the taxi speed the captain was using. Standing at attention with this mooring line and a grappling hook in my right hand, it was my job to throw this damn hook at the right time and snag the mooring line off the mooring buoy. Of course wearing the famous white hat was required during this operation. Those seaplanes had no reversing propellers, so a miss with the hook meant another approach for the captain and a cruise around the bay again for everybody.

It was not a great place for a young man susceptible to seasickness. After two more missed approaches to the mooring, I could almost hear the captain swearing and screaming up in the cockpit above the sound of the four engines. I was so cold and sick by now that I was about to vomit over the side of the plane; not the Image Pan Am wished to project to the world.

Finally some other numbered officer arrived who probably was a professional cattle roper in a prior life. He caught the mooring on the first attempt, secured the "vessel" and informed me that the captain was highly upset and planning to take an active interest in my future with that airline."

At least at Tigers it wasn't necessary to use a grappling hook, and years later in the warm cockpit of a 747 it made both of us appreciate what fate had dealt us.

Jack Bliss probably wished he had a grappling hook as he saw the runway sliding by.

JACK BLISS: With my crew, first officer Al Avey and second officer C. F. Peterson, we flew into Harrisburg, Pennsylvania, to pick up our load of 146 head of breeding cattle destined for Shannon, Ireland. Harrisburg did not have a runway long enough to allow the DC-8 to take off with enough fuel to reach Shannon, so we planned to stop at JFK to fuel up. Our cabin load was so heavy that we would land at JFK only about 3,000 pounds under maximum landing weight. We knew we had very little extra performance available.

While approaching JFK, there were several thunderstorm cells, which were permeating the entire area. By using our radar, and with the cooperation of New York Center, we were able to avoid them by a routing to the south around JFK for an approach to the southwest using runway 22L. Inbound over the outer marker there was an area of intense rain ahead and somewhat to the right on final, but not anything too unusual.

The actual ceiling seemed to be clearly defined near 3,000 feet with good visibility underneath, and with the surface wind southwest at 10. It was obvious we were going to fly through some rain on final approach. I turned on the windshield bleed air[1] and reviewed my previously calculated minimum ground speed target of 140 knots.

As we proceeded into the area of rain, the cockpit noise reached a very high level with the heavy rain and with the bleed air on. It also sounded like there was some hail mixed in, and there was occasional lightning too. There was enough turbulence to keep my attention, but nothing disturbing. I would classify it as moderate and continuous, in fact so continuous that I was distracted from my usual practice of constantly monitoring the ground speed. This was so serious a mistake that it nearly became fatal.

When just 400 feet above ground level, with the airspeed rapidly increasing through 189, I forced myself to take my concentration from the instrument panel to the ground speed indicator on the INS near my right knee. It was indicating a rapid reduction through 120 knots, and I pushed the throttles forward to maximum power and tried

---

[1]The DC-8 does not have windshield wipers, but uses high-pressure air from the engines to keep the windshields clear.

to maintain our position on the glide slope. I was pushing forward on the yoke, but trimming nose-up with my left thumb since I was sure we would soon need maximum nose-up help.

We broke out in the clear at just about 300 feet, but that was where I almost lost it. The airspeed instantly dropped to near 115 knots (our stall speed) while the airplane entered a severe crosswind from the right. Without pilot input it simply weather-cocked more than 35 degrees to the right, while I shoved the throttles the remaining distance to the stops. If I had not pre-trimmed nose-up against all that nose-down yoke pressure with a high airspeed, I do not think it would have been possible to keep the airplane out of the approach lights.

We came across the runway threshold with the nose gyrating around a point far to the right of the runway heading, and no one could have convinced me that we could stay in the air. I kicked full left rudder and luckily got the right main gear onto the runway at the same time the nose swung back to runway heading. We did not get landing spoilers, because the throttles against the stops disarmed them. With the nose gear then on the runway, full right aileron, using differential reverse and brakes, we stayed on the runway. I calculate that we landed with at least an 85-knot crosswind.

I warned the Control Tower of the dangerous wind shear condition and recommended a change in traffic direction.

The Controller said, "We were indicating wind right down the runway at 15 knots when you landed."

I replied, "I don't care what you're indicting. I'm just telling you that you have such a dangerous wind shear on the approach that you should change the traffic to land to the northwest."

CHAPTER 42 TIGER TALES 399

Moments later Eastern Airlines Flight 66, a Boeing 727 passenger flight, hit the same wind shear and crashed into the approach lights on 22L. On impact, part of the supporting structure of the approach light system impaled the aircraft cabin. 112 people lost their lives in the crash. The 727 was not equipped with an Inertial Navigation System and could not detect the sudden wind shift.

This load of cattle could probably have used a little of that wind shift.

TOM PIERCHALA: Don Hassig was Captain, Gordon Swanson was First Officer and I was Second Officer. We showed up at Anchorage operations to take a cattle charter nonstop to Mactan, on the island of Cebu in the Philippines.

The operations agent advised Don that one of the cows way back in the rear cabin had rolled over and died on the flight up from Chicago. He said that it was not possible to off-load her due to time considerations.

Don was concerned because some authorities take a dim view of dead animals arriving in their country. The agent assured him it would be O.K. so off we went.

Sure enough, when we landed at Mactan, an argument broke out between two groups of workers about the cow.

Don got real worried! He asked our agent, "What now, are we about to go to jail?"

The agent said, "No problem. One group is from the Health department, who wants to bury it, and the other group wants to eat it!"

We went to the hotel and later were at the pool having a few San Miguel's when the chef started to barbecue some beef strips for the guests.

You have to wonder?

Sounds like this could have been on the same trip.

BAR STORY
By
TOM PIERCHALA: Don Hassig, Gordon Swanson and myself got back into Anchorage from the Pacific. We had stopped in Tokyo and each of us bought a crew bottle at the duty free store.

Getting off the aircraft I dropped my bottle of gin and it cracked and started to leak! Gordy was quick thinking as usual and grabbed a plastic trash bag from the galley and we put the bottle in it. By the time we got to customs the gin was sloshing around in the bottom of the bag for all to see.

The customs guy looked at this with surprise and said, "I know you're supposed to break the seal on the bottle before you bring it into the country, but this is ridiculous!"

We went to the hotel and Don got a bucket of ice and a jar of olives. Gordy and I strained the gin thru a washcloth right into the ice bucket and we made one giant martini! No sense in wasting good booze.

CHAPTER 43 HIGH HOPES— LOW CEILINGS 1976

B-747

DC-8-

GOLDY: At a 25 year Silver Tiger banquet in 1976, I was authorized by our pilot group to present to Bob Prescott a seniority list with his name in the number one slot. Duke Hedman was #1 on the seniority list, and he was there to help with the presentation.

Duke took off his coat and tie and handed them to me. He was wearing a tee shirt with a big #1 on it. He took off the tee shirt and presented it to Bob, who put it on while receiving a standing ovation.

Later Ralph Hedden pretended great indignation as he said, "Sure, I've been number two most of my years with Tigers. Now when Duke retires I'll still be number two!"

In March I left San Francisco on what was supposed to be a round-the-world trip. Dick Bentley was the captain and John Michel the second officer. Our flight originated out of Amsterdam, Holland, so we rode a KLM flight there from San Francisco.

We departed Amsterdam with a DC-8 bound for Hong Kong with a fuel stop and crew rest in Teheran, Iran. We stayed in the Sheraton Hotel downtown. This was when the Shah was still in power, and there was law and order. The people were friendly with Americans, and most everyone seemed to be prosperous. Teheran seemed like most any other modern bustling city, but like many places in the Mideast, there was hardly any grass anywhere. There were few trees to be seen either, just sand and rocks.

We took a long walk through the city streets that evening and checked out a few open-air shops. For dinner we went to a small out-of-the-way place that had been recommended to us. It looked like a meat market, but we made our selection from the glass case, and then sat at a small table in the corner while our dinner was being prepared. It tasted a lot better than it looked.

We departed Teheran the next day for a 10 hour and 45 minute flight to Hong Kong. While we were in Hong Kong our schedule was changed, and we headed back west again. We flew a planeload of electronic parts from Hong Kong to Brussels, Belgium. Because of our heavy load, we made several fuel stops. The first was in Kuala Lumpur, Malaysia, then Bombay, India, where we went to a hotel for a crew rest. We arrived in Bombay in late morning, and it took two hours to go through customs and get to the hotel.

The hotel was not too bad, I guess, but it had huge windows and no shades. To make matters worse, the room was painted white, so the glare from the sun plus the street noise made it almost impossible to sleep in the daytime. That's all a part of airline flying but you never get used to it.

When we left Bombay, we flew to Bahrain in the Persian Gulf, where it took almost four hours to get refueled. From there we flew to Ankara, Turkey, for another fuel stop. No one in Ankara seemed to know we were coming, so no services had been arranged. After a long delay we managed to get a weather briefing, a flight plan and the airplane refueled. We departed Ankara and flew to Brussels, Belgium, where we finally got a good night's sleep.

We stayed in a very nice hotel, and the next morning I went down to the restaurant for breakfast. I ordered ham and eggs and explained in detail to the French waiter how I liked them. When it was served, he proudly lifted the silver cover from the plate with a flourish. I agreed that it was indeed a fine looking hamburger. I had long ago learned that when other languages are involved, you order what you want, and eat what you get.

Thirteen hours from the time we landed in Brussels, we were on our way nonstop to Newark, New Jersey.

Bentley said, "Je-su-s Christ! We fly halfway around the world and back again, and all we've seen is airports. We could have done that in the flight simulator!"

When you return from a long trip, you walk into the crew room, turn in your paperwork, and ask, "What's new?"
You hope for more good news than bad, or at least to come out even. This time the news was bad. Bob Prescott had always been a trim athletic looking guy who seemed to be the picture of health. We were completely taken by surprise with the news that Bob had cancer.

ANN MARIE PRESCOTT: Bob was diagnosed with cancer of his larynx. And you know, of course, that I am a physician in a sense, and had been involved with a form of medicine all my life. It was a very hard thing for me to stand by and see how quickly Bob took on the orthodox prescribed system of cancer treatments, which was "Cut, Burn and Poison." [1] From the first moment he was diagnosed, he couldn't wait to begin radiation.

---

[1] Meaning surgery, radiation and chemotherapy.

This was a new concern for us. We never considered what the Flying Tiger Line might be like without Bob Prescott. Now we had to face the possibility.

In the meantime John Keenan and his crew thought we might have to do without them.

"Quarantined in Torino"

TOM CONSTABLE: It all started in Amsterdam, Holland, with one of those famous charter flights. The Captain was John Keenan, I was the F/O, Paul Phillips was the S/O.

We flew to Genoa, Italy, and laid over, then flew to Kano, Nigeria. When we arrived the red dust was blowing out of the Sahara Desert, which gave the natives an unusual hue. At first we thought that red hair was normal in this region, but we soon found out that the red dust covered everybody and everything.

We left the aircraft (a DC8-63) and started the long drive to the hotel. On the way we got in a traffic jam that was caused by a minor accident. The local cops took care of the offender by beating him with a crop. We continued on to the hotel after an hour and a half delay. When we arrived at the hotel we were greeted with the news that they had only ONE room. We were tired but so disgusted with the situation in Kano that we decided to return to the airport and fly back to Italy, which we thought would be much nicer.

We headed for Torino, Italy, our intended next stop. Everything went well. We got hotel rooms and in spite of our fatigue (30 hours with no sleep) we went to a restaurant and had a fine meal. Just as I was drifting off to sleep the telephone rang. It was the local authorities, and they wanted us to report to their office at the airport. I thought it was a bad dream.

CHAPTER 43   TIGER TALES   405

Now we were really tired. John Keenan was so mad and tired that he would not talk, so I served as the spokesman for our group, and I might say without much luck.

They were concerned that we had come from an African country which was a cholera area, and that all five of our shot records revealed that our cholera vaccinations had expired, and that we had landed at an airport that was an entry point from Africa.

They wouldn't let us go back to the hotel, instead, they sent us to a hospital to be quarantined.

We were taken to a fortress/castle-like stone building. This was to be our home for how long we didn't know. When we entered we noticed the sign above the door written in Italian, "(Hospitalia por la Terminalia Infirmina" just a guess at what it actually said). Which we translated to: "Hospital for the Terminally ill."

This didn't make us feel any better about our situation. We didn't know what was going to happen to us. Once inside, we had to wait for our room to be readied and as we waited, Paul and I in our advanced stage of punchiness noticed some children's toys. Being children ourselves, we started joking around with some puppets and other toys. Our silly antics awakened a few of the children and at first we felt bad, but when they started laughing we felt like we brought a little joy into their lives.

So, we hammed it up for them and continued our cheerful little show. They sat up in their beds and clapped for us, which egged us on for more. Finally we were moved to another ward, so we had to end our show business career. It made us feel good that we had brought some smiles to some doomed little folks.

While we were waiting there, I went to sleep on what turned out to be an operating table. That is usually not a good idea, but I woke up with nothing missing. We were then shown to one room for all of us to occupy. Before we could go to bed, the nurses had to carry a very emaciated old fellow out in a sheet with all kinds of tubes dangling from him.

Everyone rushed into the room to get some shut-eye and guess who got the bed that had just been vacated, that's right, me.

Well, things looked very bleak indeed. We had exhausted all avenues of reason with these folks, so we did what desperate men do when they are in captivity, they plan an escape. In fact we had two plans, an A and a B plan.

Plan A was to go across the hall to the lavatory, climb out the window and down the outside wall to the moat and scale the outer wall, make our way to the airport and fly our DC-8 to freedom.

Plan B: John Keenan had a bottle of Scotch or bourbon, and in our delirium we thought that if we drank it and got drunk enough they would throw us out, just like in a bar. Well, you can see what sleep deprivation will do to a persons thinking.

We slept well and when we awoke we were very hungry, but all they fed us was boullion soup and two zwaibach toasts.

Paul Phillips and I, being well versed in Spanish, served as best we could as interpreters, since no one spoke English.

I contacted our embassy but they would not help us. The head doctor, a lady, suggested that I talk to the British Air Attaché, which I did and they were successful in gaining our release.

We beat a hasty retreat to the airport and flew back to Amsterdam.

CHAPTER 43   TIGER TALES

Occasionally changes in weather conditions and other problems make it almost impossible for Flight Operations and Crew Scheduling to keep track of each other. Flight Operations decides where the airplane should go, and Crew Scheduling makes sure a crew is there to fly it. With Captain Al Silver and Second Officer Jay Cotting, I flew a trip into Haneda Airport in Tokyo and went to the Tokyo Hilton, where we were supposed to have a three-day layover. The next day we had an unexpected trip out of Nagoya, so we were rushed to the train station and put on the Bullet Train to Nagoya. It was the fastest ride I ever had that close to the ground. When we arrived in Nagoya we found that our airplane had been diverted to Tokyo because of weather, so we rode the next Bullet Train back to Tokyo. We didn't get anywhere, but at least we made good time and saw a lot of the countryside.

Bob didn't get to see much of anything...

BOB BAIRD: This trip sounded easy, maybe too easy! I was to fly an empty passenger DC-8 from Anchorage to Yokota AFB, Japan. When we arrive at Operations, I find out the company chief pilot and DC-8 chief pilot, along with their spouses and several other headquarters types are along for the ride. They're headed for Singapore to look over one of the 747s we are buying and other things as well, I guess.

   They're lounging around Operations as we do the paperwork, and I note the forecast weather is VFR, so against my better instincts I plan on minimum fuel for the leg as there is a big drive on to not carry any more fuel than "they" think you will need.

The chief pilot comes over to see the weather, and I show him the forecast. He is happy.

Many hours later we're off the coast of Japan. It's just after dark and a nice night. We can see the lights of many small Japanese towns. The chief pilot comes into the cockpit and pulls the jump seat down and settles in it. I detect the faint smell of alcohol, and I know the crowd in the back has been very relaxed on the long over-water leg.

He leans forward and says, "I'll sit up here for the landing but relax, this is not a check ride."

Great, I think silently, but wouldn't you rather be in the back with your wife?

About a hundred out of Yokota, Tokyo Center hands us off to Yokota approach.

"Cleared to descend and expect the ILS 36 Approach."

About 50 DME approach calls and requests our speed in the descent. We advise him and then he asks if we can speed it up somewhat. Yes we can, we reply. What's up?

The controller now says, "The tower has just advised me of a fast moving fog bank off the departure end of 36 and they expect the field to go below minimums very soon!"

Well they have my full attention now, that's for sure. I push the speed up to the limit and ask them to keep me advised. At the same time I ask the second officer to contact the company and get our alternate weather. He does this quickly and gives me the bad news.

"Every station, Tokyo, Atsugi, etc, are below minimums in fog."

Looking towards Tokyo from the cockpit I can see this myself, as the lights of the city are a faint glow through the low fog cover.

At this point the second officer says, "We have about 9600 pounds of fuel remaining."

CHAPTER 43   TIGER TALES

I realize we aren't going very far if we don't make Yokota. I can now see Yokota also, and the fog has moved about half way down the runway, but the approach end is still open. We are still indicating about 290, and I now reverse the inboards to get us slowed down. I ask for a short approach as I have the runway in sight, and approach grants this and asks us to now contact the tower. Checklists are accomplished and as speed decreases gear and flaps are selected.

I plan a 3-4 mile turn on to final and will keep the descent up a little higher then normal to capture the glide slope. Turning base leg I lose sight of the runway and ask the first officer to keep me advised. He says to keep it coming around and the fog is darn near covering the runway. The ILS is alive, and I roll to the runway heading and look up to see the fog now covering the runway with just a dim glow of the approach lights.

I have the rabbit in sight. The SO calls, "Fuel, 9000 pounds."

I try to engage the autopilot CAT TWO approach but it isn't having any of that, so I will hand fly it. Things are happening real fast. We are still a few hundred feet above the fog bank, and it appears to be 4-500 feet thick. I quickly brief the first officer on call outs, to call the Radar altimeter all the way down through 200 feet in 10-foot increments if he can. He rogers that as we enter the dark gloom.

I have the airplane pretty well set up and just hold it there, no power adjustments until minimums, then start bringing off the power slowly. Everyone just sits tight as we go through 100 feet. We all know there isn't enough fuel to go anywhere else even if the weather permitted it.

At the 30 feet call everything is still lined up, and I bring the power back and attempt to establish a flare attitude. I see a runway light flash by and at the same time we touch down firmly. Max braking and all four in reverse, I still see one runway light at a time as we come up on it. It is just black gray with no visible signs of anything, earth, sky, nothing.

We ask for the tower to send a follow me to help us find the ramp. Some 30 minutes later he finds us, and we taxi very slowly to the ramp which took another 20 minutes at least.

The chief pilot unstraps and puts his hand on my shoulder. "Good job Bob, we really don't need the autopilot, do we?"

I am thinking just the opposite but I don't say anything. My mouth is too dry to carry on much of a conversation.

BAR STORY
by

DOBBIE: Andy Chambers and Frank Graff got into an altercation in a bar in Salt Lake City, so they went out in the parking lot to settle their differences. I went out to separate them and try to make peace. When I finally succeeded, they went back to the bar arm in arm. Then I noticed my watch was missing. It had been torn from my arm and stepped on by one of the protagonists. They were the best of friends again, and all I had for my trouble was a ruined watch and a torn shirt.

CHAPTER 44   COCKPIT TO BOX OFFICE?   1976

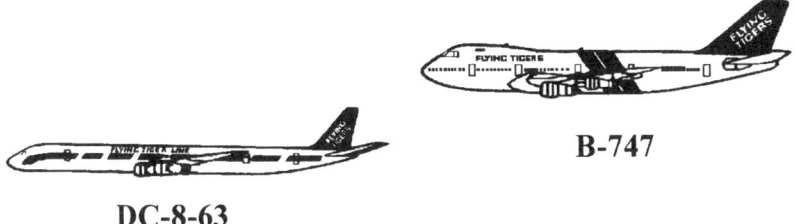

B-747

DC-8-63

Laws and customs change as time goes by. A big change in aviation was the hiring of female pilots. Here again, Tigers was in the forefront.

NORAH O'NEILL: A panel of four Flying Tiger captains conducted my final pre-hiring interview with Tigers. Oakley Smith, Dick Stratford, Al Grant, and Dick Keefer were gathered behind a large imposing desk in an office as I entered. I was so nervous that the airplane photos on the walls of the office, the window hangings, the view from the window itself, and the men's clothing were just a blur to me.

    I was wearing a suit with a modest skirt that my mom and I had purchased for the event. Mom had come from San Diego to Los Angeles to hold my hand through the days allotted to the interview process. My Alaskan bush-flying wardrobe of padded coveralls and mukluks, of jeans and turtlenecks and hiking boots had not seemed suitable for a big city interview.

    The Tiger pilots introduced themselves and shook my hand. I was glad for my Navy Captain Dad's early lessons in the proper way to shake hands. Step forward while extending your hand, always maintaining eye contact; squeeze firmly; break the hold crisply. Three of my interviewers had obviously gotten the same hand-shaking lesson as I had, but the fourth turned our hand clasp into a bone-crushing, macho contest of "he who cries out in pain first loses." Luckily, I had a high pain threshold, and our contest appeared to be a draw.

They invited me to be seated. I regretted the nylons and heels I was wearing. I was not used to them, and I spent seconds dumbly wondering how to arrange my hands and legs.

My mom and I had struggled to get my waist-length bright red hair in something that turned out to be a cross between a French roll and a bun. I was sure it was going to spill out of its pins at any moment, and look "unprofessional," whatever THAT was. I didn't have a role model for this interview and I was inventing each moment, each action. I didn't know what kind of questions I would be asked. I assumed that there would be many technical aviation questions—about engines and aerodynamics, Federal Aviation Agency rules and regulations, about licensing and instrument flying.

I was certain that they would ask about my hours in the air and experience level. I had acquired many hours in very few years, and I thought that my flight time would look like "Parker pen" time. Some pilots have padded their logbooks with fictitious flight time in order to get hired.

Oakley Smith, Vice President of Flight Operations, carefully explained to me that laws had been passed making it illegal to ask a woman any questions in an interview that were not asked of male applicants. He supposed that I, of course, was aware of this.

I had been buried in the Alaskan bush for a long time, totally immersed in flying and living, almost literally in airplanes, so I was woefully ignorant of current events.

"That's interesting," I said, "I wasn't aware of that law. But, surely, if you've never interviewed a woman pilot before, there must be some questions you would like to ask about how I might work in an all male workplace. You have my permission to ask me anything you want."

CHAPTER 44   TIGER TALES   413

In my youthful naiveté, I had not a clue to the doors I had just given them leave to open.

"Well, thank you for your understanding," the youngest of the panel said to me with a smile. "Tell me about your periods."

I was drawing a blank.

"How are your periods?" he elucidated. "How do they affect your reliability at work? How do they affect your flying? I noticed that you took four days of sick leave in the last three years. Were those sick days because of your periods?"

I was definitely NOT following the questioner's logic. (This was before I learned that "male logic" could have an oxymoronic quality.) My brain raced with the implied math of how many days in my period I had had in the previous three years, at 7 days a month times 12 times 3. Surely if I had problem periods, I would have missed more than four days of work.

"I have never missed work because of being in my period," I stated truly and firmly.

He couldn't let the subject go. I surmised that he was married to someone who must have to take to her bed for days at a time. I had heard of such women, and sympathized with them, but I was not one of them.

"Can you honestly say that your periods have NEVER affected your flying?" he pressed on.

I thought of an incident in Alaska that had occurred a few months back. I was flying an empty airplane home to Fairbanks after a very long day on a cross-state cargo charter. I was very tired and was mildly troubled by menstrual cramps.

At the same time, another of Alaska Central Air's pilots was also returning home in an empty plane after an unusually long day of back-to-back medical evacuations on the Alaskan Pipeline. He fell asleep in the cockpit and overflew Fairbanks. His plane headed toward the mountains beyond. What saved his life was that one of his engines quit because of fuel starvation. The subsequent yawing of his plane awakened him just before he would have flown into the side of the rising mountains.

I thought of that night in Alaska, and looked my nagging questioner in the eye. "Oh, yes, my period HAS affected my flying. My cramps have kept me awake on long, boring freight runs."

They asked about my plans for marriage and children. I thought I would do that someday, yes. They wondered if I would quit then, to stay home and raise my children.

"Wow," I responded, "have a lot of your pilots done that? I mean, produced a child, and then leave it up to someone else to feed him and send him to college? It doesn't sound very responsible, and I like to think that I shoulder my obligations better than that."

They asked whether I liked to party. I wanted to say what they wanted to hear, but I did not know what that was. In the Alaskan bush, on call 24 hours a day, there wasn't much time for going to parties. I had sometimes gone anyway, hoping that the phone would not ring at an inopportune time. "Hoping" had not worked out very well for me.

In the previous year, I had been unavailable for a medivac flight because I was at a party. Even if they had found me, I was in no condition to go to the airstrip. Fortunately, they had found an able-bodied pilot who successfully flew the injured pipeline worker to the hospital. But I was the one who should have flown, and the plane departed with one pilot, not the two required by pipeline rules. I made up an elaborate lie about where I had been, a lie so extraordinary that it just might be true.

My chief pilot, John Baleski, had said, "Don't insult me by repeating your story, and I won't insult you by calling you a liar. Clean it up, Norah."

CHAPTER 44   TIGER TALES

And clean it up I had. I quit drinking altogether.

So I told the interviewers that I liked to party, but I no longer drank alcohol, so I did not think going to parties would interfere with my flying.

Oakley Smith wanted to know what I was going to do when someone made a pass at me in the cockpit.

"In the cockpit?? Surely there isn't time for that?" I exclaimed.

"It WILL happen," Captain Smith said firmly. "What are you going to do?"

The men all laughed, and sat up straighter awaiting my answer. In Alaska, most of my flying had been done alone, no other pilot and no autopilot on board. One might entertain oneself with romantic fantasies of a sexual nature, but doing something about it en route was an impossibility. If I were on a two-pilot crew, we usually had passengers on board, and our cockpit was open to their perusal. We tried to present a professional presence.

I was especially conscious of passenger eyes on me, because so many of them had, in the three years with Alaska Central Air, expressed open horror that a girl might be in charge of the plane. Some had even asked for a refund on their tickets, or had postponed their flights until a man could fly them. One of the main reasons that I had applied to Flying Tigers was because they were the world's largest cargo airline, and I never wanted to fly passengers again.

I had illusions about what flying for a "real" airline meant. I thought it meant total professionalism and a goodbye to many of the problems I had had because I was a "girl" pilot. My education in that area was just leaving grade school and getting ready for junior high. I thank God I did not know that then.

Meanwhile, these men were waiting for an answer to a question I had not dreamed of being asked. This was not a pilot question, but a woman question. I answered as a woman.

"I would handle a pass in the cockpit, just the same way I would handle a pass on the ground."

"So what do you do on the ground?" a man asked.

" I say either "yes, please" or "no, thank you."

Next, the men explored how I had racked up so many flight hours in so short a time. With relief, I produced my logbooks and my pay stubs. A job-seeking pilot might fabricate flight hours, but no employer would have paid him for them. I could prove my previous three years of flying. I think they were relieved to know that I really had flown as much as I said I had.

Dick Stratford said, "Someone with thousands of hours in the Alaskan bush has to be either very, very good, or very, very lucky. I hope that you are both."

We then swapped stories about flying in Alaska, which several of them had done. This led to the only fun I had in the interview. I got to listen to them hangar fly. Hangar flying is sitting safely on the ground (often in an aircraft hangar or "garage" while waiting for the weather to improve) and telling stories about how a pilot cheated death by bringing an airplane home against insurmountable odds. Or the stories could be about some fantastic natural phenomena that only pilots get to experience. I have yet to meet a pilot who can resist hangar flying at any given opportunity.

So these guys did some hangar flying and I listened in fascination as one of them told a story about flying the DEW Line in Alaska during a whiteout. A "whiteout" is a description of visibility commonly encountered on the North Slope (where the land descends down from the Brooks Range into a relatively flat area that ends with the Arctic Ocean in Alaska).

The North Slope is snow-covered for nine months out of the year and has little in the way of prominent landmarks. When it snows, the horizon, where land meets sky, disappears into unending white, above and below. In that area of very few and very primitive navigational aids, a whiteout has been deadly for many pilots. In fact, some of the most prominent topographical marks shown on aviation maps for the area are wrecks of old planes.

The story I was told was about a Flying Tiger crew flying a C-46, a WW II vintage cargo plane, into a camp on the slope. They entered a whiteout, yet somehow miraculously found the airstrip they were searching for. Unfortunately, they saw it just as it passed beneath them, and they had to turn the plane, configure it for landing, and then find the strip again. Magnetic compasses are worthless on the Slope because of deviation errors, so their seeing the airstrip again was a combination of sheer luck and good piloting. As they paralleled the runway, flying their downwind leg, they had no way of knowing that they were above a low ridge. They began their descent, lost sight of the runway, and motored on blindly. One of them noticed that their airspeed was bleeding off (decreasing) and they added power. Their airspeed did not increase, but went to zero. Some other odd things happened to their instruments, especially to their engine readouts. They assessed their situation, which was dire, and prepared themselves for the worst. It took long minutes for them to realize what had happened.

They had flown their airplane into the ground. The billowing cushion of snow had prevented them from feeling the ground contact, and their view from the cockpit window had not changed one iota—it was still zero. They had made a good landing, if one went by the common pilot's definition—anyone you can walk away from is a good landing.

I had flown C-46s out of Fairbanks and was in awe of anyone who could fly them well. They were the most difficult planes to land and park that I had ever been in. While those Tiger pilots talked about captaining the C-46, I wanted more than anything to be able to fly with them one day, and to hear more of their stories. To me, they were history come alive.

As their hangar flying abated, one of the men noted that I had C-46 time (a measly 200 hours), and he asked me how much fuel a C-46 held. I realized, in a panic, that I did not know. Here I was finally being asked a technical aviation question and I DID NOT KNOW the answer. My brief dreams of maybe becoming an airline pilot were flying out the window of possibility.

I explained, with sinking hope, that the C-46s that I had flown were oil tankers, and were flown visual flight rules only during the summer in order to replenish the heating fuel oil storage tanks of remote villages. We were always at maximum gross weight and fueled the plane with a minimum amount of gas to get to the destination. I had never seen the C-46 full of gas. I could tell the men the number of gallons I had pumped into the tanks in order to reach Lake Minchumina and other spots, but I didn't know the answer they wanted.

"I don't know how many gallons of fuel the C-46 held," I said squaring my shoulders. I was going to take the flunking of this interview like I imagined a man would and the least I could do was learn from the experience. I forced a smile, when I felt like tearing my hair out and gnashing my teeth. I controlled the urge. Even then I knew that crying was inappropriate behavior. Instead, I calmly asked the panel of my judges what the correct answer was.

"Captain Smith, you captained the C-46. How much fuel did it hold?"

"Damned if I can remember," he replied. "Do any of you know?"

They did not. I was amazed. How could these gods of Tiger aviation not know the answer to a question they had asked?

The time they had evidently allotted for my interview was up. They stood to see me out. I had no idea of what impression I had made on them. I didn't know that it was not cool to ask, so I did ask. "Do I have the job?"

They had surprised looks on their faces. "We'll call you if you get the job," they promised.

Mom and I spent two more days together in Los Angeles, while I underwent rigorous physical examinations and testing. There were other young pilots at the medical facility that had also had interviews.

I assumed we were all undergoing the same tests, until an embarrassed doctor said, "Uhmm. We're not sure what to do here. We have never examined a female pilot before, and there are no spaces on the examination sheet for reporting your, umm, gynecological condition. I should, I guess, do a breast exam. Or, do you, by any chance, do your own? Um, "he went on, "and I guess I should do a pelvic exam, or do you have regular pap smears done? We could perhaps have your gynecologist send his latest report?"

Poor man, I thought. I arranged to have my gynecologist send the paperwork.

Then the waiting began. I passed my 27th birthday in August of 1976 still waiting. Summer was our busiest flying season in Fairbanks, and I was, thankfully, flying almost around the clock during our days of 18 hours of sunlight. In September, I did not hear from Tigers. In October, my phone's ringing at 2 a.m. awakened me. I automatically sat up in bed, a ploy I had discovered helped me further waken and sound lucid for late night medivac calls.

I answered the phone and heard a man's voice that I did not recognize. I could hear the sound of music and glasses clinking in the background, unmistakable bar noises. I could barely understand the caller; there seemed to be the crackle of long distance on the line. Also, either his speech was slurring badly, or my hearing was not yet as awake as my eyesight. He just wanted me to know, he said, that Tigers was going to hire me, that I would become their first woman pilot. He wanted to be the first to tell me. I started to ask him a question and he hung up.

As the days after the late night call passed, I began to doubt that it had even happened, or if it had, it was just a local pilot making a cruel crank call. I never learned who made that call. Weeks later, I received my official notification from the Flying Tiger Line. I had been hired and was to report to ground school in Los Angeles on Dec. 1, 1976.

In the meantime I was still bush flying. I was at 11,000 feet southbound to Anchorage when a tiny dot of an airplane showed over the water in the distance. I could hear its pilots communicate with air traffic control. It was a Flying Tiger DC-8, four-engine jet.

"Hey, Tiger 41, do you know that your cockpit is about to be changed forever?"

I recognized the voice on the radio to be D.G. Creamer, a man who was flying a plane to Anchorage about ten miles in trail of my plane. Oh, no, I thought. What the hell is D.G. doing?

"Uh, Aircraft calling Tigers, say again," responded the Tiger pilots.

"Tiger 41, you guys just hired a woman pilot," D.G. elaborated over the ATC radio frequency.

There was a momentary silence on the air, presumably while the shocked Flying Tiger pilots were sucking on their oxygen masks in order to rule out auditory illusions caused by oxygen-starved hypoxia.

"NO WAY," they chokingly responded.

D. G.'s laughter rang on the airwaves. "Yeah. It's true. She's flying the plane just ahead of mine. She starts Dec. 1. You guys will never be able to call it a cockpit again. It's about to become a box-office!"

CHAPTER 44 TIGER TALES 421

This was not the way I would have chosen to have the Tiger pilots learn that I had been hired. But that news was forever out of my hands. And D.G.'s laughing words that day were going to follow me for the rest of my career. No matter how hard I tried to be just one of the guys, no matter how much I changed myself in a effort to keep "their cockpit" the same for them, the fact remained that I was a woman. I could prove that the airplane could not tell the difference between the control inputs of someone with "inside plumbing" from a pilot with "outside plumbing". But I would learn the hard way that proving my abilities was not enough.

Cockpit? Box-office? What the hell does he mean?

BAR STORY
by

BOB ZALUSKY: Whisperin' Jim Martin, Dick Stuelke and I were sitting in a bar having a few and talking. A fellow came in and sat at a table...decent looking guy wearing a coat and tie. Wasn't bothering anybody. Whisperin' Jim seemed to take a serious dislike to the guy's tie. Without saying a word, he got up, took a jackknife out of his pocket and cut the guy's tie off. Then he handed it to the guy and went back to his seat.

The guy looked at his tie in disbelief. Then looked at Jim. His face began to turn red as his anger rose. He stood up. When he did, Dick and I stood up also. Now this guy was average size and looked like he could take care of himself, but both Dick and I were considerably larger. The guy looked at us and sat back down.

Jim just couldn't leave it alone. The guy jumped up again, ready to paste old Jim. Stuelke and I got up again.

The poor guy was really agitated, but after glancing at us once more he sat down again.

That goddamn Jim had to pick on him again, and this time when the guy got up, Stuelke and I just sat there. He knocked Jim down, and then looked over to see if we were still sitting. We were, so he commenced to beat the whey out of old Jim, who sure as hell had it coming.

CHAPTER 45 "EMERGENCY DESCENT" 1977

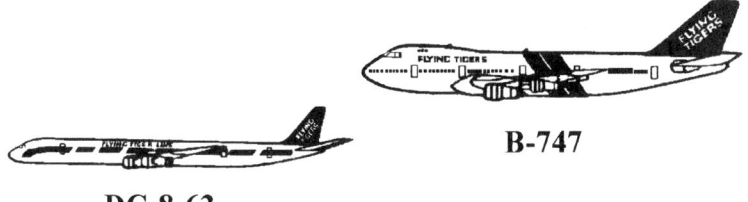

I started the year with a few unusual DC-8 trips. In January with Captain Orville Prevost and Second Officer Frank Maguire, I had a trip to Moses Lake, Washington, where we picked up a load of cattle for delivery in Tokyo, Japan.

In February with Captain Paul Crowley and Second Officer Kip Cutting, I flew a round-the-world trip. First we took a load of purebred Holstein dairy cattle from Moses Lake to Shannon, Ireland. When we were over Hudson Bay, Canada, we lost control of the cabin pressure.

We were flying at 29,000 feet, so Paul grabbed his oxygen mask and yelled, "Emergency descent!"

I slapped my mask on, got on the radio and told Center of our problem and that we were descending to 10,000 feet. We had no oxygen masks for the cows, so we had to quickly get down to an altitude where they could breathe. After dumping fuel down to our maximum landing weigh of 275,000 pounds, we landed at Bangor, Maine.

The cattle had given off so much moisture in flight that the air conditioning system outflow valves had frozen. This happens occasionally when hauling live-stock. We had the valves thawed out while the airplane was being refueled and then we were on our way again. We landed in Shannon, where another crew took the flight on to its destination in Poland.

The next day we flew a six and one half hour trip from Shannon to Teheran, Iran, where we stayed at the Teheran Sheraton again. The dining room next to the lobby had a large portrait of the Shah and his wife on one wall. On another side was a room divider of plate glass mirror.

Our flights usually arrived in the morning, so we sat there and ate a breakfast washed down with cold beer. It was a good time to relax and talk. When pilots are flying they talk about women, and when they are in a bar, they talk about airplanes.

Talking, like flying, is thirsty work, so considerable quantities of liquid refreshments are often required. Two Tiger crewmembers on another flight really cracked the place up one morning. I won't mention their names, but their initials are rumored to be Chuck Griffith, and Hank Bates. Anyway, as the story goes, they somehow managed to get into a knock-down-drag-out. They're both good old-fashioned saloon brawlers, and finally one of them threw the other through the plate glass wall. Nothing like making a shattering impression in a foreign country. (If Chuck and Hank are not the guilty parties, it doesn't really matter, because they're probably guilty of something else that they didn't get caught at.)

The following day we had a flight of over 11 hours to Hong Kong. After a day and a half rest, we flew to Kao Cheung, Taiwan, then to San Francisco via Tokyo.

It's just as far around the world as it ever was, but it's a lot easier now and besides, we don't have to load and unload the cargo.

GOLDY: Ralph Hedden and I met on a trip somewhere after not seeing each other for a couple of years. We had a

lot to talk about and were really enjoying our conversation. We reminisced about the old days when we used to help load freight, work 24 hours straight and do whatever it took to keep the company going.

One of the new pilots listening said, "You guys were out of your minds. I would never have done those things."

I said, "If we hadn't done it then, you wouldn't have a job here now."

The big Circle T, which had been on the tails of Tiger airplanes since 1961, was replaced by the words FLYING TIGERS. We also got three more Boeing 747 tails on which to put the names. I checked out as a 747 first officer and flew international routes for the rest of the year.

All through the year Bob Prescott was still undergoing treatments for cancer.

ANN MARIE PRESCOTT: I remember one time when we were in the hospital in New York. They had done surgery to rearrange the muscles of the neck so they could take part of some of the speech, so he wouldn't have to go with one of those horns, you know.

And he looked at me and said, "You know I don't mind dying, but this is so undignified."

And that was so Bob. He was not afraid of anything. He was someone who looked fear in the face. Anything he might fear he went right into. It was the indignity of picking his body apart piece by piece that really got to his strong, wonderful energy.

Bob was against deregulation of the airlines. We went to Washington to fight deregulation, and Bob could hardly talk, you know. He could only whisper by then.

And you know Fred Smith was really pushing deregulation because that would suit Federal Express to a tee, because they didn't have to go through all the regulations that were set up for anybody to fly bigger equipment, right? And he was courting everybody in Washington at the time. He was the one that started all the deregulation effort.

When he met Bob on the floor at the hearing he came up and was so profusely complimentary to Bob. "You have been my hero all my life, etc etc."

Bob said, "If I'm such a (expletive deleted) hero, why did you start all this? It's going to be a jungle out there."

But the interesting thing was, on the way home Bob said, "One day that young whipper snapper will make a bid for Tigers."

That year Bob was presented with a very prestigious award from the ALPA.

GOLDY: Bob Prescott was made an honorary member of the Air Line Pilots Association. To show how rare this honor is it had been bestowed on only two other airline presidents, and to General Jimmie Doolittle, and Charles Lindberg.

ALPA president J. J. O'Donnell flew out to LAX to present a plaque to him. Tom Cotton and I were there for the presentation.

This next crew didn't win any awards, and it's a wonder they didn't get arrested for smuggling honeybees.

BOB McCULLOCH: Elgen Long was the captain; I was the first officer and Mike Firth the second officer, on a DC-8 freighter going from Seattle to Anchorage. We had two deadheading flight attendants with us, Kay Montgomery, who married Jim Vinson, and Marsha Hayes. On the number one pallet we had 100 three-pound boxes of honeybees. The two flight attendants were asleep in the deadhead compartment. Soon they started yelling and raising hell. One of the boxes had broken open, and there were bees everywhere.

We said, "Come up to the cockpit if you want to."

"Hell no! We're all covered up with blankets and we're not coming out for anything!"

Before we could get the door closed, the damn cockpit was also full of bees. There are a hell of a lot of bees in a three-pound box.

The bees were all over everything, but the second officer used his head. He turned down the cabin temperature control until the bees were immobilized. Of course by then it was so cold in there that we weren't so spry either.

We called ahead and had a beekeeper meet us in Anchorage. After we landed and parked the airplane, we were still covered with groggy bees. We walked very gingerly down the ramp, until the bees warmed up and flew off. Our nerves took a beating, but no one got stung.

A gin sling can fix a sting, but rum and Coke can rock the boat, so Gohm stayed home...

PAUL REBSCHER: I had a passenger flight to Okinawa with Captain Elgen Long and First Officer Jim Gohm. We had a two-day layover, so Elgen suggested we go sailing. You can never get an entire crew to agree to anything, but Elgen and myself from the cockpit and Cheryl, Marilyn and Bridget from the cabin crew wanted to go. The sailboats were very small, so it was decided we needed two. Elgen and Cheryl got in one boat and Marilyn, Bridget and myself got into the other. I was the only one in our boat who had ever sailed, so I was driving.

Now Bridget never goes anywhere without some sort of refreshments. This day she had cans of Coke and a good supply of rum miniatures from, I wonder where?

I watched Elgen sail smartly about, turning ever so smoothly with no problems. Every time we "came about" some sort of emergency arose, somebody getting knocked overboard by the boom, or tangled up in the lines. Of course, it could be that our ample refreshments had something to do with it. It was a great day and nobody got killed or even hurt.

Fred didn't get killed either, but he sure dug a hole for himself.

FRED ENFIELD: Below is a cartoon I drew at the request of our lawyer(s) in Washington, DC, for the purpose of positioning it as the first page in Flying Tiger's case submission in the Domestic Southern Tier Rights Case.

But we did win the case.

CHAPTER 45 TIGER TALES

The lawyer convinced Bob Cashman, who was spearheading the preparation of Tiger's case, that the cartoon would make an impact on the CAB. Bob asked me to think up and draw a cartoon that would depict loss of freight service in the industry by depending solely on the PAX carriers.

Impact indeed! Impact grew into pure indignation on the part of top executives of several of the other carriers in the case. The CAB, as well, felt the tactic was unprecedented.

After several calls between lawyers, the cartoon was officially removed as a Flying Tiger submission.

By this time Norah was all checked out and flying the line. Now she knew what all those knobs were for.

NORAH O'NEILL: The DC-8 had two large, round control trimming knobs on the central control pedestal between the captain and the copilot. The round metal backs of these knobs popped off so maintenance could reach inside them. These metal circles became picture frames for artwork clipped from Playboy and Hustler magazines. The captain would pop off a metal circle, look at the nude, female photo inside, and proclaim, "Nice stuff."

During my first year with Tigers, I was their only woman pilot, and I was closely scrutinized by my fellow pilots. Many of them later told me that they hoped to torture me enough so I would just quit, and Tigers would not repeat their stupid woman pilot experiment.

Shoving pornographic photos up my nose was one of their forms of torture. Actually, I did not mind looking at nude artwork at all. It was quite easy to agree that most of it was nice stuff. What I did get tired of was having scrapes on the end of my nose from the guys' enthusiastic sharing of the metal circle. Since I was trying very hard to fit in with the men I worked with, and prove that my presence would not interfere with any of their sacred male cockpit rituals, I decided that verbally complaining to them was not appropriate.

Instead, I bought Playgirl magazine for the first time, and carefully clipped rounded photos of male genitals. I inserted these photos in the trim knob covers. Not too long after I started my redecorating, I was delighted to have this experience.

I reported for a flight, and during the cockpit setup, the captain pulled a trim knob cover off, briefly glimpsed at it, and pronounced, "Nice stuff." As he extended his arm to push the photo under my nose, a shocked look appeared on his face as he realized what he had seen.

"Oh my God! We have a pervert working for us!"

I grabbed his wrist, before he could jerk his hand back, and took a long look at a tiny flaccid penis.

I said, "pretty nice, but pretty small. I wish women wouldn't tell so many lies about how size doesn't matter."

No one ever shared a trim knob photo with me again.

CHAPTER 46   SOME BAD NEWS   1978

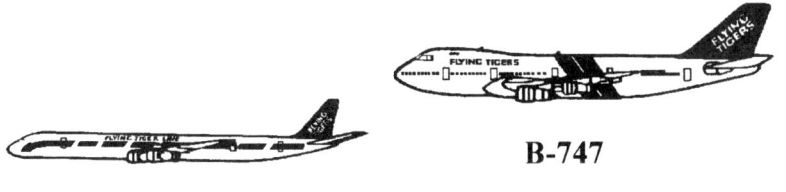

B-747

DC-8-63

In January EL AL, the Israeli airline, had a landing accident with one of their cargo planes, so they contracted with Flying Tigers for a 747 freighter and flight crews to move a backlog of freight. Captain Vern Wastman, Second Officer George Rimmer and I flew to Tel Aviv on EL AL. There were two other crews on the operation, so the airplane could keep a constant schedule.

Our first trip was from Tel Aviv to Teheran, Iran, a distance of only about 800 nautical miles, but due to the Arabs and Israelis not speaking to each other, we could not fly direct. We had to fly northwest, then north to clear the Syrian and Iraqi airspace, before going east toward Iran. This made it a trip of almost 1,300 miles. We were on the ground in Teheran about two hours, and then flew the same route in reverse back to Tel Aviv.

Turkey and Greece were not talking to each other either, so when we left Nicosia control going into Ankara control, Nicosia wouldn't tell Ankara we were coming. On our return trip Ankara wouldn't tell Nicosia we were coming. Makes it real interesting sometimes.

The next day we flew from Tel Aviv over Athens and Thessalonica, Greece, then Sarajevo and Zagreb, Yugoslavia, and on to Cologne, Germany. After two hours on the ground we again retraced our steps to Tel Aviv.

When the last flight of the contract was completed the airplane was flown back to the States. There were not enough seats on the airplane for all the crew members who were going home, so I agreed to lay over and take EL AL to New York the next day. Actually, I was bribed with a first-class ticket.

Sometimes you can call on all your experience and plan and use your best judgment and still things can go all to hell.

I was with Captain Larry Luccio on a trip from Tokyo to Anchorage, and Guy McAlister was the second officer. We had been unable to get our flight-planned altitude because of traffic, so we were behind on fuel by a considerable amount.[1]

As we approached the Alaskan coast, Center advised all aircraft that a fog bank had moved over the Anchorage Airport and it was closed. We didn't have enough fuel to descend at Anchorage, make a missed approach, then climb back to altitude and fly to Fairbanks and have any fuel reserve. To compound our problem, our 747 had been dispatched with one autopilot inoperative. This meant we could not shoot a Category II approach even though both Larry and I were qualified. Cat II approach minimums are 100 feet of altitude versus 200 feet for other ILS approaches.

I was flying the leg, so Larry looked up from his paperback novel and said, "Whatcha gonna do now?"

---

[1] At a lower altitude a jet burns more fuel, and also an eastbound flight can expect less tailwind.

CHAPTER 46   TIGER TALES

I said, "If the airport is still closed when we reach our descent point, I'll get a clearance direct to Fairbanks (our alternate airport)."

I guess this made sense to Larry, so he went back to his book. About 120 miles out, Center advised that the fog bank had moved off the airport. There were three DC-8s ahead of us in a holding pattern. The first one was cleared for the approach and we were cleared down to 10,000 feet.

"Looks like we lucked out." I said as I started down. A few minutes later the first DC-8 missed the approach. Then the second one missed.

Larry put his book away. Then the third DC-8 missed the approach.

Larry said, "Whatcha gonna do now?"

I slid my seat forward one notch and said, "I guess I'm going to hand fly a Cat II approach."

On the Boeing 747, the cockpit is so high and so far forward of the main landing gear that pilots cannot accurately judge the distance from the wheels to the runway. For that reason it is standard practice for the second officer to monitor his radar altimeter on final approach.

He begins his callouts at 50 feet and each 10 feet of descent thereafter. The prudent pilot listens not only to the callouts, but also to the tone of the second officer's voice. If the callouts are rapid and his voice is rising in inverse proportion to the distance from the ground, immediate corrective action is indicated.

After we entered the fog, I stayed on the instruments while Larry monitored and watched for the runway lights.

He kept saying, "Perfect, keep it coming down, you're right on."

Then Guy called out in a calm voice, "50—40—30—20—10 (feet)," and we landed right on the runway centerline. I don't really know what our altitude was when Larry saw the runway...and I didn't ask.

It seems that our president and company founder, Bob Prescott, spent his life doing battle. He fought the Japanese Zeros and the ice and altitude of the "Hump" in China. He fought the C.A.B.[2] and the major passenger carriers for the right to form an airline. He won all but his last battle. In March, one month after Flying Tigers became the world's largest airfreight airline, he lost his battle with cancer and died at his home in Palm Springs, California.

ANN MARIE PRESCOTT: Tigers was really a pilot's airline. Bob loved his pilots, it was wonderful. I'll tell you something that really touched my soul when Bob died. After the funeral we came back to our house, and a group of pilots made a circle around me.

And they said, "You know, we used to be Bob's pilots, but now we are Ann Marie's pilots."

That was such a touching moment, it was so sweet. You guys were a wonderful support system for the airline and for Bob. One reason Bob was so loved was that he never built a wall between himself and his pilots. He was one of them.

Some years earlier Bob had made the following comment, which shows how he felt about his employees.

---

[2]**Civil Aeronautics Board.**

CHAPTER 46   TIGER TALES   435

BOB PRESCOTT: Whether or not tigers like to be called people, people seem to like being called Tigers. More than anything else, for whatever reasons, the airline always has attracted unusual personalities, men and women with more than the normal amount of imagination, ingenuity, energy...and...guts.

We lost two more AVG men, Bus Loane and Tommy Haywood. Tommy had been in poor health since the heart attack he suffered on Wake Island in 1959.

We also lost Wayne Peake, the friendly fighter pilot, to lung cancer. Wayne tried to quit smoking for years, but never could...until now. He was a native of North Carolina, and he had a long driveway up to his home on a mountain. A sign at the bottom proclaimed "Peake's Pike."

Wayne held a strong affection for Israel since the days when he flew fighters for them in 1948. He still had many good friends there, including Ezer Weizman, now Defense Minister, and Mordecai Hod, now president of EL AL, the Israeli National Airline.

When he learned that he had but a short time to live, he asked Lamont Shadowens, vice president of operations, if arrangements could be made for him to be buried in Israel. Because Wayne was not Jewish this was not easy, but with some effort his wishes were carried out. His body was flown to New York on a Tiger airplane, then to Israel on EL AL. Wayne was noted for his impromptu poetry. Larry Partridge sent the following to me in Wayne's handwriting.

Canto the first
Wherein the mechanical ills of the aircraft are outlined...
There's a flutter in the rudder as we shudder through the

sky...And the autopilot is inop. but it's on the DMI.[3]
The PCUs[4] are surging, but the prop domes have been bled...
The radar just paints circles - I wish I'd stayed in bed...

Canto the second
Wherein the physical ills of the crew are outlined...
There's a bloody pain emerging from my autopilot thumb
And my poor old head is throbbing like a drum;
I've smoked so many cigarettes while tooling through the breeze
I've developed fits of coughing—and a mild asthmatic wheeze

Canto the third
Wherein the emotional ills of the crew are outlined and a possible panacea for the night's trials and tribulations is discovered...
The stewardess brought hot coffee, but I spilled it in her shoe...
My apologies were rebuffed with a "to hell with you!"

Canto the last
The weather is terrible, but I hardly could care less...
I'm playing it by ear just now—by ear—by god by guess...
One ray of hope still shining tho, and it may just pull us through...
Our ETA is twelve-thirty—the bars don't close till two...

                                                 Wayne (Omar) Peake

---

[3] Deferred maintenance item.

[4] Propeller control unit.

CHAPTER 47   SOME GOOD NEWS   1978 PART 2

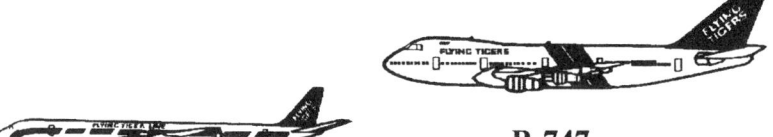

B-747

DC-8-63

Bob Zalusky says he has had a pretty dull life, hardly any excitement at all, but I did manage to pry the following from him. I guess the only good news here is that the bad news didn't get any worse.

BOB ZALUSKY: The only problem that I can recall was when I was arrested in Iran. It was a year before the hostages were taken, but of course I didn't know that then. I left New York with a DC-8 load of F-14 parts for Teheran, and when we arrived, the weather was 200 feet and one-quarter mile. They cleared me for the ILS, and I broke out and landed.

As soon as we touched down the tower began screaming at me, and I saw a row of red painted barrels on the runway ahead of me. I immediately jammed the throttles full forward and left the flaps full down. I held it on the ground until the last second, then pulled back and cleared the barrels. When we were safely airborne, I milked the flaps up and retracted the gear.

I found out later that we were supposed to fly the ILS, which is on the left runway, which we did. Then we were supposed to make a dogleg and land on the right runway, which has no ILS. Because of poor radio reception and even worse use of English, we did not receive that information. Also because of the low visibility, we never saw the other runway.

Our alternate airport was Isfahan, but the weather there was zero-zero, so we headed for Shiraz. According to our calculations we would arrive there with almost zero fuel. When we were near the airport, a hole appeared in the clouds, and we could see the runways. When I pushed the nose over to descend, the engines began to flame out. I had to make a flat descent, so the fuel pumps would remain immersed in fuel. After all that and a safe landing, we were arrested for landing at Shiraz without permission. I knew we had to get word to the company somehow, and I had noticed a telephone in the hall next to the men's room on our way in. There we were, under arrest, with soldiers standing all around us with guns.

I signaled to my copilot and he said, "I have to use the restroom."

So he left the room, but instead of going to the restroom, he called the company in Los Angeles.

We had another airplane inbound from New York with another load of F-14 spare parts, and when the company learned of our predicament, they told him to return to New York.

Of course this news reached the big wigs in Teheran, who until this point were unaware of our problem in Shiraz. In a few moments the phone rang, and it was plain that the commander was in a lot of trouble.

Finally, he slammed the phone down and said, "Captain, I don't know what you did, but I'm just about to be shot."

"What are you talking about?" I asked.

"Just what did you do? Did you send a message to your company?"

I said, "Yes."

"How did you do that?"

"My copilot called when he went to the bathroom."

"Well," he said, "I'm in a lot of trouble now"

I said, "Well hell, you told me we would all go to prison, and I didn't think we would like your prison. What in the hell else could I do? You were threatening me. All I wanted to do was to call the company and let them know where we were and what was happening. I have a right to do that, but you wouldn't let me."

"Those were my orders," he said.

"Well, I can't help what your orders were. My orders were for my copilot to get the message out and he did."

By this time it was too late to go anywhere, so with an armed guard, they took us to a hotel.

The cargo was destined for Isfahan and the next morning the weather was clear, so we flew up there and landed. There was not a soul on the airport, not a soul. We had to climb down the escape rope to go get a ladder, and then we hot-wired a forklift to get it started so we could off-load the airplane. We off-loaded the entire DC-8 load of F-14 parts onto the ramp. We did, the flight crew. Just as we were getting ready to leave, a jeep came racing up to us with a full colonel on board who ran up the ladder and into the cockpit.

"Captain," he said, "let's get out of here." He pointed to the jeep and said, "Don't let them on."

So we fired up and flew up to Teheran, and of course in Teheran the red carpet was out. All the big brass were there and said they were so sorry that we had all that trouble in Shiraz and promised that the commander would be punished.

I told them, "Hell, it wasn't his fault, he was just doing what you guys told him to do."

They looked puzzled and said, "We didn't tell him anything."

We were told sometime later that it was the head of the Iranian Airlines who had given the order. He was upset because Tigers got the contract to haul the F-14 parts, so he canceled our landing permits.

Anyway, flying over there can be an experience. But,

you know, in spite of all the funny airports, bad weather and aggravation, I still loved every minute of it. Of course it helps when you fly with the best damn bunch of guys in the world.

After the death of Bob Prescott, Wayne Hoffman named Joe Healy president of Flying Tigers. Joe had been with the company almost from the beginning, starting as a forklift driver in Newark, New Jersey.

Tom Grogean was named president of Tiger International, and Captain Dick Wilson, with the company since 1951, was named director of flight operations.

There was a huge expansion that year, and the company hired about 200 new pilots. This put me in line to move up to a captain's seat. Of all the events in a pilot's life, the most important and the most memorable is the day he checks out as captain. Everything else is just a prelude to that accomplishment. I went to the Flying Tiger training center in Los Angeles for two weeks of ground school, and then began DC-8 simulator training.

Not all pilots in initial upgrading to captain make the grade. If the pilot busts his check ride, he can fly as first officer for six months and try again. If he busts his third check ride, he is out of a job, no matter how much seniority he has. This is on each pilot's mind and adds to the pressure his own ego has placed on him. As is said among pilots, we are often our own worst enemies.

I finished my simulator training and was set up for my checkride with the F.A.A. This was the most important checkride of my life, and I'll have to admit my mouth was pretty dry when I strapped myself into the left seat of the simulator. After the checkride was in progress, I was too

CHAPTER 47 TIGER TALES

busy to worry about it.

I completed the four-engine work, and then had an engine fire, so I had to shut it down and make an instrument approach on three engines. Then the other engine on the same side failed, so I had to make a two-engine approach and landing. In between these problems the electrical system developed a short circuit and filled the cockpit with smoke. The landing gear unsafe light came on and the flaps wouldn't extend. Then the pressurization system failed, and I had to make an emergency descent.

When the simulator checkride was over and the F.A.A. examiner was satisfied, I was very tired but a happy man. I was scheduled for the airplane checkride the next afternoon at 4 p.m., but I didn't worry about that. Compared to the simulator, flying the airplane is easy.

We took off from Los Angeles and flew to the Palmdale area for the checkride. After we returned to Los Angeles, the F.A.A. examiner was filling out my new air transport pilot's license with a DC-8 type rating.

He signed it and handed it to me saying, "You look tired, maybe you could use a big steak and a couple of beers. After all, you're a captain now, you can afford it."

I said, "I'm sure going to take your advice, but I may not stop at two beers."

I didn't. But first, as I walked toward the hangar I reminisced about how some critical decisions had brought me to this point in my life. How not taking bad advice can be as important as taking good advice...like in 1959 when I went to school to get my aircraft and engine mechanic's license.

A couple of guys I worked with in the engine buildup shop said, "Why are you going to all that trouble and expense? They don't pay you any more money."

I got the license anyway and in 1960 I transferred to the flight line.

Same guys: "What in hell are you going up there for? You have to climb ladders and work out in the cold rain and the hot sun."

In 1961 when I accepted an overseas assignment as a maintenance rep, same guys: "Why in hell are you going over there? You'll have to work day and night and you won't get any overtime pay because you'll be on salary."

While I was in the Philippines, I obtained my commercial pilot's license and instrument rating. When I came back to the States in 1965, these same guys were still singing the same song.

"What in hell did you spend all that money for? No one is going to hire you as a pilot. You're too damn old and don't have enough experience."

Then in 1966 when the company put me on as a copilot, same guys, "Hell they're not going to let you fly the airplane. You'll just sit there in the right seat and talk on the radio. Besides, they don't pay new copilots nothing, and every winter you'll get furloughed."

Now, as I walked through the hangar and the engine buildup shop, I was stopped and congratulated by several of my old friends for making captain.

The same two guys shook my hand and said, "You sure are lucky."

A few days later I was talking to my mother on the phone and she asked, "Well, is it Captain Moldrem now?"

"Well yes, Mother, it is, but you can just call me Sir."

CHAPTER 48   A BOEING SNOWPLOW?   1979

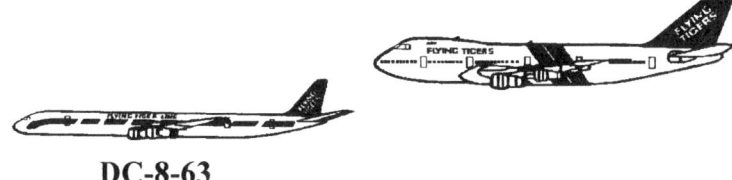

DC-8-63

Though I had been a senior first officer on international, I was now a junior captain flying domestic routes. Once in a while a trip can be memorable enough, or humorous enough to tell about. This particular trip was from Boston to Detroit. It was the first officer's leg, and though he was a good pilot, he made a terrible landing at Detroit. As a result he had to absorb a certain amount of good-natured kidding.

We arrived at the Hyatt Regency Hotel at 11:30 p.m. The bar closed at midnight, so we agreed to meet at the elevator in ten minutes, so we could get a cold beer.

When I entered my room I saw that the table was set for three. There was a bottle of Pinot Noir and a complete spread of cold cuts, cheeses and fruit. I looked around suspiciously, and then called the front desk.

The desk clerk said, "Yes sir, that room was set up for some VIP's, but they didn't show up. We are short of rooms tonight, so who's to know that you enjoyed a good bottle of wine?"

I thanked him very much and called my crew.

"Forget the bar, come on over to my room instead."

Soon there was a knock on my door, which I opened with a flourish and waved them toward the table.

The second officer said, "My goodness, how did you have this set up so quickly?"

The first officer, who was obviously upset about something said, "That's nothing, you should see what he did to me. He had me put in a room for the handicapped. It has railings around the bed and in the bathroom. I don't mind a little kidding about my landing, but I think this is going too far."

I had a tough time convincing him that I had nothing to do with that, so I called the front desk again. The desk clerk assured him that I was not the guilty party and there really were no other rooms available.

Sometimes the classroom is available, but you just can't find the answer…

BOBBIE THARP: I was in my last recurrent training class before I retired, when Bob Gilbert and Ray Elliot insisted on taking me out to lunch. Some lunch, they took me to several topless bars and my lunch consisted of pitchers of beer. We got back late and I still had to take the written test. I sat down at the desk and they put this exam in front of me. I looked at it and blinked my eyes a few times, but it didn't help. I didn't know the answers to any of the questions. It seemed to be about airplanes we didn't even fly.

Come to find out, I had been set up with a phony exam. The whole thing was done during lunch hour while I was being kept out of sight.

Hassig flunked his test too. It was in Urdu.

DON HASSIG: We had this trip into Teheran. My copilot was Marty Lewis, the engineer was Garrett Wight and Oscar Vaughn was along as our mechanic. We laid over and got legal in Teheran, and when we got back out to the airport, they had a flight plan for us. I had made this flight a couple of times before, and the flight plan was always to

CHAPTER 48   TIGER TALES

go south until we were over the water then turn toward Bombay, India. This time we were flight planned to go almost due east over Kabul, Afghanistan; Northern Pakistan; New Delhi, India; then over Rangoon. I didn't think anything about it.

We fired up, they gave us a clearance, and we took off. Of course it was 4:00 in the morning. We had been in the air only a little while when we were told that Karachi would not accept our flight plan as filed. They said we would have to fly overhead Karachi. So we discussed this a little bit, and it seemed there was no other alternative, so we headed in that direction. Then after a while they said we would have to land in Karachi. We said, no we didn't want to land at Karachi. We were empty and had plenty of fuel.

They came back and said we had to land at Karachi because we didn't have overfly rights. Well, we yakked back and forth, and told them we did have overfly rights. They demanded the overfly right number, so Marty read them his American Express card number. It was a nice try, but they didn't buy that. By now we were almost overhead, and at one point they said they would send fighters up if we didn't land. Maybe they would have and maybe they wouldn't, but we didn't want to take the chance. So what the hell, we went down and landed.

I said, "Everybody count your money, we may need it to get out of here."

Between the four of us we had about $400. So we went inside, and I started making out the international flight plan. The official there came out and greeted us, so I said, "Why did you make us land?"

He said. "We wanted some money."

I said, "All you had to do was bill us."

"Yeah, but if you land we know you have to pay it."

It was hot and we were thirsty, so Marty said, "I'll buy everyone a Coke."

The official said. "I'll get the Cokes."

He sent an underling who soon came back with two Cokes for Marty and me. None for the other two guys.

So I finished the flight plan and asked him, "Where do I file this?"

He said, "Well, first you have to pay the landing fee."

"Okay, I'll sign for it"

"No, we must have cash."

"Tigers always has credit anywhere."

"Not here. We must have cash."

"I don't have it."

I knew we had to go through Pakistani Airways for a handling fee, and that would take money also.

So I said, "I'll give you a personal check."

No, he wouldn't take that. So I offered him a credit card, but he wouldn't take that either.

Then he said, "Come with me and bring your checkbook. We will go over to the terminal and cash a check at one of the money changing windows."

I said okay, so we went there, and they didn't even say no, they just stared at us like we were nuts.

I said, "Well, you might as well take my check, or we're going to be here for days until the company can get the money here."

Nothing doing, so we hashed it around for about an hour or so.

Finally he said, "Well I'll let you sign for it on one condition."

"What's that?"

"If you write a letter saying that if Flying Tigers don't pay it, you'll pay it."

"Okay."

Now I had to go Pakistani Airways to pay the handling fee, and he wanted $300 in cash.

I said, "But they let me sign for the landing fee."

He said, "They did???"

"Yeah, they did."

"Just a minute."

He went and checked with this guy and came back and said, "You will have to write me a letter too."

So I wrote another letter, and we were ready to go.

The official said, "Captain, I helped you out of a very serious problem."

"Yes, I guess you did."

"Now I think you should give me a tip."

"How much?"

"Ten bucks."

"Okay," and I gave him a ten.

Then he looked at Marty and said, "And you owe me two bucks for the Cokes."

If you fly long enough, you're bound to have a mechanical problem of some kind. I had a night flight from San Francisco to Cleveland, with a stop in Chicago. We left Chicago just after sunrise for the short hop to Cleveland. I reduced power for the descent into Cleveland Hopkins Airport where I had been cleared down to 6,000 feet. As we approached the assigned altitude and I added power to level off, the number two engine remained at idle.

The engine would not respond to any change in throttle position, so I shut it down. I didn't want it to do something unexpected while we were landing.

As required by the checklist I said, "First officer, shut down number two engine, second officer, monitor the shutdown."

The first officer said, "Number two throttle closed," and put his hand on the fuel shutoff lever.

There was no response from the second officer. Then we heard a loud crash back in the galley area, and the second officer yelled, "Number two what?"

We both turned around, and there was the second officer standing in the cockpit doorway. He had been putting things away in the galley and was not aware of the problem. He was eating a roast beef sandwich and stood there with his mouth open and the gravy dripping onto his tie.

The first officer and I finally stopped laughing enough to get the engine shut down and the checklist completed. We informed the tower of our problem, so the emergency equipment would be standing by. After a normal landing, the mechanic determined that the fuel control unit was faulty, so they replaced it.

The first officer said, "I wonder what the training department would say about our performance this morning? It never works that way in the simulator."

The company has always responded to the needs of unfortunate people, and the following was no exception.

HAL EWING: There were these horrible pictures of starving babies in Cambodia when Pol Pot's regime fell apart. A possible relief flight was set up with the Civil Defense Director of Los Angeles County, Mike Regan. The people in the Los Angeles area had donated the food. Archie Hall and I went to the company with the idea of loading it on a DC-8. We could deliver the food in Phnom Penh, then fly the airplane to Bangkok where it was going to pick up a charter anyway. The Company agreed. I flew the trip with First Officer Lee Gunderson and Second Officer Davis.

CHAPTER 48   TIGER TALES

There's more to this story later, but for now...

Captain Dick Petrick began his aviation career by building model airplanes back in Missouri. He always assumed he would become an airplane mechanic, but then he noticed that in the movies the pilot was always the one who got the girl. Being a clever and sensible fellow, he decided he would learn to fly.

The most memorable event Dick had with Tigers happened in 1979. He was off duty at home in San Francisco and took an emergency alert when a captain went on sick leave. The flight was from Seattle to New York with a stop in Chicago. Dave Hooker was the first officer and Don Singer the second officer.

The weather at O'Hare Airport in Chicago was zero-zero and was forecast to be down at their arrival time. With that in mind they put on extra fuel and planned to overfly O'Hare. When he approached the Chicago area, the weather had improved slightly.

Approach Control said, "Tiger, I can clear you for an approach if you can accept runway 9 left."

"Negative. We are too heavy for that short runway. We'll require 9 right."

"With the traffic we have, we can't give you 9 right for about 45 minutes."

"Okay, then give me a clearance on to New York."

They received the clearance and were climbing out when the controller said, "Tiger, we have a break in the inbound traffic. Can you accept an immediate approach to 9 right?"

"Sure," he said, so they turned him right in.

He was following a United Airlines flight that slowed to a final approach speed that Dick couldn't get below, due to the heavy weight of the 747.

Approach Control said, "Be prepared for a possible missed approach."

United landed and cleared the runway quickly, so Dick was cleared to land. At this time it was snowing very hard, and with the snow on the ground it was like a whiteout.

Visibility was so poor that Dick said to Dave, "I'm going to stay on the gauges until touchdown."

They landed and the spoilers came up and the engines went into reverse. Suddenly there was a panic shouting on the radio, "Stop Delta! Stop!" At that time Dick became aware that a Delta passenger flight was taxiing across the runway right in front of him. He was crossing left to right so Dick moved to the right to keep from hitting him. He thought that with all the shouting the Delta pilot might stop, but he continued across.

All Dick could do was go off the side of the runway. When he did, he thought there was a possibility that he could get by him then get back on the runway. But the right wing gear sheared off when it hit a snow bank, then the nose gear collapsed followed by the #2 engine being torn off, so that was the end of that.

What he was worried about now like every one else was fire. George Mulcahy, a deadheading second officer, quickly opened the door then called out, "No fire!"

Dick Petrick received a total of four awards for saving the lives of 115 Delta passengers. One award was from the City of Chicago Aviation Department, and one from the F.A.A. Dick also became the second Tiger pilot to re-

CHAPTER 48 TIGER TALES 451

ceive the prestigious Daedalion Award, the first being Greg Thomas in 1957.

It takes a lot of guts to wreck a 747 on purpose, but 115 Delta passengers lived.

Dick said, "The fourth award was the most important to me: the Robert W. Prescott Award."

Flying Tiger management established this award in honor of company founder and president, Bob Prescott, after his untimely death.

Bad luck always comes in pairs?

BOBBIE THARP: The same day in Anchorage, a 747 had a nose gear collapse. Two 747s out of service at the same

time, meant some pilots would have to go back to the DC-8s. I had enough seniority that I wouldn't be affected, but I only had a few months left before retirement, so if I volunteered to go back on the DC-8, I could fly with my son, Ernie, a Tiger copilot.

I ran this by crew control and they O. K.'d it. It's a once in a lifetime chance for a father and son to fly together on a crew. I flew with Ernie for six solid months all around the world and we had a ball.

Among our trips was one to Dhahran, Saudi Arabia, where we were to get legal, then ferry the airplane to Pisa, Italy.

Dhahran was not a pleasant place to lay over. Everything was very expensive and they wanted $50.00 to put a bag of ice on the airplane. We said, "Forget it, you keep it."

Then I talked it over with the crew, "How would you like to go on to Pisa same duty time? We would be legal to do that, and a layover there would be a lot better."

Everyone agreed, so after the airplane was off-loaded, we took off for Pisa, Italy. There we had a nice hotel and a great Italian dinner.

After our crew rest we went to the airplane and were all ready to depart when the Italian airport personnel went on an impromptu strike. We sat there for three hours before we could take off for Amsterdam.

There were more changes in the company. The Reliance Investment Group bought a substantial number of Tiger International shares. We did not realize the significance of this at the time.

Bill Bartling, one of the ten ex-AVG company founders, passed away. He had served as vice president of operations for many years before retiring for medical reasons. President Joe Healy left the company, and Tom Grogean took over that position.

When a pilot nears the mandatory retirement age of 60, he might become overly sensitive to comments about age.

DON HASSIG: A short time before I reached the magic age of 60, I was on a Pacific trip. My second officer was a new hire in his early twenties and was on his first international trip.

We were leaving Tokyo in a DC-8 and taxied out behind a Pan Am 747. Several airplanes were landing so we had to wait. Finally there was a break in the landing traffic, and the tower cleared the 747 into position and to be ready for an immediate takeoff. The 747 crew acknowledged this, but then didn't move for several seconds.

I said mostly to myself, "Come on, Pan Am, let's move it."

The second officer said, "He's probably so damn old that he can't even see the runway."

I turned to him and said, "Now just a God-damn minute. He can't possibly be much older than I am, and I can assure you that I can see the runway."

He turned red and started apologizing and was obviously very embarrassed. The first officer made some comment about what a good idea it is to make brownie points with the captain, especially when you are still on probation.

Rex Tripp, affectionately called Sexy Rexy, also retired this year after a long and successful career. Rex started out as a crop duster in California. He was a professional in the business and became quite an authority on chemicals, in some cases by accident. In the early days he occasionally experienced spatial disorientation due to the effects of breathing Parathion. One day when his head was relatively clear, he quit that line of work and hired on with Tigers.

One time many years ago Rex had an ulcer, so he went to the doctor.

The doctor asked, "Do you drink or smoke?"

"Well, I drink martinis."

"Oh my goodness," said the doctor, "martinis are the worst thing for an ulcer. You will just have to give them up."

The word got out among all the pilots that Rex was not supposed to drink martinis.

One day Rex was in a bar in Honolulu holding a drink, when his copilot walked up.

He said, "Rex, isn't that a martini?"

"Yes."

"But you're not supposed to drink martinis," he said accusingly.

"I like martinis," Rex answered, "and if the God dammed ulcer don't like it, it can leave."

Which apparently it did, because Rex has had no further trouble from it.

I don't know if this next story is completely true, or only partly. Knowing Rex, I'd go with the former:

The story was that Rex overdosed on his favorite ulcer remedy at Hickam Field one night. It seems that the Military Police were trying to arrest a couple of drunken sailors when Rex decided to intervene.

CHAPTER 48   TIGER TALES   455

"I'm Lieutenant General Tripp! You guys get the hell out of here and leave these fellows alone!"

Then he supposedly went to the brig and tried to turn all the prisoners loose. During this time he had commandeered a staff car and had half of Hawaii mad at him. No one seems to know how he got out of it, but a letter was sent to Bob Prescott detailing all of Rex's offenses.

When Bob finally got to the bottom of the list he rubbed his jaw thoughtfully then said, "No it can't be true. No one could have done all that in one night, not even one of my pilots."

WISH YOU WERE IN A BAR STORY

Captain Emmet Flood was noted for not showing a great deal of respect for thunderstorms.

A new copilot commented, "Looks like thunderstorms ahead. What are you going to do?"

Flood's response supposedly was, " Ignore 'em."

Soon they were in the weather, and the sky was lit up with lightning, and the turbulence increasing severely. Emmet was fighting the yoke with both hands trying to keep the airplane right side up, and charts and coffee cups were flying all around the cockpit.

The copilot, who was hanging on for dear life, shouted, "Looks like you're having a hell of a time ignoring this one!"

There's something fishy about this next story.

HARRIE GRIFFIN, SFO flight line mechanic: Jim Archer, Nelfie McGraft and I went fishing in the bay before our shift started. Jim and Nelfie went back to the airport to depart the 9 p.m. flight to New York. Right after they left, I hooked a 37-pound striper. I went back to the airport, laid the fish on a tug and drove it out to the airplane.

The crew was in the process of starting the engines, but when the captain looked out and saw that monster fish, he came back down the ladder to see if it was real. By the time he was through admiring it and asking questions, the DC-8 departed late.

When an airplane is delayed it has to be someone's fault. Now, was it a maintenance delay because I caught the fish, or a crew delay because the captain looked at it?

Jim suggested it should be a weather delay, because it was good weather for fishing.

CHAPTER 49   ARABIA TO AFRICA   1980

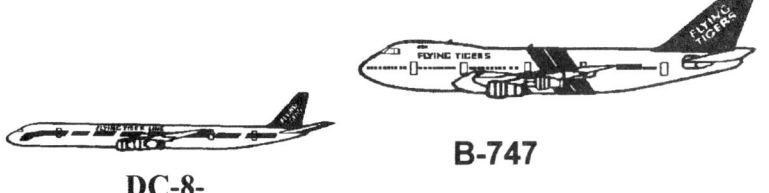

B-747

DC-8-

By May I finally was back on international flying. On the 17th I went up to Anchorage, Alaska, and was there when the Mount St. Helens Volcano in Washington State erupted on the 18th. The next day I flew a military passenger flight to Travis AFB, California. We passed just to the west of Mount St. Helens, so we all had a good view of the volcano as we flew by.

The extent of the destruction was far greater than we expected, in spite of the news reports. It looked like half of the cone was completely gone, and the trees were stripped away from what was left. No one in the cockpit said a word. We just stared at the mountain. Then a flight attendant came in and summed up our feelings with two words, "My God!"

In June I flew a trip to Sydney, Australia, stopping in Honolulu, Hawaii, for a crew rest. The next day we flew to Nandi in the Fiji Islands for a fuel stop, then on to Sydney. Howie Harder was my first officer and W. C. Harvey, the second officer. We had a great layover in Sydney. We went on a harbor tour, walked through the old penal colony area and went through the opera house. We also drank a lot of beer. The beer and the food were both excellent.

We stayed in Sydney three days then flew a charter flight through Manila, Philippines; Nagoya, Japan; Anchorage, Alaska; and San Francisco.

July 1st found me on my way from Travis AFB, California, across the mid-Pacific on a military cargo flight. My crew was Greg Cotton and Rick Campbell. We landed at Hickam Field, Hawaii, for a crew rest, and 12 hours later we flew an eight-hour flight to Anderson AFB, Guam, arriving early in the morning.

The sky was clear, and the island looked as peaceful and colorful as a tourist brochure. It was really beautiful. The hotel consisted of several cottages, and the grounds were covered with hibiscus and other tropical plants. I walked down to the cliff overlooking the shore and gazed out over the ocean. The only sound to be heard was the crash of breakers onto the beach.

The next day we flew to Subic Bay in the Philippines, then up to Clark Field. This was my first trip into Clark Field since I'd upgraded to captain. My old friends there were very happy for me. I wished I could have stayed to visit for a while, but schedules don't wait.

We lost another of our AVG men, Cliff Groh. Cliff was the youngest of the ten pilots who founded the airline. Some say he never did grow up, but I guess it doesn't matter. He provided a lot of laughs through the years.

This next crew had nothing to laugh about and neither did their passengers.

AL MOBLEY: We left out of Seattle in a Boeing 747 bound for Anchorage with a load of pregnant dairy cows. As we leveled off in cruise, the outflow valves froze up, and we lost control of cabin pressurization. We had to make an emergency descent so the cows could breathe. They all sur-

CHAPTER 49   TIGER TALES   459

survived and none of them complained, so I guess we did all right.

The most exciting news of the year (for the rest of us) was the acquisition of Seaboard World Airlines. With their routes to Europe and the Middle East added to our Pacific routes, we now could provide round-the-world service. The bad news was that the combined debt load of Tiger International and Seaboard nearly broke our backs.

It was the profit generated by the Flying Tiger Airline that allowed the formation of Tiger International in the first place. Now, with sky-high interest rates and record high fuel prices causing slim profit margins, Tiger International showed little concern for the airline. The comment was heard that they would get rid of the airline before they would let it drag down Tiger International. A real morale booster. Then they used some more of our money to buy Hall's Motor Freight, a trucking company.

Bad weather or mechanical problems are not unusual and are accepted as a part of flying. It's the little things like overlooked paperwork or what should be unnecessary red tape that is so exasperating. Shad gave up his position as vice president of operations and went back on the line. He may have escaped some of the paperwork, but not the frustrations.

Sometimes ingenuity prevails.

SHAD: We took off from London for Chatereaux, France, then we found out we didn't have the General Declaration on board. This is considered a serious offense and can result in a fine if not worse. So I got a blank General Dec. from the ship's papers, filled it out and took a silver dollar and made an imprint and rubbed a lead pencil over it to look like an official seal. It was accepted with no problem at all.

There's always someone who has to mess up a good deal.

BOB BAIRD: In October of 1980 I was living the good life. I was about number three on the DC-8 captains list and was flying seven Honolulu turns a month. These started out as a leg from SFO with a 24-hour beach layover then back to LAX. Good deal! Somebody in crew scheduling must have gotten wind of the fun we were having, so they changed this to same duty time trips over and straight back.

I had been getting a lot of calls from Freddy Lynch telling me I needed to be on the 747, so I gave in and bid it.

After finishing the systems ground school, I headed up to Vancouver in early November for flight simulator training. The simulator was set up as a 747-100. John Lamping was my instructor pilot for this bit, and things went well, as John was a heck of an instructor pilot. You always felt comfortable with him.

Halfway through the course we had a week's break for some reason and then went down to DFW to finish off in Braniff's 747-200 simulator. I picked up Bob Poindexter there as instructor pilot, and he did a nice job with me also, and I finished up on schedule.

I then had about a ten-day break waiting for an airplane to be freed up for the airplane check ride, so early in December about five of us new guys plus a Company Check Pilot in the right seat and the FAA in the observer seat launched for Palmdale. It was a typical day on the high desert, clear and a million, and a 25-30 knot gusting crosswind. What a day! I was the last guy in the seat and was

CHAPTER 49   TIGER TALES   461

already worn out from the thrills of the previous new guy's feats of daring in that wind! Somehow we all were typed on the big bird and now waited again for our IOE'S (Initial Operating Experience).

Towards the middle of the month I started my IOE with Ron Lee as coach, and we had a fine time except for losing number three at about 600 feet coming out of Anchorage with a load of passengers. We dumped fuel and returned to sit about five hours while a fuel pump was replaced.

We had just about enough duty time left to take it to Travis AFB. I had a little trouble with one of the male flight attendants. He wanted everybody to get off and go back to the hotel, so I left him behind and had an uneventful trip on down south.

I sort of wondered about the reliability factor on the engines as a result of losing one so soon after moving on to the 747, but in the next 14 years I had only one other failure, which speaks for itself. The Big Boeing was and is a wonderful airplane. The systems were fairly easy, and with multiple redundancies we seldom had any problems requiring us to abort a leg and return or divert.

The three autopilots did a superb job and were a great comfort when actual CAT-II conditions were encountered. The airplane also was very light on the controls as compared to the DC-8, and easy to fly, though it could be a handful in strong crosswinds due to the large sail effect of the slab-sided fuselage and large vertical fin. I flew the DC-8 ten years as captain and almost fifteen on the 747. I really don't know which I liked most, though I think the DC-8-63 was the best looking jet transport built. Whatever the case, Tigers had two winners with them.

What makes flying interesting is that no two trips are ever the same. Some flights are more different than others...

EDDIE RUHL: Flying at Tigers was the most interesting flying I've ever done in my life, especially the charters. This story takes place during the "Baggage Hadj." It's a great example of how the most seemingly insignificant event of a day can be the one that saves your life.

Every year Moslem pilgrims go to Mecca for the Hadj, and we sometimes had contracts to fly pilgrims to Jedda, and then fly them home again after the Hadj. We had to take them to Jedda because a non-believer cannot go to Mecca.

It seems that the pilgrims buy a lot of things to take home with them at the Hadj, so much that they couldn't possibly put it all in the bellies as baggage, so they chartered freighters to haul all the baggage home. This particular year we had the contract to haul the baggage back to Nigeria.

Their baggage claim system was quite interesting and very simple. As each Hadji left Nigeria at the beginning of his pilgrimage, he was issued a large kit bag with a plastic window on the side. These bags were color coded as to the departure city, red for Kano (pronounced Karno), green for Sokoto etc. Each pilgrim then had his picture taken and inserted into the plastic window for future identification purposes. After the Hadj, each pilgrim tied all of his baggage together in a huge bundle the size of a large Volkswagen with the color-coded bag and photo visible on the outside of the bundle. The bundles were then segregated by the color of the kit bag and piled up at the airport in huge mountains. I'm not talking hills here, I'm talking mountains.

CHAPTER 49 TIGER TALES

Each mountain was bound for a particular city in Nigeria. The bags were then loaded onto freighters and flown to their respective cities. Meanwhile, the pilgrims had flown back on the passenger birds and set up camp, waiting for their bags. When the freighters arrived and were offloaded, the bags were again piled up and the pilgrims rooted through them, rolling these huge bundles over, looking for their picture. When they found it, they hauled it to their camp, took down the tent, loaded up the camels, truck or whatever they had and went home. I think about this sometimes when I'm tempted to grumble about waiting too long at the baggage carousel!

Anyway, I happened to be on one of the baggage charters and deadheaded to Jedda just before Thanksgiving. Howard Harder was the captain, I was the copilot, Bill Niven the second officer and Bryan Gurrel was the charter rep. I forget the name of the mechanic who was on board.

We crew rested in Jedda, spent a day roaming around the old city and found a shipyard where they were building dhows, the big, wooden ships that still sail all over the Red Sea and Indian Ocean. They were building these huge, wooden ships with no power tools, just bare feet to hold the logs, an adz to shape them, an "Indian drill" to bore holes for pegs and a mallet to drive in the pegs and the caulking.

We had Thanksgiving dinner at a little walkup stand in the souk. I forget the name in Arabic, but in New York they're called gyros—sliced lamb on pita bread, with onions and a yogurt sauce— delicious.

We got legal and were scheduled to depart to Sokoto, Nigeria, the next afternoon. When we got to the airplane, it was blistering hot out on the ramp. The DC-8 was loaded to the gunnels with freight and fueled for Sokoto. This is where the trouble began. All of the prior flights down had been bound for Kano, which is a fairly large city by the local standards and had a well-established airport with fuel available. We were the first flight scheduled to go to Sokoto, which was just a bit farther, and also had no fuel.

The plan was to fly to Sokoto, off-load there and then fly back to Kano for fuel. That meant we had to tanker enough fuel to be legal to make the empty ferry to Kano. None of the previous flights had had to tanker fuel, so they had been able to carry close to 100,000 pounds of baggage. The people working the charter at Jedda just loaded us up with the same amount of bags as they had the Kano flights. As a result, by the time we added the tankered fuel and the fuel for the extra distance to Sokoto in the first place, we were legal on the weight and balance, but performance-wise we were way too heavy to get off the runway in Jedda.

We explored all kinds of options but finally concluded that the only way we could go was to off-load about 20,000 pounds of bags and make our takeoff at dawn when the air would be at its coolest. We got the plan all set up with the charter people, who were very upset because we wouldn't just go anyway and went back to the hotel. When we came back out in the morning the weight and balance showed that they had taken off 20,000 pounds of freight, but when I looked at the load it looked just the same, as far as I could tell. Howie got the lead man up there and quizzed him, but he insisted they had downloaded and taken bags off to lose the 20,000 pounds.

We looked it all over and agreed that if they were lying about the load, we would still be able to get airborne, assuming no engine failures, but that we would probably end up short on fuel at Sokoto. So we gave it a shot, and by the time we rotated and left the ground, I was really praying we didn't have so much as a hiccup from those engines. It was pretty clear already that the load was heavier than the

CHAPTER 49　　TIGER TALES　　　　　465

weight and balance said, and when we leveled off and checked the power required to hold altitude and speed, it confirmed that we were just about 20,000 pounds heavy.

The result was that we burned most of the fuel that was meant for the ferry to Kano, just getting to Sokoto. More on that later.

Before we departed Jedda, the charter agent on the ground had told us there was to be one passenger to ride with us to Sokoto, if Howie would take him. The gentleman was a Nigerian, a middle-aged man named Abu Ahnk III. At least that is how he introduced himself. He was very well spoken, dressed in a long, flowing, blue robe and had several long vertical, parallel scars on each cheek, which we later found out were signs of rank.

We welcomed him on board and did our best to make him comfortable, not exactly an easy task in the old DC-8 sometimes. We offered him food and drink and chatted a bit on the way. When we got to Sokoto, the weather was beautiful. Clear skies, great visibility, not a cloud anywhere. The Sokoto Airport had two navigation aids, an NDB and a VOR. We were descending to the VOR, looking for the field, when we spotted the airport well off from where our chart said it should be. There was no doubt it was the right airport, so Howie went on in visually and landed.

We had been promised that there would be a forklift available that could off-load the baggage pallets, but when we taxied to the only ramp there, all we saw was one Cessna 172 and a wheezy looking little forklift that couldn't even reach the deck of the DC-8. There was no power cart for electrical power, but there was a rather suspect little air cart. It's possible to start the DC-8 on battery electrical power, but you absolutely have to have a functioning air cart to make a start.

There was a huge crowd of the biggest, strongest looking young men I had ever seen in my life. They all had broad shoulders and looked like they had spent their entire lives lifting weights, which in fact, they probably had. Most were wearing only shorts, no shirts, and they were a very impressive sight.

As we shut down the engines, and Howie and I shuffled the charts around to start figuring how we were going to legally file out of there with the limited fuel remaining, Bill went back to open the door.

No sooner had he swung back the door than absolute pandemonium broke out on the ramp. The entire crowd of these large, powerful looking men began leaping around and shouting and the whole mass charged the airplane. Like two guys singing the chorus to the same old song, Howie and I both started yelling, "Close the door! Close the door!" We had no idea what had made those guys so mad, but whatever it was we didn't want to find out. But it was too late.

They had already put up a ladder and were storming onto the airplane. It took a minute or two to figure out what had happened, but as it turned out, Abu Ahnk III was a very important person. He was the Sultan's personal representative to the Hadj, and no one there had known he was going to be on our airplane. We waited for quite some time while every one there came up the ladder and paid their respects to our passenger. We were very glad we had treated him kindly!

But operationally things had taken another downturn. The forklift we saw was the only one there was, so it was decided that the only way to off-load the bags was to daisy chain them off, one by one—all 100,000 pounds of them. The good news was the crowd that had stormed the airplane was available for just such a task, and they set right to work. The bad news was it would take the best part of the day, even for them.

Fuel-wise we were supposed to file to Kano with Lagos for the alternate. Lagos, of course, also has fuel. But we didn't have enough fuel to get to Lagos in a pinch, so we filed to Kano with a return to Sokoto as our alternate. We had enough fuel for that, but if we actually had to return to Sokoto, we would be really screwed—stuck in the middle of northern Nigeria out of gas. But it was the only way, so that's what Howie decided.

Now Howie and I are both big general aviation guys. We love old airplanes and little airplanes. We wondered if we could get our hands on that Cessna that was sharing our ramp. We thought it might be fun to go out and fly around the desert chasing camels or who knows what, so I called the Sokoto tower (yes, they really had a tower) and made inquiries as to who owned the Cessna and how we could get in touch with them. He told us, with great difficulty due to a severe language barrier, that it belonged to the Sokoto Flying Club, but we couldn't figure out how to reach them.

As we were sitting there talking this over, a car pulled up and two Europeans stepped out. They came on board and introduced themselves. One was a Dutchman and the other was English. They were engineers out there building the airport and trying to get it into full operation. They were also the entire membership of the Sokoto Flying Club.

They had a VHF radio in their car and had heard us asking the tower, so they had driven over. We never did actually get to fly the Cessna, but we had a very pleasant chat, and while we were talking, the Dutchman leaned over my shoulder to look at the VOR approach plate that was still clipped to my yoke. He laughed and commented that

Jepessen had not made the change yet. They had moved the VOR because the locals kept stealing it! He took a pencil out of his pocket, leaned way over my shoulder and made a wavy little X on my chart and told us that was where it was now. That explained why the airport had not seemed to be in the right place when we came in, but we didn't really think too much about it at the time other than to make a mental note to brief the next crew. That was the first important event that happened during that conversation.

While we were talking, Howie noticed the Englishman staring at one of the five or six large, lovely cheese trays that had been put on board as part of our catering at Jedda. When Howie asked if he would like some cheese, the Englishman was embarrassed and apologized for staring. Then he explained that Nigeria had passed a law prohibiting the importation of cheese to protect the domestic cheese industry, but then had never started a domestic cheese industry. As a result, cheese was unobtainable in Nigeria, and Europeans love their cheese. Hearing that, Howie promptly gave them all the cheese on board and promised to send more down on the next flight.

We had made two friends, and that was the second important event that happened during that conversation.

It took all day to off-load the bags but we were not bored. Abu Anhk III came back and invited us on a tour of Sokoto and took us to his home and introduced us to his wives—all four or five of them. By the time we got back to the airport, the bags were growing another mountain just like the ones in Jedda, and the pilgrims were swarming over it, each searching for his picture.

When all was done, we closed up the cargo door, the mechanic fired up the wheezy little air cart and we did a battery start on one engine, then used the cross bleed to start the other three. It was my leg this time, and I took off into the same crystal clear sky that we had enjoyed all day. But as we climbed out headed for Kano, we saw the strangest sight ahead. There were no clouds exactly, but the sky just seemed to gradually fade from blue to a strange shade of yellow/brown. At about eight thousand feet, we plunged into this weird sky, and the visibility went to zero.

We later found that this was the Harmattan, an annual dust storm that comes down from the north out of the Sahara, and it had chosen just this minute to arrive. This changed the situation from a nice visual approach at Kano, to a very low minimums, instrument approach situation. The next thing we learned was that as soon as the Harmattan hit, the airport at Kano had shut off the ILS approach and gone home. The visibility was way below minimums for any other approach at Kano, so with Howie's concurrence, I turned around and dived back for Sokoto.

We hoped to get there before the dust storm arrived. Sokoto had two approaches, a VOR approach, which was no longer valid since the VOR was not where it was depicted on the chart, and an NDB. If we lost the race with the dust storm, we would have to fly the NDB, a very non-precise approach, for we no longer had enough fuel to go anywhere else.

We lost the race. In the few minutes it took to turn around and get to Sokoto, the dust storm had arrived. The minute that happened, the NDB, the only navaid we had an approach for, also went off the air. The only navaid that stayed up was the VOR, and the only depiction we had of where it was located was the wavy, penciled in X on my approach plate that the Dutchman had scratched while leaning over my shoulder.

There was no published approach for it, so Howard and I looked over the old approach plate with the X, looked at the altitude of the terrain depicted and made up an approach. We drew in a procedure turn, made up the minimum altitudes, figured some timing, and headed for the VOR.

Howard was the captain, and he certainly had every right to take the airplane and make the approach himself, but Howard is the kind of captain all the copilots like to fly with. He is not only a superb pilot himself, but he gave his copilots the freedom to be confident in themselves. He just asked me if I thought I could do it. I said yes, I could, and that was that. I flew the approach.

Everything from there on was very strange and full of questions. I'd never operated a jet engine in a dust storm before and really had no idea what kind of abrasive grit we might be flying through. How would the engines react? And this whole approach was based on that wavy, pencil mark on my chart. When we had flown out our timing and reached the missed approach point, would the airport be there? And even if we were in the right place, was the visibility good enough for us to even see it?

Luck was with us. The engines kept running and just before we reached the missed approach point, Howie called out the field. It was off to the right and just ahead, almost right under the nose. Under normal circumstances there is no way in the world we would have tried to make a landing from where we were. But the visibility was only going down, and there was no reason to believe we could do better next time.

Fuel was now getting really critical, so I called for full flaps, chopped all four throttles to idle, and as Howie called out "Slip it," I pushed the nose down and put the DC-8 into as hard a slip as I would a J-3 Cub. We developed a sink rate that would give me a heart attack all by itself in any other circumstance, but we got lined up on center line and sort of auto rotated down. At just a couple hundred feet I started to take out the slip and flared to trade the excess airspeed for reduced sink rate. We went across the threshold high and fast, all four throttles still hard against the stops.

Just then we noticed that workmen, who apparently had not known we were coming back, covered the runway. They scattered to the sides flinging tools as they went. There was no room to finesse the landing, and I just planted it on. We touched down hard, pushed the nose down and went to full reverse and maximum braking.

Just about the time the nose wheel touched down, a small flock of goats, maybe ten or fifteen, dashed out onto the runway right in front of us and then scattered on both sides. The airplane stopped before the end of the runway and the first thought I remember thinking was that we were going to be here for a long time.

We taxied back to the ramp we had just left and shut down all but one engine. Bryan used the HF radio to call Berna Radio in Switzerland, to phone patch Ned Wallace in Charter Operations in Los Angeles. When he got Ned on the phone the conversation was very brief. Bryan simply told him we were back on the ground in Sokoto, we were out of gas and we would call back tomorrow. He closed with, "The situation in Sokoto is untenable!"

Without even waiting for a reply from his boss, he shut down the last engine, killing all electrical power and the radio.

The wavy little pencil X that the Dutchman had scribbled on my approach plate had saved our lives. If he hadn't done that, we would have flown the VOR approach as published and ended up at the missed approach point, in the middle of bare desert. We probably would have reflown that approach, going lower and lower and looking for the airport until we ran out of fuel and crashed in the sand.

Now it was time for Howie's gift of the cheese to save us again. We took another little tour of Sokoto, this time looking for lodgings and found that what was available was way beyond grim by our spoiled Western standards. Foodwise, a trip past the market and all the butchered animals hanging on hooks, covered with flies, made quite an impression.

Just as we were deciding that we would be camping out on the floor of the DC-8, our new friend, the Englishman and the Dutchman, showed up and invited us to stay with them. They put us up, fed us, had our laundry done each night and took us all around Sokoto.

As it turns out, we were there four or five days while the charter folks tried to figure out how to get fuel to us. Each morning we would go out to the airplane, battery start one engine and use the HF radio to phone patch Charter Ops to see if there was any news. Then we spent the rest of the time touring around the area, drinking beer, going to local wrestling matches, having a grand old time and meeting other expatriates who lived there. It was one of these expats, a fellow from Rhodesia, who introduced us to his monkey who liked to have sex with cats, but that is another story.

In the end the company conned the Nigerian Air Force into driving a fuel truck all the way to Sokoto, and we finally made the hop to Kano, refueled again and made the return to Jedda. From then on every trip to Sokoto carried 20 kilos of cheese, along with the Hadj bags.

To this day, whenever I've run into Bryan Gurrel, he has commented on that hard landing I made in Sokoto. I personally consider it the best one I have ever done, or likely ever will do.

CHAPTER 49   TIGER TALES

Well, I went to Saudi Arabia the following month on the same operation. Thanks to the previous crew's experience, we didn't have the same problems...we had different problems.

First Officer Ken Stolting, Second Officer Bill Drennan and I flew a DC-8 from New York to Paris, France. While we rested in the Sheraton Hotel in Paris, Captain "Gibby" Gibbins and his crew flew the airplane on to Jedda.

The next evening we boarded Air France on a flight to Jedda arriving about midnight. Flight crews are not required to have visas in Saudi Arabia, as is the case in most other nations, and we had none. The normal procedure was for us to give our passports and crew declaration form to the immigration officer.

We arrived in Jedda as passengers, so we didn't have a crew declaration form. The official on duty acted like it was his first day on the job and was terrified of making a mistake. He took us to his supervisor's office, but the supervisor was nowhere to be seen. We were told to sit and wait, and in about 20 minutes the official came back and saw that we were still waiting. He looked perplexed for a moment, then walked over and looked behind the large desk. We got up and looked also, and there was the supervisor, in full uniform, sound asleep on the floor.

The official woke him and explained our predicament. He spoke in Arabic, but it must have sounded something like this, "These men say they are Flying Tiger pilots from America, who arrived in Jedda from France without an airplane, to fly trips for Saudi Arabian Airlines to Africa."

The supervisor yawned and rubbed his eyes until he made his decision. He could not begin to solve a problem of this magnitude, so he ordered us put in detention until his superior came on duty the next day.

There we were, tired and ready for bed. Instead, we spent the night in detention under the watchful eye of a camel driver nervously holding a submachine gun. There were no windows in the room, just one door, which contained the stone-faced guard.

There were several swarthy people of dubious character in there with us. Some looked like they should be locked up permanently, or maybe hanged. Then there were a few women with small children. They looked worried and tried to keep the children from fussing. We felt sorry for them.

Another small group of men seemed genuinely scared half to death. Every little while they rolled out their prayer rugs and made an extra supplication to Allah. I thought of trying that myself, but after considering the results they seemed to be getting, I decided to hell with it. Our highly motivated guard, (probably motivated because his sergeant had an even bigger machine gun) wouldn't let us out to make a phone call or retrieve our bags.

About eight o'clock in the morning our agent came through the airport bringing Gibby and his crew from the hotel to fly the trip that day. He managed to get us released, but by then our bags could not be found.

We went to the Meridian Hotel, which had suffered a broken sewer pipe during the night, so we had to climb over ditches and walk on planks over raw sewage to get to the lobby. There we each bought a toothbrush, toothpaste, one razor and one can of shaving cream, which we shared.

CHAPTER 49   TIGER TALES   475

Ken, my copilot, had been down with a bad cold or the flu or something, and he thought he was over it when he left home for this trip. I guess he wasn't, because I caught it. I was so sick the next day that I didn't care if I lived or died. I think it was Ken who brought me cold drinks. I was very weak the next day when the agent called with our final alert for our first trip to Africa.

Ken did most of the paperwork while I sat in my seat sipping cold water. It stayed down, so I guess I was cured. We took off from Jedda and turned southwest to cross the Red Sea, then flew over Khartoum in the Sudan. From Khartoum west to Lake Chad the weather was clear, and I looked down upon what appeared to be ancient caravan trails. One could spot small mud huts clustered in the sand. They could only be found by letting your eyes follow a track until it came to something.

There was a war going on in Chad, and all of its air traffic communication and navigation radios were shut down. We navigated with our inertial system and broadcast our position and altitude in the blind. British Airways had flights through the area, and we traded information and pleasantries as we passed.

Sokoto, Nigeria, was somewhat primitive, but the people were very friendly. They were tall and well built and seemed to be healthy and industrious. A very impressive man came out to meet the airplane. (Probably the same guy mentioned in the last story.)

I had the impression that he was the mayor of Sokoto.

He wore long flowing robes and raised his arms high as he said, "Welcome to my country."

He took us on a sightseeing trip to town while the airplane was off-loaded. It seemed that most of the men's faces were decorated with deep scars from their forehead down to their cheeks. These were tribal or warrior symbols of some kind. This man wore glasses with plastic frames with cuts on them that perfectly matched the scars on his face. He took us to a restaurant and bar, which was straight out of "Casablanca." It had open louvered windows and large slow-moving ceiling fans.

The mayor was the kind of man who commands genuine respect. We would have liked to have had the opportunity to know him better.

From Sokoto we flew to Kano for fuel, then flew back to Jedda. We and the other crew flew on alternating days, so on our day off Ken and Bill went back to the airport to fill out a missing bag report.

When they described our bags, an Air France employee ran out of the room and returned with the bags. They had been sitting in a back room the entire time.

Two days later we made our last roundtrip to Nigeria, and the following morning we boarded a Swiss-Air flight for Geneva, Switzerland, the first leg of our trip home.

Saudi Arabia is a dry country, and I don't mean just the sand. You can't get a drink there. After takeoff the Swiss-Air flight attendant announced in a thick German accent, "First ve haff beer, den ve haff breakfast."

It seemed that everyone on the airplane responded with cheers...including the Arabs.

Turns out that booze is not the only no-no in Saudi Arabia.

NORAH O'NEILL: In 1980, I blundered into the largest social/cultural error I have ever made. Usually, when I was

CHAPTER 49 TIGER TALES

assigned to fly to a country I had never been to before, I visited my local library and did basic research. I tried to know ahead of time about local customs, money, food and historical sights. I memorized hello, please, thank you and I am lost, in the appropriate language. When I was called to fly to Riyadh, the capital of Saudi Arabia, I got three hours notice, and I did not do my homework.

Our hotel was a welcome five-star relief after a long flight and a limo ride through the 105-degree desert. We have often joked about how the most dangerous segment of flying was getting from the airport to the hotel. This ride was not an exception to that rule. Our driver appeared to think that the dotted yellow line in the center of the road was for straddling, not for demarcating lanes.

As my captain cheerily whistled, "Follow the Yellow Brick Road," I concentrated on the sights to the right of the road, rather than the terrorizing view of what was happening in front of the car.

The air conditioning in my elegant, marble-lined room was malfunctioning. While I waited for house maintenance, I saw a beautiful swimming pool from my window. Perfect, I thought, and slipped into a very modest, one-piece, black swimsuit, and body-covering, floor-length caftan.

I was the only guest on the pool terrace. Passing a woman's changing room, I selected a lounge to drop my towel and robe on. I loved having a pool to myself for laps and I joyfully dove in.

Within minutes, the hotel manager and two of the security staff were beside the pool, calling to me. The manager said I must leave the pool immediately. I was confused and thought there must be some type of joke that I was not getting.

"Why?" I asked.

"Adult women are not allowed to swim in pools in Saudi Arabia!" he responded, his agitation clearly growing.

"But there are women's changing rooms here. What are they for?"

"European women are allowed to sunbathe, but not to go in the water," he explained.

"Who would want to sunbathe in this heat, and not go in the water?" I asked, still treading water.

The manager's patience was over. He signaled to the bouncers to go in and get me. That got my attention, and I quickly swam to the side and climbed out under my own power. The situation was much graver than I could ever have guessed. Had I been reported in the pool, the manager could have lost his job and the hotel could have been blackballed. The three men escorted me to my room.

On the way I asked more about local rules, looking for some logic I could follow to stay out of trouble. I knew flight attendants who had dated Saudi princes in Europe. They said the Saudi men shed their inhibitions when they changed their robes for western attire.

I asked the manager, "So it's okay for a Saudi Arabian man to sleep with me, but not to swim with me?"

The manager replied, "Perhaps, Miss O'Neill, you should just stay in your room for the rest of your visit."

I took his advice. I heard later that they drained the pool.

CHAPTER 50   HORSE FLIES?   1981

B-747

DC-8-63

In the spring Tiger Air Service, a subsidiary of Tiger International, had three 747 passenger planes for lease and no one to lease them. Flying Tigers, never hesitant about seizing an opportunity, started a scheduled passenger service between New York and Tel Aviv with a stop in Brussels, Belgium. Due to a desire to maintain our reputation as airfreight specialists, the Flying Tiger name was not used. The passenger operation was instead called Metro International, though the flights were handled by Tigers and were operated by Tiger pilots and flight attendants.

Of course Tiger employees didn't work all the time. We sometimes worked just as hard having fun.

J. D. Johnson put on a rodeo and barbecue about once a year. He leveled off a piece of ground behind Ron Way's house near Burson, California, and made an airstrip so Tiger pilots with private airplanes could fly in. Many put up tents or rolled out sleeping bags and camped under the wings while they were there.

J. D. JOHNSON: Any time a bunch of Tigers get together to have a good time, the spirits seem to flow freely. Booze and bull riding just don't go together. During one bull-riding event, Art Vance got thrown and broke his wrist. Then I got bucked off and sent to the hospital with two broken ribs. Oakley Smith was next up to ride. He was the director of flight operations at the time, and he got on the P.A. and announced that no more Tiger pilots would ride

the critters.

He said, "At this rate we won't have anyone left to fly the trips on Monday."

There were as many as two thousand people at the rodeo. Several flew up from Los Angeles.

A lot of our guys did some interesting things. Paul Crowley raced cars, Jim Nezgoda flew gliders, Freddy Wofford and Art Vance raced airplanes and Mark Devereaux flew ultra-lites.

There was a great diversity in the things Tiger pilots were involved with on their time off. J. D. Johnson, Ron Way and I all had ranches within a few miles of each other.

J. D. raised cattle, I raised Beefalo and boarded horses and Ron Way raised oat hay. He had built-in customers. Later, Ron converted his place into a pistachio orchard, so J. D. and I had to go out of the cattle business. We couldn't afford to feed them pistachios.

Tiger International was still on a buying binge. They bought Warren Transport, another trucking outfit, and Texas Railway Car. Before they could spend all our money, we set up a new modern European Cargo Hub at Heathrow Airport in London.

It seems like I always got more than my share of livestock charters. I can't imagine why. This one was with First Officer Mike Todd and Second Officer Bob Patterson. A DC-8 load of draft horses had arrived in Tokyo from France, and we flew it to its destination, Kagoshima, Japan. The flight was routine except that every time one of the 2000-pound horses stomped its feet, the whole airplane shook.

CHAPTER 50 TIGER TALES 481

The only problem we had took place after we arrived in Kagoshima. There was a Mediterranean fruit fly scare in the United States, and the Japanese authorities were afraid that fruit fly eggs might be on board. After a long delay they made us wade through a large tray with about an inch of smelly disinfectant of some kind before we could get off of the airplane. The horses were sprayed, and then I think they were put in quarantine for a while.

The horses were shipped to Japan live, then slaughtered for horsemeat. Through the years we have also flown many loads of live cattle. The Japanese cannot afford to import processed meat because of their high import duties.

As I recall, we had 38 horses on board tied in stalls. When the horses and stalls were unloaded, the cabin was cleaned and deodorized. It must have taken a lot of deodorant.

We stayed in Kagoshima for three days. This was not a usual stop for foreign carriers, and hardly anyone there spoke English. We ate our meals in the hotel, and then wandered around town on our own during the day. We boarded a ferry and went to a resort island, which is an active volcano. That burned up an afternoon anyway.

The hotel was on a cliff with a great view of the harbor. We walked down to the city on well-worn concrete steps. There were a lot of steps, so I decided I would count them when we climbed back up. I lost count at either 200 or 500, I don't remember which.

When we left, we ferried the airplane to Osaka, where we had a charter flight to New York for a computer company. That was my last International trip for a while.

Bobbie had one more.

BOBBIE THARP: My last trip with the company was an international trip, and out of Tokyo, crew control set me up with my son, Ernie, as my second officer. To land in San Francisco on my last flight, with my son on my crew, and be greeted by so many people, then have a party in my honor, had to be the highlight of my career.

A Fast Cow Ship To China

MIKE HOWE: We had a cattle charter from Minneapolis to Canton, China. The flight stopped in Anchorage and then Narita, Japan. Everything was pretty normal until we landed at Canton, then things were a little different. People were riding bicycles under the wings as we taxied in, things like that. Also we noticed a whole line of small Chinese army trucks of a size that would hold about two Holstein cows each. It seemed like there were at least a hundred bicycles riding up to the airplane, and they all had paperwork of some kind that had to be signed. The handling agent there spoke English, so he had things lined up pretty good.

The Chinese didn't waste a thing. Women swept up the cow manure and put it in bags, and the men tore down the wooden shipping pens and stacked the wood for other uses. The whole thing—cows, crates and manure—disappeared in about 30 minutes.

We didn't know how much the ground handling and everything else would cost, so our agent had a lot of cash with him. Also each hotel had its own currency window that took American money and issued us script. It took about two hours to check into the hotel because of the bureaucracy. We went through about six people. One guy

CHAPTER 50   TIGER TALES   483

gave us the room number; the next guy gave us a key and so on. It was a beautiful western-style hotel. The Chinese were preparing for western business, so the hotel staff had been taught English.

In the dining room we ordered anything we wanted. We had no idea of the cost, but it was really wonderful. The food and the service were superb. **The total bill for the entire crew, agents and mechanic was $37.00.**

They had cows coming out their nose

The next morning the agents and mechanic went out to the airport to get the airplane ready for departure. They should have stayed in bed. There was no one at the airport but the guards, and they wouldn't let them on the airplane. We arrived out there about 7:00 a.m. in a pouring rain. Here were our guys huddled under the wing in the cold. It took another two hours before we signed enough papers to get the airplane off the ground.

Changes in our lives usually come a little at a time, and so it was with Tigers, though it didn't seem that way. One day we just realized it already had happened. The entire character of the company had changed.

Bob Prescott, Bill Bartling, Tommy Haywood, Bus Loane and Cliff Groh had all passed on. Duke Hedman, Dick Rossi and Catfish Raine had reached the mandatory retirement age of sixty, along with many other pilots from the World War II era.

The hard drinking, all-night partying fighter pilot attitude was pretty much a thing of the past. (Except for a few incorrigibles who shall here remain nameless.)

One young captain said his crews wouldn't even have a drink with him. I suspect there may have been some other reason, because I seldom had that problem.

There was also a definite change in smoking habits. A group of us were sitting in the crew room in Chicago one night when someone remarked, "I remember when you could hardly see across this room due to the cigarette smoke, now they've all quit smoking."

We counted up the pilots we had lost to cancer or heart problems and who had been heavy smokers. We found that most of them had not just quit smoking, they had died.

The younger crewmembers were much more health conscious than we were. They might have one or two beers, then go to a gym and work out. I figured that if I was that healthy, I'd probably hurt myself.

CHAPTER 51   BOEING 747 CAPTAIN   1982

B-747

DC-8-

I had been a DC-8 captain for the last three years, and that winter I had an opportunity to bid the Boeing 747 as captain. The position available was in New York, and I didn't want to move there. There was usually a reduction of business after the first of the year, and as I would be the junior 747 captain, I had a good chance of being bumped back to DC-8 captain in San Francisco. However, I would have obtained my 747 type rating in the process, which is most important. My plan worked pretty well. I won the bid, went through school, passed the type rating check ride on December 20, and was home for the holidays.

I was set up to depart Los Angeles on a trip to Europe for my Boeing 747 initial operating experience (I.O.E.). This required 25 hours of line flying with a check captain on board. Dennis King was the check captain, Mike Barber, the first officer, and Steve Toon, the second officer. With a check captain along watching your every move, one wants everything to go smoothly, but it seldom does. On this trip nothing went like it was supposed to.

We left Los Angeles at 1:00 a.m. for Chicago, where the instrument landing system (ILS) was out of service, so I had to shoot a non-directional beacon (NDB) approach. No big deal, just something we don't do every day.

From there we flew to Houston, Texas. We were on radar vectors for an approach to runway 14 at Houston International, but the headings they were giving us didn't make sense.

I said, "Dennis, ask approach to verify the runway. It looks like we're being vectored for runway 26."

While he called approach, I reduced power and prepared for an immediate descent.

Approach Control said, "Oh! Oh! We changed the runway to 26, and I forgot to tell you. Can you still make it?"

I had already motioned to Dennis for gear down and full flaps, so he said, "That's no problem, we'll make it," as he retuned the ILS frequencies for 26.

We slept during the day, and at 11 p.m. we departed Houston for Brussels, Belgium, with a fuel stop at Gander, Newfoundland. When we were about an hour out of Gander, the weather went down, and the field was closed.

Dennis said, "What are you going to do now, Captain?"

The field could be open again by the time we would arrive, but we were only making a fuel stop, and we could get fuel at our alternate airport just as well.

I said, "Get me a clearance direct to Stephenville."

It was my first time in Stephenville, and while the airplane was being serviced, we had one of the best breakfasts we ever had anywhere. The bacon must have been a quarter inch thick; the eggs cooked just right, a huge mound of fried potatoes with onions, and a plate of hot biscuits. All this was washed down with a bottomless mug of strong steaming coffee.

Five and a half hours after we left Stephenville, we landed in Brussels in a driving rain. On final approach we took a lightning strike, which nearly blinded us. After we parked at the ramp, we inspected the airplane, but we found no damage.

CHAPTER 51   TIGER TALES   487

Our return trip was scheduled out of Frankfurt, Germany, to Dover, Delaware, so we rode on a Lufthansa flight to Frankfurt the next day. Our flight to Dover was almost nine hours, so that completed my I.O.E. I was now a qualified Boeing 747 captain.

On January 13 an Air Florida Boeing 737 crashed in Washington, D.C., while taking off in a snowstorm. It was the first of eight major airline disasters to occur in the eighties.

The storm covered the entire East Coast with snow and ice. Two days later I did some ice-skating with a 747 while departing JFK for Boston. A 747 is very vulnerable to crosswinds while taxiing on ice due to its large fuselage and vertical stabilizer. For example, a Japan Airlines 747 passenger flight was once blown off the taxiway and down a steep bank in Anchorage, Alaska. As I recall, there were no passenger fatalities, but the airplane was practically destroyed.

We taxied out early in the morning. There had been no traffic, and the icy taxiway was covered with a couple of inches of snow, which gave some traction. There was a stiff quartering headwind on the active runway, which gave us a quartering tail wind while taxiing to the runway. The airplane was relatively light, not carrying a heavy fuel load for such a short flight. I taxied very slowly, but still had to use differential reverse thrust for steering.

Several aircraft had landed on that runway, so the loose snow had been blown off of the icy surface. The tower reported, "braking action poor."

What this really means is, "It's slick as snot out there, so you better be careful!"

We waited on the taxiway with the wind at our back until we were cleared for takeoff. When we got our clearance and turned left, the wind caught the vertical fin and the airplane began to slide on the ice and to weathervane into the wind. We knew that would likely happen, so I applied enough power on the left engines to control the turn until we were lined up on the runway, then I advanced all four throttles, but maintained less power on the right side as necessary for steering. By the time we reached eighty knots, we had rudder steering and the rest of the takeoff was normal. I don't recall being all that enthusiastic about the whole thing at the time, but thinking back now, it was kind of fun.

In March I departed New York with a Metro International passenger flight to Brussels with Frank Maguire and G. Jacoban. Every seat on the 747 was full. I had 474 passengers, two deadheads and 17 crewmembers, for a total of 493 people.

There was a light rain when we landed at Brussels, so with the wet runway the tires didn't even make a squeak. I greased it on smoothly and taxied to the ramp. When I opened the cockpit door I was surprised, then embarrassed as the passengers gave me an ovation. The following day we flew a return passenger trip from Brussels to New York.

People have asked, "Isn't it much more difficult to fly a plane load of passengers? The added responsibility must be tremendous."

No, it is not. Once the cockpit door is closed, it makes no difference what is behind you in the cabin. The responsibility for the safety of your crew, the company's airplane and the customer's cargo, is as great as it can get.

CHAPTER 51   TIGER TALES   489

To put it another way, if I keep my butt in one piece, everyone behind me should be in pretty good shape.

It was fun while it lasted, but in March I was bumped off the 747 and would again be flying DC-8s out of San Francisco.

Captain J. D. Johnson, being senior to me, was still flying Metro trips.

CHERYL LEE METCALF: I was the senior flight attendant on this Metro International 747, and J. D. Johnson was the captain. We worked New York to Brussels and on to Tel Aviv where we crew rested, then worked back to Brussels where we crew rested again.

We were getting on the airplane the next morning, when we discovered that most of the aircraft lavatories were stopped up because the passengers had put soft drink cups, newspapers etc. in them.

J. D. went back into the terminal and made the announcement that all passengers would have to use the terminal restroom before boarding the airplane. That was a mistake because now the passengers thought they wouldn't be able to use the bathroom again for the next six or seven hours until they reached New York, so they refused to board the airplane. The flight was delayed until the lavatories were fixed.

During this same year that I made my first trip as a 747 captain, Larry Luccio made his last.

LARRY "DAD" LUCCIO: The biggest event I can recall when flying the 747 was when my son, Gary, was my copilot. We went to Milan, Italy, and that was a real pleasant trip for me.

Then, of course, there was my retirement trip. Ernie Rice had been flying with me all that month, and he was willing to let Gary make that last trip with me to Europe and back. I sure appreciated that. It was the finest gift I could have received on the last trip of my career. What a great way to end 32 years with the Flying Tiger Line.

Barney Boydstun was senior to me also, and he was still flying 747s out of New York. He had a Metro International passenger flight en route from Brussels to JFK. He would rather have had plugged up toilets.

BARNEY BOYDSTUN: My first officer was John Drake, second officer, Don Maxwell, and we had a check second officer on board, Tom Witt. We had a full load of passengers, so we cruised at 33,000 until we burned off enough fuel to climb to 35,000. When we leveled off the second officer moved the throttles back very slightly and number two went POW! I shut it down real quick.

Of course now we had to descend again. When we were all squared away we checked the engine readings on number two. They were normal. We thought the problem might have been a compressor stall, which happens once in a while. So we restarted the engine and it immediately went wild, so we shut it down again.

A flight attendant ran up and said, "Fire came blasting out of that engine and lit up the whole sky! Most of the passengers were asleep, but they're wide awake now."

A few seconds later the second officer tapped me on the shoulder and said, "Look at this!"

The engine oil quantity was zero and the temperature was pegged out at the top.

I said, "Well, we're going to get a fire," which we did shortly after.

CHAPTER 51   TIGER TALES   491

I shot the bottle to it and the fire went out, but nothing else changed. It was still out of oil and it was still hot.[1] We knew it would likely catch fire again, and I only had one fire bottle left. I had to get this thing on the ground as soon as possible. I called Gander and got a clearance direct to the airport. The engine did catch fire and again we put it out with the last bottle. We were now 125 miles out of Gander, Newfoundland, so we began our descent heading for the airport at about mach 1. The fire ignited again and burned all during our approach. After we landed, the fire trucks followed as we rolled out and said it appeared that the fire had gone out.

After the passengers were deplaned, we went out and looked at the engine. There was nothing inside the cowling but molten metal. We later found out that a bearing failure had caused the engine to loose its oil.

That's about the only thing in my entire career that I can recall that made my hair stand up a little bit.

Barney has real tough hair.

BAR STORY

DON SANDERS: An airplane arrived in Anchorage that we were supposed to take to Tokyo, Japan, for a fuel stop and then on to Osan, Korea. However, there was a typhoon directly over Tokyo, so we devised a plan whereby we off-loaded a couple thousand pounds of freight, so we could add enough fuel to go direct to Osan.

Well, we did that but we arrived in Osan ahead of schedule, so our regular hotel rooms were not available. We stayed in a crummy hotel where the rooms cost about

---

[1] When a jet engine is shut down in flight, the airflow keeps it " windmilling," and there is no way to stop the rotation.

five dollars a night.

We told the agent, "Okay, we'll take the rooms, but with all the money the company is saving, we want what beer we drink included in the hotel bill."

The beer came in one-liter bottles, and after one of those I went up to bed. I never could drink much beer. The rest of the crew had no such difficulty it seems. When we checked out, there were 13 liters of beer on the bill.

Meanwhile back at the ranch...
Well, how did you think I got to SFO and back?

CHAPTER 52   **FATIGUE**   **1982 PART 2**

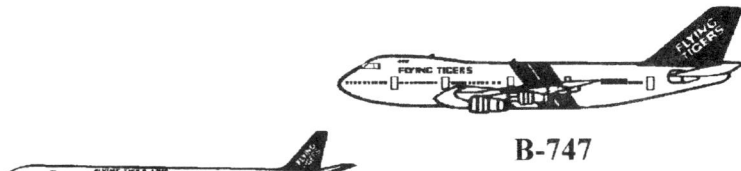

B-747

DC-8-63

I thought I had been tired before, but this was ridiculous. I was on layover in New York and had 18 hours until my next trip. I was feeling kind of tired, so after a good prime rib dinner, I hit the sack about eleven p.m.

I was sound asleep when the telephone rang.

"Captain, we need to change your schedule. A pilot went on sick leave, and we would like you to take the cargo flight to London in the morning."

I mumbled okay. I felt like I had just gone to sleep, but after all, he said in the morning, so I can still sleep the rest of the night, right? Wrong. I was sleeping soundly when the phone rang again.

"This is your four-hour final alert, it's two a.m. and the Limo will pick you up in one hour for a six o'clock departure."

I sat on the edge of the bed and tried to figure out how much sleep I'd had. I knew that if I canceled now they'd never get a reserve pilot in time to make schedule. So I decided what the hell, I'd take a shower and see how I feel. I felt pretty good as I rode to the airport, but I knew it was going to be a very long day. I didn't know how long.

After I checked the weather and completed the paperwork, I was informed that the airplane would be late arriving due to bad weather in Chicago. My crew and I tried to sleep in the reclining chairs in the crew room, but had little success. As it turned out, our flight didn't depart until noon, which meant we would land in London just before our 14 hours duty time would expire.

I talked it over with my crew. I had not flown with either of them before. They both lived on the East Coast and had been scheduled for this flight, so I thought they should have had a good night's sleep.

"Hell," the first officer said, "it's only about a six-hour flight to London, then we can go back to bed."

I rechecked the weather forecast for the new arrival time. The forecast was for low ceilings, poor visibility and fog. The nearest airport with a decent forecast was Brussels, Belgium. I added 20,000 pounds to the fuel load, then picked up my flight kit and walked out to the ice-covered ramp.

When we taxied out, there were about 20 airplanes in line ahead of us, so it was another half hour before we were cleared to the runway.

I looked back at the fuel gauges and said, "Good thing we put on the extra fuel, we've already burned 6000 pounds and we're still on the ground."

After takeoff I made the usual call, "Gear up." As I continued the climb I felt a buffeting which became more pronounced as the airspeed increased toward 250 knots. I looked over at the landing gear handle and indicator lights, then shook my head.

The procedure was for the first officer to raise the gear handle to the up position until the gear was retracted and the indicator lights were out, then the handle should be placed in the halfway or off position. Apparently he had placed the gear handle from the down position directly to the off position, which did not retract the landing gear.

CHAPTER 52   TIGER TALES   495

I said, "Put the landing gear handle in the up position."

"Up?"

"Yeah, up. Then the gear will retract, this buffeting will stop, the noise will go away and the gear warning lights will go out."

He had an incredulous look on his face as he took hold of the gear handle and moved it to the up position. Sure enough, the gear came up, the buffeting stopped and the warning lights went out.

He then returned the handle to the off position. A full minute went by in silence and then he said, "I can't believe I did that!"

"Christ," I said under my breath, "I guess I'm not the only one who's tired. I wonder how the second officer is doing."

I glanced back over my shoulder and said, "How's chances for a cup of coffee when you get the time?"

"Sure thing, how do you take it?"

"Black."

"Same here," said the first officer. "Looks like I'll need all the help I can get."

The second officer went back to the galley and then quickly returned.

"There is no coffee," he said. "The airplane hasn't been catered. We have three frozen dinners on board, but that's all. I saw them bring the meals while I was busy checking the fuel, and I forgot to check the galley."

I sat there for a moment and didn't even cuss. I engaged the autopilot, unbuckled my seat belt and went down the stairs to where the crew bags were stored. I retrieved a jar of instant coffee from my suitcase and made my way back to the flight deck. I set the jar of coffee on the second officer's table, and then quietly returned to my seat.

It was 9:30 p.m. London time when we began our approach to the Heathrow Airport. The weather had gone below minimums several times in the last hour, but now Heathrow was reporting 200 feet and a half-mile on runway 27. Fatigue had really set in now. My eyes burned and my mouth was too dry to spit. As the 747 descended, the fog moved back over the airport.

I missed the approach and completed the missed approach procedure.

My thoughts were interrupted by a cheerful call from London Control, "We are showing 1200 RVR[1] on runway 9 now, Sir. I'll give you vectors and you'll be number one for the approach."

I said, "Sorry, I will require 2000 RVR." (Due to my not having 100 hours of captain time on the 747.)

About a minute later he came back with his same cheerful voice, "Looks like the RVR has just come up to 2000 Tiger. You are cleared for the approach."

I was so tired that I decided to shoot a coupled approach. This means the approach and landing would be made by the autopilots, auto-throttles and auto-land system. To complicate matters, the airplane had been dispatched with one of the three autopilots inoperative. On final approach at about 500 feet above the ground the two remaining autopilots apparently disagreed, and one of them tripped off. With only one autopilot working, it will automatically trip off when the airplane descends to 150

---

[1] Runway Visual Range.

CHAPTER 52 TIGER TALES 497

feet above the ground if the selector is in auto-land. The reasoning is that it would be safer for the pilot to either land, or to fly the missed approach manually, than to trust one autopilot.

I forgot to switch the selector from auto-land to ILS, so at 150 feet the autopilot did kick off, and I landed the airplane manually. But sometimes even the best training can't keep you out of trouble. In normal auto-land operations after landing you disconnect the autopilot and the auto-throttles at the same time. This time when I landed the airplane I didn't have an autopilot to turn off, so I didn't turn off the auto-throttles either.

I retarded the throttles to idle, and as was my habit, slid my hand forward to pull the inboard engines into reverse as soon as the main wheels touched the runway, waiting until the nose wheels were firmly on the ground before reversing the outboard engines. (in case one of them didn't go into reverse.)

In this case I was in effect holding the inboard throttles closed, but as the auto-throttles were still engaged, both outboard throttles moved forward. The second officer saw the number one throttle moving forward, so he reached up and pulled it back to idle. In the darkened cockpit he didn't see number four which was on its way to full power.

The airplane went into a sudden and violent skid to the left. As I countered with full right rudder and right brakes, the first officer yelled auto-throttle, and pulled the number four throttle back to idle. I disconnected the auto-throttles as I fought to keep the airplane on the runway.

While taxiing the two miles to the cargo terminal, we watched the right brake temperature indicators rise from the green to the yellow caution range, and then into the red. I taxied slowly and did not touch the brakes again, but after we parked at the ramp, four of the overheat safety plugs melted and four tires on the right main gear went flat.

We made the limo ride to the hotel in silence. Each man reflecting on the events of the day in his own way.

One of the most serious things a pilot has to contend with is fatigue. You do your best to arrive for your flight well rested, but when the phone rings at midnight and the flight leaves at three in the morning...

ART VANCE: I might as well get this off my chest. I have to tell somebody, so here goes. It probably wasn't all my fault. We had this old DC-8-61 that didn't have INS or much of anything else. Miami is not the best place to try to sleep in the daytime. Though we tried, we did not get a good rest.

We departed Miami about ten o'clock at night and flew to Atlanta. So far so good, but the problem was we had to sit in Atlanta about four hours. After we were good and tired, we finally took off for San Francisco about five in the morning.

My crew was Copilot Chuck Chambers and some forgotten flight engineer who probably quit after that flight. Soon after we leveled off, we started falling asleep, so we decided to take turns staying awake. This old airplane had one of those autopilots that, if the turn knob was in the centering detent, it would go into about a one-degree bank.

After a while, when it was my turn to stay awake, I remember making a small heading correction with the turn knob, whereupon I fell asleep. Now all three of us were

CHAPTER 52 TIGER TALES

asleep.

It was dark when I dozed off, and when I woke up the sun was in my eyes. I tried to digest that fact for a few seconds. Why, after coming up in the east for the last umpteen million mornings, did the sun decide to come up in the west?

Suddenly I was terrified. When I looked out the window would I see ocean or dirt? I got my nerve up, looked out and saw dirt. I was sure thankful for that because I remembered the story about a crew, I think it was United or maybe American, who went to sleep, flew past LA, and woke up out over the Pacific ocean. They barely had enough fuel to get back to land.

I clicked off the autopilot and rolled the airplane into an 89-degree bank, probably, and pulled some Gs coming around. Chuck woke up pretty quick, and the engineer began hollering something. He couldn't raise his head off the table because of G forces. It seemed like only about two seconds, and I had made a 180-degree turn to the left and was again heading west. But where were we? As it turned out, we were still heading for the same VOR station we were before I went to sleep.

Center came on right after I leveled the wings and said, "Tiger, did you just make a 360-degree turn?"

I motioned to Chuck not to pick up his microphone. I had to think fast. Then I borrowed a line from old John Newcomer. He landed a DC-8 in Syracuse one time. It was the right airport, but unfortunately, the wrong runway.

As he taxied in, ground control called and said, "Tiger, you just landed on the wrong runway!"

John motioned to his copilot to not answer.

Then John picked up his mike and said, "Are you mad?"

Ground Control, apparently surprised by the question hesitated then said, "...No."

So here I am in the same situation, so I picked up my mike and said, "Yes, I'm afraid we did. Are you mad?"

He said, "...No."

I lived in fear of my mailbox for a few weeks after that.

Fatigue wasn't Ron's problem. He just had this terrible itch. Ron Way and J. D. Johnson were overheard having the following conversation:

Ron Way: I finally got the hankerin' for a new car so bad that the other day I went out and bought one.

J.D. Johnson: Hell, if I had known you had got to feeling that way, I'd have come over to your house and set with you for a spell.

CHAPTER 53   WAY DOWN—WAY UP   1983

B-747

DC-8-63

Most of my flying during the year was on domestic routes with several flights to San Juan, Puerto Rico. San Juan is a nice layover town—decent climate, good restaurants and beaches.

On September 1, I arrived in Atlanta, Georgia, en route to San Juan when I heard that the Russians had shot down a Korean Airlines 747 with the loss of 269 lives. We had flown that route, North-Pac 1, many times. There was a lot of discussion about the various ways in which a pilot could wander off course.

WAY DOWN

Captain Ron Way claims he wasn't lost. He says he was supposed to take this load of cattle to this little island somewhere in the Indian Ocean.

RON WAY: This DC-8 cattle charter landed in Tokyo for a fuel stop and crew change. I flew it to Cocos Island after a fuel stop in Singapore. We had to transit Singapore between 10 p.m. and 2 a.m. because during that time a certain type of mosquito was dormant.

We delivered the cattle to Cocos Island, which was a quarantine station operated by the Australian Government. They were fussy about what kind of insects or other critters might be on board with the cows.

Brad Eaton was my first officer, Mike Flemons, my second officer, and we had Jim Archer along as our mechanic.

We were carrying our bags from the airplane to the little hotel nearby when a group of Aussies hailed us from a small open-air bar.

"Hey, Mates, would you like a beer?"

"We'll change out of our uniforms and be right back!"

We had three or four rounds of beer, and then a case appeared on the table.

One of the Aussies explained, "The bar will be closing soon, and we don't want to be caught short."

These guys were divers from Perth, and they were re-working the moorings along the dock for the supply ships. We had a few more beers, and then the doctor for the Island came over. He invited us to his house for dinner and a little going away party later. His replacement had arrived, and he and his wife were leaving the next day.

Before the night was over, everyone was pretty well oiled, and one of my guys made a move on the doctor's wife.

Then I heard someone say, "Sure we can take you along with us to Singapore tomorrow."

I figured it would all work itself out before we left, so I chose not to get involved. It's just as well. Our destination was changed to Taipei.

When we were ready to leave the next night, it was raining cats and dogs. We had a portable power unit with us, but Jim couldn't get it working. We found out that the Australian Navy had one in a shed.

One of the guys in their office said, "Yes, there is one down there, but we can't give you permission to use it. The keys are right there on the wall."

We got the thing out of the shed, but the air outlet fitting was different than ours. Jim took the fitting off our unit, and after we got the engines started, he changed it back and put their unit back in the shed.

I still had a case of Kiwi beer with me when we left, and I was lucky. When I got back to San Francisco, I discovered only one six-pack was missing.

WAY UP

In October Captain Ron Burson and his crew, First Officer Bill Gallogy and Second Officer Ken Halls began their takeoff roll at Frankfurt, Germany. Then things started looking up...

RON BURSON: The first officer was making the takeoff when, at about 50 to 60 knots, the aircraft's nose pitched up abruptly. As I started to ask Bill what the hell he was doing, he yelled, "YOU GOT IT!" (It's company policy that the captain initiates all rejected takeoffs. The crew found themselves sitting about 50 feet in the air as the tail of the B-747 scraped along the runway.)

I grabbed the controls and during the rejected takeoff the nose of the aircraft oscillated around the horizon as I tried to regain control and stop without driving the nose wheel through the runway. Reverse idle caused an abrupt nose down, and forward idle caused an abrupt nose up. When I came out of reverse the first time, the rudder deflected full right, further compounding our control problems. (Severed hydraulic lines just forward of the stabilizer screw jack resulting in complete loss of hydraulic pressure evidently caused this in all four hydraulic systems, along with trapped pressure on one side of the rudder.)

With the rudder full right, which we were not aware of at the time, the airplane started to turn right in addition to pitching up and down. I tried to control it with asymmetric power and reverse and forward idle. We drifted off the left side of the runway and onto the grass after which the airplane continued in a straight line. I was afraid we might cross the other runway, which had an aircraft on short final, so I asked Bill to advise the tower of this possibility.

The controller said, "Tiger, the whole airport is yours!" There was lot's of laughter in the background.

Not so funny from up here

I let the tail down on the grass, and we slid to a gentle stop. The dust was settling, but our hearts were still pounding. I called the tower and asked for the fire trucks.

He said, "The trucks are rolling up to your nose right now. Tiger, that was the funniest show we have ever seen!"

It wasn't so funny from where we sat.

It was impressive to see the military fire trucks come around the left side and the civilian fire trucks on the right side at the same time. That was good service.

When we first started the takeoff roll, Art Hilts, the charter agent, had heard a loud snap down in the main cargo floor. He had started down the ladder to see what it was when I initiated the rejected takeoff. He changed his mind, knowing that if a pallet were loose, it would come forward during our stop and run him down.

We found that a pallet had come loose, and during acceleration, it had gone aft through the pressure bulkhead. What looked like smoke from an electrical fire was coming from the area, so we opened the left upper deck access door intending to bail out. A quick look at the ground some 40 feet below changed our minds, and we decided to brave the smoke, which turned out to be only misting hydraulic fluid. Mechanic, Luis Betancourt, who was riding with us, confirmed this.

When I stepped to the ground from the aft door, a small German man who did not speak English met me. He took my hand and shook it with great vigor while saying, "Danke Schoen!" I asked our agent, who had now arrived, who this guy was, and he said it was the airport manager.

Lookin' up

The agent said, "He had been in his car near several 747s at the passenger terminal, and we had been aimed directly at him and at the terminal several times during our wild ride. He thought sure we were going to smash into the passenger terminal."

After the initial debriefing by the local gendarmes (local police and the German equivalent of our FAA), the Frankfurt Tiger Station Manager set up transportation to the hotel and told us to drink and eat as much as we wanted and sign it to the company (probably knowing we wouldn't have much of an appetite).

During our unwinding at the hotel, I jokingly said, "Bill, I'm not going to give you any more takeoffs or landings."

Bill said, "It doesn't matter. I'm never going to fly with you again anyway!"

I hope he was joking. All in all, it was a ride I will never forget. Some people pay good money for a lot less excitement than that. I was fortunate to have a very good crew that day.

It is my understanding that some high company official wanted to terminate all of us, but our vice president of flight operations, Dick Wilson; director of flight training, Oakley Smith; and director of flight operations, Ron Hall, would not hear of it. They did finally acquiesce to giving Second Officer Ken "Salty" Halls 30 days off for failing to properly check the pallet locks.

According to Ed Hale, who has held almost every position in the maintenance department and was now its director, the flight came in to Frankfurt with a load of cargo destined for Amsterdam. Unknown to the crew, it had a few pieces to be unloaded in Frankfurt. The loading crew unlocked a couple of pallets to move them out of the way, and then moved them back when they were done. Then there was a shift change, and no one locked the pallets in position.

When the second officer accomplished his preflight, he had no idea anyone moved any cargo, so he did not physically recheck the pallet locks. Still, he was legally

CHAPTER 53 TIGER TALES 507

responsible, so he was given 30 days off. Due to an oversight, or the use of common sense, whichever you prefer, the 30 days off was <u>with pay</u>.

By the end of the year John Flynn was named company president replacing Tom Grogean.

In the winter I found myself skating on the ice again, this time in a DC-8 in Dallas. The runway had been sanded, so the landing was normal, but now we had to get off of the runway and try to get to the Tiger cargo ramp. We didn't make it. We cleared the runway, but the taxiways were solid clear ice.

We called Tiger Operations, and they said, "We don't have a parking space for you, so don't come in to the ramp. It is so icy in here that the maintenance guys can't get enough traction with the tug to push the outbound airplane out. It could take an hour till we can get you in."

There was no use sitting there burning fuel for an hour, so I called ground control and told them we were going to shut down the engines, and that we would be on the taxiway with no lights and no radios. We sat there in the dark for a while, and then I noticed that the wind was picking up. I remembered how easily the wind moved the 747 in New York last year.

We sat there for maybe another five minutes when my first officer said, "We're moving! Look the whole damned airplane is sliding right off the taxiway!"

"That's right," I said, "and with the engines stopped they won't be damaged if they scoop up any snow."
They weren't. When the right main landing gear slid to the edge of the pavement, the airplane stopped.

After they got some sand on our ramp area, the tug finally got the other airplane pushed out and ours towed in. Our maintenance guys had a rough time that night.

Crew control must have taken pity on me, because they gave me a trip to New Zealand so I could thaw out. George Beck was my first officer, and Kevin Kramer, my second officer. We went from San Francisco to Honolulu to Nandi, Fiji Islands, to Auckland, New Zealand.

While in Auckland my crew and I went for a walk along the beach. We were unaware that the beaches were topless, and as we walked along, we kept tripping over each other. We finally grabbed a taxi and went back to the hotel, before we got run over by a truck or something. The scenery was really lovely.

PAUL REBSCHER: My best trip ever was in 1983, with Captain Walt Sahaydak and Second Officer George Foreno, from New York to Anchorage. The airplane was going on to Korea, and two of the flight attendants were deadheading to Seoul for Christmas shopping (typical flight attendants). Due to lack of space, one of the girls was being bumped in Anchorage. We were going to the Captain Cook for our layover, so it had nothing to do with us.

The girls had spent most of the trip from New York in the cockpit, and we had a good time. After I got to my room, I called the office and asked which girl had been bumped. They said Miss Hart, and that she had gone to the Captain Cook to rest. I called her room and made a date for lunch after a much needed nap. We went to La Mex where the Margaritas flowed like water, and we had a wonderful afternoon. I went on my way the next day and she went hers. In September '87 we were married.

CHAPTER 54   SNOW AND MORE SNOW   1984

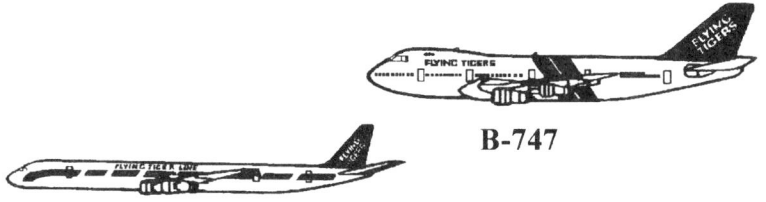

B-747

DC-8-63

In January, to start the year off, I rode Pan Am from San Francisco to Zurich, Switzerland. First Officer Guy Lopez and Second Officer Mike Broome and I enjoyed a pleasant layover in Zurich. It was cold and windy, so we didn't get a chance to tour the city, but the hotel accommodations were very good. The lobby was well appointed with deep carpets and comfortable sofas. The social hour before dinner was well represented by an affluent clientele.

The next evening we took off for Charlotte, North Carolina. Our DC-8 was fully loaded, so we had to land at Shannon, Ireland, for a fuel stop, then continued on to Gander, Newfoundland, for another fuel stop. While preparing to depart Gander, the auxiliary hydraulic pump burned out. This pump is a required item, but fortunately it is the same type pump as the standby thrust-reverser pump, which is not required. I asked the local Canadian mechanic to swap the thrust-reverser pump with the standby hydraulic pump. We were running out of crew duty time, so we went to the local hotel for a 12-hour crew rest.

The mechanic completed the pump swap and advised Tiger Maintenance in Los Angeles. He also advised them that he did not possess an FAA mechanic's license, so he couldn't sign off the work. The maintenance coordinator was trying to figure out how in hell he could get a mechanic up to Newfoundland.

Someone said, "Who did you say the captain was?"

"Let's see. It's Captain Moldrem."

"Well hell, he's an old mechanic. He can sign it off himself."

He called me at the hotel and, of course, I said I'd take care of it.

When we arrived at the airplane for departure, the access doors to the pumps were open for inspection. I was lucky it was a warm day in Gander, 12 degrees above zero. I had to remove my coat, tie and shirt in order to crawl up inside the hydraulic compartment. Mike, the second officer, pressurized the system, and I inspected the hydraulic system for leaks. Everything checked out okay, so I signed off the Form 1. After I washed my hands, put on my shirt, tie and coat, I was the captain again.

While I was busy with such mundane affairs, Larry Partridge, John Tymczyszyn (pronounced Timchisun) and Larry Smith were engaged in international intrigue.

LARRY PARTRIDGE: We had a trip from New York to Malmo, Sweden, to pick up a load of cargo. We assumed it was a load of toys or something. When we arrived in Malmo, instead of going through customs, the officials escorted me into a meeting room full of guys in white shirts with their sleeves rolled up, and they were all puffing on cigarettes.

They told me that the Russians had gotten digital computers in pieces from a German arms dealer in Bremen, Germany. The Treasury Department agents from the States and the German authorities became aware that they were loaded on a ship, but they mishandled it, and the ship sailed. They put out an APB to all the agencies in Europe.

CHAPTER 54 TIGER TALES

The Swedes just happened to notice that the ship was coming into Malmo, so they seized it. The Swedes were holding important talks with the Russians at the time, and they didn't want to embarrass them.

They said to me, "We are giving the computers to you."

For a while I owned $1,500,000 worth of the latest digital computers. We went to the hotel fearful that somebody might hijack us.

They said, "Don't let anyone in the limo on the way to or from the hotel, and don't let anyone in your rooms."

During the night I was awakened by a phone call.

The caller said, "I'm Mister Snow, a part of the team, and I'll need a ride to the airport in the morning."

He gave me the name of his hotel. That sounded kind of strange. I said that we would check with him. We left the hotel about two in the morning while it was snowing. The first thing we asked the driver was if we could get a cup of coffee or something.

He said, "Yeah, there's a Burger King just up the street."

It was the opposite direction from the airport and, of course, all the security cars were pointed toward the airport. So we came out and turned right instead of left and put everybody in a big fit, and they lost us. We went to Burger King and got our coffee and donuts, then stopped at the hotel where Mr. Snow was supposed to be staying. I told John I would go in, and if anything weird happened, he should tell the driver to go straight to the airport.

I went inside and asked a blond gal behind the counter, "Is Mr. Snow here?"

She said, "No."

"Could you check?"

"There is no Mr. Snow here."

We left for the airport, and on the way cars began to fall in behind us. The driver remarked that this was unusual this early in the morning. It turned out that they were all security cars, which surrounded us when we pulled up to the terminal. Of course our driver didn't know what was going on. There were big Swedes with fur coats and AK 47s or what have you all around us.

Then an American came out and asked, "What the hell happened, where have you guys been?"

I said, "We just went to a Burger King for coffee."

He slapped his forehead and began bawling out the others saying, "Can't you guys even keep track of a flight crew going for coffee?"

The CIA and the Swedish Secret Service advised me that they had very reliable sources warning them of a terrorist plot (Russian and/or Libyan) to destroy our airplane on the ground or shortly after take-off. It was an opinion shared by all that the weather combined with the early hour would minimize this threat, so we should go if at all possible.

After a lot of thought combined with a dash of Tiger can-do spirit, we decided that although the margins of safety were less than we're normally comfortable with, they were still there.

We had our agent check the cargo, and it had been made to look like we were hauling a load of rocks.

JOHN TYMCZYSZYN: When we got out to the airplane about two in the morning, it was loaded to the gunnels. The cabin was full of computers, and the tanks were full of fuel. We were at maximum gross weight for the runway, and it was snowing like hell. It was really coming down, and we were the only airplane that was moving. The snowplows were out, and they were trying to clear the

CHAPTER 54   TIGER TALES

runway, but it was a losing battle.

We felt quite a bit of pressure to get the airplane out of there, no matter what. We did the preflight, had the airplane deiced and taxied out to the runway at 2:25 a.m. We rechecked the wings, and there was no way we could go, we had to be deiced again. We taxied back to the ramp. They topped off the tanks then towed us out to the end of the runway and backed us up as far as they could to give us the entire runway. We sat there with only one engine running to save fuel, while they deiced us again.

It was snowing so hard that the plows could only clear a path 25 feet wide right down the centerline. They completed the deicing, and got the plows clear of the runways while we started the other three engines.

The Treasury guy was in the jump seat right behind Larry. Larry opened the throttles, and when the power was up, he released the brakes. I have never felt such a slow acceleration in my life. Here we were tracking down that narrow 25-foot path and watching the airspeed needle slowly increase. Long before V1 (the speed at which you can no longer stop the airplane on the runway) it was obvious there would be no rejecting this takeoff, because there was no way we could stop this thing. <u>I will never, ever forget that takeoff.</u>

We reached the end of the runway before reaching VR (the speed at which if you pull back on the yoke the airplane will fly) and Larry pulled back on the yoke. The nose came up, but we were afraid the fuselage was going to smash into the light standards at the end of the runway. Obviously, it did not. I have never been that low over the lights.

None of the three of us could talk, but the Treasury man yelled, "That was bitching! God, that was great!"

LARRY PARTRIDGE: We climbed to our cruising altitude, and as soon as we were over international waters at 61 N and 10 W, the cargo was officially confiscated. The Treasury man started reading me my rights.

I said, "What the hell is this all about?"

He said, "I'm seizing these computers from you in the name of the U. S. Government."

I said, "Well, just take them, you don't need to read me my rights!"

He said, "Well, I have to play the game."

We headed for Andrews Air Base and arrived without any prior notice. The Customs man was just mad as hell. It was about 5:00 a.m. on a Sunday, and it was supposed to be his day off. He gave us all kinds of hell until the Treasury man pulled out his badge and flashed it at him. Then he said, "You're cleared, you're cleared!"

The Treasury man gave me a receipt for the computers, and we ferried the airplane to New York. That was the end of it.

Due to additional business in Europe and the Mideast, we expanded our Frankfurt, Germany, station into a Hub.

The bad news was that we canceled the Metro International operation, and the aircraft were disposed of.

The good news was that we began service to South America and Australia and added Brussels, Belgium, to our European service. So all in all the good news was a lot better than the bad news was bad.

CHAPTER 55   TIGERS IN THE JUNGLE   1984 PART 2

747-200

I won a bid for Boeing 747 captain effective June 1st, and it was just as well because the company sold all the DC-8s that fall. I would be flying out of New York when I completed my 747 recurrent training. I needed a line check, which consists of flying one trip with a check captain. They didn't have a check captain available, so they released me for vacation.

One day while still on vacation, I had a phone call from Crew Control.

He said, "We know you're on vacation and we're not supposed to call you, but we were hoping you could help us."

"Well, what do you want me to do?"

"We need you to fly a trip to London tomorrow, and you would be home the following day."

"Sure, I'd be glad to help you out."

He said, "Gee, we sure appreciate this."

"That's okay. By the way, who is the check captain?"

There was a long pause, and then he said, "Oh my God, you never got your line check, did you?"

I said, "No, I didn't. But don't forget I agreed to do you a favor, so now you owe me one."

After my vacation I did get a line check, followed by a trip to Tokyo, Taipei, Manila and Hong Kong.

In July I made my first trip to South America with First Officer Eric Ermert and Second Officer Vic Newman. We left New York for Miami, and Manaus, Brazil.

Manaus is deep in the jungle and is on the Negros River. I had seen a T.V. program about Manaus and the Opera House, which was built around the turn of the century. The hotel was quite nice and had been built by the Germans many years before. It had massive doors and planked floors with heavy furniture. A zoo containing many exotic birds and animals surrounded the hotel.

We went on a boat tour, which included a walk through the jungle. We saw natives, ate a lunch of native food and were shown several different species of piranha. The boat went a few miles down the river past Manaus to the point where the two rivers merge. The Negros River is black from rotting trees and plants from the jungle. The Solimoes River is white and flows from the mountains of Peru, according to the guide.

We stopped at the exact spot where they meet. The waters do not merge at that point, due to the differences in the temperature. The water from the mountains of Peru is much colder, of course. The guide said the black and the white waters stay separate for about five miles before they merge. The tour was very enjoyable. We stayed in Manaus three days and were glad we got to see it.

We flew the airplane to Sao Paulo, where another crew took it on to Buenos Aires, Argentina. We stayed overnight in Sao Paulo and then rode on Trans Brazil Airlines to Rio de Janeiro where we stayed for two days. Eric and I went downtown and toured H. Stern's, the big German gem company. Vic, our second officer, was sick the entire time. He thought he'd caught something in the jungle.

By our departure time Vic was ready to go home, so we left on schedule. We made a fuel stop at Curacao then continued on to Miami, Florida, and New York.

CHAPTER 55   TIGER TALES

It was hot in the jungle, but it got a hell of a lot hotter around Tiger headquarters.

DICK WILSON: It was in mid '84 that I got fired from the vice president position. I like to say I got fired. But I enjoyed my tenure. I was there over two years, which was longer than anyone else, I guess. I got along great with the union, and I had people that liked me and, I suppose, some that didn't. I stayed on working for the company in various positions.

After Dick left, Ned Wallace hired Bill Bond to replace him.

My next trip of any interest was a round-the-world trip in August with Jeff Stuffings and George Mandler. We rode a limo to Dover AFB, Delaware, and then flew a trip to Frankfurt, Germany. Just getting positioned for a trip can be exhausting. Our next flight was out of Dubai in the United Arab Emirates, but sometimes "you can't get there from here."

After a crew rest in Frankfurt, we rode Lufthansa Airlines to Heathrow Airport, London, England. After clearing customs, Jeff was put on another trip, and I had Ray Churlonis as first officer.

We took about a two-hour ride on a company crew bus through heavy traffic from Heathrow to the London Gatwick Airport where we had reservations on a British Caledonia flight to Dubai. It was a very nice flight and we enjoyed the excellent service, but it was a long and tiring day.

Our departure from Dubai was scheduled for 4 a.m., destination Singapore. The flight was a sub-service flight for Lufthansa, and their ground personnel fueled the airplane. Unfortunately they had a mix-up converting kilograms to pounds and the aircraft was over-fueled.

I requested the defueling truck, and they took off all the fuel the truck would hold. This left me with an aircraft weighing 823,000 pounds, which was the maximum taxi weight. I checked the runway limit at the current temperature of 84 degrees, and it was good for 824,000 pounds. The maximum structural weight for takeoff was 820,000 pounds, and we were presumed to burn 3,000 pounds of fuel during taxi out to the runway. We were legal to go, but we had to go immediately. At four o'clock in the morning, it was as cool as it was going to get. If it got any warmer, we would not be legal for takeoff.

We started the engines and taxied to the active runway. I held the brakes and opened the throttles, and when we were assured that all engines were producing full power, I released the brakes.

At that time three of the engine over-temperature warning lights came on. These warning lights illuminate five degrees centigrade before reaching the maximum engine exhaust gas temperature. By this time the airplane had barely started to roll. I said to George, "If any engine starts to overheat, reduce power to keep it within limits and tell me if you do that."

The engines stayed below the red line as we began what seemed like the longest takeoff roll I ever made.

We reached takeoff speed and lifted off, but the heavy aircraft would neither climb nor accelerate. I was afraid to retract the landing gear, because of the additional drag when the huge gear doors open. In the glare of the landing lights, we watched sand dune after sand dune disappear under the nose. When the airspeed inched up to V2 I

CHAPTER 55   TIGER TALES   519

called "Gear up." After we got the landing gear retracted we could accelerate enough to retract the flaps. Then we were on our way. When we crossed over Bombay, India, we were still climbing. The remainder of the flight was routine.

The point of this story is that there was no problem. Nothing went wrong. No failed engines, no blown tires, yet this was one of those situations where the combinations of circumstances make your palms sweat a little.

Soon I was off on another round-the-world flight with Dennis Flanagin and Al Woodall. We went to Dover, Delaware, then Frankfurt, Germany, Hanover, Germany, Kuwait International, Kuwait, and Sharjah, United Arab Emirates. Twelve hours after landing at Sharjah, we took off on a nonstop seven hour and 15 minute ferry flight to Hong Kong.

Since the airplane was empty, we were flight planned at FL410 (41,000 feet). Later, dispatch decided to tanker fuel because it's cheaper in the Mideast than in Hong Kong, so all of the tanks were filled. Our flight plan did not reflect this weight change, but it was on the weight and balance form. I saw it, but it didn't register.

We were climbing through 40,000 feet when I realized the airplane couldn't fly that high with the additional weight of the extra fuel. I leveled off as I called center and informed them that I had to descend immediately to FL370. (The maximum altitude we could hold at our present weight)

The cheerful British voice said, "One moment sir..."

I knew he had to check for conflicting traffic, but one way or another we were going down before encountering a jet-upset, and that would be very soon.

As the airspeed began to decay, he called back, "Tiger, you are cleared to descend and maintain FL 370."

Our recurrent training includes jet-upset recovery, but it would have been damned hard to explain my getting into one.

In many parts of the world radio communications are very difficult. English is the international aviation language, but Iraqi, Japanese, French and Chinese English have no relation to each other. In the Mideast people speak pretty good English, but the problem is often poor and inadequate radio coverage.

Communications were good over India, but after Chittagong, Bangladesh, and over Burma, north of Mandalay to Lashio, Dennis had a tough time of it. He was finally able to establish contact with Kunming when we crossed the Chinese border. We flew over Kunming and Canton then descended into Hong Kong.

We had the opportunity to luxuriate in Hong Kong for an entire 24 hours, during which time we paid our respects at Ned Kelly's Saloon. We must have had at least ten hours sleep before departing for Tokyo, where we were on the ground exactly one hour before taking off for Anchorage.

The company was in serious trouble due to a worldwide recession, in addition to high interest rates on the debts Tiger International had run up buying other companies.

FRANK MAGUIRE, ALPA chairman: I may have a slightly jaundiced view of the events to come. I was convinced that Steinberg's[1] intention was to sell the company.

---

[1] Sol Steinberg of Reliance Investment Group that bought a large amount of Tiger International stock in 1979.

CHAPTER 55 TIGER TALES

I pretty much viewed everything that was going on during that whole period as preparation for doing exactly what he did. Not that I'm any genius, but the signs seemed pretty obvious to me.

I had a conversation with John Flynn in the Midway Hotel in New York. John, by the way, did not do a bad job. It's just that he was captain when the ship started sinking. He was back there trying to sell DC-8s to UPS. What he did was pull the 747s out of Europe, where they were losing their shirts because the yield was so low, and put them on the more profitable Pacific. The cash sale of the DC-8s is what kept Tigers alive.

That fall the company bought a fleet of less expensive 727-100s. Things looked so bleak that winter that I went into the Christmas tree business just in case.

The company had to sell the DC-8-63s because of the government anti-noise regulations, which went into effect the end of the year. We did not have the money it would take to re-engine them to meet the new noise standard, so UPS bought them and had them re-engined. After the modification, they were designated DC-8-73s.

The Tiger Face logo became well known in international airports around the world

CHAPTER 56 "THIS IS BAGHDAD CONTROL" 1985

B-747-200

In January the Ethiopian Famine was in the news. Tigers again volunteered to help.

HAL EWING: We already had the 1979 relief flight to Cambodia under our belt, so we talked to Steve Hanks and anyone else who had to be involved in it. At the same time there was a gal named Marilyn Folkes from JFK, who was doing a lot of organizing of relief efforts, getting food together and collecting money and what not. She had been trying to sparkplug a deal along exactly the same lines, where the company could send a relief flight.

I should mention that I had been doing a lot of relief work in different places, so I knew many people in the relief business—the Red Cross, and Salvation Army and so forth. I talked to Marilyn, and we kicked it upstairs till it got to Lewis Jordan. Lewis bought the deal, and that's what made it happen. Tigers would provide the airplane. Others would donate the food, fuel and provide volunteer help. Several organizations previously mentioned and also a government agency called Interaction helped with the project.

We took off out of Kennedy with 281,000 pounds of food. It was probably the largest load ever hauled on the 747. We landed at Brussels, Belgium, for fuel and then went on to Addis Ababa.

We had two complete crews on board. Randy Patterson and I were captains, Chuck Cozad and Mick O'Connor, the first officers and Paul Zahner and Charlie Gallardo, the second officers.

The weather at Addis Ababa was crappy with gusty winds. The airport is built on a mesa with a drop-off at both ends of the runway. It's over 8,000 feet above sea level, which caused us considerable concern. Our maximum tire speed is 195 knots and due to our heavy landing weight, our ground speed on approach was 220 knots. The runway is 14,000 feet long, and we needed every foot of it. Another thing that was not exactly a confidence builder was that there were wrecked airplanes at both ends of the runway. But we had no problems.

We were on the ground about three hours while the cargo was off-loaded. Then we ferried the airplane to Dubai, where it could continue on its next revenue trip, and we went to the Holiday Inn in Sharjah for a well-deserved rest.

Now to back up a bit. Volunteers had done all the work of loading, mechanical work and everything else. I worked in the warehouse for a couple of days helping to prepare the load. While running across the floor, I managed to sprain my ankle. It gave me a lot of trouble, but I sure didn't want to miss the trip.

Now on our layover in Sharjah we had a lot of congratulatory drinks, starting out in the Frontier Bar. Then, when it closed, a hospitality suite was set up for us. We were playing Musical Trivia, which is a game where if you can't answer the question you have to sing the song. Everything was going fine until Paul Zahner refused to sing Soldier Boy. Mick was going to sit on him till he did, but Paul jumped out the window. Mick went out after him and was chasing him around the roof when Mick sprained his ankle.

Mick was my first officer, but we figured it would be okay. I had sprained my right ankle, and he sprained his left. If we lost an outboard engine, whoever had a good leg

CHAPTER 56   TIGER TALES   525

to stand on the rudder would fly the airplane.

About three weeks later Steve Hanks called up and said, "You're not going to believe this, but we're going to do it again. We've got another airplane, and this time we're going to the Sudan."

So we threw everything in high gear and went hell for leather again. We had the same crews except that Randy Patterson now had Freddie McClurkin as his second officer.

This time the weather in Brussels was down, so we went to Frankfurt, Germany, for fuel. They were not going to let us land because we got there at night during the curfew.

Mick O'Connor was on the radio, and he kept telling them about our load of food for the starving kids until they said, "All right, all right, we don't want to hear any more of this. You are cleared to land."

From there we flew to Khartoum, Sudan. This trip was a real ball buster. The company needed the airplane in Taipei, Taiwan, for a scheduled trip. So after an 11-hour wait while the cargo was off-loaded we flew to Dubai for a fuel stop, and then went on to Taipei.

I didn't have all that excitement, only two uneventful trips to Europe, then a trip from Anchorage to Tokyo. The Tokyo trip was not uneventful. Dennis Flanagin was my first officer, and Dom Ciorciari, my second officer. When we arrived at the Anchorage Airport, I spoke to the crew that had just brought the airplane in from Los Angeles.

The captain said, "On takeoff roll we felt a vibration in the nose gear, but it wasn't too bad."

When we began our takeoff roll, I was expecting some vibration. As a result, when it began I didn't worry about it too much. By the time we reached 80 knots the vibration was so bad that I aborted the takeoff. By the time we got the airplane stopped, several of the instruments and radios had shaken loose from the second officer's panel.

We taxied back to the ramp and reported the trouble to the maintenance people. They checked the gear over and couldn't find any problem, so they changed the nose wheel and tire assemblies and greased the landing gear fittings. We prepared for another takeoff, and when we started down the runway, the same thing happened again. This time after we brought it back to the ramp we went to the hotel.

The next morning the airplane was still there. Maintenance had replaced a couple of bearings so we tried it again. There was still a vibration but it was not quite as bad. I continued the takeoff and we went to Tokyo.

On the landing roll at Tokyo we again had severe vibration. After the airplane was off-loaded our maintenance people towed it to the Japan Airlines hangar. They removed the entire nose gear assembly from the airplane and took it apart.

When it was repaired and reinstalled they called me at the hotel in the middle of the night to ask if I would come out and do a high-speed taxi check. They wanted to be sure it was fixed before it was loaded with cargo. Dennis, my first officer and I went out and made three high-speed runs down the runway. There was no vibration.

We went back to the Narita View Hotel and back to sleep. That morning we made our scheduled departure for Anchorage. Dennis and I received a nice letter of appreciation from the chief pilot.

CHAPTER 56   TIGER TALES

Boeing 747 at Tokyo, Japan

We had more changes upstairs. Robert Jenson replaced Hoffman as president of Tiger International, and Sol Steinberg became a member of the board of Tiger International. None of this was viewed as cause for celebration.

"This is Baghdad Control"

In April I left New York with Mike Rooney and John Englehardt for a round-the-world-flight. We took Flight 10 from New York to Brussels, Belgium, and were scheduled to take Flight 10 to Dubai the next night. This is where the trouble started.

Flight 10 was a scheduled flight between New York and Singapore with stops at Brussels and Dubai. Flight operations wanted this particular flight to terminate in Bangkok, Thailand. This required a change in flight numbers. All of our paperwork was for Flight 10 except for the flight plan, which was for Flight 12. As we were only flying the flight as far as Dubai, we didn't notice the change of flight numbers.

Red 19 is a very heavily traveled air route through Saudi Arabia and Bahrain. Where the route is close to Iraq, it is controlled by Baghdad control. When we approached Turaif, Saudi Arabia, Baghdad control called us. The lady controller informed us that Tiger Flight 12 did not have overfly rights on Red 19. She said we had to return to Brussels. Of course we had neither enough fuel nor the inclination to do that. Through all of this, Mike did a fine job on the radio. He did everything but ask her for a date.

Finally she asked if we could accept a clearance from Turaif to Al Shigar to Hail, all in Saudi Arabia, then Route Amber 1 to Dhahran. From there we could continue to Bahrain and Dubai on Red 19. After a quick check on the additional distance in order to figure our fuel reserves, I accepted the clearance.

When we arrived at Dubai there was a stiff wind blowing out of the north. As we were arriving from the northwest this meant we had to fly south of the airport to circle around to land to the north. This used even more fuel. Mike planned and flew the approach perfectly, and after we landed we had almost an hour of fuel remaining. I wonder, maybe he did ask her for a date.

CHAPTER 56   TIGER TALES

Talk about being out of sight...

JOHN CIGANKO: It was the night of May 17, 1985. 747 freighter flight 71 Tokyo-Taipei-Singapore. Captain B. G. O'Hara, myself as first officer and Joe Femmenino, second officer. The Tokyo-Taipei leg was routine and we departed Taipei at 1800 local time. After level off at cruise altitude flight conditions were: a moonless night, very little cloud cover, lots of stars with an occasional flicker of lightning in the distance. A nice night for an airplane ride.

About two hours south of Taipei, in the mysterious way that these things come about, the cockpit conversation drifted around to the ghost of Eastern Air Lines flight 401. We had been chatting about five minutes or so, when suddenly on the right windshield there was a loud BAM BAM BAM BAM, like someone pounding on it!

Well folks it got verrry quiet in the cockpit. The three of us just sat there looking at each other, our eyes as big as saucers. After what seemed like an hour (probably four or five minutes) somebody finally said, "Wonder what that was?"

Things started to loosen up and the conversation was beginning to approach a normal state.

Then it started again, BAM BAM BAM... As it continued I started telling myself, "He was a GOOD guy."

I picked up my flashlight and shone it on the windshield. There was the windshield wiper going back and forth. The BAM BAM occurred as the blade hit the edge of the window frame. Pulling the circuit breaker solved the problem, but it still took a while for blood pressures and pulses to return to normal.

The logbook write-up simply said: right windshield wiper came on in flight—pulled circuit breaker.

It would take more than circuit breakers to fix the problems at headquarters.

Lewis Jordan replaced John Flynn as president, and Ron Hall, director of flight operations, took over Bill Bond's duties as vice president.

A number of highly qualified men resigned their positions during this time, because the board of directors would not implement the policy changes they felt were necessary to make the company competitive.

CHAPTER 57   A WOLF AT THE DOOR   1986

B-747-200

January 28 was a day I would prefer to erase from my mind. I was sitting in an Eastern Airlines plane on the ground in Tampa, Florida, and saw the space shuttle, Challenger, blow up. As I watched the explosion with the crazy vapor trails spinning off in all directions, my mind did not want to accept the obvious. Our departure was delayed while airborne aircraft were rerouted away from the area.

I rode up to New York on Eastern, and then flew a Tiger 747 flight to Miami that night. As we flew past the launch area, I could still see those vapor trails in my mind.

Tigers had space problems of a different nature. We had outgrown our Hub at Chicago O'Hare (ORD) several years before. There was not enough space available for expansion, and we had numerous flight delays due to excessive traffic congestion, especially in the winter months.

Rickenbacker Field at Lockbourne, Ohio, near Columbus, had been a National Guard Base and had plenty of open space. Tigers built a huge automated freight terminal there. In March, after the new Hub opened, practically all of our flights transited Lockbourne (LCK) where freight from or to all other stations was transloaded. There was space for five 747s and 16 DC-8s or 727s to be loaded simultaneously.

Along with the new 727 fleet came the opportunity for many of our senior first officers to check out as captain.

BOB TAYLOR, chief pilot: Randy Falde had just checked out as a 727 captain. A new captain is not supposed to give the first officer landings until the captain has 100 hours of captain experience. Randy wanted to be a nice guy, and he gave his first officer the leg going in to LCK. Randy had not been into LCK before. They were cleared for a visual approach to runway 5, but unfortunately for Randy, Bolton Field is nearby and has a runway 4. In the dark it looked about right, so they landed at the wrong airport.

That's the trouble with being a nice guy. What is it they say, "No good deed goes unpunished?" Oh well, Chuck and I didn't do any good deeds, but we could have taken some punishment anyway.

During the month of April my crew was First Officer Chuck Cozad and Second Officer Rich Oskamp. First we had a Pacific trip from New York to LCK, Seattle, Anchorage, Tokyo and Taipei. The next night we flew the infamous Iron Triangle. We left Taipei about dark and flew to Singapore, about a four and a half hour flight. After an hour and a half on the ground, we flew to Kuala Lumpur and arrived in a pouring rain.

It was Chuck's leg and he was all set up for an ILS approach. At the last minute approach control changed it to an NDB approach. There was no way we could get set up in time, so Chuck held his altitude and did a tight 360 while I set up for the new approach. There are hills all around the airport, and with the heavy rain, visibility was

CHAPTER 57   TIGER TALES   533

zero. While we were coming around, the weather went below NDB minimums, so they got the ILS going. Now we had to retune the radios again. We broke out—if you could call it that—at least we could make out the runway lights at about 200 feet.

It rained all the while we were being reloaded and refueled, so our ground people were soaked. After engine start, the mechanic jumped in his truck and drove away without showing me the landing gear safety pins. It's a company requirement that the captain see the pins before leaving the ramp. If he had not removed them I would not have been able to retract the landing gear. I hated like hell to have to do it, but I had no choice but to call the office on the radio and have him come back and show me the pins.

I flew the leg to Hong Kong where we arrived about seven a.m. We could have won a redeye contest by the time we arrived at the hotel.

Our next trip was from Dover, Delaware, to Ramstein A.B., Germany. During our layover in Germany, Chuck and I walked all over the small town of Homburg where our hotel was located. It was very picturesque with small manicured lawns and well cared for houses. We complemented ourselves for taking such a healthy walk.

Later we found out that the Chernobyl Nuclear accident had taken place on the 26th, two days before. We were only about a 1,000 miles from there. If we had known about it, we would have stayed in a local bierstube and drank German beer all day. It might have been safer.

Hank Germain would have traded places with me that day. If the radioactive cloud doesn't get you and an exploding engine doesn't do you in, you still may have to contend with the FAA.

HANK GERMAIN: It's the same old story—a heavy airplane out of Tokyo, late departure, trying to beat the curfew, and trying to get enough fuel on board to make Anchorage. The company never wanted to bump freight off in Tokyo to add more fuel because that cost big bucks. Anchorage said the weather was okay and our alternate airport, Elmendorf, is so close to Anchorage we called it the left runway. Fairbanks was also forecast to be open, so that was my ace in the hole.

We were grossed out and could barely make 27,000 feet on our initial climb. We were approaching Shemya and began our climb to 29,000 when I noticed that something just wasn't right. It was coming from number 1 engine. The parameters were okay according to the gauges, but we could feel it. Something wasn't right. We were grinding along in this slow climb and finally reached 29,000 feet.

The sun was coming up, and we were about 300 miles west of Shemya. I had just turned and looked out at the left wing when number 1 engine literally exploded. When an engine can blow smoke out forward at 600 miles an hour, you know you had an explosion.

We shut the thing down and ran the checklist, but the airplane wasn't flying. We just barely had made the climb on four engines, and it wasn't going to stay up there on three. We couldn't wait for a clearance to a lower altitude, so I turned 30 degrees to the left to get off the airway, and started down as we broadcast in the blind to warn other aircraft that we had lost an engine and were descending.

CHAPTER 57 TIGER TALES

We finally leveled off at 22,000 feet where it felt like it would fly. Through all this time we had no radio contact with anyone. We continued up the Aleutian Chain, and when we neared Adak, we made radio contact with Anchorage.

We get to Anchorage. They had the news that we had an engine shut down, but approach said, "You'll have to wait, we are congested right now."

I said, "No, we're out of gas, and we have to land now!"

So we landed, and we were all beat. We'd been up all night, and with all this going on we were tired and wanted to go to bed. We got off the airplane and this tough little guy, at least that's the impression I had, comes and says, "I'm so and so from the FAA, and I want you to know that we are violating you for descending without permission. Why did you descend?"

I said, "Go talk to those mechanics looking at that engine. Get up on the ladder and look at it."

"No, I don't want to look at it."

"I'm not going to talk to you until you do look at it."

So he finally got a ladder and crawled up and looked in the engine nacelle. Of course it looked like a jungle in there, all burned, melted and what not.

He came down from the ladder and said, "Well, I see what you mean. Geez, you guys really had something there!"

I said, "Now you know why I made an emergency descent—because that engine damn near blew off, we were at our critical altitude, and we had to descend."

"But you didn't..."

"Oh yes we did. I made a 30-degree turn off the airway and broadcast in the blind on 121.5 (the emergency frequency) and also on H. F. (High Frequency Radio). That's all you need to know. We complied with all the regulations and got the damn thing on the ground in one piece. Now I'm tired, and I'm going to bed, and I'm through talking to you or anybody else."

I got back home, and one day Dick Wilson called and said, "Hank, the FAA is violating you."

I told him the same story, and he said, "Hell, you're lucky you're not an oil spot in the Goddamn ocean! We'll send them a letter and see what happens."

Of course the FAA never ever admits that they're wrong. A month later I get a letter saying, "Due to the lack of sufficient evidence we are not pursuing this case any further."

It turns out it wasn't all that safe around Tiger headquarters either. Bob Taylor was manager of flying on Boeing 727s:

BOB TAYLOR: In 1986 the board of directors brought in Stephen Wolf, a long time airline executive. He was brought in to rebuild the airline and regain its competitiveness and its profitability.

He had three basic goals: to significantly reduce the operating expenses, some of which came out of the hides of the employees, including pilots, in the form of wage and benefit reductions; to restructure the company financially; and to put together a strategic plan that would enable the company to carve out a niche that we could defend. Part of that plan was to fly more and bigger airplanes into more places.

There are several different views of what was happening with the company during this time. Captain Ron Hall was the senior director of flight operations and system chief pilot.

CHAPTER 57   TIGER TALES   537

RON HALL: As far as what actually happened, Steinberg wanted to get $20 a share for his stock holdings no matter what it cost the employees. So Wolf had his marching orders, and he pulled it off quite well, because that's exactly what was done.

As for Wolf himself, he played poker with the pilot group. I was there when the 25% pay cut was offered to the Master Executive Council (MEC) of the Airline Pilots Association (ALPA). Prior to that time in the industry no group had ever been asked for a 25% pay cut. They had been asked for five percent or seven percent over two years, but never 25%. So naturally our pilots said absolutely no way.

He said, "Look, I need a 25% pay cut and I need it next week. You have until Friday to come back with this agreement, because after Friday I cannot go and restructure the company debt. The pilots just left the meeting and never came back.

I was with the V.P.s on the tenth floor with Wolf working out the strategy every morning at 7:30. Of course he didn't give everyone the same information. During the day I would be called up for a briefing, and other V.P.s would be called up at different times, but every morning we were all told what he wanted us to know.

A slightly different perspective from an ALPA officer and line pilot:

FRANK MAGUIRE, ALPA MEC (Master Executive Council) Chairman: Stephen Wolf came in and did what he was hired to do. Steinberg hired him to put together a saleable package. One of the ways of doing that is to beat up on your employees and get them to work for half of what everyone else is working for. Then they have some leverage when they go to sell it. Wolf did exactly what he was supposed to do. He was a hired gun. When the pilot group did not respond, Wolf came back with an ultimatum. He wanted a 54% pay cut from the pilots, or he would sell off the company assets.

RON HALL: The strategy changed after the pilots refused the 25% pay cut. Jim Cronin, one of our very young directors who became a vice president, asked for three different bids for people to come into the company and cut everything up for scrap metal, including airplanes. He came up with a stock value of $14 a share. That's the highest share price anyone could work out.

At that time no one would buy us. U.P.S. came and spent three months. They said they would not buy Tigers because the employees were too well paid. Fred Smith from Fedex came and spent three weeks, but was noncommittal.

Steinberg did not accept the $14 a share. He said, "It's close, but get six dollars closer."

Wolf came back and said he needed a $75 million package per year from the pilots. To save the company the pilots accepted a 54% pay cut.

It had taken us many years to gain the medical insurance, retirement and reasonable working conditions that we now enjoyed, so the pilots accepted the entire cut in pay in order to keep the benefit package intact.

With all the bickering and sniping going on around headquarters, one might think a trip in the clean fresh air high over the North Pacific would be a welcome change.

BRUCE OSWALD: We took a 747 MAC passenger flight from Anchorage to Yokota, Japan. My crew was First Officer Mick O'Connor and Second Officer Dave Akel. It

CHAPTER 57   TIGER TALES

was the middle of the night somewhere around Shemya in the Aleutians when our eyes began to water, and we felt a burning in our throats.

About that time one of the flight attendants came up and said, "We have some people in the rear of the airplane having difficulty breathing."

The whole thing was a mystery at that point. Shortly after that, another flight attendant came up saying, "We have a number of people on supplementary oxygen. They're having trouble breathing, and I'm afraid the passengers will panic!"

Then I remembered that when I left the hotel that morning, I heard something about a volcano erupting somewhere off the Japanese Mainland. From what I could smell, I thought it might be volcanic ash. I had the second officer increase the flow of air through the cabin. I considered turning back and landing at Shemya, but the increased airflow seemed to help, so we pressed on.

We called Anchorage and told them of the problem, then a few minutes later they called back and said they just got word that a volcano had erupted on Kamchatka. They closed that airway for the rest of the night so no one else would fly into it. We had flown through the top of the cloud of ash. Fortunately, we were in and out of it before any permanent damage was done.

YOU HAVE BEEN FLYING TOO LONG IF...

Your right arm is longer than your left, from carrying that heavy suitcase.
You get in the family car, fasten your seat belt and call for the checklist.
You come home late at night, and your dog bites you.
You crawl into bed and your wife says, "Who's that?"

CHAPTER 58   THIS LAMB IS A TIGER   1987

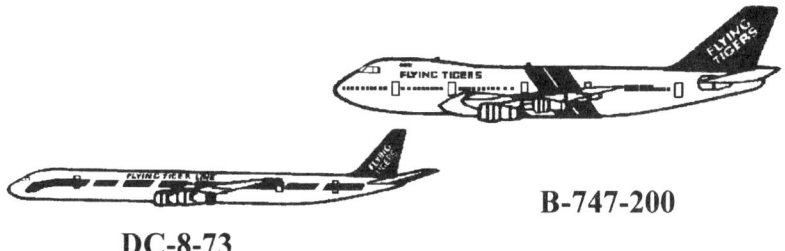

B-747-200

DC-8-73

In July I decided to give it up and retire. It seemed like 31 years ought to be enough. We have a lot of good young pilots who would love to have my seat, and I wish them well. I had a very interesting and rewarding career with Flying Tigers. I have enjoyed every minute of it: as a mechanic in Burbank; a maintenance rep in Japan, the Philippines, Viet Nam and Thailand; as a copilot on the CL-44, DC-8 and B-747 and, finally, as captain on the DC-8 and the B-747, which has to be the greatest job in the world.

July was a busy month for Ray Lamb and his crew, but I guess they thought for a minute they were not going to make it to retirement. Ray was captain on a Boeing 747 with First Officer Art Colon and Second Officer Gary Sewall.

RAY LAMB: I started this trip on July 24 and commuted to New York where I joined up with Art and Gary. Our flight sequence was from New York to Brussels to Zurich, back to Brussels then to Dubai, Sharjah, Taipei and Hong Kong, back to Taipei, then Singapore, Kuala Lumpur and back to Hong Kong.
    We had done all of that, and now it was July 31, and we were bringing Tiger Flight 66 into Kai Tak Airport, Hong Kong. We were on final approach to runway 31. The airport was reporting the wind from 190 to 240 degrees at 10 to 18 knots gusting to 25 knots with wind shear reported on

approach. Our landing weight was 518,000 pounds, which was well under maximum. Art was flying the airplane, and everything was normal. As we approached the outer marker, we selected 30 degrees of flaps. Soon after that we heard a loud BANG, and the airplane rolled and turned to the left.

Gary called out, "SPLIT FLAP!" The left inboard flap needle was indicating 20 degrees flaps and all the rest 30 degrees, so I immediately selected 20 degrees flaps. I got on the flight controls with Art as I was afraid the airplane was going to roll into an inverted position. By the use of full right aileron and right rudder, we were able to get the wings level and the turn stopped. At this point I told Art I would take control.

We had turned about 30 degrees to the left and we were below the glide slope. I added power and managed a shallow right turn to intercept the ILS course. At this time I briefly considered a go-around but quickly decided against it. I didn't believe the airplane was capable of making a go-around.

There was doubt in my mind that we would be able to get the airplane on the runway in one piece. I was using full aileron and rudder and still had only marginal control of the airplane. The quartering tail wind, turbulence and wind shear were not helping matters either. For the first time I fully understood the saying, "I had a sick feeling right in the pit of my stomach." To experience is to understand. I must have had about a quart of adrenaline running through my system.

The airspeed had increased to about 200 knots, and both Art and Gary called it out. On short final the mood changed from apprehension to total elation as it became apparent that we were going to make it. When we crossed the threshold I reduced power, flared and touched down at

CHAPTER 58   TIGER TALES

about 170 knots indicated airspeed.

I used maximum brakes and was very surprised at how quickly the airplane decelerated. We easily turned off at the Charlie hi-speed taxiway.[1] I asked Art to taxi it into the ramp because my back was in spasm. A few minutes after we shut the engines down, the tires began a series of thermal deflations due to the heavy braking. The brakes had overheated, which caused the fuse plugs in the wheels to melt and let the air out of the tires. (This is a safety feature to prevent possible tire explosions.) The ground crew really scattered. Andy, the maintenance supervisor, who was not yet aware of our problem, was mad as hell because now he had 10 tires to change. When we pointed out the left inboard flap, we were promptly forgiven.

The time from flap failure to touchdown was about two minutes. The saying is, "Hours of boredom followed by minutes of pure panic."

We went to the hotel as we were scheduled to go to Taipei, then Tokyo, in 12 hours. I got a couple of chocolate bars and a six-pack of beer and proceeded to take a hot bath while consuming the beer and chocolate.

As a result of this incident, Captain Ray Lamb and his crew became the third Flying Tiger crew to receive the coveted Daedalian Award. The others were Captain Gregory Thomas in 1957 and Captain Dick Petrick in 1979.
The following are excerpts from communications received by Ray:

---

[1] A high-speed taxiway exits the runway at a shallow angle, so an airplane can clear the active runway quickly. Taxiways are coded with letters, so Charlie would be the third exit available.

Captain Ray Lamb
Dear Ray:

It is a great honor for Flying Tigers to have you and your crew receive the Daedalian Civilian Air Safety Award for 1987. This prestigious award will be presented to you and your crew by the Order of the Daedalians at their dinner and convention in Charleston, South Carolina.

Both Don Pritchett and I are planning to attend the dinner, and Flying Tigers will provide transportation and hotel accommodations for you, your crew and wives.

Again, on behalf of our President, Jim Cronin, and all of us at Flying Tigers, congratulations on winning such a coveted award. I am looking forward to meeting you in Charleston. Regards,
Ronald Marasco
Senior Vice President Operations

Dear Captain Lamb,

The Federal Aviation Administration selected the 747 crew of Flying Tiger Line Flight 66 to receive the Daedalian Civilian Air Safety Award for 1987. As the captain of the crew I want to congratulate you. Your and the crew's flying skills averted a major and tragic accident as you prepared to land at Hong Kong's Kai Tak airport on 31 July 1987. The Order of Daedalian is grateful for the opportunity to recognize this outstanding feat of flying skill.

The Daedalian Civilian Air Safety Award will be presented at our formal Awards dinner at the Omni Hotel at Charleston Place, Charleston, South Carolina, on Saturday evening 25 June 1988.

Joseph H. Moore
Lt General, USAF (Ret)
National Commander
Order of Daedalians

CHAPTER 58 TIGER TALES

Larry Barrow's adventure wasn't caused by any mechanical failure; he's just a nosey guy:

LARRY BARROW: After many years of flying over the countryside, and especially after several trips to South America across the jungles and the Amazon, I wondered what was down there, what the people were like and how they lived.

One day I decided to ride a motorcycle from Anchorage to Argentina. I wanted to go to Manaus, Brazil, and generally follow the routes we had been flying. All together it took about six weeks.

I started from Anchorage, and the first day I rode to Whitehorse, which is about 730 miles. I left Anchorage in August, which worked out pretty well. The guys in Anchorage gave me a pair of rubber gloves, which came in handy. I had to ride through a hailstorm, and it was cold in the mountains.

Then going into Manaus, Brazil, I had a 13-hour ride mostly in the rain, which turned the red dust into mud. I had about an inch of caked mud all over the motorcycle and me when I rode up to the hotel. The bell captain wouldn't let me in, but then finally the manager did. I didn't realize I looked so bad until I looked in a mirror. One of the guys at the hotel washed the mud off the motorcycle and was surprised to find a nice bike underneath.

I changed to the local money as I went along, so I could buy food and drinks, and I could always find small hotels along the way. I usually pushed the bike into the room with me. At one place in Venezuela I went in the room and asked, "Where is the bed?"

The guy said, "Don't you have a hammock?"

There were just two hooks on the walls. I did have a hammock, but I had not used it in a hotel. The people along the way were friendly and very helpful. Of course I live in Costa Rica, so I am familiar with Central and South America.

I didn't get much farther south than Buenos Aires, because by that time the Japanese bike was trash. I had to get pulled by a car to get it started in the morning.

A Harley would have been nice, but I couldn't have carried it through some of the places I toted this one.

Meanwhile back in Los Angeles they were setting up the new DC-8-73 program.

BOB TAYLOR: I was manager of 727s until I was tapped for the DC-8-73 operation. Part of Wolf's plan was the reintroduction of the DC-8 in 1987. These were -73 models we got from Trans International Airlines. We had operated -63s in the past, but this model had new engines of much greater thrust, new pneumatic and air conditioning systems as well as new instrumentation. As a result we had to bring out a new operating manual, new ground and flight training courses, and the check personnel had to be retrained. All these things required step-by-step FAA signoffs and was a Herculean task.

There were three other people who were an immense help on this project: Al Hader, Ron Cuccio, and Russ Beltz.

Our turnaround began when these DC-8-73s came on the line. We recalled all the furloughed pilots, and then began a massive hiring program. This resulted in our people moving up to larger airplanes and many people had the chance to upgrade from second officer to first, and from first to captain. All this, of course, helped the morale of the pilots and brought back some of the old "can do" spirit of the old days.

CHAPTER 59   THE DC-8-73   1988

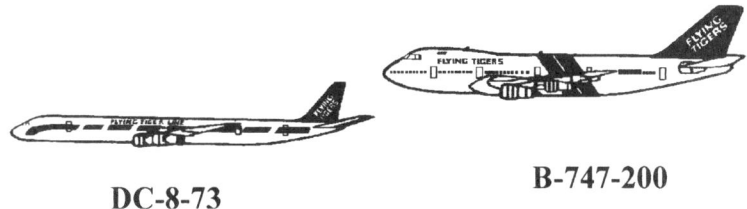

DC-8-73

B-747-200

In the first chapters of this book, the old timers told their stories of how it all began. Now the younger fellows can tell us how it ended. "Younger" being a relative term, here is Ron Hall.

RON HALL: When I was made director of flight operations, I was promised the vacant position of vice president, but I didn't get it. There were certain things I would not do as far as the pilots go. We pilots had a contract, and in my opinion, by God, the company should abide by that contract. That last 18 months was not really a very pleasant job. I went back on the line in '88.

Soon after Wolf left and went over to United, the Wall Street Journal, the L. A. paper and a few other papers interviewed me. I didn't really want to do an interview, but they stopped me in the lobby. They asked me what I thought of Carl Icahn, Frank Lorenzo and Stephen Wolf.

I figured if I told the truth I would probably be fired. And If I lied, there would be over 1,000 pilots who would never speak to me again.

So I looked these people in the eye, then looked straight at the camera and said, "I would be happy to bet one annual paycheck that these are three men that Will Rogers never met." With that I walked out.

About an hour later one of our pilots stopped me and said, "Ron, that's the worst thing you could have said. I know this will get you fired."

The papers must not have used it because I never heard a word from anyone.

FRANK MAGUIRE: One thing Wolf does deserve credit for is the acquisition of the DC-8-73s. We were running 747s around on domestic and for each DC-8 we got, a 747 became available for use on international flights where it could make some money. It had the same effect as getting a 747 at a DC-8 price. Wolf is a smart guy. In some ways...a son-of-a-bitch, but a smart guy.

In the meantime most of the guys were still overcoming adversity while trying not to lose their sense of humor, unlike some of their passengers.

GARY ROEDER: I was initially an oiler (second officer) on the 727. I was on a flight from LCK (Lockbourne, Ohio) to CLT, (Charlotte, North Carolina). When I got out to the airport, one of the load crew came up and said, "Did you know about the live animal you're carrying tonight?"
    He took me back to P-1 where the pallet with a cage of three-inch thick steel bars awaited my inspection.
    Staring back at me was a 1200-pound gorilla with eyes that said, "If it weren't for these bars I'd have my way with you."
    The handler said, "The gorilla's not in a good mood tonight." (Who is at 2 a.m.?) The front end (pilots) showed up and off we went to Charlotte. On climb-out, the air was a bit rough, even on autopilot. Well, the gorilla didn't like the way we were bumping around and started shaking his cage from side to side, to such an extent that the autopilot kicked off.
    The pilots looked back at me, so I looked at the handler in the jump seat.

CHAPTER 59   TIGER TALES   549

He said, "Don't look at me, I'm not going back there!!!"

We flew on to Charlotte making jokes about catering and in-flight entertainment for the passenger.

Upon landing, it was like the Oscars—TV—lights—everything, as we unload the latest showpiece for the zoo.

Turns out that when this 1200 pound male arrived at the zoo, waiting for him was a 700 pound mate, all fired up to make little gorillas. The sad ending to this tale is that he crushed her during the act of passion. Wish we could have given him a smoother ride, or at least let the gorilla take it out on something else other than his mate...

Of course some passenger flights have flight attendants.

GARY ROEDER: I kind of miss the passenger flights. I remember the first one I did with one of the flight attendants coming up front to serve coffee. She and I looked at each other, and I think both realized at the same time that, "Jeez she's older than my mother," and "Jeez who hired this kid?" We got along okay on that flight as long as I didn't call her mommy...

You fight your way through the weather and land at the airport safely, and then you climb into the taxi...

GLEN BORCHARD: We went into Nandi, Fiji Islands, on the second leg of a Sydney, Australia, trip and arrived in a driving rainstorm. When we got to our taxi, a right hand drive Japanese car, Joe Femmenino took the left front seat. The first officer and I were in the back seat, with me behind the driver.

Joe said, "Why is this thing running? The generator light is on."

I said, "It's running because it's a diesel."

So the driver hops in, and we take off. We can't see a thing in this rain, and the windshield wipers don't work for lack of electricity. Joe is really upset and concerned about a head-on collision. So the driver opens the window and tries to move the wiper blade back and forth with his hand, to see where he's going. Then I was getting soaked with the rain coming in the open window. It was a comical situation, although dangerous, but I had to laugh.

When we got to the hotel we couldn't get the trunk open, so the first officer went with the cab to get a pry bar, so we could get our luggage. What a morning.

Some pilots seem to have more problems with weather than others, and some have more mechanical problems. Glen has this thing about taxis...

GLEN BORCHARD: We arrived in New York about two in the morning, and the van arrived to take us to the hotel. Gone were the days of Fugazi's Limo Service. (A reliable company with real limousines that we had used for years.)

The driver said with obvious pride, "We just put a new engine in this van, and this is my first trip with it."

When we got to the toll plaza to go through the tunnel, something was very wrong. The driver had just paid the toll when the van filled with smoke.

I commanded an emergency evacuation!

The Port Authority had the van pull off to the side of the road. The mechanics had forgotten to fill the radiator after they installed the new engine, hence one cooked engine.

When the DC-8-73s came on the line in 1988, the profits started rolling in. The new engines provided much more power, used less fuel and made less noise than the older DC-8s. Still it was too late to save the company. The big money people wanted their profits so the die was cast.

ANN MARIE PRESCOTT: A strong man at the helm of Flying Tigers, I think, would have taken it through. You know the only thing that was a hitch was Stephen Wolf's actions, which nearly forced a pilot's strike. I think the memory of Bob was instrumental in avoiding that. You guys compromised yourself to do what was asked, and I know what that took. But I also know that we could have completed the cycle and gone forward, and Tigers would be in business today and very successful.

JOHN McDONALD, Vice-President of maintenance: Frank Riggins was one of those great mechanics who kept the line stations running so well. (I have always believed that the heart of an outfit like FTL was paradoxically perhaps, in the line stations rather than the head office). The following note supports this contention admirably.

I had just arrived at Tokyo when just a couple of days earlier the ground staff had to handle a rather special shipment of valuable horses. Unloading apparently proceeded normally until one of these high-strung animals caught its hoof in the doorsill protector and started to panic, kicking wildly.

All the local lads departed the scene quickly and wild confusion reigned. Enter into this scene "Big Frank" who, with the innate knowledge of horses as a farm boy, knew exactly what to do. He went straight to the wildly kicking animal and put his big arm around its neck and bit it hard in the ear. The shock quieted the animal immediately and he was able to lead it safely down the ramp. Frank talked quietly to the horse and then, still talking, led it around the tarmac until it had calmed enough to hand it over to the grooms who were with the other horses.

A wonderful example of the real "can do" spirit which was the real core of the talented group of men of which I was both proud and privileged to be a part.

BORCHARD BAD BEER BAR STORY

GLEN BORCHARD: Near the Narita View Hotel in Tokyo a tractor-trailer was parked along the road to the airport. It had been made into a Karaoke bar. The beer was terrible, but you could sing your heart out. All the airline people were in there most evenings. I never did see a rest room around there, so everybody just went outside. Just behind the trailer was a binjo ditch or flood control canal. It was at least eight feet deep and quite wide. One night Gerry Proctor went out to take a whiz and went too far. He fell into the ditch and got banged up enough that he had to deadhead home. Such is the life of a Tiger pilot.

CHAPTER 60   THE FINAL FLIGHT   1989

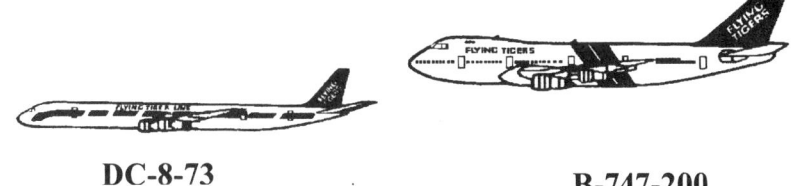

DC-8-73   B-747-200

NORAH O'NEILL: In that one second of blue and white lightning fire dancing across the windshield, the blue sky gone to charcoal, and the simultaneous bone-crushing, wing-bending turbulence, I knew we were about to die.

We were 1200 feet above the ground and our jet had just quit flying. It flashed through my head that this is how the Delta guys felt in the moments before they hit the ground in Dallas after they had flown into unrecoverable windshear.

"But I didn't do anything wrong!" my mind screamed. Then there was no time for thinking. Just reaction and flying and calling out the checklist that I had memorized; had practiced in the simulator. MAX POWER, ATTITUDE UP TO 15 DEGREES OR STICK SHAKER. MAINTAIN HEADING. MAINTAIN CONFIGURATION.

Hell, the four throttles were already firewalled. They had been shoved full forward as soon as the speed had started to bleed off to that unbelievable 45 knot airspeed loss. Didn't have to do anything about the plane's attitude either—we were in level flight with the full tooth-rattling stickshaker pounding. We were going straight ahead and my hands were glued to the controls. My left hand was pinned to the throttles by Dick's right hand mashing mine, as if our hands together could get the throttles to go further than the mechanical stops.

My right hand was on the yoke, white knuckled with the effort of holding the plane level, when the elevator control surfaces were trimmed for a 20-degree flap approach at

60% power. I didn't have a hand free to change the aircraft configuration.

The 747s massive gear was down and locked. Raising the gear would reduce drag and allow us to gain airspeed, but it would also, for too many long seconds, open the garage-door-sized gear doors and add to our drag. Twenty degrees of flaps was adding drag and lift. IF IT IS STILL FLYING DON'T CHANGE IT. That was a basic rule for extreme emergencies that we had learned from our deceased flying brothers. In one well-studied case, a DC-10 had an engine tear loose from the wing during the take-off roll. I had been in Chicago that horrible day, and was a witness to that plane's last seconds, flying its crew and passengers into eternity.

The co-pilot had been at the controls and the captain had said, "I have it" and took over control as captains were, according to the book, supposed to do during emergencies. Then the captain had begun to slow the plane to its best one-engine flying speed, as the book said to do. There was no way for him to know that the non-working engine had actually departed the aircraft, taking part of the leading edge slats with it, along with vital hydraulic and electrical lines. That slowing was the beginning of the end. He did everything perfectly and died.

We are trained that way—to drill our responses to emergencies so that when the shit really hits the fan, and we don't have time to think or assess, we will, by rote, do the right thing. Most of the time, these emergency checklists that we have memorized were put together by the manufacturer and test pilots, then periodically modified by the knowledge gained from accidents and incidents.

That heart-pounding day in the skies over the Philippines was clearly a case of the, IF IT IS STILL FLYING DON'T CHANGE IT rule.

Dick did not yell, "I have it!"

CHAPTER 60 TIGER TALES

Later, he would say that to take over had been his first thought.

His second thought, he said, was, "It's still flying, don't change it."

And so the next seconds in that shaking, howling airplane were spent voiceless in a frozen tableau. There was nothing left to be done but ride it out. Whatever fate had planned for us, we were going to meet in motionless silence. In those hour-long seconds, I thought of my children, and had a moment to offer them and myself to the care of God.

Then the airspeed indicator began to rise; I had time to trim the forward pressure out of the yoke; and the lightning stopped. The yoke quit throbbing with the stickshaker's warning of impending stall and we broke out of the clouds into a calm blue summer sky. The airspeed climbed to normal, and I began to ease back on the throttles. We no longer needed 200,000 screaming horses to push us through the sky.

"Fly the missed approach procedure," Dick commanded in a normal tone of voice, as he keyed his microphone to inform Manila tower that Tiger Flight 18 was going around for another approach.

"This man must have balls of steel," I thought wonderingly.

Dick reported, "Severe windshear on final at 1,200 feet, and loss of 45 knots of airspeed,"

Manila tower said, "Roger, turn right to 120 degrees and expect vectors for another localizer approach to runway 6."

"I don't think so," Dick replied. "We require a different runway."

Dick's cool and calm reporting of the massive windshear, did not appear to have given Manila the slightest clue that we had JUST CHEATED DEATH OF THREE PILOTS.

This flight, like most, landed safely and never made the news. Sad as it is in this business, usually due to combinations of circumstances, sometimes death wins.

The "Iron Triangle" finally claimed an airplane. We lost a Boeing 747 and its crew on approach to Kuala Lumpur. The crew was Captain Frank Halpin, First Officer Jack Robinson, Second Officer Ron Penton and Mechanic Lenny Sulewski.

What made that trip so miserable was that after a day of trying hopelessly to sleep in the din of downtown Taipei, the flight departed in the evening. Just about the time your eyes finally begin to close, it's time to go to work. I don't know for sure that it was a factor here, but I mention fatigue from my own experience, having flown the trip many times.

Frank Halpin had been a pilot with the company since 1955.

Jack Robinson was the first officer on my first trip as captain in 1978.

Ron Penton hired on as a flight engineer in 1956. He later upgraded to first officer, then to captain. When he reached the maximum pilot age of 60, he downgraded to second officer so he could keep on flying.

I didn't personally know the mechanic, Lenny Sulewski.

One cause of the accident was confusion between approach control and the crew in aviation terminology.
They apparently thought they had been cleared to 400 feet. In fact they had been cleared to two four zero zero, 2400 feet. The aircraft struck a ridge at an altitude of 438 feet and was destroyed with the loss of all on board.

CHAPTER 60   TIGER TALES   557

There were other captains who did not retire when they reached the magic age of 60. Oakley Smith downgraded to second officer and kept right on working. Dick Wilson worked at the Hub in Columbus as director of technical services and also as a simulator instructor.

FRANK MAGUIRE: No one was at Tigers by accident. We had everything from jailbirds to moonwalkers, and they all belonged at Flying Tigers. No one could have gone out and hand picked all these guys. They found Tigers.

GLEN BORCHARD: Soon after Bob Prescott died our airline began a slow decline. People were brought in who didn't care if they managed an airline or a railroad. I once saw a list of companies owned by Tiger International. There were forty some, and most were going broke. The airline was bled dry, and instead of money being put back into it, it was used for other investments. If Ann Marie (Prescott) or Oakley (Smith) had taken over, we might still be in business.

At least we got some respect. The following resolution was assed in the United States House of Representatives.

101st CONGRESS
1st Session

S. CON. RES 39

IN THE HOUSE OF REPRESENTATIVES

June 13, 1989

Referred to the Committee on Post Office and Civil Service

CONCURRENT RESOLUTION

Whereas the merger of Tiger International with the Federal Express Corporation led to the transfer of the international air cargo routes from Flying Tiger Line, Inc., a subsidiary of Tiger International, to the Federal Express Corporation, will bring to a close one of the most remarkable and distinguished chapters in United States aviation history;

Whereas the pilots of the Flying Tiger Line, Inc. bear a name which represents members of a proud and distinguished group of aviators (properly known as the "Flying Tigers");

Whereas approximately 50 years ago the Flying Tigers initially operated in the jungles of Burma, with the operations of the American volunteer group under the command of General Claire Chennault;

Whereas the tradition of proud and distinguished service by the Flying Tigers to the United States began under the direction of Robert W. Prescott;

Whereas for more than 4 decades such proud and distinguished group of aviators has steadfastly served the specialized air transportation needs of the United States; and

Whereas the Flying Tigers have provided assistance with rescue efforts in Korea, Hungary, Vietnam, Cambodia, and Ethiopia, and have conducted many other humanitarian missions:
Now, therefore, be it

CHAPTER 60   THE FINAL FLIGHT

1   Resolved by the Senate (the House of Representatives
2   concurring), That Congress commends the group of pilots
3   that bear the name Flying Tigers, a distinguished group of
4   aviators, for nearly 50 years of valued and competent service
5   to the United States.

Passed the Senate June 9 (legislative day, January 3), 1989.

Attest: WALTER J. STEWART, Secretary

Given that the pilot group had taken a 54% pay cut to <u>save</u> the company, and now that the company was making more money than ever, did the pilots receive a huge bonus? Maybe just a thank you? Not exactly, but let's not dwell on that. A story about heroes should not end on a sour note. Heroes? You're damned right they were. Hero worship? Sure, we all had it, still do, and we're not ashamed of it.

So the Flying Tiger Line comes to an end. It would be a shame if all Tiger exploits, accomplishments, adventures, and our few defeats, not to mention our Bar Stories, were forgotten. Somebody ought to write a book.

Fred Smith of Federal Express was waiting in the wings and biding his time. He is an airline person and recognized the extent of Flying Tigers assets, including routes, equipment, reputation and personnel. Prescott's prediction that one day Fred would make a bid for Tigers was correct. Fred and Bob seem to share some of the same traits. So, now that about ten years have elapsed, how did it all turn out?

Well, here's an excerpt from a letter from FedEx.

January 3, 2000
Mr. Russ Emerson
President
Flying Tigers Retirement Club
Dear Russ:

In a recent issue of FedEx "World Update" there was an article commemorating the ten-year anniversary of the Tiger acquisition. I thought you and the Flying Tiger retirees would enjoy the article.

Ten years after the FedEx purchase of Flying Tigers, the acquisition ranks among the most significant in company history.

Without Flying Tigers, FedEx would still be a formidable competitor in the express transportation industry, says Rush O'Keefe, legal department Vice President. But he believes the company would be several years behind the leadership position it enjoys today.

United Parcel Service likely would have made that a certainty by scooping up Tigers in a competitive volley clearly aimed at FedEx, O'Keefe believes. "Had that happened," he says, "FedEx would be in the same position as UPS today—playing catch-up."

On behalf of all of us at FedEx who learned so much from all of you while we were at Flying Tigers, thank you for your wisdom, leadership, and great times.

Charles B. Malone
Vice President
Business Development, Marketing & Communications.

GLOSSARY

ADF:	The radio in the airplane that is trying to find the non-directional beacon—NDB on the ground.
A.D.I.:	Anti-detonation-injection, a mixture used to keep the engine cylinders cool during takeoff.
A.L.P.A:.	Air Line Pilots Association.
A.P.U.:	Auxiliary Power Unit.
A.T.C.:	Air Transport Command.
A.T.R.:	Air Transport Rating.
A.V.G.:	American Volunteer Group 1941-42.
BLUE ROOM:	Head, or toilet when it's on an airliner.
BOGIE:	A heavy beam holding the main landing gear wheels.
BRAINBAG:	A leather flight kit that holds a pilot's maps etc.
C.A.A.:	Civil Aeronautics Administration.
C.A.M.S.:	Civilian Army Movement Systems.
C.A.T.:	Civil Air Transport (China).
C.A.T.C.:	China Air Transport Corporation.
C.A.B.:	Civil Aeronautics Board.
CHERRY PICKER:	A tall ladder usually on wheels.
C.N.A.C.	China National Aviation Corporation.
DEADHEADS:	Non-working crewmembers.
F.A.A.:	Federal Aviation Administration (Used to be CAA).
F.B.O.:	Fixed Base Operator. (Fuel, Hangars, Maint., Etc.)
F.T.L.:	Flying Tiger Line.
GRANDMA GAS:	Extra fuel put on by the flight crew for "grandma."
"HUMP"	The Himalayas between China and India.
I.L.S.:	Instrument Landing System.
I.M.C.:	Instrument Meteorological Conditions.
I.N.S.:	Inertial Navigation System.
LAX:	Los Angeles International Airport.
MAC:	Military Airlift Command.
M.A.T.S.:	Military Air Transport Service.
M.E.C.:	Master Executive Council—of the ALPA.
MINES FIELD:	What they used to call LAX.
NACELLE:	What the engines are bolted to on the wings.
N.D.B.:	Non Directional Beacon or Homer.
PAX:	To pax means to ride a passenger airline.
PBY:	"Catalina" Patrol Bomber.
P.R.T.:	Power Recovery Turbine.
R.A.F.:	Royal Air Force (British).
R.V.R.:	Runway Visual Range.
TOUCH AND GOES:	Take off and landing practice.
T.W.A.:	Trans World Airways.
V.O.R.:	The standard radio navigation facility.

Contributor's names are in **Bold** print.

Abraham, Ed, 165, 166
Adcock, John, 292
Agronin, Sam, 166, 167
Akel, Dave, 538
Alexander, George, 278
Alexander, Jim, 108, 264, 313
Allen, Ray, 19, 42, 211
Allison, Ernest, 23, 24
Amrhein, Howie, 189, 213
Anderson, R.C. "Andy", 241, 263, 273, 383
Appel, Sheldon, 279
Archer, Jim, 242, 456, 501
Arnold. Gen. Hap, 40
Avey, Al, 396
Baird, Bob, 274, 279, 331, 339, 341, 371, 381, 407, 460
Baleski, John, 414
Barber, Mike, 485
Barberra, Joe, 213
Barlow, Bob, 109, 110, 136
Barrow, Larry, 371, 381, 545
Bartling, Bill, 2, 6, 18, 19, 30, 31, 452
Bartosiewicz, Jim, 371, 381
Bassie, Carol, 353
Bates, Hank, 424
Bax, Bob, 303, 366, 381, 387
Bayne, Howard, 99, 101, 158, 387
Bazan, Joe, 381
Beck, George, 508
Belanger, Ernie, 287, 288
Bellows, Charley, 223
Beltz, Russ, 546

Benninger, Fred, 86, 320
Bentley, Dick, 90, 102, 401
Bergman, Moon, 330
Berry, Millard, 126
Berryman, Les, 41
Betancourt, Luis, 505
Bixby, Dianna, 64, 69, 71
Blackburn, Harry, 228
Blanck, Bob, 169
Bledsoe, Jim, 81
Bliss, Jack, 102, 108, 396
Bliss, Pat, 140
Bobo, Jack, 184, 208
Bock, George, 53, 329
Bond, Bill, 517, 530
Borchard, Glen, 549, 550, 552, 557
Bower, Joe, 264
Bowles, Carey, 19, 91, 92, 214
Boyd, Ken, 220
Boydstun, Barney, 490
Boyer, Ernie, 228
Brackett, Jimmy, 257, 263
Brandenberg, "Brandy" 102, 166, 185
Bredon, Arnie, 99, 211, 290, 291
Brennan, Nancy, 294
Brondum, Ted, 175, 176, 363, 366, 371, 381
Brooks, Howard, 129, 212
Broome, Mike, 509
Brotman, Jacqueline, 246
Brown, Scott, 290
Brumfield, "Curly," 164, 165
Buchanan, Jerry, 42
Buchanan, Buck, 41, 42, 43,

78, 183
Buck, Robert, 304
Buckner, Dave, 381
Burke, Dorothy, 274
Burson, Ron, 479, 503
Burt, Grady, 243
Buskey, Doug, 64, 202, 266
Calton, Joe, 203
Campbell, Rick, 458
Carr, Joe, 336
Casey, Gerry, 381
Cashman, Bob, 429
Cerniway, Hal, 240, 329
Chambers, Andy, 102, 104, 410
Chambers, Chuck, 498, 499
Chaney, Bill, 283
Chase, Allen,
Chennault, Claire, 1, 7, 11, 31, 43, 110
Christian, Frank, 299, 316
Churlonis, Ray, 517
Ciganko, John, 529
Ciorciari, Dom, 525
Ciszlac, John, 105
Clark, Hank, 213
Clasens, Tony, 269
Clemente, Geraldine, 205
Cochran, Jacqueline, 75
Cole, Roy, 240
Collins, Carol, 295
Colon, Art, 541
Colquette, "Colley," 51
Conrath, Bob, 19, 20, 75, 355
Constable, Tom, 290, 323, 404
Conway, Pat, 295
Cormier, Al, 337

Costello, Gerry, 19
Cotting, J, 407
Cotton, Greg, 458
Cotton, Tom, 75, 76, 78, 121
Cozad, Chuck, 523, 532
Crapo, David, 251
Creamer, D. G., 420
Cronin, Jim, 538
Crowley, Paul, 381, 423, 480
Cuccio, Ron, 546
Cullen, Jim, 146, 147
Cuppet, Joe, 51, 59
Curran. Bill, 228, 256
Cussen, Jeannine, 189
Cussins, George, 121
Cutting, Kip, 423
Danielson, Danny, 70
Davis, 448
Dayton, Robert, 189
Delman, Rick, 263
Devereaux, Mark, 160, 381
Dewey, John, 41, 59, 193, 285
Dickinson, "Curly," 90, 102, 103
Dobson, "Dobbie," 55, 65, 68, 106, 132, 211, 212, 263, 281, 360, 410
Dodd, Art, 381
Donahoe, George, 82, 205
Doolittle, Jimmy, 426
Doty, C. K. 105
Dove, Perry, 144, 146, 147, 160, 167, 185
Drake, John, 490
Drake, Larry, 312
Drennan, Bill, 473
Drew, Frances, 109, 206
Drew, (Smith) Marilyn, 136,

149
Drumwright, Mike, 231
Drusch, Kenneth, 241
Dunn, Dick, 381, 383
Dupree, Jack, 41
DuVander, Georgianna, 211
Eatchel, Don, 184, 235
Eaton, Brad, 501
Eban, Abba, 313
Edge, George, 85, 137, 341, 387
Elliot, Ray, 444
Elliot, Wayne, 346
Emerson, Russ,
Enfield, Fred, 428
Englehardt, John, 527
Entz, Paul, 139, 155, 268
Ermert, Eric, 515
Ewing, Hal, 448, 523
Falde, Randy, 532
Femenino, Joe, 207, 213, 529, 549
Ferguson, Sandra, 347
Ferris, Brian, 280
Fine, Ina Collins, 294
Firth, Mike, 426
Flanagin, Art, 223, 307
Flanagin, Dennis, 519, 525
Flemmons, Mike, 501
Flood, Emmet, 174, 455
Flynn, John, 507, 521, 530
Foley, Bob, 338
Folkes, Marilyn, 523
Foreno, George, 508
Forsythe, Jim, 155
Foster, Linda, 276
Foster, Ray, 112, 340, 349
Frampton, Andy, 250

Franklin, Bill, 273
Franklin, Eileen (Mrs. Bill), 342
Franzone, John, 381
Frederick, Jeanine, 211
Frederickson, Tom, 381
Freedell, Ted, 381, 382
Freeman, Dave, 347
Frey, Yolanda, 205
Gallardo, Charlie, 523
Gallogy, Bill, 503
Garber, Ken, 219
Garrett, James, 246
Gaudino, Joe, 139
Gazzaway, Bob, 243
George, Bill, 338
Germain, Hank, 222, 534
Gewher, George, 312
Gibbons, "Gibby," 473, 474
Gilbert, Bob, 444
Gin, Warren Fong, 147
Glenn, John, 237, 238
Gohm, Jim, 427
Gold, Phil, 60
Goldberg, Al, 62, 87
Goldsmith, J.P. "Goldy," 40, 44 46, 49, 51, 52, 53, 55, 58, 59, 64, 66, 69, 72, 83, 84, 85, 104, 106, 111, 115, 117, 121, 125, 129, 153, 158, 175, 186, 194, 198, 227, 230, 240, 261, 319, 324, 335, 401, 424
Gordon,---, 31,
Gorham, Art, 266
Goro, Sy, 264
Gould, Carol Ann, 246, 248
Grace, Paul, 89
Graff, Frank, 71, 206, 261,

331, 410
Grant, Al, 411
Greber, Chuck, 118
Green, Michael, 241
Grey, Jack, 251
Griffin, Bob, 211
Griffin, Harrie, 456
Griffith, Chuck, 424
Griffith, Marv, 381
Grogean, Tom, 320, 337, 440, 453, 507
Groh, Cliff, 2, 8, 9, 33, 36, 38, 39, 41, 45, 60, 133, 136, 192, 458
Gunderson, Lee, 448
Gurrel, Bryan, 463
Guttman, Henry, 241
Hader, Al, 546
Hale, Ed, 184, 208, 219, 231, 246, 256, 266, 271, 306, 506
Hall, Archie, 381, 448
Hall, Ron, 284, 347, 530, 536, 537, 538, 547
Halls, Ken, "Salty," 503
Halpin, Frank, 333, 556
Hamby, Bob, 79, 80, 157
Hammer, Chuck, 133, 134, 141, 143, 216, 227, 246, 259, 292, 334
Hampton, Stan, 123, 124, 239, 318
Hanks, Steve, 523
Harder, Howie, 457, 463
Harvey, W. C., 457
Hassig, Don, 19, 21, 91, 99, 126, 228, 229, 270, 399, 400, 444, 453
Haszko, Hank, 213, 223

Hathaway, Henry, 330
Hawes, Bob, 79
Hawkins, Frank, 221, 264, 303
Hayes, Marsha, 426
Haywood, Tommy, 2, 33, 45, 51, 60, 209, 293, 304, 435
Healy, Joe, 440, 453
Healy, Ken, 383
Healy, Mike, 283
Heaphy, Bill, 395
Heckman, Fred, 91
Hedden, Ralph, 42, 52, 53, 64, 108, 130, 294, 335, 401, 424
Hedman, Duke, 2, 3, 13, 19, 28, 30, 33, 60, 209, 401, 484
Hegstadt, Paul, 254
Heller, Harvey, 125
Henderson, Ken, 64, 77, 93, 111, 174
Hengehold, Jim, 312
Hennessy, Dan, 202, 268
Herbert, Ed, 282
Hernandez, Diane, 282
Hernandez, Richard, 381
Hickman, Ernie, 211
Hicks, Charlie, 193
Hightower, Robert, 147
Hilts, Art, 504
Hinshaw, Harry, 136
Hod, Mordecai, 435
Hoey, Bill, 227, 308, 314, 317, 330
Hoffman, Wayne, 309, 320, 335, 337, 440, 527
Holmes, Johnny, 60, 240, 281
Holmes, Red, 32
Holt, Henry, 210
Hooker, Dave, 449

Hopkins, D, K., 170, 171
Hopper, Hedda, 39
Houge, Marge, 354
Howe, Mike, 482
Hughes, Morgan, 158, 241, 242, 299, 351
Hunt, Thomas, 280
Huntington, Gene, 258, 263
Huntington, Pappy, 116, 299, 301
Ice, Bill, 68
Icahn, Carl, 547
Jackson, Frank, 310, 311
Jackson. Mike, 303
Jacoban, G., 488
Jarvis, Len, 320
Jarvis, Ralph, 313, 351
Jenkins, Bob, 201
Jennings, Buck, 299
Jenson, Robert, 527
Jewett, Darrel, 243
Johnson, Euginia, 189
Johnson, J. D., 381, 479, 480, 489, 500
Johnson, Ken, 381
Johnstone, James, 241, 242
Jolly, Earl, 228, 239
Jordan, Lewis, 523, 530
Jorgensen, Stan, 339
Kangieser, Jerry, 362, 381, 384
Keefer, Dick, 333, 411
Keenan, John, 404
Kelly, Paul, 31, 255, 278
Kennedy, William, 243
King, Dennis, 485
Kleen, Merle, 233
Kocisko, George, 186

Koken, Treso, 295, 296
Koret, Dick, 278
Korth, Bill, 60
Korty, Ray, 73, 207
Kramer, Kevin, 508
Kyle, Lee, 295
Lagerquist, John, 334
Lamb, Ray, 541, 543
Lamping, John, 79, 89, 158, 170, 172, 176, 199, 460
Lane, "Skip," 60, 188
Lange, Milt, 53
Laughlin, Link, 2, 18, 32, 40, 41
Lawson, Art, 182, 183
Le Clere, Lou, 83, 84, 86, 205
Lee, Ron, 461
Lenarsic, Glenn, 310, 311
Lewis, Marty, 201, 212, 444
Lewis, Doc, 35
Libra, R. J., 205
Lightner, Joe, 228
Lindberg, Charles, 426
Lindsey, Woody, 219
Loane, Bus, 2, 15, 20, 435
Long, Elgen, 50, 53, 57, 94, 180, 192, 343, 426, 427
Long, John, 40, 44, 50, 53, 64, 71, 72, 76, 79, 81, 90, 91, 92, 335
Lopez, Guy, 509
Lorenzo, Frank, 547
Lowe, Ed, 76, 91
Lowe, Robert, 205
Lowe, Wayne, 156, 241, 242
Lowe, W. C, 118
Luccio, Gary, 489
Luccio, Larry, 87, 93, 130,

213, 432, 489
Lynch, Freddy, 460
Machado, Tony, 58, 74, 147, 148
Maguire, Frank, 423, 488, 520, 537, 548, 557
Maguire, Mar, 149
Maiuro, Tony, 212, 213, 214, 215, 221, 223
Mandler, George, 517
Marasco, Ronald, 544
Marble, Frank, 263
Martel, Norm, 381
Martin, Bob, 319
Martin. Jack, 118, 121, 270, 292, 293, 319, 335
Martin, "Whisperin' Jim," 144, 421
Maxey, Dick, 281
Maxwell, Don, 490
Mays, Vern, 281
McAlister, Guy, 189, 432
McClarty, Jack, 184, 235, 283, 302
McClellon, Clayton, 243
McClendon, E. Kelly, 118
McClendon, Gary, 118
McClendon, Kelly, 118
McClendon, Rosemary, 118
McClung, Tom, 231
McClurkin, Freddie, 525
McCulloch, Bob, 426
McDevitt, Dave, 381
McDonald, John, 551
McElroy, Dave, 277
McGowen, George, 306
McGraft, Nelfie, 456
Mckenzie, Bill, 323

Merrill, B. M, 118
Messenger, George, 175
Metcalf, Cheryl Lee, 489
Metcalf, Dwight, 319
Meyers, Harry, 207
Michel, John, 401
Middle, Rick, 382
Millican, Ray, 242
Miranda, Ernie, 258, 263, 365
Mitchell, Gen. Billy, 191
Mitchell, Ralph, 19, 23, 211, 298, 299, 320, 382
Mitchell, Tom, 241
Mobley, Al, 51, 55, 60, 139, 458
Moldrem, L. J. "Vern," 181, 219, 222, 225, 238, 253, 257, 259, 261, 271, 285, 297, 302, 305, 308, 310, 314, 315, 319, 320, 324, 330, 334, 337, 347, 387, 401, 423, 431, 440, 443, 457, 473, 480, 485, 488, 493, 501, 507, 509, 515, 525, 531, 541, 556
Montgomery, Jim, 394
Montgomery, Kay, 426
Moon Chin, 25
Moore, Joseph, Lt. Gen. 544
Moore, Lloyd, 229, 303
Morris, Jack, 136, 216, 352
Morris, Manny, 320
Morrow, Frank, 223
Mosher, Sam, 30
Mroczec, Walt, 184
Mudd, Ruth, 246
Mulcahy, George, 450
Muller, Hildegarde, 243
Mulvaney, Harold, 352

Murray, John, 71, 221, 246, 248
Myer, Glen, 60, 134, 143
Nau, George, 184, 243
Neathery, Bowles Cynthia, 92, 96, 97, 98, 206, 221
Newcomer, John, 108, 174, 197, 198, 328, 499
Newman, Vic, 515
Nezgoda, Jim, 480
Nicholson, Sam, 246, 248, 249
Niven, Bill, 463
O'Brian, Bob, 277
O'Conner, Mick, 523, 538
O'Donnell, Charley, 307
O'Donnell, J. J., 426
O'Hara, B. G., 529
Okicich, Pete, 303
Olsen, Richard, 147
Olson, Janet, 32, 53, 54, 58, 77, 90, 122
Olson, John, 251
Olson, Roy "Curly", 261, 262, 320
O'Neal,"Oney," 175
O'Neill, Norah, 411, 429, 476, 553
Opeggard, Bob, 235
Orlicky, Bill, 320
Ortega, Chris, 219
Oskamp. Rich, 532
Ossello, Jim, 350
Oswald, Bruce, 538
Pacini, Joe, 381
Palomar, B. J., 189, 205
Parker, Robert, 246
Parsons, Willy, 164

Partridge, Larry, 320, 324, 326, 363, 381, 435, 510, 514
Patterson, Bob, 480
Patterson, Randy, 523
Pattison, Bill, 156
Peake, Wayne, 158, 216, 270, 286, 315, 435, 436
Penton, Ron, 289, 556
Peralta, Pete, 66
Perrault, Al, 220
Perrine, Anne, 38
Perrine, Edith, 38
Perry, Paul, 172
Peters, Art, 113
Peters, Frank, 105
Peterson, C. F., 396
Peterson, Fred, 381, 387
Petrick, Dick, 449, 543
Petros, Jerry, 333
Pfeifer, Al, 40
Phillips, Paul, 404
Pierchala, Tom, 399, 400
Pinke, Ed, 74, 132, 137, 186, 187, 189, 223, 232, 319, 335, 343
Pinny, John, 34
Pistole, Larry, 2
Poindexter, Bob, 460
Pong, 24
Popp, Bill, 381
Ports, Mel, 269, 381
Pot, Pol, 381, 448
Powell, Doc, 166, 235
Powers, Jimmy, 83, 84, 164, 165
Prendergast, Art, 18, 25, 165, 183
Prentiss, Carl, 287, 289, 290

Prescott, Ann Marie, 245, 255, 278, 309, 337, 403, 425, 434, 551, 557
Prescott, Bob, 2, 3, 13, 19, 27, 30, 33, 43, 45, 130, 245, 278, 304, 309, 310, 335, 401. 403, 426, 434, 435
Prescott, George, 28, 44
Prescott, Helen Ruth, 27, 245, 337
Prescott, Jim, 287
Prescott, Peter, 278, 337
Prevost, Orville, 423
Pritchett, Don, 544
Proctor, Gerry, 552
Pryor, Charley, 88, 110, 180, 215, 231
Rader, Karl, 164, 251
Rademacher, "Rod," 51
Rafferty, Joe, 46, 49
Raine, Catfish, 2, 8, 9, 17, 25, 27, 32, 33, 35, 36, 42, 44, 45, 75, 169, 209, 484
Rebscher, Paul, 318, 328, 335, 427, 508
Reed, Pete, 280
Reese, Tommy, 64, 129
Reeves, Fred, 231, 242
Regan, Mike, 448
Regina, Angelo, 381
Reiter, Chrystel, 243
Reubens, Berangere, 189
Rice, Ernie, 313, 490
Richards, J, 136, 268
Riemer, Dick, 268, 381
Riggins, Frank, 277, 381, 551
Rimmer, George, 431
Rinne, Pete, 91

Ristaino, John, 233
Roberts, Bill, 324
Roberts, Walter, 338
Robbins, Doug, 82, 151
Robinson, Jack, 556
Robinson, Robbie, 137
Roeder, Gary, 548, 549
Rogers, Roy, 50
Rogers, Will, 547
Rooney, Mike, 527
Rosbert, Joe, 2, 5, 6, 9, 15, 29, 33, 34, 43, 44, 74
Rossi, Dick, 2, 6, 7, 14, 19, 20, 21, 71, 72, 94, 95, 156, 157, 180, 211, 264, 484
Rovegno, Joe, 290, 339
Royall, Sam, 239, 310, 339, 381
Ruhl, Eddie, 462,
Russell, Jack, 64, 115
Sahaydak, Walt, 201, 508
Sanders, Don, 71, 74, 132, 146, 275, 294, 491
Sanders, Jim, 130
Schoumaker, John, 263
Scamans, Bill, 189, 249
Sensabaugh, Brent, 358
Sewall, Gary, 541
Seymour, Art, 49, 74, 78, 89, 91, 127, 145, 285, 335
Shadowens, Lamont, "Shad," 122, 123, 124, 318, 435, 459
Shaw, Doug, 264, 265, 349
Shelton, Ben, 207
Shelton, Gil, 152
Shilling, Erik, 2, 11
Shroeder, Paul, 228

Sidney, Spence, 335
Silver, Al, 60, 102, 104, 407
Simms, Ginny, 335
Singer, Don, 202
Skaggs, Willy, 235
Slack, Gregory, 381
Smillie, Bill, 235
Smith, Fred, 425, 538, 560
Smith, Larry, 510
Smith, Mel, 89, 112, 176, 282
Smith, Noah, 148, 244
Smith, Oakley, 19, 102, 104, 195, 196, 280, 284, 347, 368, 381, 382, 411, 479, 557
Smith, Ted, 105
Snoke, Chuck, 285
Snyder, Wayne, 19
Soloman, Jack, 102, 103
Souers, Bob, 93, 223, 233
Squires, Bill, 170, 268
Starker, Betty, 211
Steinberg, Sol, 520, 527, 537, 538
Steiner, Curt, 60
Stevens, Wally, 184
Stilwell, Gen. Joe, 11
Stolting, Ken, 473
Story, Dick, 47
Strassle, Art, 223
Stratford, Dick, 19, 20, 25, 64, 131, 133, 197, 212, 213, 214, 233, 411
Stubbs, "Stubby," 51
Studer, Jack, 41, 181
Stuelke, Dick, 19, 20, 25, 57, 107, 186, 194, 228, 229, 292, 334, 421
Stuffings, Jeff, 517

Sulewski, Lenny, 556
Sullivan, Tommy, 176, 237, 361, 381
Swan, Jack, 316
Swanson, Gordy, 399, 400
Swartz, Grant, 381, 384
Sweeley, Mike, 310
Taggart, Dick, 109, 110
Talley, Kirk, 102
Talkington, Jack, 71, 139, 155, 159, 173
Taulbee, Harry, 74, 75
Taulbee, Jay, 75
Taulbee Roseanne, 75
Taylor, Al, 381
Taylor, Bill, 66
Taylor, Bob, 532, 536, 546
Taylor, Gene, 192, 237
Tharp, Bobbie, 47, 52, 72, 73, 87, 90, 107, 111, 115, 118, 120, 121, 132, 151, 158, 163, 164, 180, 187, 194, 199, 287, 354, 394, 444, 451, 452, 482
Tharp, Ernie, 357, 394
Thomas, Greg, 189, 191, 243, 452, 482, 543
Thomas, Jim, 51
Thompson, Bill, 41, 50, 51, 120, 220, 226, 257
Thompson, Starr, 81, 102, 104, 164, 203, 250, 305, 346
Tjosaas. Will, 351
Todd, Mike, 480
Tomuro, Tommy, 307
Toon, Steve, 485
Towne, Gerry, 102
Towner, Bill, 131, 211, 212, 381

Treft, Monte, 82, 338
Trimble, Rhuel, 182, 220
Tripp, Rex, 203, 204, 298, 302, 453, 454
Tune, C, 303
Tymczyszyn, John, 510, 512
Urnezis, John, 194, 297
Vachon, Dave, 164, 220, 329
Valour, Johnny, 186
Vance, Art, 479, 480, 498
Van Der Velde, Father Franz, 176
Vaughn, Oscar, 444
Vendini, Russ, 250
Ventresca, Dominic, 147, 148
Vinson, Jim, 426
Waldo. Buck, 266
Wallace, Ned, 517
Wall, Herb, 50, 71, 76, 91
Walmsley, Barbara, 211, 243
Wanzer, Jack, 111
Wassum, Patricia, 243
Wastman, Vern, 121, 431
Waterbury, Claire, 71
Watkins, H. P., 102, 395
Way, Barbara (Graham), 294
Way, Ron, 269, 310, 480, 500, 501
Weil, John, 55
Weizman, Ezer, 435
Welsh, Billie, 69
White, John, 101, 346
White, John Jr., 381
Wibben, Jack, 157, 163
Wight, Garrett, 444
Wilkins, Willy, 211, 342
Wilson, Dave, 269
Wilson, Dick, 128, 192, 319, 440, 517, 536, 557
Winterberg, Jim, 363, 381
Wisbar, Gloria, 141
Wish, Bob, 243
Witt, Tom, 490
Wofford, Freddy, 480
Wolf, Stephen, 536, 537, 538, 546, 547, 548
Wong, 17
Woodall, Al, 519
Woodmansee, Janet, 118
Woodward, "Woody," 91, 99
Zahner, Paul, 523
Zalusky, "Ski," 57, 113, 114, 116, 128, 130, 153, 155, 188, 201, 249, 269, 354, 387, 421, 437
Zimmerman, 250
Zopfi, Bob, 211